W9-DCO-200

Basic Psychotherapeutics: A Programmed Text

Basic Psychotherapeutics: A Programmed Text

by

C. Warner Johnson, M.D.,
John R. Snibbe, Ph.D.,
and Leonard A. Evans, Ph.D.
all of University of Southern California School of Medicine
Los Angeles, California

New York • London

Copyright © 1980 Spectrum Publications

All rights reserved. No part of this book may be reproduced in any form, by photostat, microform, retrieval system, or any other means without prior written permission of the copyright holder or his licensee.

SPECTRUM PUBLICATIONS, INC.
175–20 Wexford Terrace, Jamaica, N.Y. 11432

Library of Congress Number: 80-16115

ISBN: 0-89335-114-8 (Cloth)

ISBN: 0-89335-128-8 (Paper)

Foreword

This book provides instruction in applying basic treatment strategies to patient care. Emphasis is placed on teaching diagnostic skills, and especially, the therapeutic management of emotionally disturbed patients. This book is intended as a companion text to Basic Psychopathology: A Programmed Text, which focuses more on teaching the description and observational skills for diagnosing common psychopathologic syndromes.

Basic Psychotherapeutics gives pragmatic suggestions for treating a variety of psychopathologic disorders, many of which are newly classified in the Diagnostic Statistical Manual - III (DSM-III) published by The American Psychiatric Association. We have adopted the terminology and many, but not all, of the diagnostic criteria used in DSM-III. The treatment recommendations proposed are eclectic in nature and the information presented is non-theoretical and patient centered.

Basic Psychotherapeutics is divided into three parts. The first reviews basic data collection procedures and treatment skills; it includes chapters on interviewing, the mental status examination and pharmacologic, psychologic and behavioral therapy. The next section includes chapters on commonly encountered psychiatric syndromes such as schizophrenic, affective and anxiety disorders. The final chapters are presentations of special clinical interest, such as the management of suicidal patients, psychiatric emergencies, treating the dying patient and his family, and others. The content material is likely to be of special interest to a variety of health care related professionals including students of medicine and nursing, social workers, police officers, educators, religious counselors, and paramedics which are called upon to regularly evaluate and treat persons experiencing emotional disorders. This book is introductory in its scope and well suited for persons who are desirous of basic instruction in psychotherapeutics, but it can also serve effectively as a basic review for those preparing for certifying examinations in medicine, psychiatry, nursing and social work.

The format of Basic Psychotherapeutics facilitates learning because of its unique instructional design. Each chapter begins with an introduction to the topic and provides you with a conceptual frame of reference. Next, come learning objectives which highlight the essential things to learn. These are followed by content information necessary to achieve the stated objectives. Each content area is followed by a self-assessment exercise consisting of clinically oriented questions, which if completed, will indicate your learning progress. A closing paragraph summarizes the major content points of each chapter and is followed by a list of references which can be used if you wish to pursue the topic in greater depth.

Basic Psychotherapeutics is introductory in its scope, but provides a solid foundation upon which fundamental treatment skills can be developed. Although this book contains information necessary for you to accomplish the intellectual mastery of the stated learning objectives, we have found that our students learn the material best when it can be related to patient-centered learning experiences which transform the didactic knowledge into actual clinical skills.

The particular order in which this text is read is left to your discretion and interest. However, in most cases, we recommend that you initially read the first section which introduces basic terminology and general methods of evaluation and treatment. After these chapters are understood, you then can move on to other chapters of special interest or importance.

Contents

We would like to express our appreciation and admiration to Mrs. Shirley McElwee and Miss Viktoria Weiss for typing and collating the manuscript, and to our families for their encouragement and support throughout the preparation of this book.

Part I
Basic Psychotherapeutic Procedures

CHAPTER 1. ABBREVIATED PSYCHOLOGICAL ASSESSMENT

Many persons coming to you for care will develop emotional distress from time to time, and for this reason, it is important for you to develop skills for evaluating their psychological status. A psychological evaluation of this type can be accomplished by conducting a specially designed interview, the principles of which you can easily learn and use with your patients.

Numerous authors have described the principles and techniques typical of good psychological interviewing. However, most of these descriptions involve a comprehensive psychological evaluation which takes fifty minutes or longer to complete, an amount of time which often may not be available to you. A practical alternative to a lengthy interview is an abbreviated one that has limited objectives, a focused format, and can be completed in twenty minutes or less. Using the principles outlined in this chapter, you will be able to establish the most appropriate interviewing methods and goals in keeping with the time available.

LEARNING OBJECTIVES

By the time you complete the material in this chapter, you should be able to do the following and apply the information to written case histories:

1. List the three general goals of an abbreviated psychological assessment.

2. Identify four psychopathologic conditions important to diagnose during rapid psychological assessment.

3. Determine the appropriate use and timing of open- and closed-ended questions.

4. Construct one open-ended and one closed-ended question for each of the following topics:

   a. sleep patterns
   b. use of medication
   c. prior psychiatric treatment

5. Identify good and poor interviewing tehcniques in a written case vignette.

6. Identify the special interviewing techniques useful with patients who demonstrate:

   a. intense feelings (anger, sadeness, anxiety)
   b. prolonged silences
   c. excessive talkativeness
   d. using words of unclear meaning

7. Characterize each of the interviewing phases of abbreviated psychological assessment in terms of:

   a. predominant phrasing and timing of questions
   b. degree of verbal activity by the interviewer
   c. the type of information sought

8. Distinguish between important and unimportant areas of basic information which should be obtained during an abbreviated psychological assessment.

9. Make tentative diagnoses and prescribe appropriate recommendations for patients portrayed in case vignettes.

GOALS OF ABBREVIATED PSYCHOLOGICAL ASSESSMENT

Skillful interviewing utilizes an approach which is fexible and can be readily adapted to the needs of you and your patient. Eventually, you will develop your own interviewing style, but initially it will be helpful for you to follow established principles of effective information collection. Since time is so limited during an abbreviated psychological assessment, it is important to work efficiently toward achieving three major goals: (1) enhancing rapport with your patient, (2) establishing an adequate data base by which to diagnose psychopathology if it is present, and (3) making appropriate therapeutic recommendations. Although data collection is of central importance, keep in mind that a well-conducted interview also can be a therapeutic experience. Frequently when a patient is able to express his personal worries and feelings to an interested listener, he will feel less alone and emotionally distressed. It is comforting for him to know that someone cares enough to listen.

PSYCHOPATHOLOGIC CONDITIONS IMPORTANT TO DIAGNOSE

One primary goal of an interview is to determine whether sufficient psychopathology is present to pose a substantial threat to your patient's emotional or physical well-being. Of particular significance in this respect is the presence of an organic brain disorder, a functional psychosis, a state of intense depression or marked anxiety.

The early detection of an organic brain disorder is important for at least two reasons. Because the brain is an organ highly sensitive to changes in physiology, the appearance of symptoms of an organic brain disorder may provide an early signal of disease elsewhere in the body. Such symptoms deserve careful evaluation. Secondly, patients with an organic brain disorder are intellectually impaired and often demonstrate deficits in judgment for even routine activities. Therefore, appropriate arrangements for patient supervision and care are indicated. The presence of an organic brain disorder is common in medically ill patients, and the condition is likely present in persons who show impairment of general intellectual functioning, recent memory and orientation.

Patients with a functional psychosis rarely present an actual danger to themselves or others. However, the presence of a psychosis introduces the possibility that the patient may react impulsively or with poor judgment in a way that may cause them harm. When a psychosis is diagnosed, therefore, further psychiatric evaluation is indicated. Symptoms of bizarre or disorganized thinking patterns, excessive or inappropriate affect, hallucinations and/or inappropriate behavior are suggestive of functional psychosis.

Serious depression with resultant suicide now ranks among the ten most frequent causes of death in our country. Persons who have experienced a major loss, older patients and those with chronic debilitating illnesses are at special risk. For these reasons, it is vital to detect early signs of severe or increasing depression and take appropriate therapeutic measures. A patient who appears sad, expresses feelings of hopelessness and apathy, and/or complains of a disturbance of sleep, weight loss and persistent fatigue may be experiencing a depressive syndrome.

Finally, persons who are under considerable emotional stress, including medically ill and hospitalized patients are especially susceptible to a variety of anxiety and tension states which may complicate their treatment. Symptoms of underlying anxiety (which include feelings of apprehension, generalized muscle tension, restlessness and such somatic complaints as "dizziness," palpitations and shortness of breath) are often responsive to appropriate medication and supportive measures. The discerning therapist is frequently able to rapidly alleviate their patient's feelings of anxiety.

Now complete Self-Assessment Exercise #1 beginning on the following page.

Self-Assessment Exercise #1

1. In addition to building doctor-patient rapport, the goals of an abbreviated psychological assessment are to:

   a.

   b.

2. During an abbreviated psychological assessment it is important to establish whether or not four psychopathologic conditions are present. For each of the patient descriptions below, write in the name of the diagnostic syndrome which it suggests.

   a. The patient is a 38-year-old man who is three hours post-operative after surgery for a peptic ulcer. He demonstrates mental confusion, has an impairment of recent memory and is disoriented to time and place. He seems somewhat apprehensive and restless.

      Diagnostic syndrome: ____________________

   b. An 18-year-old teenager describes feelings of vague apprehension, "dizziness" and is restless following admission to the hospital. Her speech is rapid and she asks many questions about her prognosis and treatment.

      Diagnostic syndrome: ____________________

   c. Four days following the birth of her first child, a 24-year-old woman became increasingly withdrawn and unresponsive. In spite of reassurance to the contrary, she insisted that her baby had been kidnapped and murdered. Her thought pattern was hard to follow as she jumped from subject to subject. However, she was well-oriented to time, person and place.

      Diagnostic syndrome: ____________________

Self-Assessment Exercise #1 (Continued)

d. A 45 year-old man complained of chronic fatigue, loss of appetite and weight. He related the onset of symptoms to the loss of his job three months earlier. He sat slumped in his chair and rarely gestured as he spoke. At times he seemed to be stiffling tears.

Diagnostic syndrome: ______________________________

When you have completed this exercise to the best of your ability, check your answers with those on the following page.

Self-Assessment Exercise #1 – Feedback

1. The major goals of an abbreviated psychological assessment are:

   a. building therapist-patient rapport

   b. establishing an adequate data base by which to diagnose psychopathology, if it is present

   c. making appropriate therapeutic recommendations

2. The diagnostic syndromes suggested by the cases are:

   a. the presence of mental confusion, deficits of recent memory and disorientation suggests an organic brain syndrome

   b. the symptoms of vague apprehension, restlessness, rapid speech and "dizziness" are consistent with a diagnosis of a state of anxiety and/or tension

   c. the patient's withdrawn behavior, delusional beliefs and disorganized thinking patterns in the absence of disorientation indicate a functional psychosis

   d. the patient describes and demonstrates many symptoms suggestive of a depressive reaction, i.e., chronic fatigue, loss of appetite and weight, decreased motor activity and a sense of sadness.

If your answers are reasonably close to those above, please continue with the reading on the next page. If not, please reread the preceding material.

OPEN- AND CLOSED-ENDED QUESTIONS

With time in short supply during an abbreviated assessment, the type and quantity of your verbal interventions should be carefully planned. Even the wording of questions takes on special significance when you realize that each of your spoken interventions leaves less time available for your patient. By careful phrasing of questions it is possible for you to guide the direction of the interview and subtly control the quantity and content of your patient's verbal responses. Developing skill in the use of open- and closed-ended questions will facilitate your ability to collect information.

An open-ended question is one phrased to evoke an elaborative and unstructured answer. These questions use minimal verbal intervention from you, but require the patient to respond spontaneously at some length. Examples of open-ended questions are: "What sort of problems have you been having?" or "What happened then?" or "What were your growing up years like?" It is difficult for patients to reply to such questions without revealing a good deal about themselves. Open-ended questions help maximize your patient's verbal responses and are of special value for obtaining data about his mental status and the underlying theme of his history. These questions are particularly useful with patients who need some prompting in order to express themselves. For example, "How have you been feeling?" will yield more information than "Have you been feeling depressed or anxious recently?" Likewise, "Would you tell me about your marriage?" is preferred to "Do you have a happy marriage?"

This type of question helps guide the interview and diminishes the dominance of the interviewer. Correspondingly, it gives little direct emotional support to the patient and may not be appropriate with persons who are anxious, show signs of psychological disorganization or are overly talkative.

Closed-ended questions require a more specific and briefer response from your patient and are useful in obtaining factual information. Closed-ended questions call for more verbal activity on your part and correspondingly limit what your patient can say. Examples of closed-ended questions are: "What medications are you taking?" or "How many times have you been depressed before?" These questions tend to increase your control of the interview and thus cause your patient to assume a more passive role in the evaluation process. Questions like this add considerable structure and goal-directedness to an interview and can be used effectively with patients who are overly anxious, excessively talkative or psychologically disorganized.

Now complete Self-Assessment Exercise #2 beginning on the following page.

Self-Assessment Exercise #2

1. Designate whether open- or closed-ended questions would be most appropriate for handling each of the following circumstances:

O = open-ended C = closed-ended

______ a. the patient appears to become increasingly apprehensive, rambling and disorganized in relating the history.

______ b. a young woman is very talkative and tends to dwell on non-essential details at great lengths.

______ c. the interviewer would like to elicit the patient's feelings about her spouse.

______ d. inquiry about the orientation and recent memory of a patient with suspected organic brain syndrome.

______ e. encourage a silent patient to verbalize more.

______ f. obtaining specific detail about suicidal ideation.

______ g. making an unobtrusive assessment of the patient's mental status.

______ h. seeking detailed information about the patient's current medical treatment.

______ i. questions which allow the interviewer to be <u>least</u> verbally active.

Self-Assessment Exercise #2 (Continued)

2. In addition to mental status and history findings, you should obtain at least cursory information in the following areas. Construct one open- and one closed-ended question for each.

   a. sleep patterns

      open-ended:

      closed-ended:

   b. use of medications

      open-ended:

      closed-ended:

   c. prior psychiatric treatment

      open-ended:

      closed-ended:

When you have completed this exercise to the best of your ability, check your answers with those on the following page.

Self-Assessment Exercise #2 - Feedback

1. For the following circumstances:

O = open-ended C = closed-ended

__C__ a. the patient appears to become increasingly apprehensive, rambling and disorganized in relating the history.

__C__ b. a young woman is very talkative and tends to dwell on non-essential details at great lengths.

__O__ c. the interviewer would like to elicit the patient's feelings about her spouse.

__C__ d. inquiry about the orientation and recent memory of a patient with suspected organic brain syndrome.

__O__ e. encourage a silent patient to verbalize more.

__C__ f. obtaining specific detail about suicidal ideation.

__O__ g. making an unobtrusive assessment of the patient's mental status.

__C__ h. seeking detailed information about the patient's current medical treatment.

__O__ i. questions which allow the interviewer to be <u>least</u> verbally active.

Self-Assessment Exercise #2 - Feedback (Continued)

2. Examples of open- and closed-ended questions for each of the following areas of information are:

   a. sleep patterns

      open-ended: "What changes have you noted in your sleeping habits?"

      closed-ended: "Are you sleeping alright?"
      "Have you noticed any changes in your sleeping habits?"

   b. use of medications

      open-ended: "What medications or drugs are you using now?"
      "What response to the medications have you had?"

      closed-ended: "Are you using any drugs or medications?"
      "Have you noted any dizziness, dry mouth or blurring of vision because of the medicines?"

   c. prior psychiatric treatment

      open-ended: "Could you tell me about your previous psychiatric treatment?"

      closed-ended: "Have you had prior psychiatric treatment?"

If your answers are reasonably close to those above, please continue with the reading on the next page. If not, please reread the preceding material.

GENERAL PRINCIPLES OF INTERVIEWING

Your interview should be thoughtfully planned from its inception. Your first task is to create an environment which facilitates communication by taking all measures to assure your patient's comfort and privacy. It is when patients feel at ease and sense your undivided attention that they are more likely to speak openly about themselves. Be sure to convey a nonjudgmental attitude toward your patient. Generally, it is best to take a seated position which is in easy view of the patient. Sights, sounds and other distractions which may interfere with the interview should be excluded as much as possible. It is important for you to focus full attention upon your patient's mental status, history recitation and behavior; and for that reason, note taking during the interview is generally not advised. Try to maintain an attentive facial expression. Nod when appropriate, lean expectantly toward your patient, and make occasional empathic responses. These actions will convey a feeling of support and interest. Speaking slowly and deliberately to your patient will create the effect of having more time available than actually may be the case.

Special Techniques

Occasionally during the course of an interview, your patient may demonstrate intense feelings of sadness, tearfulness, anger or anxiety. This display of emotion may make you and the patient uncomfortable. However, if he seems reasonably stable do not actively suppress these feelings. On the contrary, it may be quite therapeutic for your patient to openly express feelings, and in most instances he should be encouraged to do so. One way to do this is to describe your perceptions of what he is feeling and add a statement which will permit him to express it. As a general rule, help your patient appropriately deal with any intense feeling as it arises, even if time for collecting factual history is lost in the process. Reckoning first with troubled feelings will strengthen your patient's rapport with you.

Example:

Interviewer: "I get the impression that you feel quite angry now. Can you tell me about it?",
or
"You don't have to fight to hold back tears here. It's alright to cry. I wonder what makes you feel so sad."

If a patient shows markedly rising tension or other feelings which may be overwhelming, you should actively redirect the focus of the session to more neutral or factual topics. Focusing on biographical or factual information will provide the structure and diversion needed to help your patient regain emotional equilibrium.

Occasionally, a patient may ramble excessively or dwell on irrelevant details. You can intervene by adding structure to the interview and/or using closed-ended questions. For example, you could say, "I see that what you are talking about is important to you. However, we have limited time and I would like to focus on other areas, too. Could you tell me about...?"

Brief pauses can be handled without verbal intervention by patiently waiting. Other responses which may help if your patient becomes silent are to restate his last spoken phrase or simply saying, "And then?" or "Go on." This action generally is sufficient to evoke a resumption of his history. If your patient has persistent difficulty in volunteering information, then you should become more active. Reflecting out loud in a supportive way about your patient's hesitancy often will help.

Example:

Interviewer: "I get the feeling that it is hard for you to talk right now. It is often difficult to talk about ourselves to others, even if they are trying to help and understand. Perhaps you would like me to ask some questions for awhile."

Patient: Nodding assent.

Interviewer: Responds by asking <u>open-ended</u> questions.

During the interview your patient may use words which may have special significance but are not clear in meaning. For example, he may say, "I feel troubled." or "I had a 'nervous breakdown'." It is then appropriate to quizzically repeat the key word or phrase and imply the need for further clarification.

Example:

Patient: "I feel 'nervous' most of the time."

Interviewer: "Nervous? In what way?"

Now complete Self-Assessment Exercise #3 beginning on the following page.

Self-Assessment Exercise #3

1. Read through the case vignette below. Then in the columns provided list the doctor's responses which represented a good interviewing technique. Similarly, list those responses which indicated a poor technique.

   Case:

   A 32-year-old man was taken to an emergency room for evaluation of injuries sustained in a home accident. After introducing himself, the doctor began inquiring about the patient's injuries while escorting him to an examination cubicle. After arriving at the examining room, the doctor closed the door and asked the patient to be seated. Twice during the evaluation, the doctor took telephone calls and consulted once with the nurse. While the patient described his injury the doctor remained standing, writing detailed notes of the patient's history.

   Good interviewing technique:

   Poor interviewing technique:

Self-Assessment Exercise #3 (Continued)

2. In the space provided, list the letters corresponding to the techniques most appropriate for you to use with each of the patients described below. More than one response may be used for each of the patients.

a = use closed-ended questions
b = use open-ended questions
c = comment on the patient's feeling and encourage its open expression
d = direct the patient to a more emotionally neutral topic
e = continue with the data collection without comment
f = interrupt the data collection to deal with the patient's affective distress
g = have the pateint explain words of unclear meaning

______(1) A middle-aged woman seems on the verge of tears as she talks about her husband's death.

______(2) As the young man tells his story of "seeing visions of God," he shows increasing anxiety, restlessness and disorganized thinking.

______(3) The elderly man talks without interruption about historically insignificant details.

______(4) A teenager gives non-verbal indications of irritation at being brought for consultation against his wishes.

______(5) A depressed middle-aged man rarely volunteers information about himself and often remains silent unless prompted by questions.

______(6) During the middle phase of the interview, the patient mentioned being "treated for a chronic illness."

When you have completed this exercise to the best of your ability, check your answers with those on the following page.

Self-Assessment Exercise #3 - Feedback

1. Interview responses indicating:

   Good interviewing technique

   introduced self to patient
   personally escorted patient to interviewing room
   closed door of interviewing room to promote privacy

   Poor interviewing technique

   began inquiry before patient was seated and privacy establishe
   allowed interruptions of interview in the form of telephone calls and consultation with the nurse
   remained standing
   took notes during interview

2. The technique which you should use for the following patients are:

   a = use closed-ended questions
   b = use open-ended questions
   c = comment on the patient's feeling and encourage its open expression
   d = direct the patient to a more emotionally neutral topic
   e = continue with the data collection without comment
   f = interrupt the data collection to deal with the patient's affective distress
   g = have the patient explain words of unclear meaning

b c f (1) A middle-aged woman seems on the verge of tears as she talks about her husband's death.

a d f g (2) As the young man tells his story of "seeing visions of God," he shows increasing anxiety, restlessness and disorganized thinking.

a e (3) The elderly man talks without interruption about historically insignificant details.

f (4) A teenager gives non-verbal indications of irritation at being brought for consultation against his wishes.

Self-Assessment Exercise #3 – Feedback (Continued)

b c f (5) A depressed middle-aged man rarely volunteers information about himself and often remains silent unless prompted by questions.

g (6) During the middle phase of the interview, the patient mentioned being "treated for a chronic illness."

If your answers are reasonably close to those above, please continue with the reading on the next page. If not, please reread the preceding material.

CONDUCTING THE INTERVIEW

For most interviews it is helpful to divide the time into three portions, each characterized by different goals, format and the amount of your verbal intervention.

The Initial Phase

The initial phase of the interview is especially important because it establishes the pattern of communication and type of patient-interviewer relationship that will follow. During the early phases of the interview, a central task is to encourage your patient's spontaneous discussion of his problems. After a word of greeting and brief statement of the purpose of the session, you should pose an opening question which allows your patient broad latitude in topic selection and yet focuses on what is troublesome. Initial questions such as, "What sort of problems have you been having?" or "What's been troubling you recently?", show that the focus for discussion is your patient's distress but also allow him to select the specific themes of the interview and elaborate upon them in his own way. The most revealing data are often obtained when your interventions are kept to a minimum. This relatively unstructured approach to information collection helps to establish the patient as an active collaborator in the evaluation process. Furthermore, you may be perceived as a very special person by your patient, someome whom he wants to please. If your questions are focused too early in the session, your patient may follow your lead and talk about what he thinks you want to hear rather than provide a self-selected history.

Whatever the patient says early in the interview is usually very important. When given a chance to do so, most troubled persons will reveal the major theme of their distress within the first few minutes of an interview. During the opening phase, you should act primarily as a guide-facilitator who helps your patient define his difficulty and express feelings and worries. By careful listening, you usually can identify the theme of your patient's difficulty, formulate a tentative diagnosis, plan strategic questions for later use, and unobtrusively perform a mental status examination.

Generally, open-ended questions and a relatively unstructured interviewing style should be used during the opening phase. Many patients experience considerable emotional relief when they are able to express themselves uninterruptedly to an interested, objective listener. Your full attention at this time will help build trust and rapport. When your patient is developing a major trend of thought, it is best not to interrupt it for details. Any gaps in information can be noted and returned to later in the session. Of course, the relatively unstructured approach to interviewing must be modified if your patient is mute, mentally confused or disorganized.

The Middle Phase

It is unlikely that your patient will supply all of the data needed for evaluation without some direction. Therefore, a change in your approach is indicated for the middle portion of the interview. By initial careful listening and observation you should be able to formulate a tentative diagnosis and start a more focused approach to information collection. During this middle phase of the evaluation, you should become more directive, verbally active and rely more on closed-ended questions. It now becomes appropriate to gather specific details relating to your patient's distress and psychological state. A working knowledge of commonly encountered psychiatric syndromes is necessary in order for you to formulate definitive questions. For example, if early in the interview your patient was unable to describe in detail recent life events and gave a somewhat disorganized history, you should suspect the presence of an organic brain disorder and ask focused questions about memory, orientation, etc. Similarly, if your patient alludes to feelings of depression or demonstrates unusual anxiety, then these areas warrant further exploration. In addition to evaluating your patient's chief difficulty and determining whether or not psychopathology is present, you should also inquire about recent changes in daily habits, thinking, behavior and feelings.

With time at a premium, other questions should be selected on a priority basis. Generally, collection of information most pertinent for an abbreviated psychological assessment emphasizes current rather than past history, that is, identifying factors which at the present time affect your patient. One or two questions in key areas will yield information important for establishing appropriate recommendations for your client's case. It is quite helpful to correlate your patient's physiological status with those of the mental status examination and present history. Therefore, you should routinely inquire about any changes in sleep, appetite, weight, and general level of physical activity. Likewise, it is pertinent to ask about current medical problems, if medications or drugs are being used, and any current or past treatment for psychiatric problems. As time permits, obtain at least cursory information about key areas of your patient's life which may either be a potential resource or source of stress. This includes a brief review of current living conditions, the quality of interpersonal relationships (marriage, friendships, etc.) and capacity to function daily at home and/or at work.

Closing Phase

The third stage of the interview is reserved for summarizing the findings and making specific recommendations. You should be more verbally active than during the earlier phase of the evaluation. Your patient's rapport and trust in you are optimal at this point, and questions about sensitive and personal material can now be raised. Since it is important to focus and terminate the session, use closed-ended questions much more frequently.

It is a good policy to advise your patient of the approaching end of the interview a few minutes in advance of its conclusion. Encourage him to raise any final questions or express other concerns which might have been overlooked. After completing the information collection, present a brief summary of the pertinent findings phrased in layman's terms and make specific recommendations to your patient. In general these final recommendations take one of three forms. If the information gathered is insufficient for a definitive disposition or diagnosis, recommend a second consultation with that purpose in mind. If significant psychopathology is diagnosed, then arrange for referral and/or treatment. It is at this time that specific recommendations about routine activities, work, relationships and the prescribing of medication can be handled. If you are convinced that no psychological problems exist, then the session can be terminated with the recommendation that no further follow-up is needed.

Good interviewing technique calls for you to end the session on an optimistic note by pointing out some positive aspect of your patient's situation, for example the treatability of the condition, the availability of significant resources and so forth.

Now complete Self-Assessment Exercise #4 beginning on the following page.

Self-Assessment Exercise #4

1. Based on the information presented in this chapter, circle the best opening statements by which to begin an abbreviated psychological assessment.

   a. "You seem in pain. Would you tell me more about it?"

   b. "Your doctor told me about your heart condition. In what way has it been troubling you?"

   c. "What sort of worries have you been having?"

   d. "What's been troubling you recently?"

   e. "Will you tell me about yourself?"

   f. "When did your troubles start?"

   g. "What brought you here?"

Self-Assessment Exercise #4 (Continued)

2. Match the letter representing the phase of an interview appropriate to each of the actions and/or statements made by the interviewer.

a = the opening phase of the interview
b = the middle phase of the interview
c = the closing phase of the interview

_______(1) The time of least verbal intervention.

_______(2) The time of greatest verbal intervention.

_______(3) "What changes have you noted in your daily routine?"

_______(4) "Based on what you told me about yourself, I think you are experiencing a depressive reaction. If you are agreeable, I would like to prescribe some medication which may be of help."

_______(5) "Have you had any previous psychiatric treatment?"

_______(6) "I wonder if you have any questions you would like to ask before we stop."

_______(7) "What medications are you currently taking?"

_______(8) "I think we should schedule a second meeting."

_______(9) Identification of the major theme of the patient's difficulty.

______(10) "What sort of problems have you been having?"

Self-Assessment Exercise #4 (Continued)

3. It is important to obtain as much relevant information as possible during an abbreviated psychological assessment. For each of the following areas, indicate whether it is relatively important (A) or relatively unimportant (B) to gather data in these areas.

_____ a. a cursory mental status examination

_____ b. a work record over the past 10 years

_____ c. a history of early familial relationships

_____ d. details of recent medication use

_____ e. details of the patient's present problems

_____ f. evaluation of recent memory and orientation for a patient who gave a rambling history which suggests general intellectual impairment

_____ g. a thorough mental status examination for patients who describe performing unusual behavior and express eccentric ideas

_____ h. current living arrangements

_____ i. current medical treatment

_____ j. past medical history

Self-Assessment Exercise #4 (Continued)

4. At the close of an abbreviated psychological assessment, it is important to make appropriate recommendations to the patient. Read through the following case vignettes and then, using the principles presented make: (a) a tentative diagnosis, and (b) an appropriate recommendation.

   a. A 23 year-old woman was interviewed in an emergency room for 20 minutes. She had been involved in an automobile accident. She received a slight head injury and seemed very apprehensive, restless and at times mentally "confused." Her history was related in a rambling fashion and she did not supply many details of the accident or of her life in general. The history and evaluation seemed incomplete at the end of the 20-minute period.

      Tentative diagnosis:

      Recommendations:

   b. A man in his late twenties requested brief consultation with you. He appeared slightly disheveles and manifested a somewhat blank facial expression. His history was disjointed, hard to follow and focused on feelings that he was under surveillance by the F.B.I. and the Mafia. He did not show evidence of disorientation or recent memory impairment.

      Tentative diagnosis:

      Recommendations:

When you have completed this exercise to the best of your ability, check your answers with those on the following page.

Self-Assessment Exercise #4 - Feedback

1. The best opening statements for an abbreviated psychological assessment include:

   c. "What sort of worries have you been having?"

   d. "What's been troubling you recently?"

   The following questions are too inferential and/or are prematurely focused:

   a. "You seem in pain. Would you tell me more about it?" -- prematurely focused.

   b. "Your doctor told me about your heart condition. In what way has it been troubling you?" -- prematurely focused.

   f. "When did your troubles start?" -- erroneously focused on time not the problem.

   g. "What brought you here?" -- doesn't deal with the patient's problem.

   e. "Will you tell me about yourself?" -- is too general for a time-limited interview, when the primary concern is what is troubling the patient.

Self-Assessment Exercise #4 - Feedback (Continued)

2. The following actions/statements by the interviewer are most appropriate during:

a = the opening phase of the interview
b = the middle phase of the interview
c = the closing phase of the interview

__a__ (1) The time of least verbal intervention.

__c__ (2) The time of greatest verbal intervention.

__b__ (3) "What changes have you noted in your daily routine?"

__c__ (4) "Based on what you told me about yourself, I think you are experiencing a depressive reaction. If you are agreeable, I would like to prescribe some medication which may be of help."

__b__ (5) "Have you had any previous psychiatric treatment?"

__c__ (6) "I wonder if you have any questions you would like to ask before we stop."

__b__ (7) "What medications are you currently taking?"

__c__ (8) "I think we should schedule a second meeting."

__a__ (9) Identification of the major theme of the patient's difficulty.

__a__ (10) "What sort of problems have you been having?"

Self-Assessment Exercise #4 - Feedback (Continued)

3. During an abbreviated psychological assessment, the following areas in which to gather data are:

(A) relatively important (B) relatively unimportant

A a. a cursory mental status examination

B b. a work record over the past 10 years

B c. a history of early familial relationships

A d. details of recent medication use

A e. details of the patient's present problems

A f. evaluation of recent memory and orientation for patients who gave a rambling history which suggests general intellectual impairment

A g. a thorough mental status examination for patients who describe performing unusual behavior and express eccentric ideas

A h. current living arrangements

A i. current medical treatment

B j. past medical history

4. a. The symptoms of mental "confusion", rambling history, impaired recent memory are suggestive of an organic brain syndrome. Since this may indicate a neurological/ medical problem and data is incomplete, the recommendation should be to arrange for a more complete evaluation and/or consultation before releasing the patient.

b. Inappropriate affect (blank facial expression), a disjointed history and delusional beliefs in the absence of an organic brain syndrome suggest the presence of a functional psychosis. Further psychological evaluation and/or consultation should be ordered.

If your answers are reasonably close to those above, please continue with the reading on the next page. If not, please reread the preceding material.

SUMMARY

Developing proficiency in performing an abbreviated psychological assessment can enhance your diagnostic and therapeutic effectiveness. As a skilled interviewer you should provide an optimum environment for communication, adhere to a goal-directed format and make careful use of questions and interventions. Special attention should be given to your patient's psychological state and present history. A well-conducted interview should conclude on a positive note with lucid and helpful recommendations. The principles of good interviewing are easily learned and should be applied to patient care.

REFERENCES

Bernstein, L., Bernstein, R., Dana, R., Interviewing: A Guide for Health Professionals, New York: Appleton-Century-Crofts, 1974.

Bird, B., Talking with Patients, Philadelphia: Lippincott, 1973.

Enelow, A., Swisher, S., Interviewing and Patient Care, New York: Oxford Press, 1972.

Engel, G., Morgan, W., Interviewing the Patient, Philadelphia: Saunders, 1973.

Sullivan, H., The Psychiatric Interview, New York: Norton, 1954.

Wexler, M., Adler, L., Help the Patient Tell His Story, New Jersey: Medical Economics Book Division, Oradell, 1971.

CHAPTER 2. MENTAL STATUS EXAMINATION

Accurate diagnosis of psychopathology and effective psychological treatment depends upon the collection and systematic organization of observations about your patient's mental and physical state. The Mental Status Examination (MSE) is the evaluation process by which the necessary observations are obtained and recorded.

This chapter will describe what is meant by a mental status examination, explain why it is important, review its characteristics and suggest how it may be used in actual practice.

LEARNING OBJECTIVES

By the time you complete this chapter, you should be able to do the following and apply the information to written case histories.

1. Define the term "mental status examination."

2. List three purposes served by a mental status examination.

3. List and define the five major categories of the mental status examination.

4. Correctly define the following terms and be able to place each term in the appropriate major category of the mental status examination:

orientation	judgment	phobia
thought content	insight	obsession
level of consciousness	feeling (mood/affect)	compulsion
associational disturbance	hallucination	illusion
remote memory	recent memory	delusion
stream of thought		

GENERAL PRINCIPLES

The Mental Status Examination (MSE) is the name given to the process by which systematic observations of patient behaviors are obtained, organized, and used to make a diagnosis. The MSE should also include making an appropriate record of the observations and diagnosis.

You, as a health care professional, can readily learn to observe and describe patient behaviors demonstrated during an interview. In order to be useful, your observations must be objective (other trained observers would have described them in a way similar to yours) and reliable, i.e. if your patient exhibited the same characteristics at another time, they would be described in a similar way. Be as objective as possible in making and communicating your observations. In order to communicate effectively with other health care professionals, you should use standard terms and phrases to describe your patient's behavior. These terms are also helpful in observations concerning your patient to the scientific literature about psychopathology.

Before conducting a MSE it will be necessary for you to learn the meanings of standard-behavioral terms and acquire the skill of recognizing them in patients. It is also important to learn to prepare a systematic written record of your observations. This record will describe your patient's mental status as it occurs at a particular point in time. If the examination is repeated later, a comparison of the previous and recent findings of the MSE will give one measure of your patient's progress. This record can provide invaluable information about your patient which you may wish to pass on to a consultant.

Making and organizing accurate observations constitutes the first part of the diagnostic process. These data, when combined with your patient's history, will allow you to formulate some conclusions about a diagnosis. Keep in mind that no single finding of the MSE can by itself establish a definitive diagnosis. Rather, carefully consider all of the findings and observations which have been made. It is well to obtain additional information from relatives and other sources. Your final diagnosis should be consistent with the findings from a combination of sources.

Thus, a completed mental status examination has three general purposes. First, obtaining the data enables better understanding of your patient's psychological condition at a particular point in time. Second, the observations plus the patient's history will enable you to establish a diagnosis. Third, the MSE serves as a written record which can be referred back to at a later time.

Now complete Self-Assessment Exercise #1 on the following page.

Self-Assessment Exercise #1

1. The "mental status examination" is the name given to the . . .

   a.

   b.

2. What are the three purposes of the mental status examination?

   a.

   b.

   c.

When you have completed this exercise, check your answers with those on the following page.

Self-Assessment Exercise #1 - Feedback

1. The "mental status examination" is the name given to the:

   a. Process by which systematic observation of patient behaviors are obtained.

   b. Systematic record of these observations.

2. What are the three purposes of the mental status examination?

   a. It enables you to better understand your patient's psychological condition at a particular point in time.

   b. Your observations plus the patient's history will enable you to establish a diagnosis.

   c. It is part of the patient's written record which is available for review at a future time.

If your answers are reasonably close to those above, please continue with the reading on the next page. If not, please reread the preceding material.

MENTAL STATUS CATEGORIES

The findings of the MSE are recorded under the following five major categories: (1) appearance, (2) behavior, (3) feeling (affect and mood), (4) perception, and (5) thinking. These categories may be further subdivided into specific descriptors (terms) which further describe your patient's behavioral characteristics. As stated above, the descriptors should be those which other trained health care professionals would use. A suggested MSE form is shown in Table I. This type of form can help organize your thoughts and assist in the systematic recording of patient behaviors.

In the next sections of this chapter several behavioral descriptors will be defined so that when they are demonstrated by your patient, you can recognize and record them appropriately. Combining the descriptors included in all of the categories with the findings of a comprehensive history should enable you to diagnose your patient's psychopathology.

When performing a MSE be alert for the unusual and the unexpected. If you detect unusual patient characteristics attempt to find out why they are present. Atypical findings which your patient can logically explain may be a "normal" response to an acute personal stress. An intense, but transient, grief reaction following the death of a spouse is an example of a normal reaction to loss.

Each of the five categories and their associated descriptors will now be discussed.

Appearance

Appearance refers to your patient's mode of dress and his external physical characteristics. It is important to discover in what ways your patient appears out of the ordinary, strange or different. In making these judgments, consider the culture and socioeconomic environment in which your patient is living. You should ascertain if he is physically unkempt or unclean. Determine if the clothing is atypical, seductive or bizarre and if it is disheveled or dirty. Also, look for any unusual facial or bodily characteristics, e.g., scars, deformities, weight extremes, etc.

Avoid becoming mislead by your own cultural and socioeconomic frame of reference in making your judgment. Gaining broad experience in observing differing groups of persons and studying their varied social mores will help you to objectively evaluate your patient's appearance.

Now complete Self-Assessment Exercise #2 on the following page.

Self-Assessment Exercise #2

1. List the five categories which make up the MSE:

   a.

   b.

   c.

   d.

   e.

2. Define the first category:

3. List several descriptors for this category:

When you have completed this exercise, check your answers with those on the following page.

Self-Assessment Exercise #2 - Feedback

1. The five categories of the MSE are:

   a. appearance

   b. behavior

   c. feeling (affect and mood)

   d. perception

   e. thinking

2. Appearance refers to the way a patient looks (external physical characteristics) to you during a MSE.

3. Major descriptors of appearance are:

   a. physically unkempt or unclean

   b. clothing disheveled or dirty

   c. clothing atypical, seductive or bizarre

   d. unusual physical characteristics; scars, deformaties, weight extremes, etc.

If your answers are reasonably close to those above, please continu with the reading on the next page. If not, please reread the preceding material.

TABLE I

MENTAL STATUS EXAMINATION

APPEARANCE		
BEHAVIOR	Posture	
	Facial Expression Suggests	
	Body Movements	
	Speech	
	Doctor-Patient Relationship	
FEELING (AFFECT AND MOOD)	Appropriate-ness	
	Predominant Mood	
PERCEPTION		
THINKING	Level of Consciousness	
	Intellectual Functioning	attention span: intelligence:
	Orientation	
	Memory	
	Insight	
	Judgment	
	Thought Content	
	Stream of Thought	

DIAGNOSIS: ____________________

AS MANIFESTED BY: ____________________

MENTAL STATUS CATEGORIES (CONTINUED)

Behavior

The second MSE category is entitled Behavior. Behavior refers to the manner in which the patient conducts himself (both verbally and non-verbally) during the interview. It is more complex than the Appearance category and frequently used subcategories are shown in Table I.

The patient's posture during the interview can be instructive. Determine if the posture is slumped, rigid, tense or inappropriate in some way. Your patient's posture should generally correlate with the feeling and ideas expressed.

Also evaluate your patient's face for signs of anxiety, fear, sadness, anger, elation or unusual blandness. Especially note expressions which do not match with the ideas expressed, for example, smiling while describing a particularly sad or traumatic event.

Your patient's body movements during the interview also are informative. Note if the movements are fast, slow, infrequent, continuous, or if they are inappropriate to the ideas and feelings expressed.

When evaluating speech, consider the loudness, speed, and quality. With regard to the quality of speech look for profanities, grammar, slurring, stuttering, etc. Speech which is excessively loud or soft or unusually fast or slow should be noted. Again, cultural and socioeconomic conditions should be considered when making your judgments.

Careful evaluation of your patient's verbal and non-verbal behavior and noting your own feeling responses will enable you to determine the nature of his relationship with you. It is important to determine the overall pattern for relating to you, that is, whether your patient is cooperative, controlling, passive, hostile, seductive, suspicious, and so forth. The therapist-patient interaction forms the foundation for any treatment program. Continuously monitor the relationship and strive to keep it an optimal one.

Several behavioral characteristics which are diagnostically useful have been discussed. Practice using them to describe your patients.

Now complete Self-Assessment Exercise #3 beginning on the following page.

Self-Assessment Exercise #3

Using information abstracted from the following history, complete the Appearance and Behavior categories of the MSE below:

> Mrs. Arthur, a woman in her early 60's, was brought by her husband for psychological evaluation. He reported that Mrs. A had become increasingly apathetic and withdrawn over the past six weeks. In addition, she ate little and had great difficulty in sleeping. At the time of the interview, Mrs. A was dressed in a soiled nightgown and wore slippers. Her hair was disheveled and her fingernails long and untrimmed. She wore no makeup. Her face was deeply lined with furrowed brow and downturned mouth. Mrs. A walked very slowly to her chair and once seated assumed a slumped position rarely moving or gesturing. Her verbal responses were given in a barely audible monotone. Mrs. A gave the impression of being deeply preoccupied with her thoughts, and appeared oblivious to many questions asked of her.

<table>
<tr><td>APPEARANCE</td><td colspan="2"></td></tr>
<tr><td rowspan="5">BEHAVIOR</td><td>Posture</td><td></td></tr>
<tr><td>Facial Expression Suggests</td><td></td></tr>
<tr><td>Body Movements</td><td></td></tr>
<tr><td>Speech</td><td></td></tr>
<tr><td>Doctor-Patient Relationship</td><td></td></tr>
</table>

When you have completed this exercise, check your answers with those on the following page.

Self-Assessment Exercise #3 - Feedback

APPEARANCE	physically unkempt and unclean, hair disheveled, long fingernails, no makeup; clothing disheveled and soiled	
BEHAVIOR	Posture	slumped
	Facial Expression Suggests	face lined, furrowed brow, downturned mouth
	Body Movements	walked slowly, rarely moving or gesturing
	Speech	barely audible monotone
	Doctor-Patient Relationship	often unresponsive, unable to answer questions

If your answers are reasonably close to those above, please continue with the reading on the next page. If not, please reread the preceding material.

MENTAL STATUS CATEGORIES (CONTINUED)

Feeling (Affect and Mood)

The category of Feeling refers to your patient's emotional state, and for our purposes, includes both the affect and his mood (the sum total of feelings over the duration of the interview). While a feeling is not directly observable, it usually can be inferred from the patient's appearance and behavior during the interview. We will be concerned especially with the two subcategories of appropriateness and predominant mood as indicated in Table I.

Evaluate the appropriateness of your patient's feeling responses in terms of their type and intensity. Observe carefully the appropriateness of the feeling being shown with respect to the general context of the interview as well as the ideas being expressed. Marked discrepancies should be noted.

In addition to the appropriateness of the expressed feelings, it is important to define the predominant mood, i.e., which feeling best characterizes the patient when considering the interview in its entirety. Look especially for subtle or obvious signs of anger, anxiety, depression or unusual euphoria. Note fluctuations in spontaneous expression of feeling during the sessions. Also determine if your patient's feeling changes abruptly in response to a minimal stimulus. Unusual blandness (blunting) or marked intensity of feeling are significant.

Now complete Self-Assessment Exercise #4 on the following page.

Self-Assessment Exercise #4

Using information abstracted from the three histories below, complete the Feeling category of each MSE below:

Case #1

Psychological evaluation was requested for an elderly hospitalized woman. She began crying in response to questioning about the reason for her hospitalization. Her tearfulness ceased abruptly when asked about her home and family. Her crying immediately resumed when her medical problem was again mentioned. The woman became noticeably irritable if she was asked details about her illness.

FEELING (AFFECT AND MOOD)	Appropriate-ness	
	Predominant Mood	

Case #2

A 26 year-old man described feeling that his flesh was being burned away by "evil rays" beamed at him from a helicopter flying over his home. He pointed to some old scars on his arm. Although he described feeling fear and puzzlement, his voice remained a dull monotone without inflection.

FEELING (AFFECT AND MOOD)	Appropriate-ness	
	Predominant Mood	

Self-Assessment Exercise #4 (Continued)

Case #3

A college student was brought to the dispensary by his roommate because of "nervousness." The student had just been informed by his fiancee that their engagement was terminated. He described feeling intense apprehensiveness which he could not explain. The student was restless and fidgety and frequently changed positions in the chair. His pupils were dilated, his voice quavery and fearful, and he seemed frightened.

FEELING (AFFECT AND MOOD)	Appropriate-ness	
	Predominant Mood	

When you have completed this exercise, check your answers with those on the following page.

Self-Assessment Exercise #4 - Feedback

Case #1

FEELING (AFFECT AND MOOD)	Appropriateness	feelings are appropriate to content but excessive
	Predominant Mood	variable and labile; sadness and irritability

Case #2

FEELING (AFFECT AND MOOD)	Appropriateness	inappropriate to content
	Predominant Mood	dulled; blunted

Case #3

FEELING (AFFECT AND MOOD)	Appropriateness	appropriate to content
	Predominant Mood	apprehension and fear

If your answers are reasonably close to those above, please continue your reading on the next page. If not, please reread the preceding material.

MENTAL STATUS CATEGORIES (CONTINUED)

Perception

This category concerns the manner in which your patient experiences the world via his five senses (vision, hearing, touch, smell, and taste) during the MSE and in the immediate past history.

Illusions and hallucinations are two types of perceptual disorders which may indicate the presence of psychopathology. Illusions are brief misinterpretations of actual stimuli, for example interpreting the sound of wind in the trees as a voice. Hallucinations are perceptual experiences in the absence of any real, external stimuli. Seeing or hearing things which no one else can are representative of hallucinations. Illusions and hallucinations usually reflect visual or auditory misperceptions. The sense of taste, smell, and touch may be involved. Illusions may be experienced from time to time by normal individuals, especially when they are fatigued or under emotional stress. However, the presence of hallucinations generally is indicative of a serious psychopathology, usually psychosis.

Now complete Self-Assessment Exercise #5 on the following page.

Self-Assessment Exercise #5

Using information abstracted from the following history, complete the Perception category of the MSE:

A seriously ill middle aged black woman was receiving treatment for kidney failure in an intensive care unit. The nurse noted the woman was apparently conversing with someone, although no one was near her bed. When asked about what she heard, the patient responded that she was talking with her dead sister who was giving her advice. The patient then directed the nurse's attention to some specks of lint on the bed sheet insisting that they were "bugs" and that they should be removed.

PERCEPTION	

When you have completed this exercise, check your answers with those on the following page.

Self-Assessment Exercise #5 - Feedback

PERCEPTION	auditory hallucinations--hearing her dead sister visual illusions--specks of lint were perceived as "bugs"

Be sure that you clearly understand the difference between an illusion and a hallucination. The patient demonstrated both. She was hallucinating when she was hearing her dead sister speak. She experienced an illusion (visual) when she misperceived specks of lint as "bugs."

If your answers are reasonably close to those above, continue with the reading on the next page. If not, please reread the preceding material.

MENTAL STATUS CATEGORIES (CONTINUED)

Thinking

The category of Thinking encompasses a wide range of complex intellectual functions and abilities. An assessment of many of these different functions is needed to establish the presence and type of psychopathology which may be demonstrated by a particular patient. The subcategories which should be explored during an MSE are listed in Table I. Briefly look over the section on Thinking.

An important subcategory of thinking which must be assessed is your patient's level of consciousness. Level of consciousness refers to cognitive alertness and ability to perceive and respond appropriately to the environment. Note whether your patient seems fully awake, drowsy, lethargic or unconscious.

Under the subcategory of intellectual functioning, are two areas to assess -- attention span and intelligence. You should evaluate your patient's attention span, that is his ability to consciously maintain his thinking on a particular subject over a period of time. You should observe whether your patient can carry an idea or a simple activity to its natural end. A patient's inability to "attend" to a particular idea or activity for an appropriate length of time can signify the presence of some form of organic brain impairment or emotional stress. Indicate whether your client's attention span seems within the normal range or is impaired. Assess and record your patient's level of general intelligence. Intelligence can be estimated during the interview by determining the extent of formal education, your patient's type of work and noting the vocabulary and ability to use abstract ideas and perform simple calculations. Be sure to note any significant deviation from average intelligence.

Orientation refers to the accuracy of an individual's awareness of time, place, and self. In general, people should be able to state accurately who they are, the present date, and their approximate geographic location. If you suspect that such is not the case with your patient, specifically question to determine the extent and type of disorientation present.

You also should determine if impairment exists in your patient's immediate, recent or remote memory. We shall define memory with respect to time as follows, "immediate" means being able to remember questions just asked, "recent" means an accurate recall of events which have occurred within the past month, "remote" refers to the capacity to recall events which occurred longer ago than one month.

Now complete Self-Assessment Exercise #6 on the following page.

Self-Assessment Exercise #6

Using information abstracted from the following history, complete the specific subcategories of the Thinking category of the MSE below:

> A 21-year-old woman was hospitalized for evaluation after being found wandering about in a park in a "confused" and disheveled state. While awaiting examination the patient was noted to drift off to sleep when left alone, would become more alert in response to noisy stimuli or persistent questioning. Her speech was difficult to understand and she "forgot" the questions while attemtpting to answer them and asked for them to be repeated. She was unable to give details of her early life and schooling. In spite of hospital personnel and medical apparatus being in plain view, she misidentified the hospital as a train station and maintained that she was "somewhere east of the Mississippi." Although she knew her name, she misidentified the date by several months. The woman was unable to supply the details of her recent problems except that a short time earlier she ingested large quantities of drugs and alcohol.

THINKING	Level of Consciousness	
	Intellectual Functioning	attention span: intelligence:
	Orientation	
	Memory	

When you have completed this exercise, check your answers with those on the following page.

Self-Assessment Exercise #6 - Feedback

THINKING	Level of Consciousness	variable; alternately alert and drowsy
	Intellectual Functioning	attention span: diminished; would lose point of questions intelligence: no data
	Orientation	disoriented to time--misidentified date; oriented to person--knew her name; disoriented to place--thought she was "somewhere east of the Mississippi".
	Memory	both remote and recent memory impaired--unable to give details of early life and recent problems

If your answers are reasonably close to those above, please continue with the reading on the next page. If not, please reread the preceding material.

MENTAL STATUS CATEGORIES (CONTINUED)

Thinking (continued)

The four remaining subcategories of Thinking include insight, judgment, thought content and stream of thought.

Insight refers to an individual's ability to recognize the presence of psychological problems and his personal role in bringing them about. Attempts should be made to determine if your patient acknowledges that there is a problem and the degree to which he either accepts responsibility for it or tends to blame it upon something or someone else.

To cope satisfactorily with daily life, people must continually make decisions and thereby demonstrate their judgmental ability. During the MSE you should determine whether your patient is able to make sound decisions (good judgment) about every day life or if he is inclined to actions which are impulsive, imprudent and unwise. It is important to consider the intellectual functioning level and socioeconomic situation when making an assessment of your patient's judgment.

Another aspect of thinking to be evaluated is the thought content. Attempt to discover those ideas which your patient wishes to discuss; his major interest and preoccupations. You should look for the presence of one or a combination of the following types of thinking which are pathological:

a. obsession: a persistent or repetitive idea which cannot voluntarily be excluded from your patient's mind.

b. compulsion: a repetitive unwanted urge to perform an act that is contrary to your patient's wishes or standards.

c. phobia: an intense and unrealistic fear of an object or situation.

d. depersonalization: feelings of unreality, strangeness or change either in the environment, the self, or both.

e. suicidal or homicidal ideation: thoughts relating to harm of self or others.

f. delusions: fixed, false beliefs which are not amenable to logical intervention and are not culturally approved.

MENTAL STATUS CATEGORIES (CONTINUED)

The final subcategory of thinking is stream of thought, which refers to the way in which your patient's expressed ideas are related. If your patient shows a disordered continuity of ideas, gives a rambling history, jumps unpredictably from subject to subject, or combines thoughts which do not belong together, then he is demonstrating an associational disturbance. An associational disturbance may be observed when the speed of thinking is accelerated, slowed or highly variable.

Now complete Self-Assessment Exercise #7 on the following page.

Self-Assessment Exercise #7

1. Using information abstracted from the following history, complete the specified subcategories of the Thinking category of the MSE:

> A man in his early thirties was brought by the police for evaluation. During the interview he spoke very rapidly and seemed tense and restless. Manifesting great apprehensiveness, he described feeling that the FBI was out to get him, was reading his thoughts and beaming messages into his head using long distance radar waves. He could not explain the motives behind the alleged actions of the FBI and the doctors' assurances to the contrary left the patient's ideas unchanged. He rejected the statement that he might be ill in some way and he planned to go to the FBI office and issue a formal complaint. The patient complained that he experienced unwanted ideas of harming himself continuously, despite his attempt to think of other things. The story he told was hard to follow because he jumped from topic to topic. In spite of his apparent mental confusion he rapidly and accurately gave a chronological history of the events leading to his coming to the hospital and identified the date and the name of the hospital where he had been admitted.

THINKING	Insight	
	Judgment	
	Thought Content	
	Stream of Thought	

Self-Assessment Exercise #7 is continued on the following page.

Self-Assessment Exercise #7 (Continued)

2. Match the patient's statements from column B with the terms listed in column A:

COLUMN A

_______ 1. insight

_______ 2. compulsion

_______ 3. phobia

_______ 4. delusions

_______ 5. obsession

_______ 6. judgment

_______ 7. associational disturbance

COLUMN B

a. "I know that every time a policeman goes by he is reading my mind with radar and ESP."

b. "It may sound silly, but I refuse to enter small rooms or caves. I get terribly frightened that I'll smother or something."

c. "One must be strong. The philosophical cosmos shall endure... but even Jesus can walk on water and I can't do that. But I will when the sun shines. Your eyes are blue, aren't they?"

d. "The ideas that I'll harm my child keep coming back over and over again. I can't seem to get them out of my mind."

e. "I realize that my fears of showing angry feelings play an important part in my relationship with others."

f. "Everytime I hear an argument I have to start counting things... if I don't I get very nervous."

g. "I wanted so much to buy a color T.V. but my bank account could not stand the expense. I guess I'll have to wait awhile."

When you have completed this exercise, check your answers with those on the following page.

Self-Assessment Exercise #7 - Feedback

THINKING	Insight	impaired--he claimed that he was not "ill" in any way
	Judgment	impaired--he planned to act upon his erroneous beliefs about the FBI by filing a complaint
	Thought Content	obsessions--experienced unwanted ideas about self harm; suicidal--experienced ideas of self harm; delusion--experienced unchangeable false idea about the FBI
	Stream of Thought	impaired--spoke rapidly and jumped from topic to topic

2. e 1. insight

f 2. compulsion

b 3. phobia

a 4. delusion

d 5. obsession

g 6. judgment

c 7. associational disturbance

If your answers are reasonably close to those above, please continue with the reading on the next page. If not, please reread the preceding material.

SUMMARY

The Mental Status Examination describes a patient in terms of his appearance, behavior, perception, feeling and thinking. This information, when combined with the findings of your patient's history, will enable you to correctly diagnose the presence of psychopathology. It will be necessary for you to conduct many MSE's, preferably under professional supervision, before you can accurately and reliably perform this type of psychological evaluation.

A carefully performed MSE can provide very useful information for recognizing in patients the presence and type of psychopathology. In this book we will place particular emphasis on your learning the MSE findings typical of common psychopathologic syndromes. In addition, there are other findings often needed to refine the diagnosis, estimate prognosis and enable definitive treatment. We recommend that you consider these findings as you evaluate patients.

For example, it is worthwhile to note the nature and severity of stress factors which may have caused or aggravated the symptoms. Do they seem proportionate to the type and intensity of abnormal findings? It is significant if relatively minor stress results in severe symptoms. The duration of psychopathology is also important. Usually, the longer that symptoms persist, the greater the impairment which they cause. Also evaluate the degree to which symptoms interfere with routine functioning -- is the patient able to carry on in spite of anxiety or depression or is he unable to work or care for himself? Finally, try to formulate a picture of your patient's life adjustment, i.e., the quality of social relationships, work performance and ability to meet basic needs prior to the onset of his symptoms. Premorbid adjustment is often a reliable indicator of the ultimate prognosis, irrespective of the severity of current psychopathology.

REFERENCES

Gregory, I. and Smeltzer, D., Psychiatry: Essentials of Clinical Practice, Boston: Little, Brown and Company, 1977.

Kraft, Alan, Psychiatry: A Concise Textbook for Primary Care Practice, New York: Arco Publication Company, 1977.

Lieb, J., Slaby, A. and Tancredi, L., Handbook of Psychiatric Emergencies, Flushing, New York: Medical Examination Publishing Co., 1975.

Strub, R. and Black, F., The Mental Status Examination in Neurology, Philadelphia: F. A. Davis Company, 1977.

CHAPTER 3. SUPPORTIVE PSYCHOTHERAPY

Psychotherapy is a treatment which uses psychological means to help patients with emotional problems. By "psychological means" is meant the guidance, education, emotional support, insight and other primarily psychological methods which a therapist provides while attempting to alter in a positive way a patient's attitudes, feelings and behavior. This chapter focuses on supportive psychological techniques which are particularly effective in helping patients maintain or regain their emotional equilibrium. You will find it advantageous to become skilled in using these supportive methods.

LEARNING OBJECTIVES

By the time you complete this chapter, you should be able to do the following and apply the information to written case histories.

1. Briefly contrast uncovering and supportive psychotherapies with respect to indications and goals.

2. List three patient characteristics which may interfere with psychotherapy.

3. Define psychotherapy and list three premises basic to it.

4. List four therapist characteristics important for psychotherapy.

5. Define and describe the following supportive psychotherapeutic techniques and indications for their use:

   a. directive guidance
   b. nondirective guidance
   c. environmental intervention
   d. ventilation
   e. reassurance
   f. education
   g. diversion

A COMPARISON OF SUPPORTIVE AND UNCOVERING PSYCHOTHERAPY

As mentioned before, psychotherapy principally uses psychological methods for the treatment of emotional disorders. This type of treatment depends greatly on effective verbal communication, patient-therapist cooperation and the patient's intellectual intactness. Patient-therapist collaboration and achieving insight into causative factors are more necessary for a successful outcome in psychotherapy than for drug or behavior therapy. In the latter instances, a desirable change in the patient is sought primarily through the use of selected chemicals or behavioral conditioning, respectively, and psychological factors are given less emphasis.

Many clinicians find it useful to distinguish between uncovering and supportive forms of psychotherapy. A brief description will help to discriminate between the two. Uncovering psychotherapy (intensive, reconstructive or psychoanalytically-oriented therapy) is characterized by extensive treatment goals such as alleviating long-standing emotional problems or attempting to bring about major personality alterations. This form of treatment often involves extended personal exploration and relearning on the part of the patient and may take months or years. Extensive training and experience are necessary for a therapist to become skilled in this type of therapy. A detailed description of the techniques and theory involved is beyond the scope of this book, and if you are interested in learning more about uncovering psychotherapy, please refer to the readings listed at the end of this chapter.

The goals of supportive psychotherapy are more modest and are directed toward providing symptomatic improvement and reestablishing the patient's usual adaptive behaviors. This is not to imply that supportive psychotherapy is just a stop-gap measure or that it is "second best" to uncovering psychotherapy. Quite the contrary is true because for many persons the use of supportive techniques may constitute the most appropriate treatment approach. Supportive psychotherapy is particularly effective with patients who are experiencing an acute crisis and need temporary bolstering. However, these techniques are equally useful for chronically disturbed persons who can function adequately when provided with ongoing support. Supportive techniques are easier to learn and apply than the uncovering ones.

PATIENTS NEEDING SPECIAL CONSIDERATION

For most emotionally disturbed persons, implementation of one or a combination of the psychotherapeutic techniques to be described will result in symptomatic improvement. However, for some patients supportive psychotherapy by itself may not be sufficient to produce a symptom remission. It is important for you to identify those patients who are likely to need supplementary treatment. Three patient characteristics which require special handling are intellectual impairment, lack of motivation and overly intense feelings.

Intellectual impairment will reduce your patient's capacity to make use of supportive psychotherapy. Emotionally disturbed persons who simultaneously show impairment of their intelligence, memory, attention span and abstract thinking ability, typically have difficulty in retaining and integrating all new experiences, including psychotherapy. This is not to say that such patients will not benefit from a supportive treatment program. However, for the most part, these individuals will respond more favorably to behavior therapy and/or medication which are not so dependent upon an intact intellect for a therapeutic response.

If your patient is not motivated for help or is unwilling to collaborate with you, the treatment process is seriously hindered and little can be accomplished. Patients who feel coerced into treatment, are quite suspicious or feel little need for personal change, are poor candidates for supportive psychotherapy. They may respond better to a psychopharmacologic and/or behavioral approach.

A patient who is <u>unable to control his feelings and behavior</u> initially may respond better to drug and/or behavioral techniques. After regaining behavioral and emotional control, he then may be amenable to supportive methods. Psychotherapy should be tailored to fit your patient's particular needs; sometimes supportive therapy works best, at other times prescribing medication or behavior modification may be the treatment of choice.

BASIC PREMISES OF PSYCHOTHERAPY

Although there are many different theories and approaches used in psychotherapy, most share some basic premises.

A first premise is that <u>the patient is capable of changing</u>--that he is not unalterably destined to relive his past in the future. If a patient desires to change, he can learn new responses and influence the course of his life. This belief represents a statement of hope and serves as a foundation for all therapeutic efforts. Periodically, by one means or another, you should emphasize the expectation that a favorable change can be effected. Without this belief being held by you and your patient alike, the therapeutic momentum is difficult to sustain.

Secondly, <u>prospects of a better future exert a powerful effect on present motivation and behavior</u>. For this reason, the treatment goals and potential benefits should be outlined early in therapy. Usually your patient's trials and tribulations can be borne more easily if he can envision a time when circumstances will be improved. During therapy your patient often must learn to delay present, short-term satisfactions and wait for future, longer-lasting ones. Positive future expectations supply a strong incentive for initiating behavior changes in the present.

A third important premise is that <u>your patient should feel motivated</u>

for change. Psychotherapy can be a tedious and stressful process which depends greatly upon your patient's willingness to work to achieve particular treatment goals. Maintaining your patient's motivation deserves your careful attention. It is to be expected that your patient's motivation will wane from time to time. When this happens, reestablishing your patient's desire to change takes precedence over all other therapeutic work.

Now complete Self-Assessment Exercise #1 beginning on the following page.

Self-Assessment Exercise #1

1. In the space provided, for each of the following items indicate whether supportive "S" or uncovering "U" psychotherapeutic techniques are indicated.

______ a. personality reconstruction

______ b. short-term crisis

______ c. ongoing maintenance of functioning

______ d. resolving complex or deep-seated emotional problems

______ e. dealing with an acute grief reaction

2. Define psychotherapy and list the three premises upon which it is based.

3. For each of the following patient characteristics, in the space provided write a "C" if the characteristic is compatible with supportive psychotherapeutic techniques and an "I" if the characteristic may interfere with supportive psychotherapeutic techniques.

______ a. the patient claims not to have any psychological problems

______ b. the patient is anxious, disoriented and shows signs of mental confusion

______ c. the patient is immobilized by deep depression

______ d. the patient seeks help because of feelings of episodic, severe anxiety

Self-Assessment Exercise #1 (Continued)

______e. the patient expresses fear that the therapist may be involved in a plot against him

______f. the patient describes feeling that her family coerced her to seek therapy

When you have completed this exercise to the best of your ability, check your answers with those on the following page.

Self-Assessment Exercise #1 - Feedback

1. S = supportive U = uncovering

U a. personality reconstruction usually requires intensive and prolonged psychotherapy

S b. short-term crisis is likely to respond to supportive psychotherapy

S c. ongoing maintenance of a patient can be accomplished by supportive psychotherapy

U d. resolving complex and/or deep-seated emotional problems usually calls for uncovering psychotherapy

S e. a grief reaction can usually be handled by supportive psychotherapy

2. Psychotherapy involves the treatment of emotional disorders by psychological means, i.e., utilization of the therapist-patient relationship and verbal communication. This type of therapy is based upon the premises that: the patient is capable of changing, future expectations exert a positive effect on present patient behavior, and the patient is motivated for help.

3. C = compatible with supportive psychotherapy techniques
I = likely will interfere with supportive psychotherapy techniques

I a. the patient denies having problems and is not motivated for treatment

I b. the patient is intellectually impaired and probably could not collaborate effectively with the therapist

I c. the patient is overwhelmed by depression and probably could not participate in the treatment program

C d. the patient seems motivated for treatment

I e. suspicious patients find it difficult to collaborate closely with the therapist

I f. the patient seemingly lacks personal motivation for therapy

If your answers correspond closely with those above, please continue reading on the next page. If not, please reread the preceding material.

IMPORTANT CHARACTERISTICS OF THE THERAPIST

Research has shown that the therapist's attitudes and characteristics significantly influence the therapeutic relationship and outcome.

From the patient's standpoint, a vital factor in treatment is your interest and desire to help. Patients are better able to tolerate changing life situations (and treatment) when they sense that their therapist is genuinely interested in their well-being. Conversely, if a patient perceives a waning interest or indifference on your part, the working alliance and treatment may be seriously jeopardized.

Patients are very sensitive to the nuances of your attitude toward them and the therapeutic encounter is subject to the same tensions, frustrations and fluctuations as any other close relationship. However, it is your responsibility as the helping figure to monitor your own feelings and handle them in a way which will not interfere with the patient's progress. If you detect in yourself a persistent loss of interest or aversion to working with a particular patient, every effort should be made to rectify those feelings. If this cannot be done, then seek consultation with another colleague about the problem or refer the patient to another therapist.

Ideally, you should strive to maintain an attitude of flexibility in dealing with patients, especially with respect to selecting treatment goals and methods. In the therapeutic encounter, you serve as the expert who directs treatment. However, psychotherapy also is a collaborative effort, and your patient's needs and capabilities deserve thoughtful consideration. Early in treatment you should work out with him mutually agreeable objectives and ways to achieve them. Frequently the treatment goals and/or procedures will need revision and you must be willing to make appropriate changes. When dealing with complex human beings whose needs are ever changing, no one therapeutic approach will work with all patients (or even a single patient) all of the time.

The process of psychotherapy depends greatly upon open and meaningful communication between the therapist and patient. In this regard, it is vital that you respond nonjudgmentally towards your patient, and create an atmosphere in which he literally can talk about anything and everything.

Emotionally troubled persons often are plagued by feelings of shame and guilt about some of their feelings, behaviors and thoughts. Anticipating possible criticism from their therapist, most patients initially are reluctant to talk openly about personal matters. Their reluctance to communicate can be overcome gradually if they perceive the therapist to be understanding and noncritical. During the course of treatment, your patient may discuss matters that evoke feelings of discomfort, anger or even revulsion in you; but it is vital that you set your personal feelings aside and try to present a nonjudgmental attitude. To do otherwise will likely inhibit your patient's communication.

Most patients are highly influenced by a therapist's authority and knowledge, and usually adopt his prognostic viewpoint as their own. For this reason, you should make a concerted effort to convey a feeling of optimistic confidence about both the treatment method and outcome. This does not mean that unrealistic promises or expectations should be given the patient. But it does imply that your patient's therapeutic morale will be greatly influenced by yours. Studies have shown that a patient's therapeutic response to a medication is significantly related to their perception of the therapist's expectations about its effectiveness. The same principle can be applied to the therapeutic outcome.

In summary, you should demonstrate concern, a flexible approach to treatment, a nonjudgmental attitude and optimism about the treatment and prognosis.

Now complete Self-Assessment Exercise #2 beginning on the following page.

Self-Assessment Exercise #2

1. List the four therapist characteristics which are important for psychological treatment.

2. Briefly describe how the following therapist's statements/behaviors may not be in keeping with the recommended therapist characteristics.

   a. "I really don't know whether the medicine will help you, but try it anyway. It probably won't do any harm."

   b. "I'm really surprised that you would spank your child like that. No wonder you feel guilty."

   c. The therapist persists in reading the patient's chart while the patient relates the history.

   d. "I know you've been under a lot of pressure lately, Mrs. Smith, but we agreed that you must reduce your eating and lose weight. If you don't, someday you are going to get sick because of being fat."

When you have completed this exercise to the best of your ability, check your answers with those on the following page.

Self-Assessment Exercise #2 - Feedback

1. Four characteristics of the therapist which are important for psychological treatment are: an expressed therapeutic interest, a flexible approach to treatment, a nonjudgmental attitude and therapeutic optimism.

2. The following therapist's statements/behaviors are not in keeping with the recommended characteristics in the following ways:

   a. The therapist's uncertainty about the value of the medication has been conveyed to the patient. This doubt may adversely affect the patient's response to it. If the therapist has uncertainties about the drug (or treatment approach), either another medication should be selected or the doubts not conveyed to the patient.

   b. The therapist's statement is highly judgmental and is likely to accentuate the patient's guilt and hinder further discussion. Although the therapist may not condone the patient's actions, he should not make critical statements that may restrict open communication.

   c. The therapist may be perceived as being more interested in the chart than the patient. Full attention should be given to the patient while he narrates his history.

   d. The therapist periodically may have to readjust treatment goals according to the needs of the patient. Threats or insisting that the patient adhere to previously established goals may be counterproductive. A more flexible approach is indicated. The diet may be resumed after Mrs. Smith's tension has subsided.

If your answers correspond closely with those above, please continue reading on the next page. If not, please reread the preceding material.

SUPPORTIVE PSYCHOTHERAPEUTIC TECHNIQUES

There are several therapeutic techniques which will provide emotional support for troubled patients. Seven of these techniques and the indications for their use will now be discussed. They may be utilized singly or in combination for brief or extended periods depending on the needs and the goals of treatment.

Directive Guidance

This treatment technique calls for you to intervene with your patient in an active and directive way. Capitalizing on your authority and experience, give specific advice about your patient's problems and ways to solve them; to varying degrees "direct" his life. This therapeutic approach is particularly effective with a person who, by himself, is unable to make and enact important life decisions. For an individual overwhelmed by an acute emotional stress from which he soon will recover, direct intervention is needed only temporarily. As soon as the patient is again self-determining, relinquish your directive role. For other patients whose judgment and coping behavior are chronically impaired because of severe emotional disorders, mental retardation, organic brain disease, etc., supportive guidance may be indicated for an indefinite period.

As is the case with other forms of treatment, directive guidance may cause complications if it is not used appropriately. By keeping the following principles in mind, however, you can minimize problems caused by this form of treatment.

If enhancing your patient's capacity for self-determination is a goal of psychotherapy, directive guidance should be utilized only to the degree and for the time that it is absolutely necessary. Many individuals find it very gratifying to turn various life decisions and problems over to their therapist for solving. This approach, if overutilized, may encourage excessive dependency.

Generally, your advice should be presented in the form of a "recommendation" or "suggestion." It is important that you carefully regulate the use of your authority and directiveness in accordance with your patient's needs. Definitive recommendations are suitable for anxious or disorganized patients but are not appropriate for individuals who are capable of self-determination. Most persons react negatively if they feel that the ideas of others are being arbitrarily imposed upon them.

As a rule, you should avoid advising your patient to initiate life changes which are potentially irreversible or may be fraught with far-reaching consequences, for example, recommending a divorce or major vocational change. Your patient later may hold you accountable if problems arise.

Nondirective Guidance

In this form of treatment, you purposely give little or no direct guidance to your patient with respect to making decisions or initiating action. Instead, present a clear summary of the problem, offer some options for resolving it and leave to your patient the decision of which course of action to take.

Nondirective guidance is useful for promoting independence and self-determination; its use assumes that the patient is mentally and emotionally capable of making and carrying out sound judgments. This method is generally contraindicated for patients who are psychotic, intensely anxious or who, for other reasons, are so disturbed that their judgment is seriously impaired.

Briefly described, this method consists of encouraging your patient to discuss at length what is troubling him. By means of careful listening and observation, you should be able to identify the theme of his difficulty. You are then in a position to summarize the facts of the problem and suggest constructive ways of handling it.

Throughout the encounter, you should function as an interested, objective and nonjudgmental figure who is authoritative, but not authoritarian. For this reason, a nondirective approach is of special value for patients who may respond negatively to persons they perceive as an authority figure. Adolescents, juvenile delinquents or others who strongly resist "being told what to do" are candidates for nondirective guidance.

The following interview segments illustrate the technique.

Mrs. Jones: "I'm sick and tired of having to work so many extra hours. The boss keeps asking me to do it, and I hate to turn him down. I'd quit the job entirely, if I didn't need the money right now."

Therapist: "It sounds like you are feeling overworked, but are hesitant about saying 'no' to your boss. (A summarizing statement.) Right now it looks like you can either quit and do without the money, talk with him about it and see if some alternative solution is possible, or just keep with what you have been doing. (Listing options for possible action.) What action do you think is best to take?" (Decision is left to the patient.)

Miss Reynolds: "I don't know whether to get married or not. We have been engaged for several months and I love him, but what if it doesn't work out? Still, if we wait too long, he may lose interest in me. I don't know what I should do."

Therapist: "It seems that you are puzzled about what to do about getting married. You are concerned that if you marry now it may be premature, but waiting may not help either. I wonder if some other option might be possible, such as talking the matter over with your fiance to see how he feels--or perhaps getting some counseling before you decide. What do you think might help?"

This treatment method is based on the belief that the responsibility for making and carrying on important life decisions should rest with the patient, and it assumes that he is capable of good judgment.

Now complete Self-Assessment Exercise #3 beginning on the following page.

Self-Assessment Exercise #3

By each of the patient descriptions below, place a "D" if a directive guidance approach is indicated, or an "N" if a nondirective guidance approach is indicated.

______a. the patient seems overwhelmed after being involved in an auto accident

______b. the young woman suffers from moderately severe mental retardation

______c. a 50-year-old banker states he is bored with his work and questions whether he should change his vocation

______d. the young man is unable to make routine decisions because of intense anxiety

______e. a widow, after overcoming her grief, must decide whether to sell or keep her home

______f. a "normal" student is puzzled as to whether she should attend a local or distant college

______g. a decision about living arrangements must be made regarding an elderly man who is subject to periodic confusion and memory loss

______h. the woman has completely recovered from a depression and is uncertain whether she should return to work or stay longer at home

______i. a teenager requests advice for selecting a career

When you have completed this exercise to the best of your ability, check your answers with those on the following page.

Self-Assessment Exercise #3 - Feedback

D = a directive guidance approach is indicated
N = a nondirective guidance approach is indicated

__D__ a. the patient seems overwhelmed after being involved in an auto accident

__D__ b. the young woman suffers from moderately severe mental retardation

__N__ c. a 50-year-old banker states he is bored with his work and questions whether he should change his vocation

__D__ d. the young man is unable to make routine decisions because of intense anxiety

__N__ e. a widow, after overcoming her grief, must decide whether to sell or keep her home

__N__ f. a "normal" student is puzzled as to whether she should attend a local or distant college

__D__ g. a decision about living arrangements must be made regarding an elderly man who is subject to periodic confusion and memory loss

__N__ h. the woman has completely recovered from a depression and is uncertain whether she should return to work or stay longer at home

__N__ i. a teenager requests advice for selecting a career

If your answers correspond closely with those above, please continue reading on the next page. If not, please reread the preceding material.

Environmental Intervention

This technique refers to a variety of interventions which you can make to alleviate sources of stress arising from your patient's environment, i.e., work, home or school. Various emotional problems or feelings of insecurity may inhibit your patient from taking corrective action to improve his own life circumstances. When such is the case, it may be necessary for you to initiate stress-reducing changes in the environment.

Your interventions may be presented in the form of definitive action (such as personally arranging for a medical appointment, a change of housing, telephoning an employer, etc.), or as recommendations given to your patient to carry out (for example, suggesting a vacation from a stressful job). This treatment approach is effective for reducing short-term environmental stress. Generally, it is of little value when dealing with complex emotional problems, and carries the risk that your patient will perceive the "bad environment" as the principle cause for his personal distress, and not recognize his own role in the difficulty. Environmental intervention must be used judiciously with persons who easily become dependent, since they may come to rely unduly upon you rather than themselves to solve life problems.

Ventilation

In this procedure you should actively encourage your patient to express previously surpressed emotions and ideas. The pent-up feelings and thoughts often have been kept from expression because of your patient's guilt or shame, or simply that no interested listener was available to him. The verbalization of potent feelings usually results in a marked reduction of emotional tension, and many persons describe feeling that their problems seem more tangible and manageable once they have been put into words. Furthermore, it can be therapeutic for a patient to experience your nonjudgmental support in response to feelings which he feared would be "unacceptable."

Tearfulness, anger and intense fears and worries are the most common affects expressed during ventilation. As a rule, you should attentively listen and not interrupt your patient's verbal flow during the outpouring of emotion. Collecting details of his history is best left until later in the interview, after the expression of feeling has run its course.

Ventilation is a procedure which should be used selectively. It is most helpful with patients who recently have experienced an emotional crisis or personal catastrophe and are in need of an opportunity to express their feelings about it. Patients with psychotic symptoms or who, during the interview, show signs of rapidly escalating tension, disorganized thinking and behavior, generally should not be encouraged to dwell on powerful feelings or potentially disruptive thoughts. To do so may further accentuate their disorganization. Instead, their attention should be diverted to more neutral and reality-oriented topics.

Reassurance

Giving reassurance and encouragement to a distressed person is a common method of providing support. However, by virtue of your authoritative knowledge and experience, reassurance given by you as the therapist carries much greater significance than that supplied by friends or relatives. In fact, well-timed and thoughtfully given reassurance is a very effective psychotherapeutic technique.

It is likely that all patients benefit from periodic expressions of reassurance given by the therapist, but it is especially helpful for those who feel socially isolated by their problems and doubt their ability to cope with them. Even individuals who have been quite self-sufficient in the past may need special support when faced with new situations or a personal crisis.

Reassurance can be explicitly stated in words, but it is also meaningfully conveyed by your continuing interest, optimistic approach and availability. It is a therapeutic tool which is most effective when used selectively in terms of specificity of need, timing and frequency.

As a rule, you should await giving reassurance until you have a clear understanding of your patient so that the intervention can be focused on specific needs. However well-intended, general statements of reassurance such as "don't worry," or "you have nothing to worry about," or "everything will be alright" provide little support and tend to discourage further communication by the patient. Reassurance will be more effective if your patient first has thoroughly expressed his worries, doubts and anxieties. Otherwise, these intense, but unexpressed, feelings may interfere with your patient's ability to attend to your remarks.

Some emotionally needful patients may seek reassurance continuously, perhaps to overcome self-doubts or seek attention. In such cases, you should assess and treat those aspects of your patient's emotional life which are responsible for the persistent need for reassurance.

Education

Educating patients is an integral and important part of psychotherapy. Indeed, for many therapists, treatment consists primarily of providing information and experience needed by patients for learning better ways to solve problems. A well-informed patient is more likely to make correct judgments about himself and the world, than one who lacks basic information.

As the therapist, your first task is to determine whether your patient is having difficulty resolving his problems because he lacks basic information and particular life experiences. A good starting place is to explore his understanding of his problem. It then will become clear where you should focus your efforts. Don't equate your patient's years of formal education or intelligence with his capacity for understanding or dealing with personal difficulties. Even in today's enlightened society, it is not rare to find individuals with little understanding about the determinants of their behavior. Others may intellectually "know" the facts, but are unable to practially apply the knowledge which they possess. In both cases, the therapist can serve a vital role as educator.

Sometimes your patient's educational needs are primarily informational. For example, your patient may not know where to apply for welfare benefits or understand the nature of his physical illness or the reasons for following your recommendations. Providing basic information may be of great help. A recent study indicates that patient compliance with physician recommendations is surprisingly low. One reason for the poor compliance may be that most physicians fail to provide their patients with meaningful explanations about the illness and treatment. Patients are less likely to follow recommendations if they don't understand their purpose.

For some patients, the education needed is experiential in nature; accordingly, therapy should be planned to provide problem-solving by means of direct personal experience. Helping an inhibited patient learn to express feelings more openly or arranging job training for an occupationally unskilled client exemplifies this treatment approach.

Intense feelings can interfere with retaining and applying new information. Whenever the education process is likely to evoke strong feelings in your patient, such as providing information about his forthcoming surgery, he may have difficulty in retaining the material and repeated explanations may be needed. Verbal descriptions should be supplemented by written explanations, diagrams, pictures, etc. whenever possible. If, after a number of attempts to educate your patient about a particular subject and his perspective remains unchanged, emotional factors are likely responsible. You then must search out the disturbing feelings and deal with them. Only then will your patient be able to assimilate the information provided.

Diversion

The technique of diversion consists of your redirecting a patient's thinking and/or behavior away from disturbing areas into more therapeutic ones. Intense feelings often can interfere with adaptive behavior and persons who are emotionally disturbed may worsen if they are allowed to dwell upon upsetting feelings or thoughts. Some patients become so preoccupied with personal problems that they neglect other important areas of their life which in turn causes more difficulty.

Making use of your authority and expertise, you can often discreetly divert a patient's attention away from disturbing topics to less upsetting ones. For example, if during the consultation your patient shows increasing disorganization or anxiety while talking about a particular subject, you should firmly but tactfully change the topic of discussion. After this is done, your patient often will show immediate improvement. When working with persons who are emotionally unstable, it is important for you to assess their capacity to deal with strong feelings and carefully adjust their exposure to them.

Some individuals become morbidly withdrawn and preoccupied following a personal catastrophe or loss. If these symptoms persist, it is often therapeutic to recommend that they engage in activities which will divert them from their preoccupations. This approach likewise is useful with patients experiencing a psychosis, particularly if they are engrossed with disturbing ideas or hallucinations. Encouraging their participation in structured activities which promote social interaction and focus their attention on things external to themselves frequently will reduce the intensity of their symptoms.

Providing diversion is particularly valuable for patients experiencing pain or who are hospitalized because of medical problems. Research has demonstrated that medically ill patients are easier to manage, complain less frequently about their illness and need less pain medication when their attention is diverted from their illness.

Diversion, then, is a useful therapeutic tool which can be used for a variety of psychopathologic and medical conditions.

Now complete Self-Assessment Exercise #4 beginning on the following page.

Self-Assessment Exercise #4

1. Match the type of supportive psychotherapy to the description of the therapist intervention/statements. Each therapeutic approach may be used more than once or not at all.

   a. environmental intervention
   b. ventilation
   c. reassurance
   d. education
   e. diversion
   f. directive guidance
   g. nondirective guidance

_______(1) "I think it's most important that you not drink alcohol while you are taking the medication."

_______(2) The therapist changes the direction of the interview when the patient seems increasingly distraught.

_______(3) "It seems to me that a vacation from your job is in order. I recommend a week at the beach or mountains--where it's quiet and restful."

_______(4) "It's no sin to feel angry. Go ahead and get it off your chest."

_______(5) "You can either seek counseling, break up the relationship or wait and see what happens. What would you like to do?"

_______(6) "I'd like you to read the pamphlet on high blood pressure. I think it will help you understand your condition better."

2. Match the following psychological techniques to the patient behaviors described. Each approach may be used more than once, and each patient may require more than one type of intervention.

   a. environmental intervention
   b. ventilation
   c. reassurance
   d. education
   e. diversion
   f. directive guidance
   g. nondirective guidance

_______(1) The emotionally distraught woman markedly worsens as she continues to talk about her husband.

_______(2) The patient does not understand the nature of his physical illness.

Self-Assessment Exercise #4 (Continued)

______(3) The man makes a great effort to suppress his tears as he describes the recent death of his wife.

______(4) Immediately after the death of her husband, the woman does not seem to know how to proceed with handling legal matters regarding his estate.

______(5) The patient is very fearful of undergoing surgery.

______(6) The client asks whether or not to go ahead with the divorce.

When you have completed this exercise to the best of your ability, check your answers with those on the following page.

Self-Assessment Exercise #4 - Feedback

1. a. environmental intervention
   b. ventilation
   c. reassurance
   d. education
   e. diversion
   f. directive guidance
   g. nondirective guidance

f (1) "I think it's most important that you not drink alcohol while you are taking the medication."

e (2) The therapist changes the direction of the interview when the patient seems increasingly distraught.

a,f (3) "It seems to me that a vacation from your job is in order. I recommend a week at the beach or mountains--where it's quiet and restful."

b,f (4) "It's no sin to feel angry. Go ahead and get it off your chest."

g (5) "You can either seek counseling, break up the relationship or wait and see what happens. What would you like to do?"

d,c (6) "I'd like you to read the pamphlet on high blood pressure. I think it will help you understand your condition better."

2. a. environmental intervention
   b. ventilation
   c. reassurance
   d. education
   e. diversion
   f. directive guidance
   g. nondirective guidance

e (1) Since the woman is becoming increasingly distraught, it is best that she be diverted to a more neutral topic than talking about her husband.

d (2) Since the patient does not understand the nature of his physical illness, some sort of education approach is indicated.

b (3) Ventilation is indicated since the man is struggling to suppress his sadness. As a general principle, it is more therapeutic to have the patient express his feelings rather than keep them inside.

Self-Assessment Exercise #4 - Feedback (Continued)

_d,f_ (4) Education and directive guidance. Following a personal catastrophe, many individuals have trouble making up their minds and at least temporarily need some sort of guidance. As soon as they improve, responsibility for decision-making should be returned to them.

_c,d_ (5) Reassurance and education. This approach is indicated when the patient seems to be overwhelmed and/or needful of positive support by the therapist. Some education about the contemplated surgery may help to reduce fears.

_g_ (6) Nondirective guidance. When a patient requests advice about major and potentially irreversible life decisions, it is best for the therapist to not give definitive suggestions. Instead, he should describe the problem and enumerate the options available. Only under extreme circumstances should the therapist give direct advice about such an important life matter.

If your answers correspond closely with those above, please continue reading on the next page. If not, please reread the preceding material.

SUMMARY

Supportive psychological techniques often are effective in helping your patients who are emotionally disturbed. These treatment methods are relatively easy to learn and apply, but should be used strategically and selectively according to your patient's needs.

REFERENCES

Barten, H., Brief Therapies, New York: Behavioral Publications, 1971.

Mendel, W., Supportive Care, Santa Monica: Mara Books, 1975.

Patterson, C., Theories of Counseling and Psychotherapy, New York: Harper and Row, 1966.

Rogers, C., Client-Centered Therapy, Boston: Houghton-Mifflin and Company, 1965.

Wolberg, L., Short-Term Psychotherapy, New York: Grune and Stratton, 1965.

Wolberg, L., The Technique of Psychotherapy, New York: Grune and Stratton, 1976.

CHAPTER 4. BEHAVIOR THERAPY

Behavior therapy is a treatment approach that is designed to modify specific patient behaviors. Its goal is to reinforce adaptive behavior and reduce maladaptive ones by applying principles of learning theory and experimental psychology. This chapter presents some of the basic principles of this commonly used treatment method.

LEARNING OBJECTIVES

By the time you complete this chapter, you should be able to do the following and apply the information to written case histories.

1. Define behavior therapy.

2. Contrast behavior therapy with supportive psychotherapy.

3. List indications for behavior therapy.

4. List some contraindications for behavior therapy.

5. List and briefly describe the six behavioral therapies below and the indications and contraindications for their use.

   a. token therapy
   b. desensitization
   c. biofeedback
   d. aversive therapy
   e. contractual therapy
   f. modeling techniques

GENERAL PRINCIPLES OF BEHAVIOR THERAPY

Behavior therapy (behavior modification) is aimed principally at changing what the patient does rather than what he thinks or feels. In contrast to uncovering psychotherapy (dynamic psychotherapy or psychoanalysis), relatively little emphasis is placed on exploring a patient's psychological life or the historical antecedents of their problem. In behavior therapy it is sufficient to substitute new adaptive behavior patterns for older, maladaptive ones. Furthermore, behavior modification is a more structured and focused procedure with respect to treatment goals than many psychological therapies.

Most behavior therapies possess a similar format. Usually, one or more target behaviors (those which are to be changed) are identified and treatment goals reflecting the desired behavioral alterations are established. A therapeutic approach is designed which promotes the desired behavioral response, for example, to act more assertively, to decrease smoking, or to eat less. Appropriate rewards are administered in a way which reinforces the desired behavior. Records are often kept to chart the patient's progress. In time, and with practice, the new response gradually replaces the old one and becomes part of the patient's behavioral repertoire.

Indications for Behavior Therapy

Behavior therapy is most likely to succeed in persons who are highly motivated for change, when a positive therapist-patient relationship exis the patient is intellectually and emotionally capable of collaborating in the treatment and the problematic areas are easily identified and few in number. However, some behavior techniques can be adapted success fully to persons who have considerable intellectual or emotional impairment (i.e., mental retardation, psychosis, severe personality problems etc.). Indeed, for many such persons, behavior modification may be th most appropriate therapy. It is equally effective with adults and childre

Circumscribed problem areas such as drug or alcohol abuse, well-defined fears or phobias, temper outbursts, lack of assertiveness, faul grooming or eating habits, couples therapy, and difficulties with weight control, exemplify conditions which may respond to behavior therapy.

This treatment method is less effective with individuals who have numerous or ill-defined behavioral disturbances, and who are overwhelmed by intense feelings. In the latter instance, the administration of appropriate psychotropic medication may be needed first to reduce the level of feelings which otherwise would interfere with treatment. Similarly, behavior modification may not be as appropriate as tradition psychotherapy with persons for whom more extensive or psychological-type goals are indicated.

Before selecting any therapeutic approach, you should carefully consider the patient's characteristics and needs, and accordingly match the with the appropriate behavioral, drug or psychological treatment method.

Now complete Self-Assessment Exercise #1 beginning on the following page.

Self-Assessment Exercise #1

1. Define behavior therapy and briefly discuss its goal and basic principles.

2. Contrast behavioral and uncovering psychotherapy for each of the following categories.

	BEHAVIORAL THERAPY	UNCOVERING PSYCHOTHERAPY
focal point of therapy		
importance of developing insight		
importance of extensive exploration of past history		
definitiveness of treatment goals		

Self-Assessment Exercise #1 (Continued)

3. In the space provided, for each of the following patient symptoms, place an "A" if behavior therapy is appropriate or an "I" if behavior therapy is inappropriate.

______a. a young woman with persistent, non-specific depression

______b. a ten-year-old boy with an intense fear of dogs

______c. a grief stricken middle-aged woman whose husband died three days earlier

______d. a young adult with a marked fear of flying

______e. a college student who seeks help for lack of assertiveness

______f. a mentally retarded child who has not learned to groom himself properly

______g. an overweight teenager who deals with emotional stress by eating

______h. a lawyer who experiences episodes of intense anxiety without discernable cause

______i. a middle-aged man who is experiencing intense feelings of guilt, depression and hallucinations

When you have completed this exercise to the best of your ability, check your answers with those on the following page.

Self-Assessment Exercise #1 - Feedback

1. Behavior therapy is a treatment which is concerned with modifying a patient's behavior. Using principles of learning theory and experimental psychology, it systematically makes use of various rewards and/or punishments to encourage repetition of target behaviors.

2.

	BEHAVIORAL THERAPY	UNCOVERING PSYCHOTHERAPY
focal point of therapy	changing behavior	changing the patient's psychological and emotional perspective
importance of developing insight	little importance	considerable importance
importance of extensive exploration of past history	little importance	considerable importance
definitiveness of treatment goals	specific behavioral goals	treatment goals are often vague and/or not specific

Self-Assessment Exercise #1 - Feedback (Continued)

3. An "A" answer should be given for the following patients because behavior therapy is appropriate for them; the described problems are concerned with specific fears, inhibitions and are primarily behavioral in nature.

   b. a ten-year-old boy with an intense fear of dogs

   d. a young adult with a marked fear of flying

   e. a college student who seeks help for lack of assertiveness

   f. a mentally retarded child who has not learned to groom himself properly

   g. an overweight teenager who deals with emotional stress by eating

An "I" should be assigned to the following patient symptoms because behavior therapy is inappropriate for them; the symptoms are not clearly related to specific behavior and/or the symptoms are primarily affectual rather than behavioral in nature.

   a. a young woman with persistent, non-specific depression

   c. a grief stricken middle-aged woman whose husband died three days earlier

   h. a lawyer who experiences episodes of intense anxiety without discernable cause

   i. a middle-aged man who is experiencing intense feelings of guilt, depression and hallucinations

If your answers correspond closely with those above, please continue reading on the next page. If not, please reread the preceding material.

TECHNIQUES USED IN BEHAVIOR THERAPY

The following techniques, singly or in combination, are commonly employed for the treatment of behavioral problems. They are presented here more to acquaint you with an overview of the basic types of behavior modification than as definitive instruction in the subject. Some of the simpler approaches can be adapted easily to patient care in general, while others require specialized training. Selected references regarding behavior modification are listed at the end of the chapter.

Token Therapy

This therapeutic technique emphasizes giving tangible rewards to patients when they have demonstrated a designated behavior. The "reward" usually is in the form of tokens, points or coupons, which later can be exchanged for objects or experiences such as candy, cigarettes, or special privileges valued by the patient.

To implement this system, an agreement between the therapist and patient is made which: (1) clearly defines the patient behavior that is expected, (2) establishes the interim reward (token), and (3) defines the ultimate reward for which the token can be exchanged. Undesirable or counterproductive behavior is purposefully neither punished nor rewarded. Emphasis is placed on having the therapist reward positive behavior and show indifference (not punishment, per se) towards an undesirable response. Usually only one or a few target behaviors should be chosen for modification at one time.

This therapeutic approach is especially applicable to self-help projects such as improving personal hygiene, reducing socially inappropriate behavior, reducing weight and others. Token systems work best in structured environments, i.e., classrooms, day care centers, institutions and other settings where it is possible to closely monitor and support the patient.

After the new behavior pattern has been firmly established, most patients should be weaned gradually from the token system. Hopefully, their new behavior will have become self-perpetuating and the tokens replaced by the rewards of enhanced self-esteem and sense of accomplishment. For other patients with chronic behavioral problems, a token system approach may be needed indefinitely.

Desensitization

This therapy is designed to help a patient overcome fears, phobias (unrealistic fears) or aversions to particular stimuli (objects or situations) by gradually decreasing his sensitivity to them, i.e., desensitization. This therapeutic approach is based on the belief that physical relaxation and the experience of fear or anxiety cannot exist simultaneously in the same person. Briefly, the patient is first taught to relax by maintaining calm, pleasurable thoughts and purposefully decreasing his muscle tension. The patient is then exposed to the feared stimulus in graduated increments. He is asked to maintain a state of physical relaxation and mental calm while being confronted by that which is feared. The physical tension and feelings of anxiety which were formerly experienced when he was confronted by the fearful stimulus, gradually are replaced by calmness and muscle relaxation.

This therapeutic method can be exemplified by the patient who seeks to overcome an aversion to snakes. The patient is first taught to physically relax and maintain peaceful thoughts. A treatment regimen is designed which calls for the patient to imagine that a snake is gradually brought closer to him. As the distance between the patient and the snake lessens, he is instructed to deliberately practice muscle relaxation and focus on calming thoughts. After extensive practice of imagining the threatening situation and becoming desensitized to it, the same technique may then be duplicated by using a real snake.

Desensitization methods can be effective for overcoming various inhibitions or fears such as riding elevators, flying, or public speaking. This method is most effective for modifying specific fears rather than global or pervasive ones. Treatment progress depends greatly on patient motivation and a trusting relationship with the therapist.

Biofeedback

Recent research has shown that it is possible to learn control over body physiology in ways which formerly were believed not possible. By means of biofeedback monitoring devices, an individual can learn to influence basic physical functions such as heart rate, blood pressure, muscle tension, brain wave patterns, skin responses and others.

Typically, this method utilizes a mechanical signal such as a light, tone or buzzer which is activated by a predetermined physiological change in the patient's body. Using the sensory signal as a guide, the patient can be trained to use relaxation and other techniques to influence a specific physiologic response. When the patient is able to control the physical response in the desired fashion, he receives confirmation of his success by the electronic monitoring device; this communication (feedback) serves as his "reward." Ideally, the patient eventually will be able to maintain the desired response without reliance upon the feedback apparatus; but periodic retraining sessions may be necessary.

The application of biofeedback principles can be illustrated by a patient for whom a reduction of systolic blood pressure below 150 is desired. The patient first is thoroughly instructed about the biofeedback method including relaxation techniques, the role of the electronic monitoring device and the treatment goals. He is then attached to the biofeedback apparatus which emits a tone when a pressure of 150 is exceeded. As the patient relaxes and his blood pressure drops below 150 the tone stops. By receiving this direct feedback, the patient gradually is able to learn to reduce his blood pressure level. Immediate feedback provides evidence of the patient's ability to influence his body functioning, builds confidence and reinforces the behavior.

Biofeedback techniques are used widely in research as a means of alleviating headaches, high blood pressure, seizures and other physiological symptoms that, in part, are stress related. The technique requires sophisticated technology and a high level of patient motivation; it works best with physical symptoms that easily can be electronically monitored. Although still in experimental stages of development, biofeedback offers much promise for the treatment of selected medical problems in the future.

Now complete Self-Assessment Exercise #2 beginning on the following page.

Self-Assessment Exercise #2

1. Briefly describe the following behavioral therapies and give an example of a patient problem to which it could be applied.

   Token Therapy

   Desensitization

   Biofeedback

When you have completed this exercise to the best of your ability, check your answers with those on the following page.

Self-Assessment Exercise #2 - Feedback

1. Common behavioral techniques are:

 Token Therapy consists of giving tokens as a reward for performing a specific behavior; the token can be saved and exchanged later for a desired object or privilege; token therapy is useful for developing new behavior patterns such as encouraging grooming, performing various work assignments, etc.

 Desensitization is a regimen which combines muscle relaxation techniques and gradual increasing exposure to a threatening stimulus (object or situation) in order to overcome specific fears and phobias; for example, the fear of being confined in small areas.

 Biofeedback is concerned with modifying physiological responses by means of combining relaxation techniques and feedback of the patient's biological state; it is applicable to regulation of blood pressure, muscle tension states, and others.

If your answers correspond closely with those above, please continue reading on the next page. If not, please reread the preceding material.

Aversive Therapy

Under special circumstances, aversive therapy is of value for changing patient behaviors. In contrast to the treatment approaches previously described which reward specific patient responses, aversive therapy brings about change in the target behaviors by associating them with some type of "punishment." Behavioral change is achieved because the patient wishes to avoid the unpleasant consequences which have followed undesirable actions.

In aversive therapy the punishment can be physical (i.e., a mild electric shock or medically induced nausea and vomiting) or psychological (verbal reprimands, social isolation, etc.). After sufficient training sessions to establish an aversive response, just the memory of the aversive experience is strong enough to inhibit the undesired behavior.

Aversive therapy as a treatment technique is somewhat controversial and is usually reserved for behaviors that are seriously maladaptive and/or resistent to change. It has been used to treat conditions such as intractable head-banging in psychotic children, alcoholism, compulsive smoking and others. Avèrsive treatment may generate considerable hostility and negativism in some patients and should be performed only by specially trained therapists.

Contractual Methods

Selected behaviors can be altered as a result of a specific agreement or "contract" between the therapist and patient. The target behaviors and incentives for performing them are clearly specified and when the patient responds in the desired way he receives a reward. In some respects, establishing a behavioral contract is similar to the token system described earlier. However, this technique is more sophisticated in that the contract is often written out and the patient's progress charted graphically. The written and visual representations provide both the patient and therapist with the conditions of the contract, the problem areas, rewards, punishments, and progress.

According to Stuart (1971) an effective contractual arrangement contains several elements: (1) a detailed statement of privileges or rewards to be gained by the patient as he fulfills his responsibility, (2) provisions for monitoring these responsibilities, (3) sanctions to be applied if responsibilities are not met, (4) bonuses given for extraordinary performance, (5) establishing a minimal level of rewards so that the patient always receives something just for trying, (6) a means for the patient to constructively respond to punishments, (7) a feedback mechanism to enable the patient to assess his progress in problem areas. Contractual techniques have been used successfully with a variety of behavioral disorders including drug abuse, underachievement in school, weight reduction programs, and others.

Modeling

Modeling is a therapeutic technique which consists of having the patient repeatedly imitate specific behaviors (such as expressing angry feelings or practicing self-assertion) which first are purposefully enacted by the therapist. After carefully evaluating the patient's history, the therapist identifies the major problem and enacts a behavioral solution to it. Thus, the patient has an opportunity to observe the authoritative therapist demonstrating how to successfully handle the problematic situation. The patient is then encouraged to practice the behavior. Initially, the patient may experience some discomfort, but with repetition his uneasiness will decrease. With sufficient practice and encouragement from the therapist, the patient is asked to try new behavioral responses in "real life" situations. The patient regularly should review progress with the therapist for evaluation and comment. Modeling is particularly effective with patients who are inhibited about expressing self-assertiveness or strong feelings, or who lack experience in managing particular social relationships.

Now complete Self-Assessment Exercise #3 beginning on the following page.

Self-Assessment Exercise #3

1. Briefly describe the following behavioral therapies and give an example of a patient problem to which it could be applied.

   Aversive Therapy

   Contractual Therapy

   Modeling

Self-Assessment Exercise #3 (Continued)

2. In the space provided, indicate the appropriate behavior therapy for achieving each of the treatment goals listed below. A therapeutic approach may be used more than once, and more than one may apply to a single goal.

a. token therapy
b. desensitization
c. biofeedback
d. aversive therapy
e. contractual therapy
f. modeling

__________ (1) to overcome fear of riding in elevators

__________ (2) to reduce inhibitions about expressing angry feelings

__________ (3) to reduce current muscle tension headaches

__________ (4) to help children keep their room orderly

__________ (5) to decrease a rise in blood pressure due to stress

__________ (6) to reinforce good grooming behavior

__________ (7) to control compulsive smoking

__________ (8) to increase self-assertiveness

__________ (9) to reduce fears of public speaking

__________ (10) to encourage group therapy participation for a socially withdrawn patient

__________ (11) to develop good study habits

__________ (12) to encourage your child to take medication regularly

__________ (13) to decrease head-banging in an autistic (psychotic) child

__________ (14) to stop uncontrolled alcohol consumption

When you have completed this exercise to the best of your ability, check your answers with those on the following page.

Self-Assessment Exercise #3 - Feedback

1. Basic definitions of common behavioral techniques:

   Aversive Therapy seeks to stop undesirable behavior by administering unpleasant emotional or physical stimuli; it is indicated for intractable alcohol dependency and behavior unresponsive to other approaches.

   Contractual Therapy attempts to modify behavior by establishing an agreement (contract) between the therapist and patient which sets forth in detail the target behavior, various rewards and punishment for performing the correct response; this therapy can be applied to a variety of behavioral problems which need reinforcement, such as weight reduction programs, enhancing study habits, etc.

   Modeling is a treatment form in which the therapist models a behavioral solution to the patient's problems, e.g., overcoming excessive deference to others by firmly stating personal preferences; the patient is then encouraged to initiate the therapist's behavior first in the latter's office and, after sufficient practice, in "real life" situations; this therapy works well with patients wanting to overcome behavioral traits which interfere with social interactions or who lack particular experience involving personal relationships.

2. The following represents the appropriate behavior therapies for achieving the treatment goals listed:

   a. token therapy
   b. desensitization
   c. biofeedback
   d. aversive therapy
   e. contractual therapy
   f. modeling

a, b (1) to overcome fear of riding in elevators

b, e, f (2) to reduce inhibitions about expressing angry feelings

c (3) to reduce current muscle tension headaches

a, e (4) to help children keep their room orderly

c (5) to decrease a rise in blood pressure due to stress

a, e (6) to reinforce good grooming behavior

Self-Assessment Exercise #3 - Feedback (Continued)

a, d, e (7) to control compulsive smoking

a, e, f (8) to increase self-assertiveness

b, f (9) to reduce fears of public speaking

a, b, e (10) to encourage group therapy participation for a socially withdrawn patient

a, e (11) to develop good study habits

a, e (12) to encourage your child to take medication regularly

a, d (13) to decrease head-banging in an autistic (psychotic)

d, e (14) to stop uncontrolled alcohol consumption

If your answers correspond closely with those above, please continue reading on the next page. If not, please reread the preceding material.

SUMMARY

Behavior therapy is a form of treatment which attempts to modify problems in behavior by systematically applying principles of learning, rewards and punishments. It is most effective for changing target behaviors which are specific, easily identifiable and few in number. The principles of this therapy are relatively easy to learn and apply to many common behavioral problems.

REFERENCES

Agras, W. S., Behavior Modification: Principles and Clinical Application, Boston: Little, Brown & Company, 1978.

Barten, H., Brief Therapy, Behavioral Publications, New York, 1971.

Bergin, A. E., Garfield, S.C., Handbook of Psychotherapy and Behavior Change, New York: John Wiley & Sons, Inc., 1971.

Katz, R., Zlutrick, S., Behavior Therapy and Health Care, New York: Pergamon Press, 1975.

Miller, N. E., Dworkin, B. R., "Effects of Learning on Visceral Functions - Feedback", N. Engl. J. Med., 296:1274, 1977.

Patterson, C. H., Theories of Counseling and Psychotherapy, New York: Harper & Row, 1966.

Stuart, R. G., "Behavioral Contracting Within the Families of Delinquents", J. of Behavioral Therapy and Experiemental Psychiatry, Vol. 2, pp. 1-11, 1971.

Taylor, C. B. Farguhar, J. W., et al, "Relaxation Therapy and High Blood Pressure", Arch. Gen. Psychiatry, 34:339, 1977.

Wolpe, J., The Practice of Behavioral Therapy, New York: Pergamon Press, 1973.

CHAPTER 5. PHARMACOLOGIC THERAPY

Among the most significant advances in the treatment of emotional disorders has been the development and use of psychotropic (mind acting) drugs. These drugs, which include the various tranquilizers, anti-depressants and others, have revolutionized the therapeutic approach for a wide spectrum of emotional disorders ranging from schizophrenic and affective disorders to common states of tension and depression. Psychotropic drugs comprise the most frequently prescribed medications in our country today. When carefully selected and administered, they constitute a major therapeutic tool for the alleviation of symptoms due to emotional distress. Because of their effectiveness, potential risks and widespread use, it is important for you to become familiar with these drugs.

LEARNING OBJECTIVES

By the time you complete this chapter, you should be able to do the following and apply the information to written case histories.

1. List and describe the basic principles to follow when prescribing psychotropic medications for patients.

2. Identify and define the common abbreviations used in drug prescriptions.

3. For each of these common psychopathologic conditions:

    a. schizophrenic disorders
    b. manic disorders
    c. major depressive disorders
    d. anxiety disorders
    e. insomnia

list the:

(1) indications for drug therapy
(2) drugs commonly prescribed
(3) usual starting, maintenance and upper limits of dosage for outpatients
(4) contraindications
(5) common side effects
(6) complications

4. Define the following terms:

psychotropic
pseudo-Parkinsonism
major tranquilizer
neuroleptic
side effects
contraindications
hypertension
functional psychosis
complications
akathesia
dystonia
analgesics
hypotension
cardiac arrhythmia

BASIC PRINCIPLES FOR PRESCRIBING PSYCHOTROPIC DRUGS

Prior to 1960, medications used to control symptoms of psychopathology produced their main therapeutic effect by sedating the patient. As a consequence, the patient's intellectual functioning, coordination, and ability to function often were compromised greatly. Furthermore, patients frequently became physically and psychologically dependent on the drugs. Modern psychotropic drugs have the advantage of being able to reduce many of the symptoms associated with emotional disorders without seriously impairing the patient's alertness, coordination or cognitive functioning. Relatively few of these newer medications are physically habituating, but they are potent drugs and may cause significant side effects and/or medical complications. (A side effect is defined as a common, undesirable effect produced by the drug. A complication is a syndrome or disease caused by the drug.) For this reason, you should always adhere to the following basic principles before prescribing a psychotropic drug.

1. Be thoroughly knowledgeable about the drug including its specific indications for use, dosage, contraindications and associated side effects.
2. Specifically inquire about your patient's existing medical condition and current use of <u>all</u> other medications, including those not requiring a prescription.
3. Determine your patient's response to previously administered psychotropic drugs and if any allergies or hypersensitivities developed.
4. Seek consultation with an experienced psychiatric colleague if uncertainties exist about either your patient or the drug prescribed.

Once a drug is selected, it is important to advise your patient and/or responsible family member:

1. about the name, purpose and dosage of the drug prescribed
2. about potential side effects and possible complications
3. not to take <u>any</u> other medications or alcohol without first consulting you
4. to avoid any activity (e.g., driving, working around machinery, etc.) which may prove hazardous if drug induced drowsiness or decreased coordination is present
5. to discontinue the medication and immediately call you if <u>any</u> unusual behavior or physical symptoms occur

An untoward drug reaction may occur at any time and it may be necessary to enlist the aid of interested relatives or friends to "monitor" your patient's drug response if he is unable to do so reliably.

Only general guidelines are available for selecting specific psychotropic drugs and their dosage; ultimately, both the drug and amount must be tailored to each patient. In this chapter, typical adult doses will be presented which often may need to be decreased for the elderly and persons with significant medical problems, and increased for individuals who are intensely disturbed. In most instances, it is best to start with a low dose of medication until the patient's response to the drug is determined. If the drug is tolerated well, the dosage then can be increased to the point of maximum effect and/or the onset of significant side effects. Medications taken by mouth usually have a more gradual onset of action than if given by injection. In order to minimize a precipitous onset of complications, the oral route of administration is preferred in all but exceptional circumstances.

Now complete Self-Assessment Exercise #1 beginning on the following page.

Self-Assessment Exercise #1

Answer the following items:

1. Before prescribing any psychotropic drug, you should:

   a.

   b.

   c.

   d.

2. Once a drug is prescribed you should specifically advise your patient:

   a.

   b.

   c.

   d.

   e.

Self-Assessment Exercise #1 – (Continued)

3. Describe what action you should take when a patient requires psychotropic medication but cannot be relied upon to report side effects or take the medication.

4. Describe the general rule to follow regarding the initial dosage and route of administration for a new patient or one at special medical risk.

When you have completed this exercise to the best of your ability, check your answers with those on the following page.

Self-Assessment Exercise #1 - Feedback

1. Before prescribing any psychotropic drug, you should:

   a. know the drug's specific indications for use, dosage, contraindications and associated side effects

   b. know your patient's existing medical condition and whether he is currently taking other drugs

   c. determine your patient's general response to previously administered psychotropic drugs and if any allergies or hypersensitivities occurred

   d. seek consultation if uncertainties exist

2. When a drug is prescribed, you should specifically advise the patient:

   a. the drug's name, dosage and reason for prescribing it

   b. the potential side effects and complications

   c. not to take alcohol or any other medications without first consulting the therapist

   d. avoid activities which may be potentially hazardous if alertness is compromised

   e. discontinue the medication and call the therapist immediately if any unusual behavior or symptoms develop

3. If your patient cannot be relied upon to take the prescribed medication and/or report side effects, the aid of interested relatives or friends should be sought to "monitor" your patient in these areas.

4. When a psychotropic drug is being given for the first time to a new patient or one who might present a special medical risk, it is best to start with a low dose of the medication given orally.

If your answers correspond closely with those above, please continue reading on the next page. If not, please reread the preceding material.

DRUG PRESCRIPTION DIRECTIONS

In order to understand better the material that is to follow, you should know the terms and abbreviations commonly used to designate the timing, frequency and route of administration of prescribed drugs. Most of the terms are of Latin derivation and only their abbreviations will be presented. Prescription directions should be written in the following order: the drug's name; dosage; frequency and timing of administration. The abbreviations can be written in either lower or upper case letters. A few minutes spent in memorizing these abbreviations will facilitate your learning the skills related to drug therapy.

TIMING OF ADMINISTRATION	ABBREVIATIONS
immediately	stat
every hour	qh
every 2 hours, every 4 hours, etc.	q2h, q4h, etc.
once a day	qd
twice a day	bid
three times a day	tid
four times a day	qid
at bedtime	hs
as needed	prn
ROUTE OF ADMINISTRATION	
by mouth	po
intramuscular	IM
intravenous	IV
MISCELLANEOUS TERMS	
milligram	mg
cubic centimeters	cc
tablets	tabs
capsules	caps
milliequivalents per liter	mEq/L

Now complete Self-Assessment Exercise #2 beginning on the following page.

Self-Assessment Exercise #2

1. In the space provided, write the correct definition or abbreviation for each of the terms listed:

   a. tid ____________________

   b. intramuscular ____________________

   c. every hour ____________________

   d. mg ____________________

   e. hs ____________________

   f. IV ____________________

2. In the space provided, write out the appropriate <u>meaning or abbreviation</u> for administering the following drug prescriptions:

   a. chlorpromazine (Thorazine) 25 milligrams to be given immediately by intramuscular injection

      ____

   b. diazepam (Valium); 10 mg hs, po

      ____

   c. imipramine (Tofranil) 75 milligrams at bedtime, to be given orally

      ____

   d. fluphenazine (Prolixin) decanoate 25 milligrams (1 cubic centimeter) immediately, intramuscularly

      ____

When you have completed this exercise to the best of your ability, check your answers with those on the following page.

Self-Assessment Exercise #2 - Feedback

1. Definitions and abbreviations:

   a. tid — three times a day

   b. intramuscular — IM

   c. every hour — qh

   d. mg — milligram

   e. hs — at bedtime

   f. IV — intravenous

2. Drug prescriptions:

   a. chlorpromazine (Thorazine) 25 milligrams to be given immediately by intramuscular injection

      chlorpromazine 25 mg stat IM

   b. diazepam (Valium); 10 mg hs, po

      diazepam 10 milligrams to be taken at bedtime, orally

   c. imipramine (Tofranil) 75 milligrams at bedtime, to be given orally

      imipramine 75 mg hs po

   d. fluphenazine (Prolixin) decanoate 25 milligrams (1 cubic centimeter) immediately, intramuscularly

      fluphenazine decanoate 25 mg (1cc); stat; IM

If your answers correspond closely with those above, please continue reading on the next page. If not, please reread the preceding material.

MODERN PSYCHOTROPIC MEDICATIONS

The remainder of this chapter contains information basic to the drug therapy of the following pathological conditions: anxiety, functional psychosis, depression and persistent insomnia. A summary of each condition will precede a discussion of the drugs commonly prescribed to treat it (a table summarizing pertinent information is included). For each medication; dosage range, contraindications, side effects and complications will be reviewed. The dosages recommended are average amounts and may need to be decreased or increased depending on variables such as the patient's age, physical state, intensity of symptoms and response to therapy. Both generic and trade names are used; often a prescription is less expensive for the patient if the medication is prescribed in generic terms. The information is introductory and not an exhaustive presentation of psychiatric drug treatment; therefore, only a few representative drugs will be discussed. The medications selected for presentation here are those which are well-studied, widely used, and possess unique qualities felt important for the purposes of this chapter. You are encouraged to first become proficient with a few medications and then expand your knowledge and experience with others. Side effects and complications usually become more severe and frequent as the drug dosage is increased. Therefore, it is suggested that you carefully reassess your patient and/or seek consultation before prescribing amounts of medication which exceed the recommended upper dosage limits for outpatients. References at the end of the chapter should be consulted, if further detailed information is desired.

Anti-Psychotic Medications

The functional psychoses are a group of serious emotional disorders which do not have identifiable organic cause. These psychoses are characterized by impaired reality testing and abnormalities of thinking, feeling and behavior of sufficient intensity to interfere with normal functioning. The group of drugs used to treat common psychoses and associated symptoms are often interchangeably called anti-psychotics, neuroleptics or major tranquilizers. (In practice, the term "tranquilizer" is a misnomer, since these medications reduce tension and anxiety, but rarely produce a feeling of euphoria or calm.) These drugs are quite different from the minor tranquilizers and hypnotic-sedatives with respect to the indications for use, side effects and complications. In contrast to anti-anxiety drugs, the anti-psychotic medications can increase muscle tone, lower the threshold for seizures and produce little or no drug dependence. These drugs, even more than the minor tranquilizers, accentuate the effects of other medications including sedatives, analgesics (anti-pain drugs), anti-hypertension drugs and others. Many inhibit nausea and vomiting, a characteristic which is not typical to either sedative-hypnotic or anti-anxiety drugs. Major tranquilizers are potent drugs which frequently cause a variety of side effects, some of which may present difficult management problems, Although anti-psychotics often cause a sedative effect, they do not generally produce anesthesia or severely compromise intellectual functioning. As compared with most sedative-hypnotics, anti-psychotic medications are not habituating or particularly lethal even when taken in large quantities.

There are few absolute guidelines for selecting particular anti-psychotic medications or dosage, and the drug treatment for each patient must be individualized. Even if a patient fails to do well at one dosage level or with one drug, he may improve with a different drug or dosage. Response to major tranquilizers is somewhat unpredictable. Some patients show dramatic improvement rapidly, others progress slowly, and some may show little change or paradoxically even get worse. In the same patient some symptoms rapidly resolve while others remit gradually. Typically, improvement is most rapid during the first days of treatment, but progress may continue gradually for several months before a therapeutic plateau is reached. As a rule, the symptoms of psychoses which are characterized by an abrupt and recent onset, an intensive affective component, and marked behavioral changes are more likely to respond to drug treatment than those which developed insidiously or have been chronic. It is clear that considerable patience by you and your patient may be needed when using anti-psychotic medications. Basic information about the neuroleptics is summarized in Table I.

Target Symptoms:

Major tranquilizers provide symptomatic relief--not cure, but they are very effective in the treatment of a wide variety of psychoses including the group of schizophrenic disorders, manic and bipolar disorders, paranoid disorders and others. The anti-psychotic drugs often are used for alleviating such symptoms as acute delusions, belligerence, hyperactivity, intense anxiety, hallucinations, social withdrawal, disorganized thinking, excessively intense or blunted affect and impulsive and/or inappropriate behavior.

Literally dozens of anti-psychotic drugs are available for use, each with intrinsic advantages and disadvantages. The medications selected for presentation here are representative of chemically different groups which are unique with respect to potency, specificity for particular target symptoms, side effects and proven effectiveness. If therapeutic improvement does not occur in four to six weeks or if side effects become especially problematic with one drug, another may be chosen to replace it. The drugs that will be presented here are chlorpromazine (Thorazine, Chlor-PZ), thiothixene (Navane), fluphenazine (Prolixin,

Permitil) and haloperidol (Haldol). After allowing for differences in relative potency, all are equally effective and are available in tablet, capsule, liquid or injectable forms (IM use only). Although lithium carbonate possesses anti-psychotic properties with respect to manic and bipolar disorders, it distinctly differs from the other major tranquilizers and will be considered separately.

Chlorpromazine

Chlorpromazine (Thorazine, Chlor-PZ) is representative of most other major tranquilizers with respect to indications, side effects and complications. It will be described in detail and properties unique to the other drugs in this section will be noted and discussed.

Indications:

Chlorpromazine is useful for treating symptoms of psychosis including severe anxiety, agitation, restlessness, hyperactivity and diminished emotional control (belligerence, impulsive behavior, etc.). It tends to be more sedating than other anti-psychotics and is effective in reducing nausea and vomiting. It potentiates (increases) the potency of sedatives and most pain medications (analgesics) thereby promoting a therapeutic effect while using smaller doses of drugs.

Dosage:

For outpatients whose drug response is unknown and in elderly or debilitated persons, a suitable initial dose is 25 to 50 mg tid to qid po. Dosage can be increased by 50 to 100 mg per day until the desired therapeutic effect is achieved or side effects become problematic. The typical maintenance dose range for outpatients is 100 to 400 mg per day in divided doses with an upper total dose of 600/day. For more severely disturbed patients, usually those requiring hospitalization, chlorpromazine may be given in much larger amounts.

In exceptional instances when the prompt control of severe symptoms is desired, 25 mg may be administered IM. This amount may be repeated in one to two hours if necessary. Special precautions are needed when the drug is given IM (see "Complications" below). The likelihood of side effects such as a fall in blood pressure (hypotension) increases greatly when an IM dose exceeds 50 mg. IM medications should be replaced by the oral route as soon as the patient's condition permits.

During the early phase of treatment, chlorpromazine and other anti-psychotics may be given in multiple doses tid to qid. However, as a therapeutic effect is achieved, maintenance amounts can be given bid or in a single dose at bedtime. Once optimal symptom improvement has been obtained, the total daily amount usually can be decreased by one-third to one-half. The lower maintenance dose lessens the likelihood of side effects, and in most cases is sufficient to maintain the patient. The drug can be increased if psychopathologic symptoms recur.

Contraindications:

Absolute contraindications to administering chlorpromazine include patients who are lethargic or comatose. Other potential contraindications are the presence of seizure disorder, pregnancy, disease of the cardiovascular system, liver or kidneys, or persons with a history of a previous hypersensitivity reaction to it or related drugs. You should prescribe chlorpromazine with caution if the patient is already receiving other drugs such as analgesics, anesthetics, anti-hypertension medication and others.

Side Effects:

Most patients experience some degree of drowsiness, dry mouth, and/or blurring of vision especially during the first few days of drug therapy. These symptoms usually moderate in a week or two as the patient develops a tolerance to the drug. A fall in blood pressure (hypotension) to abnormal levels along with a rapid heartbeat and dizziness may occur soon after an injection or high oral dose. In elderly or debilitated persons and those receiving anti-hypertension medications, hypotensive reactions increases in intensity and frequency. Individuals taking anti-psychotic medications also become especially susceptible to sunburn and should be advised accordingly. Skin rashes, constipation and minor gastrointestinal disturbances may occur.

Complications:

Major tranquilizers are potent drugs and may cause a variety of disturbing and potentially serious complications. These complications may require a reduction of the dosage of chlorpromazine, its discontinuance altogether and/or the substitution of a different anti-psychotic drug. Chlorpromazine may accentuate or induce cardiovascular problems. For patients receiving chlorpromazine a sudden change in posture may bring about a precipitous fall in blood pressure, a resultant dizziness and fainting or a fall. The blood pressure usually can be restored to acceptable levels by having the patient lie down with his legs elevated slightly. In rare instances, special chemicals, i.e., norepinephrine (Levophed) or neo-synephrine may be needed to support the blood pressure. Epinephrine should never be administered for this purpose since it may further lower the blood pressure.

Convulsive seizures (epilepsy) may be precipitated by anti-psychotic drugs especially if they are given in high, loading doses. Persons who are at special risk, i.e., those with a head injury or who are withdrawing from drugs or alcohol, generally should not be given neuroleptics. If it is absolutely necessary to administer chlorpromazine or a similar drug, anti-convulsants such as phenobarbitol and/or diphenylhydantoin (Dilantin) should be added to the drug regimen to protect against seizures.

Some patients receiving chlorpromazine develop neuromuscular (extrapyramidal) reactions which are important to diagnose and treat.

These reactions typically are manifested as a decrease of voluntary movements, development of a rhythmical tremor, a mask-like facial expression, stiffness of the body musculature, impaired speech and a shuffling gait. Together these symptoms comprise a syndrome known as pseudo-Parkinsonism. This condition can be reversed by reducing the dosage of chlorpromazine and/or the administration of benztropine (Cogentin), 1 to 2 mg bid po or by injection (IM or IV). An alternate anti-Parkinson drug is trihexyphenidyl (Artane) given 2 to 5 mg bid to tid po. After the extrapyramidal symptoms have been controlled by these drugs for approximately three months, it is recommended that the medications be periodically reduced or discontinued on a trial basis. Studies indicate that most patients do not experience a recurrence of the extrapyramidal symptoms. Although quite effective in reducing the symptoms once they have developed, anti-Parkinson drugs should <u>not</u> be prescribed prophylactically.

During the first weeks of therapy susceptible individuals may develop symptoms of persistent physical restlessness, a feeling of inner tension accompanied by an inability to lie or sit still (akathesia). This condition is drug-induced but may be confused with a recurrence of anxiety. The anti-Parkinson drugs previously described or diphenhydramine (Benadryl) 50 mg bid to tid po may help to counteract the symptoms.

Disordered tone of the musculature (acute dystonia) in the form of involuntary and uncoordinated spasms of the tongue, mouth, cheeks, neck, body and/or limbs may occur. Occasionally a patient may experience an involuntary tongue protrusion and/or upward rolling of the eyes which he is unable to control. These distressing but reversible symptoms respond readily to IM or IV benztropine 1 to 2 mg or diphenhydramine 50 to 100 mg IM or IV. Usually the symptoms spontaneously will subside within 24 to 48 hours if chlorpromazine has been discontinued, but they are so distressing that medications usually should be given to alleviate them.

Occasionally, abnormal muscle movements persist indefinitely (tardive dyskinesia). This condition usually occurs in persons who have been treated with major tranquilizers for many months or years. Typically the disorder consists of persistent abnormal, involuntary movements of the face, cheek tongue, jaw and sometimes the extremities. Swallowing, speech and respiration may be impaired. This condition may begin during drug therapy or when medications are decreased or stopped, and it is usually unresponsive to known drugs or other treatment. Tardive dyskinesia may be precipitated or worsened by anti-Parkinsonian drugs. Prevention of this condition may be possible by occasionally changing drugs, discontinuing medication unless absolutely needed and arranging drug "holidays," i.e., temporary interruptions of drug therapy lasting a few days or longer. Keeping drug dosage reduced to the lowest levels necessary for symptom control may be effective in preventing tardive dyskinesia.

You must keep in mind that serious medical problems may arise at any time from treatment with any of the major tranquilizers. Any of the body organ systems may be affected including the liver, cardio-vascular system, blood forming organs, skin or digestive tract, and kidneys. Additionally, patients receiving psychotropic medications may develop an impairment of body temperature regulation, and they should avoid prolonged exposure to environments of high temperature. Your patients must be advised to contact you immediately at the first sign of physical illness or development of any unusual symptom.

Now complete Self-Assessment Exercise #3 beginning on the following page.

Self-Assessment Exercise #3

1. For which of the following conditions and symptoms are anti-psychotic drugs often indicated: (circle all that apply)

   a. schizophrenia
   b. retarded depressions
   c. agitation
   d. delusions
   e. mild anxiety
   f. disorganized thinking
   g. hallucinations
   h. belligerence
   i. impulsive behavior
   j. blunted affect

2. Circle each patient characteristic from the list below that may be a contraindication for using chlorpromazine and/or major tranquilizers:

   a. repeated psychotic episodes
   b. previous hypersensitivity to antipsychotic drugs
   c. is lethargic or comatose
   d. gall bladder disease
   e. liver disease
   f. receiving anti-hypertension medication
   g. receiving medication for pain
   h. presence of heart disease
   i. a woman two months pregnant
   j. a history of epilepsy

3. List the three most common side effects of anti-psychotic drugs:

Self-Assessment Exercise #3 - (Continued)

4. Briefly describe the symptoms of pseudo-Parkinsonism that may result from taking major tranquilizers.

5. List two or more drugs useful in the alleviation of neuromuscular (extrapyramidal) side effects caused by anti-psychotic drugs.

When you have completed this exercise to the best of your ability, check your answers with those on the following page.

Self-Assessment Exercise #3 - Feedback

1. Anti-psychotic drugs are indicated for treating the following conditions and symptoms:

   a. schizophrenia
   c. agitation
   d. delusions
   f. disordered thinking
   g. hallucinations
   h. belligerence
   i. impulsive behavior
   j. blunted affect

2. Patient characteristics which may be a contraindication for using chlorpromazine and/or other major tranquilizers are:

   b. previous hypersensitivity to anti-psychotic drugs
   c. is lethargic or comatose
   e. liver disease
   f. receiving anti-hyper-tension medication
   g. receiving medication for pain
   h. presence of heart disease
   i. a woman two months pregnant
   j. a history of epilepsy

3. The three most common side effects of anti-psychotic drugs are drowsiness, blurring of vision and a dry mouth.

4. Symptoms of pseudo-Parkinsonism that may result from taking major tranquilizers include decreased voluntary movements, rigidity of the body musculature, mask-like facial expression, a shuffling gait, impaired speech and a rhythmic tremor.

5. Drugs useful in the alleviation of neuromuscular (extra-pyramidal side effects are benztropine (Cogentin), trihexy-phenidyl (Artane) and diphenhydramine (Benadryl).

If your answers correspond closely with those above, please continue reading on the next page. If not, please reread the preceding material.

Fluphenazine

Another potent anti-psychotic medication is fluphenazine (Prolixin, Permitil). Although quite comparable with chlorpromazine in many respects, it is available in both a regular and a long-acting injectable form. The regular form of the drug is fluphenazine hydrochloride and the long-acting version is fluphenazine decanoate. The long-acting form is particularly advantageous for patients who are unable or unwilling to take anti-psychotic medication on a regularly scheduled basis. The therapeutic effects of a single injection of the drug may last from one to three weeks or longer.

Dosage:

Oral doses of fluphenazine hydrochloride are recommended in amounts of 1 to 2.5 mg given tid to qid or 1.25 mg by injection. Maintenance doses are given up to a total of 5 to 20 mg per day. The long-acting decanoate form of this drug is given by injection in the amount of 0.5 to 2.0 cc (25 mg/cc) q2 to 4 weeks, IM.

Contraindications and Side Effects:

The contraindications and side effects to fluphenazine regular or long-acting are comparable to those of chlorpromazine except that pseudo-Parkinson symptoms and neuromuscular disorders are more common.

Complications:

Allergic reactions of the skin and neuromuscular side effects are more common with fluphenazine decanoate than chlorpromazine. Some authorities recommend that candidates for long-acting fluphenazine decanoate be tried first on the short-acting from of the drug. If no untoward effects occur, you may proceed to the long-acting type. This precautionary procedure helps to minimize the likelihood of prolonged adverse reactions.

Thiothixene

Although the general indications for thiothixene (Navane) are similar to those of chlorpromazine, it has a different chemical structure, and there is a smaller incidence of hypotensive reactions, neuromuscular and sedative side effects. Consequently, where any of those symptoms might be particularly problematic, thiothixene may be an appropriate substitute. Like chlorpromazine, this drug may reduce nausea or vomiting.

Dosage:

Thiothixene is a more potent drug than chlorpromazine. The recommended starting dose for mild symptoms is 2 mg tid to qid po, with a maintenance range extending from 10 to 40 mg per day with the upper limits at 40 mg/day for most outpatients. An injectable form of thiothixene is available and is usually given 4 mg bid to tid IM.

Contraindications:

Contraindications for the use of thiothixene are essentially the same as those of chlorpromazine.

Side Effects:

Side effects for thiothixene are similar to those of chlorpromazine except that it is less sedating.

Complications:

Many of the potential complications from the use of thiothixene are the same as for chlorpromazine. Eye damage has developed in patients receiving high doses of thiothixene over an extended time period.

Haloperidol

Haloperidol (Haldol) is an anti-psychotic medication belonging to a different chemical group than the three described above. Haloperidol generally causes less sedation or hypotensive reactions than does chlorpromazine. For that reason, it may be of special use in treating elderly patients or those with cardiovascular disorders.

Dosage:

Initial oral dosage for haloperidol is 0.5 to 2 mg bid to tid. Maintenance doses for persons who are moderately disturbed range from 5 to 20 mg/day with an upper daily total of 20 mg/day. In instances where a rapid effect is desired, 3 to 5 mg can be given IM q2-6h up to 15 mg qd.

Contraindications, Side Effects and Complications:

Contraindications, side effects and complications are comparable to chlorpromazine except that haloperidol may cause a greater incidence of neuromuscular (extrapyramidal) disorders. Wait until the onset of such symptoms before prescribing counteracting medications, e.g., benztropine, etc.

Prescribing Recommendations

Drug therapy must be individualized for each patient according to factors such as age, severity of symptoms and intercurrent medical problems. Determine your patient's response to antipsychotic drugs which were taken previously. Prescribe the ones which have worked well before. If you prescribe a medication which is new to your patient, use a small initial dose to see how it is tolerated. If no adverse effects occur, then increase the dosage until the desired improvement is achieved or side effects become problematic.

If it is important to obtain rapid therapeutic effect, that is from one to two hours, any of the antipsychotic medications can be given IM. However, before giving medication IM, make sure there are no physical conditions (e.g., cardiovascular disease or cerebral intoxication) exist which could be worsened by the concentrated effect of injected drugs. Similarly, inquire whether your patient is taking other medications which might adversely react with antipsychotic drugs. After an IM injection, watch your patient for signs of a drop in blood pressure and dizziness or weakness associated with sudden changes in posture. It is particularly important that you avoid a sudden fall of blood pressure in patients who are elderly or are known to have cardiovascular disease. As soon as the troublesome symptoms are sufficiently controlled, switch to oral medications which are less likely to cause side effects.

Begin giving the selected medication in divided doses, two to four times a day. After several days, when it is clear that the drug is well tolerated and improvement is noted, one-third of the total daily dosage can be given in the morning and two-thirds at bedtime. In two to three weeks' time the medication can be given in a single bedtime dose, a practice which can be followed thereafter. Exceptions to this regimen are elderly persons or those with cardiovascular disease who should not receive a large dose of medication that might cause serious complications. If no significant therapeutic gain is noted after maintaining the recommended upper dosage level for four to six weeks, switch to a different drug and again follow the procedure just described.

When optimum improvement has been maintained for two to three months at a given dosage level, try reducing the daily amount by one-fourth to one-third and determine if your patient remains stable with less medication. It is a good policy to keep your patient stabilized on an antipsychotic medication for at least six months before beginning to discontinue it. To discontinue a medication, gradually reduce the dose by 30% each six to eight weeks over a several month period. Be prepared to reinstate the dosage if symptoms recur. Many patients will need antipsychotic medications indefinitely to control their symptoms, but to minimize the risk of complications, administer the least amount of the drug necessary to achieve symptom control. Include a "drug holiday" into the dosage schedule for these patients. Carefully educate your patients about possible side effects and the risks of using alcohol, other medications, or driving while under the influence of these potent drugs. Enlist the aid of family members to increase patient compliance for taking medications.

Now complete Self-Assessment Exercise #4 beginning on the following page.

Self-Assessment Exercise #4

1. Select the letter indicating the typical starting dose for out-patients from column B for each of the drugs listed in column A (the amounts of starting doses may be used more than once).

	COLUMN A		COLUMN B
______(1)	chlorpromazine (Thorazine, Chlor-PZ)	a.	1 to 2 mg bid to tid po
		b.	25 mg (1 cc) IM
______(2)	fluphenazine decanoate (Prolixin decanoate)	c.	25 to 50 mg tid to qid po
______(3)	haloperidol (Haldol)	d.	300 mg tid po
______(4)	thiothixene (Navane)		
______(5)	fluphenazine hydro-chloride (Prolixin or Permitil hydrochloride)		

2. Match one or more of the drugs below with each of the listed patient characteristics (more than one drug may be used). Place the letter for the drug in the space provided.

Drugs:

A – chlorpromazine (Thorazine, Chlor-PZ)
B – thiothixene (Navane)
C – haloperidol (Haldol)
D – fluphenazine decanoate (Prolixin)
E – benztropine (Cogentin)
F – diphenylhydramine (Benadryl)

Patient Characteristics:

______(1) an agitated patient for whom a sedative effect is particularly important

______(2) an outpatient who needs anti-psychotic medication that cannot or will not take it on a regular basis

______(3) a person for whom it is medically important that a drug-related fall in blood pressure not occur

Self-Assessment Exercise #4 - (Continued)

_______(4) after two days on haloperidol, the young man developed symptoms of tremor, rigidity of voluntary movements and a mask-like facial expression

_______(5) two weeks after beginning treatment with fluphenazine decanoate, the woman developed an abrupt onset of involuntary tongue protrusion and an upward rolling of her eyes.

When you have completed this exercise to the best of your ability, check your answers with those on the following page.

Self-Assessment Exercise #4 - Feedback

1. The typical starting doses for outpatients are as follows:

c (1) chlorpromazine (Thorazine, Chlor-PZ) 25 to 50 mg tid to qid po

b (2) fluphenazine decanoate (Prolixin decanoate) 25 mg (1 cc) IM

a (3) haloperidol (Haldol) 1 to 2 mg bid to tid po

a (4) thiothixene (Navane) 1 to 2 mg bid to tid po

a (5) fluphenazine hydrochloride (Prolixin or Permitil hydrochloride) 1 to 2 mg bid to tid po

2. The best drugs for the following patient characteristics are:

A (1) chlorpromazine--an agitated patient for whom a sedative effect is desired

D (2) fluphenazine decanoate--an outpatient who needs antipsychotic medication that cannot or will not take it on a regular basis

B & C (3) thiothixene or haloperidol (Haldol)--a person for whom it is medically important that a drug-related fall in blood pressure not occur

E (4) benztropine (Cogentin)--after two days on haloperidol, the young man developed symptoms of tremor, rigidity of voluntary movements and a mask-like facial expression

E & F (5) benztropine (Cogentin) or diphenylhydramine (Benadryl)--two weeks after beginning treatment with fluphenazine dedecanoate, the woman developed an abrupt onset of involuntary tongue protrusion and an upward rolling of her eyes

If your answers correspond closely with those above, please continue reading on the next page. If not, please reread the preceding material.

TABLE I

SUMMARY OF ANTI-PSYCHOTIC MEDICATIONS
(Major Tranquilizers, Neuroleptics)

INDICATIONS	DRUGS	ADULT DOSAGE RANGE	
Conditions: schizophrenia manic-depressive illness paranoid states involutional melancholia some depressions Symptoms: intense anxiety delusions hallucinations disordered thinking hostility behavioral disturbances blunted or excessive affect insomnia nausea and/or vomiting	chlorpromazine (Thorazine or Chlor-PZ)	Initial: 25 - 50 mg tid - qid po Maintenance: 100 - 400 mg/day po Upper Limits:** 600 mg/day IM 25 mg*	Contraindications: previous hypersensitivity or allergic reaction; coma or depressed central nervous system; liver disease; blood diseases; special caution indicated with pregnancy; performing potentially hazardous tasks, i.e., driving, machinery work, etc.; seizure disorder; concomitant use of other medications (sedatives, analgesics anti-hypertensive, etc.); cardiovascular disease Common Side Effects: drowsiness; dry mouth; blurring of vision; hypotension; susceptibility to sunburn Complications: hypotension; seizures; various neuromuscular disorders (i.e., dystonia, akathisia, pseudoParkinsonism); cardiovascular disorders; allergic reactions
	thiothixene (Navane)	Initial: 1 - 2 mg tid - qid po Maintenance: 10 - 40 mg/day Upper Limits:** 40 mg/day IM 2 0 5 mg*	
	fluphenazine hydrochloride (Prolixin or Permitil)	Initial: 1 - 2.5 mg tid - qid po Maintenance: 5 - 20 mg/day Upper Limits:** 20 mg/day IM 2.5 mg*	
	fluphenazine decanoate (Prolixin decanoate)	Maintenance: 1/2 - 2 cc (25 mg/cc) Q2 - 4 weeks	
	haloperidol (Haldol)	Initial: 0.5 - 2 mg bid - qid po Maintenance: 5 - 20 mg/day Upper Limits:** 20 mg/day IM 2 - 5 mg*	

* May cause hypotension.
** For most outpatients.

Anti-Mania Medications

Lithium carbonate (Lithane, Eskalith, Lithonate) is distinctly different from the anti-psychotic drugs previously described. It has proven eminently useful in the treatment of the manic phase of manic and bipolar disorders which is a psychopathologic state characterized by marked alterations of affect and behavior.

Indications:

Lithium carbonate is singularly effective in alleviating and/or preventing the symptoms associated with manic behavior. Typically, mania is manifested by a generalized hyperactivity, rapid speech, racing thoughts, feelings of grandiosity, euphoria, insomnia, distractibility, impulsivity and hypersexuality. These symptoms periodically occur in varying combinations and degrees of intensity. Lithium carbonate is most effective in the treatment and prevention of manic symptoms, but also may help to prevent depressive symptoms of bipolar disorders. Basic information about anti-mania drugs is summarized in Table II.

Dosage:

The dosage of lithium carbonate must be individualized in accordance with the patient's physical state, weight, severity of symptoms and kidney function. Usually the control of manic symptoms is accomplished by prescribing an initial "loading dose" of 300 mg tid to qid po (1200 mg total) followed by a smaller maintenance dose of 300 mg tid po thereafter. Since it may take five to ten days of lithium treatment to obtain the satisfactory therapeutic effect, chlorpromazine or haloperidol can be added to the treatment regimen for a more rapid control of the patient's symptoms. These major tranquilizers then can be gradually decreased (and eventually discontinued) as the therapeutic effect of lithium is achieved. The therapeutic and toxic levels of lithium in the blood are close and laboratory determination should be performed frequently to assure that the lithium concentration is maintained between 0.5 and 1.2 mEq/L. The administration of lithium ordinarily should be undertaken only if facilities are available for prompt and accurate blood level determinations. Because lithium carbonate is effective in preventing manic recurrences, unless toxic symptoms preclude doing so, it should be prescribed indefinitely for individuals who are prone to that condition.

Contraindications:

Kidney disease which might impair lithium excretion is a contraindication to its use. Additional contraindications that mitigate against prescribing it are a previous hypersensitivity reaction, cardiovascular problems (especially if salt intake is restricted) and organic brain disease. Advanced age, medical conditions in which blood levels of sodium are reduced such as occurs with the use of diuretics (drugs that increase the excretion of urine), and special low sodium diets are relative contraindications for using lithium.

Side Effects:

The common side effects of lithium can occur at any blood level concentration and may indicate early signs of toxicity, therefore, you must be alert for them. Common early symptoms of toxicity include a fine hand tremor, frequent urination, increased thirst, nausea and gastrointestinal upsets. The benign symptoms are usually mild, transitory and generally disappear after a few weeks of therapy. If they persist or increase in intensity then lithium toxicity should be suspected. As a rule, toxic symptoms are more likely to occur if there is a significant loss of body fluids as in the instance of prolonged sweating, vomiting or diarrhea. You should keep these possibilities in mind and reduce the amount of lithium carbonate accordingly.

Complications:

If toxic levels of lithium carbonate are reached (usually above 1.7 mEq/L), decreased appetite, diarrhea, nausea and vomiting will follow. Disorders of the central nervous system including muscle twitching, tremors, loss of coordination, drowsiness, mental confusion and seizures and coma may develop. When these symptoms occur, the drug should be reduced immediately in amount or discontinued altogether. Various cardiovascular problems and thyroid disorders are associated with lithium. No specific antidote to lithium overdose is known, although supportive medical measures as described in the instructions accompanying the medication may be of value.

Now complete Self-Assessment Exercise #5 beginning on the following page.

Self-Assessment Exercise #5

1. List the psychological and behavioral findings associated with manic behavior:

2. For a patient of average height and weight who is in good physical health, list:

   a. a typical starting dose of lithium

   b. a typical maintenance dose schedule

   c. the blood concentration that should be maintained for proper effect and yet avoid a toxic reaction

3. Circle each of the following patient characteristics that may represent a significant contraindication for lithium therapy:

   a. age 63
   b. kidney disease
   c. recurrent manic episodes
   d. cardiovascular disease
   e. organic brain disease
   f. acute manic behavior
   g. concurrent treatment with chlorpromazine
   h. depression

Self-Assessment Exercise #5 - (Continued)

4. Knowing that therapy with lithium carbonate may take five to ten days before achieving maximum effectiveness, what drug regimen would you prescribe for a young woman who is in an acute manic state?

5. List six signs of lithium toxicity.

When you have completed this exercise to the best of your ability, check your answers with those on the following page.

Self-Assessment Exercise #5 - Feedback

1. The psychological and behavioral findings typically associated with manic behavior include generalized hyperactivity, racing thoughts, rapid speech, feelings of grandiosity, euphoria, insomnia, distractibility and impulsive behavior.

2. For a patient of average height and weight and in good physical health:

   a. the initial starting dose of lithium is 300 mg tid to qid po

   b. the typical maintenance dose is 300 mg tid po

   c. the blood concentration level that should be maintained in order to achieve maximum effectiveness and yet avoid toxicity is 0.5 to 1.0 mEq/L.

3. The following patient characteristics may represent a contraindication for lithium therapy:

   a. age 63

   b. kidney disease

   d. cardiovascular disease

   e. organic brain disease

4. Since the therapeutic effect of lithium carbonate might not be achieved for several days, you should augment the drug with either chlorpromazine or haloperidol until the patient's symptoms are under control.

5. Signs of lithium toxicity include decreased appetite, diarrhea, nausea and vomiting, tremors, mental confusion and various cardiovascular or thyroid disorders.

If your answers correspond closely with those above, please continu reading on the next page. If not, please reread the preceding material.

TABLE II

SUMMARY OF ANTI-MANIA MEDICATIONS

INDICATIONS	DRUGS	ADULT DOSAGE RANGE	
Conditions: manic disorder; bipolar disorder Symptoms: hyperactivity racing thoughts euphoria pressure of speech impulsivity grandiosity belligerence, irritability	lithium carbonate (Lithane, Eskalith, Lithonate)	Initial: 300 mg tid - qid po (to achieve 0.5 - 1.0 mEq/L) Maintenance: 300 mg tid po (to maintain 0.5 - 1.2 mEq/L) Upper Limits: variable--the amount needed to maintain 0.5 - 1.2 mEq/L IM not available	Contraindications: hypersensitivity; renal disease; cardiovascular disease; organic brain disease, treatment with diuretics Common Side Effects: gastrointestinal disorders; drowsiness; tremor; increased urination Complications: diarrhea; vomiting; neuromuscular disorders (tremors, decreased coordination, slurred speech, etc.); thyroid disorders; increased blood sugar

Anti-Depressant Medications

Anti-depressant medications (sometimes called psychic stimulants, mood elevators, or psychic energizers) comprise a variety of chemically different compounds that may alleviate symptoms of depression. From the numerous drugs available, three tricyclic anti-depressants will be discussed in detail and a brief comment made about the efficacy of other types.

Indications:

Symptoms of depression may arise from a variety of different causes including a reaction to drugs (especially sedatives, narcotics, or hormones), medical disorders (viral infections), grief reactions, or in conjunction with diverse psychopathologic conditions such as schizophrenia and major affective disorders and others. It is even more difficult to predict which patients and depressive symptoms will respond to anti-depressant medications than it is for either anti-anxiety or anti-psychotic drugs For many depressed patients, medications are neither effective nor needed; for still others, anti-depressant medications may play an integral part in the therapeutic regimen. In any case, your first task is to recognize the common signs and symptoms of depression. You should suspect the presence of depression when some combination of the following symptoms are found; persistent apathy or sadness, thoughts of self-harm, self-recriminations, guilt, tension and irritability, and slowing of thought, speech and motor activity. These psychological symptoms are often accompanied by varying degrees of loss of appetite and weight (although overeating may occur in depression), tearfulness, sleep disturbances (too little or too much), constipation, and decreased sexual activity and interest.

There are indications that anti-depressant medications are most effective in the so-called "endogenous depressions," that is those which are prolonged, do not seem to have a well-defined etiology, do not respond to environmental or psychological intervention and occur in an individual whose history shows a satisfactory premorbid adjustment. Major depressive disorders which are characterized by agitation, self-recriminations, restlessness, and unfounded suspiciousness are classified "endogenous" by some authorities. In general, depressive symptoms associated with a situational loss (such as grief following the death of a loved one, or divorce, etc.) are caused by medications (hormones, sedatives) or accompany depression caused by a chronic affective disorder, are less likely to respond to specific anti-depressant medications. Basic information about anti-depressant medications is summarized in Ta

Medications Commonly Used

From the many medications available, tricyclic anti-depressants and a selected few of the major tranquilizers currently appear to be the most effective and safest drugs for the treatment of depression. Stimulants such as amphetamine and methylphenidate (Ritalin) are of little value and possess several undesirable side effects including the potential for habituation. Another group of anti-depressant drugs, the monamine oxidase inhibitors (MAO's) are unpredictable in effect and present potentially serious side effects. The stimulants and MAO inhibitors are not recommended for general use and will not be discussed further. There is some evidence to show that chlorpromazine, thiothixene and perhaps a few other neuroleptics are of value in the treatment of restlessness, anxiety, agitation or hostility which may be associated with depression. (Please refer to the earlier description of chlorpromazine regarding the dosage, side effects, etc.).

Three of the most commonly prescribed tricyclic anti-depressants will be presented here: amitriptyline (Elavil), imipramine (Tofranil, Presamine), and doxepin (Sinequan, Adapin). For the most part, all three are very comparable in effect, dosage and side effects and, therefore, they will be discussed collectively. Amitriptyline and doxepin are the most sedating and imipramine the least sedating of the three medications, a distinction worth remembering if you want either to induce or avoid sedation of your patient.

Dosage:

Each of the drugs can be administered in a starting dose of 25 mg tid po. Lower initial doses are recommended for persons who are elderly, debilitated or medically ill. If no untoward effects develop within a few days, the dosage may be increased at the rate of 50 mg per day until a total daily dosage of 150 mg is achieved. In contrast to other psychotropic drugs, anti-depressants have a slow onset of action and significant therapeutic effect may not occur for two to four weeks. Therefore, if no beneficial effects are noted within two to three weeks, the dosage may gradually be increased to a total of 200 mg per day, which is the upper limit for most outpatients. Anti-depressants are rarely given by injection.

After an optimal response has been attained and no further improvement is demonstrated, efforts then should be made to reduce the maintenance level of the drug by approximately one-half. This can be accomplished by gradually reducing the medication at the rate of 25 to 50 mg every other week. The therapeutic effect is usually maintained even though the medication being given is significantly less. Maintenance doses should be continued for four to six months after the patient has remained symptom-free. Thereafter, it can be discontinued gradually. If a relapse occurs, drug therapy should be reinstituted and maintained for an indefinite period.

Many clinicians advocate administering all or a large part of the total daily dose at bedtime. By so doing, many of the unpleasant side effects including drowsiness, dry mouth, etc. can be minimized. Other therapists recommend that the total daily dose be divided in two, with one-half being given at bedtime and the rest during the day.

Contraindications:

Tricyclic anti-depressants are generally contraindicated for individuals with known cardiovascular disease, especially those with cardiac arrhythmias, hypertension or coronary artery disease. There is some evidence that doxepin may be the safest anti-depressant medication for cardiac patients. They should not be administered simultaneously with other types of anti-depressants, especially MAO inhibitors. If MAO inhibitors are to be substituted for tricyclic drugs or vice-versa, a time lapse of at least two weeks without either medication should be instituted before changing to the new one. Tricyclic drugs are generally contraindicated for persons during pregnancy, with a history of untreated increased intraocular pressure (glaucoma), urinary retention, seizures, or those receiving most anti-hypertensive medications. Previous hypersensitivity to these drugs preclude their subsequent use.

Side Effects:

Drowsiness, blurring of vision and dry mouth are the most common side effects of tricyclic anti-depressants. Constipation and urinary retention are other side effects that occur with some frequency. Your patients should be advised in advance about the possible occurrence of these side effects and to report immediately the first signs of any unusual physical or mental side effects, such as sore throat, dizziness, etc. Specifically, your patients should be advised not to use alcohol and to be cautious about engaging in activities which may be hazardous if their mental alertness is compromised by the drug. Your patients should be told not to take other medications without first obtaining medical approval from you.

Complications:

Cardiac arrhythmias and hypotensive reactions are potential serious complications. A worsening of glaucoma may result. Occasionally a hypomanic state or schizophrenic reaction may be precipitated by these drugs. Although rare, complications involving the blood-forming organs, the liver, skin and central nervous system, may occur. It is important to remember when treating a depressed patient, that suicide is an ever-present risk. Even when improvement is in progress, suicidal attempts by taking an overdose or by other means can be made at any time by your patient. Tricyclic medications are potentially lethal drugs. Your patient, his medications and activities must be closely monitored.

Now complete Self-Assessment Exercise #6 beginning on the following page.

Self-Assessment Exercise #6

1. Circle all of the patient symptoms and conditions that are likely to respond favorably to anti-depressant medications:

   a. schizophrenia
   b. endogenous depression
   c. hyperactivity
   d. persistent feelings of depression
   e. suicidal ideation

2. Circle all of the following drugs which are recommended for the treatment of depression:

   a. chlorpromazine
   b. monamine oxidase inhibitors (MAO's)
   c. amphetamines
   d. methylphenidate (Ritalin)
   e. amitryptyline (Elavil)

3. Mr. W, a middle aged man, is diagnosed as having an endogeous depression. You decide to treat him with imipramine (Tofranil or Presamine). Indicate:

   a. an appropriate starting dose

   b. the typical upper limits of a total daily dosage

   c. expected onset of action time

   d. your course of action if no beneficial response occurs within three weeks

Self-Assessment Exercise #6 - (Continued)

4. Circle each of the following statements about tricyclic antidepressants that are true:

   a. their therapeutic effect is enhanced by MAO inhibitors

   b. contraindications include cardiovascular disease, pregnancy, and simultaneous use of anti-hypertensive drugs

   c. drowsiness, blurring of vision and dry mouth are common side effects

   d. cardiac arrhythmias and hypotensive reactions are potential serious complications

   e. has a high lethality if taken as an overdose

   f. may activate hypomanic or schizophrenic reactions

When you have completed this exercise to the best of your ability, check your answers with those on the following page.

Self-Assessment Exercise #6 - Feedback

1. The following patient symptoms and conditions are likely to respond favorably to anti-depressant drugs:

   b. endogenous depression

   e. suicidal ideation

   d. persistent feeling of depression

2. The following drugs are recommended for the treatment of depressive reactions:

   a. chlorpromazine

   e. amytriptyline (Elavil)

3. Since Mr. W has an endogenous depression and is assumed to be in good physical health:

   a. the recommended starting dose of imipramine would be 25 to 50 mg tid po

   b. the typical upper limit of daily dosage of imipramine would be 150 mg per day in divided doses to be achieved at the end of one week's time

   c. the expected onset of action of imipramine would probably be two to three weeks

   d. if he did not respond to the drug treatment by the end of the three weeks, you should gradually increase the total daily dosage to an upper limit of 200 mg per day total dosage; if there still was no therapeutic response by the end of a total treatment time of five to six weeks, then it may be well to consider placing him on different anti-depressant medication

4. The following statements about tricyclic anti-depressant medications are <u>true</u>:

   b. contraindications include cardiovascular disease, pregnancy, and simultaneous use of anti-depressant drugs

   c. drowsiness, blurring of vision and dry mouth are common side effects

Self-Assessment Exercise #6 - Feedback (Continued)

d. cardiac arrhythmias and hypotensive reactions are potential serious complications

e. has a high lethality if taken as an overdose

f. may activate hypomanic or schizophrenic reactions

If your answers correspond closely with those above, please continue reading on the next page. If not, please reread the preceding material.

TABLE III

SUMMARY OF ANTI-DEPRESSANT MEDICATIONS
(Psychic energizers, mood elevators, psychic stimulants)

INDICATIONS	DRUGS	ADULT DOSAGE RANGE	
Conditions: depression "endogenous depression" major depressive disorder	imipramine (Tofranil, Presamine) amitriptyline (Elavil) doxepin (Sinequan, Adapin)	Initial: 25 – 50 mg tid po Maintenance: 75 – 150 mg/day Upper Limits: 200 mg/day rarely given IM	Contraindications: hypersensitivity; cardiovascular disease (especially arrhythmia); use with MAO inhibitors; glaucoma; urinary retention; pregnancy; other medications
Symptoms: depressed affect tearfulness insomnia agitation loss of appetite slowing of thought, speech and action	For marked restlessness, anxiety, or agitation that is associated with depression: chlorpromazine (Thorazine, Chlor-PZ)	Initial: 20 – 50 mg tid – qid po	Common Side Effects: drowsiness; dry mouth; blurred vision Complications: hypotension; cardiac arrhythmias, suicide attempts; hyperactivity; psychosis

Anti-Anxiety Medications

Anxiety is a symptom common to a variety of emotional disorders and is defined as the emotional and physiological response to an unusual, unrecognized or imagined danger. The experience of anxiety is similar to a response of fear, except that in the latter case the perceived danger is clearly identifiable as a real threat to the well-being of the individual.

The psychological symptoms of anxiety including feelings of apprehension, "nervousness," tension, uneasiness, and if intense, fear of an impending catastrophe such as a heart attack or insanity. Anxious individuals also may complain of cardio-respiratory symptoms such as pounding heartbeat, shortness of breath and dizziness or lightheadedness. Frequent physiological concomitants are rapid heartbeat and breathing, muscular tension, tremulousness, sweating and a dry mouth. Anxiety episodes may be limited in duration or persist over long periods of time and range in intensity from mild tension to states of panic. Anxiety may occur only in specific circumstances or pervade most of the patient's daily activities. Unusually intense or unrelenting anxiety may indicate the presence of an overt or impending emotional breakdown and a thorough psychological examination is indicated to rule out that possibility.

Anti-anxiety medications encompass a variety of drugs including sedative-hypnotics (sedative or sleep inducing drugs), anti-histamines (drugs used to counteract allergic reactions), minor tranquilizers and others. They act upon the central nervous system to reduce feelings of anxiety, muscular tension and related physiological symptoms. These medications tend to produce a calming effect in part by inducing a state of sedation and drowsiness; effects which also make them useful for treating insomnia in which tension and worry are causative factors. Although sedatives and anti-histamines sometimes are prescribed to relieve anxiety, their regular use for that purpose is questionable because they tend to impair higher intellectual functions, are potentially habit-forming and may be lethal if taken as an overdose in relatively small quantities. Because of these and other limitations, the sedative-hypnotics and anti-histamines will not be discussed further. Comments will be limited to two minor tranquilizers--chlordiazepoxide (Librium) and diazepam (Valium) as indicated in Table IV.

Indications:

Chlordiazepoxide and diazepam are anti-anxiety medications frequently termed "minor tranquilizers" and are closely related chemical compounds. Although diazepam is more potent on a milligram-for-milligram basis, they otherwise possess effects and properties which are quite similar. Both are useful for relieving the feelings and physical symptoms of mild to moderate anxiety as described previously. In addition, they also possess muscle relaxant and anti-convulsant properties. For this reason, they are of particular value in the treatment of muscle spasms, muscle tension and in drug and/or alcohol withdrawal states in which seizures may occur. These minor tranquilizers also relieve restlessness associated with organic brain disorders and the anxiety and tension associated with a variety of medical illnesses. Both medications can be used to induce sleep and commonly are employed for presurgical relaxation and anesthesia. Chlordiazepoxide and diazepam are not recommended for the treatment of functional psychoses.

Dosage:

These minor tranquilizers generally are administered in oral form which has an onset of therapeutic effect occurring within two to four hours. Recommended starting doses for chlordiazepoxide is 10 to 25 milligrams bid to qid, and for diazepam, 2 to 10 milligrams bid to qid. After symptomatic improvement is obtained, many clinicians recommend that the total daily amount be reduced and given in a single dose, usually at bedtime. Some studies suggest that the minor tranquilizers are most effective when taken for short periods (days to a few weeks) and intermittently when symptoms are problematic. The therapeutic potency decreases and the likelihood of drug dependency increases if either of these medications are used at constant dosages for longer than a few weeks. The maintenance dosage range for chlordiazepoxide is 25 to 75 mg/day and for diazepam, 10 to 20 mg/day.

Under special circumstances when a rapid therapeutic effect is desired (e.g., panic states), or oral administration is not possible (e.g., vomiting associated with drug withdrawal), the drugs may be administered IM or IV. Intramuscular absorption is somewhat unpredictable, and the IV route may be preferred. Chlordiazepoxide can be given by injection in amounts of 25 to 50 milligrams and diazepam at a dosage of 2 to 10 milligrams. Injections of anti-anxiety medications usually are given q3 to 4h until symptomatic control is reached. Recommended upper limits for chlordiazepoxide is 100 mg/day, and diazepam 20 mg/day in divided doses. (Special procedures are needed for preparing and injecting these drugs and the manufacturers' recommendations should be consulted before administering them.) If your patient's symptoms of anxiety do not improve on recommended dose of the anti-anxiety medications, then prescribing a major tranquilizer may be effective.

Contraindications:

In comparison with many other psychotropic drugs, the contraindications for chlordiazepoxide and diazepam are few. These medications should not be administered to persons with a known hypersensitivity to either drug, to young children or to persons with acute, untreated glaucoma (a condition characterized by increased pressure within the eye). Chlordiazepoxide and diazepam are not recommended for psychotic patients or those who are comatose. Special care should be taken when prescribing anti-anxiety medications for persons with impaired kidney or liver functioning, the elderly and/or debilitated, and those already receiving medication for pain, insomnia, high blood pressure (hypertension), heart conditions, nervousness or depression.

Side Effects:

The most common side effects of the anti-anxiety medications are drowsiness, a sense of fatigue, decreased coordination and an unsteady gait. Each patient should be informed that such symptoms may occur, but will usually subside within a few days. Most side effects will disappear within a few days or by reducing the dosage. These drugs are well-tolerated by most patients and only in exceptional circumstances is total discontinuance necessary. If the above symptoms persist or others develop, your patient should discontinue the drug and contact you right away.

Complications:

As with any psychotropic medication, chlordiazepoxide and diazepam may accentuate or interfere with the effects of other drugs currently taken by the patient. Therefore, it is vital that you be thoroughly knowledgeable about the pharmacologic interaction between these drugs and any others that the patient is receiving. Either medication may cause drowsiness and impair the patient's performance when driving and working around machinery. Although both drugs typically raise the threshold for seizures, convulsions may be precipitated in susceptible individuals. For many physically well persons, but especially the elderly, debilitated, or those with impaired renal or liver functions, the drugs tend to accumulate in the body thereby producing an overdose effect. When taken in large amounts over an extended period of time, physical dependence may develop, and if the drug is stopped abruptly, a withdrawal syndrome may occur. Although chlordiazepoxide and diazepam are unlikely to cause death even when taken in large overdoses, discretion is necessary when prescribing any medication for patients who are depressed and are potentially suicidal.

Now complete Self-Assessment Exercise #7 beginning on the following page.

Self-Assessment Exercise #7

1. Chlordiazepoxide and diazepam may be of value when treating: (circle all that apply)

    a. tension-related insomnia

    b. functional psychosis

    c. drug/alcohol withdrawal states

    d. muscle spasms

    e. severe depressive reactions

    f. pre-operative anxiety

    g. chronic mild anxiety

2. Relative to the "minor tranquilizers," circle all statements that are true:

    a. have a low potential for habituation

    b. are highly lethal when taken in moderate overdoses

    c. may affect the action of other simultaneously taken drugs

    d. are contraindicated in comatose patients

    e. are preferred to sedative-hypnotics for the treatment of anxiety

3. Mrs. R is a 63-year-old woman who is troubled by recurrent feelings of tension, restlessness and anxiety which are not related to any medical problem. You elect to prescribe diazepam for her.

    a. What would be an appropriate route of administration and starting dose?

    b. What would you advise her about potential side effects and other measures she should take to minimize complications?

Self-Assessment Exercise #7 - (Continued)

4. Common side effects of diazepam include: (circle all that apply)

   a. restlessness
   b. drowsiness
   c. loss of appetite
   d. decreased coordination
   e. slowed reaction time

5. Each of the following patients complain of feeling anxious; indicate in the space provided, whether chlordiazepoxide should be: A - given in usual amounts; B - given in reduced amounts; or C - not given at all.

______a. a healthy middle-aged woman with untreated glaucoma

______b. a chronically sick patient

______c. a college student with a previous history of hypersensitivity to the drug

______d. a middle-aged man in good health

______e. an elderly man who is bedfast

______f. a young man who suffers from mild liver disease

When you have completed this exercise to the best of your ability, check your answers with those on the following page.

Self-Assessment Exercise #7 - Feedback

1. Chlordiazepoxide and diazepam may be of value when treating:

   a. tension-related insomnia

   c. drug/alcohol withdrawal states

   d. muscle spasms

   f. pre-operative anxiety

   g. chronic mild anxiety

2. Relative to the "minor tranquilizers," the following statements are true:

   a. they have a low potential for habituation

   c. they may affect the action of other simultaneously taken drugs

   d. are contraindicated in comatose patients

   e. are preferred to sedative-hypnotics for the treatment of anxiety

3. a. Mrs. R is an older woman and hence may overreact to anti-anxiety drugs. She should be tried on 1 mg of diazepam bid, taken orally. If no adverse reactions develop, then this dose may be increased as tolerated and needed.

   b. Mrs. R should be informed that she may experience drowsiness, a sense of fatigue, and decreased coordination. She should be told not to engage in any hazardous activities if her alertness is compromised, to not take alcohol and to immediately contact you if any unusual symptoms develop.

4. Common side effects of diazepam include:

   b. drowsiness

   d. decreased coordination

   e. slowed reaction time

Self-Assessment Exercise #7 - Feedback

5. The following represent the correct use of chlordiazepoxide:

_C_ a. Chlordiazepoxide should not be given to any person with untreated glaucoma.

_B_ b. A chronically sick patient should receive chlordiazepoxide in reduced dosage.

_C_ c. Chlordiazepoxide should not be given to persons with known hypersensitivity to the drug.

_A_ d. Chlordiazepoxide can be administered in the usual dosage to a midlle-aged man in good health.

_B_ e. Chlordiazepoxide should be given in a reduced amount to an elderly person who is bedfast.

_B_ f. Chlordiazepoxide should be given in a reduced amount to persons suffering from mild liver disease.

If your answers correspond closely with those above, please continue reading on the next page. If not, please reread the preceding material.

TABLE IV

SUMMARY OF ANTI-ANXIETY MEDICATIONS
(Minor Tranquilizers)

INDICATIONS	DRUGS	ADULT DOSAGE RANGE	
Conditions: feelings of tension, anxiety, apprehension muscle tension restlessness insomnia	chlordiazepoxide (Librium)	Initial: 10 – 25 mg bid – qid Maintenance: 25 – 50 mg/day Upper Limits: 50 – 75 mg/day IM or IV 25 – 50 mg	Contraindications: hypersensitivity; glaucoma; psychosis comatose state; other drugs; liver disease Common Side Effects: drowsiness; unsteady gait; decreased coordination Complications: cumulative effects; withdrawal seizures; drowsiness; drug dependence
	diazepam (Valium)	Initial: 2 – 10 mg bid – qid Maintenance: 10 – 20 mg/day Upper Limits: 20 mg/day IM or IV 2 – 10 mg	

Anti-Insomnia Medications

It is likely that every person periodically experiences insomnia (the inability to fall or remain asleep) without any significant untoward effects. Occasional or mild insomnia can be due to a variety of benign conditions and rarely requires medical intervention. However, persistent or severe insomnia lasting more than a few days is often indicative of significant depression or other psychological problems. You should carefully evaluate all patients who complain of recurrent sleep disturbances. All too often therapeutic attention is focused only on the presenting complaint of insomnia, and the patient sent on his way with a prescription for medication. This approach to the management of insomnia carries considerable risk for your patient. Inquire also about his psychological status, appetite, weight changes, energy levels, and so forth.

The therapeutic effect of inducing sleep is obtained only at the price of some problematic side effects. Most of the sedative-hypnotic drugs depress central nervous system functioning and create a sedating effect that also impairs the higher thinking centers and neuromuscular coordination. Indeed, these drugs, when taken in large amount, can produce a comatose state and general anesthesia especially when combined with alcohol. Still larger doses may cause death.

Several different types of drugs which can induce sleep are available. Some are useful only for their sedative effect. Others such as the anti-anxiety drugs and major tranquilizers are primarily used to treat emotional disorders, but because they possess some sedating effects can be useful for treating insomnia.

In various short- and long-acting forms, the barbiturates have been often prescribed for the treatment of insomnia. Numerous other sedative-hypnotics have been developed for the same purpose including chloral hydrate (Noctec), glutethmide (Doriden), methyprylon (Noludar), and ethchlorvynol (Placidyl).

Although the above medications may be suitable for the treatment of occasional mild insomnia, they possess properties which may limit their usefulness. Some actually interfere with sound sleep if taken on successive nights. In addition, they may significantly diminish or influence the effectiveness of other medications. All are potentially habituating, and if taken regularly, require an ever-increasing dose to produce the same sleep inducing effects. Most important, all are potentially lethal if taken in large overdoses. For these reasons, flurazepam, diazepam, or chlordiazepoxide are preferred for treating transient insomnia. Basic information about anti-insomnia drugs is summarized in Table V.

Dosage:

Flurazepam (Dalmane) in doses of 15 to 30 mg hs po induces, but does not impair deep sleep. This drug has little tendency to interfere with other drugs taken, it does not have any strong habituating properties, and it is unlikely to prove lethal even when taken as a large overdose. The chemically-related compounds diazepam (Valium) 5 to 10 mg hs po or chlordiazepoxide (Librium) 25 to 50 mg hs po have similar effects and properties. If one of these drugs cannot be given because of hypersensitivity or they are not effective, a drug belonging to a different chemical class is indicated. In this case, chlorpromazine in amounts of 50 to 100 mg hs po can be used with effect. This drug has significant sedating properties, is non-habituating, and presents very little risk from the standpoint of an overdose resulting in death. However, it does interact with other drugs which may be administered simultaneously and possesses significant side effects. (See the section on Anti-Psychotic Medications for details.)

Contraindications:

A known hypersensitivity or other untoward reaction to the sedative selected is a contraindication. Contraindications for flurazepam, diazepam and chlordiazepoxide are comparable. Since insomnia may be an accompaniment of depression, which in turn may be associated with the risk of suicide, any sedative-hypnotic drug prescribed should be carefully monitored. Liver or kidney impairment or the concomitant use of medications such as anti-hypertensive, analgesics and others may be relative contraindications. Patients should be advised not to take other sedatives, pain medications or alcohol simultaneously with anti-insomnia medications.

Side Effects:

Signs of cerebral intoxication including drowsiness, decreased coordination, unsteady gait, dizziness, and indistinct speech are common side effects. Patients also may experience a "hangover" effect in the morning following the use of sedative-hypnotics. This state of drowsiness usually subsides in a short time after awakening. Mild stimulants such as coffee or tea may alleviate the symptoms.

Complications:

Some individuals may become dependent on the sedative-hypnotics and request sleeping medication on a nightly basis. Elderly or debilitated patients are particularly susceptible to the effect of these drugs and may become confused or overly sedated. Accordingly, these persons should be started on a lower than usual dosage. Occasionally, depressive symptoms may be accentuated. Other symptoms which may result are a fall in blood pressure, dizziness, and decreased coordination. All of these symptoms are reversible simply by reducing the amount or discontinuing the drug.

Now complete Self-Assessment Exercise #8 beginning on the following page.

Self-Assessment Exercise #8

1. Match by letter the following drugs to the statements listed below. Each drug may be used more than once.

Drugs:
A - flurazepam (Dalmane)
B - chlorpromazine (Thorazine)
C - secobarbitol (Seconal)
D - glutethimide (Doriden)
E - diazepam (Valium)

Statements:

______(1) significantly impairs higher thinking centers

______(2) high lethality potential when taken in an overdose

______(3) in high doses may produce general anethesia or coma

______(4) an anti-psychotic (major tranquilizer) drug

______(5) a frequently prescribed minor tranquilizer (anti-anxiety) drug

______(6) high habituation potential

______(7) may actually impair sound sleep

2. Indicate the hs typical dosage range for each of the following medications:

   a. flurazepam (Dalmane)______________________________

   b. diazepam (Valium)______________________________

   c. chlorpromazine (Thorazine)______________________________

3. Is the following statement true or false?

   In contrast to anti-psychotic and anti-depressant drugs, it is safe for patients to use alcohol while taking a sedative-hypnotic.

   ______ True ______False

Self-Assessment Exercise #8 - (Continued)

4. List the common side effects of a sedative-hypnotic.

5. List two possible complications of taking a sedative-hypnotic.

When you have completed this exercise to the best of your ability, check your answers with those on the following page.

Self-Assessment Exercise #8 - Feedback

1. The drugs listed correctly match the statements below:

Drugs:
A - flurazepam (Dalmane)
B - chlorpromazine (Thorazine)
C - secobarbitol (Seconal)
D - glutethimide (Doriden)
E - diazepam (Valium)

Statements:

C & D (1) significantly impairs higher thinking centers

C & D (2) high lethality potential when taken in an overdose

C & D (3) in high doses may produce general anesthesia or coma

B (4) an anti-psychotic (major tranquilizer) drug

E (5) a frequently prescribed minor tranquilizer (anti-anxiety) drug

C & D (6) high habituation potential

C & D (7) may actually impair sound sleep

2. The average hs dosage ranges for the following medications are:

   a. flurazepam 15 to 30 mg

   b. diazepam 5 to 10 mg

   c. chlorpromazine 50 to 100 mg

3. The statement that it is safe for patients to use alcohol while taking a sedative-hypnotic is false. Serious potentiating effects which may result in death are associated with mixing alcohol and psychotropic drugs.

4. Common side effects of a sedative-hypnotic are those of cerebral intoxication which include drowsiness, unsteady gait, decreased coordination, and impairment of higher thinking centers.

Self-Assessment Exercise #8 - Feedback (Continued)

5. The two most common complications of taking a sedative-hypnotic are excessive sedation and the development of a dependency on the drug.

If your answers correspond closely with those above, please continue reading on the next page. If not, please reread the preceding material.

TABLE V

SUMMARY OF SEDATIVE-HYPNOTIC MEDICATIONS

INDICATIONS	DRUGS	ADULT DOSAGE RANGE	
Conditions: insomnia restlessness	flurazepam (Dalmane)	15 – 30 mg po hs	Contraindications: hypersensitivity; liver or kidney disease; history of drug abuse or serious depression Common Side Effects: drowsiness; unsteady gait; decreased coordination; "hangover" Complications: development of dependency; drug abuse; accentuation of depression
	diazepam (Valium)	5 – 10 mg po hs	
	chlordiazepoxide (Librium)	25 – 50 mg po hs	
	chlorpromazine (Thorzaine, Chlor-PZ)	50 – 100 mg po hs	

SUMMARY

Psychotropic drugs are widely prescribed and, when carefully selected, can be effective in alleviating symptoms of a variety of psychopathological conditions. Only general guidelines are available for matching the type and dosage of a drug to a given patient. Each drug is simultaneously potentially therapeutic and problematic, yielding both symptomatic relief from emotional distress and the hazards of complications and side effects. It is your responsibility to be thoroughly knowledgeable about your patient and the drugs which will be prescribed.

REFERENCES

Appleton, W. S., "Psychoactive Drugs: A Usage Guide," Dis. Nerv. System, 32:607-616, 1971.

Barchas, J., Berger, P., Ciaranello, R., Elliott, G., Psychopharmacology From Theory to Practice, New York: Oxford University Press, 1977.

Goodman, L. and Gilman, A., The Pharmacologic Basis of Therapeutics, 5th Ed., New York: Macmillan, 1975.

Hollister, L. E., Clinical Use of Psychotherapeutic Drugs, Springfield: Thomas, 1973.

Kline, N., Alexander, S., Chamberlain, A., Psychotropic Drugs: Manual for Emergency Management of Overdosage, Oradell: Medical Economics, 1974.

Physicians' Desk Reference, Oradell: Medical Economics, 1977.

Shader, R., Manual of Psychiatric Therapies, Boston: Little, Brown and Company, 1975.

CHAPTER 6. CONSULTATION AND REFERRAL

There may be times during your work with patients when you will want specialized help in establishing the correct psychological diagnosis or management procedures. Or, because of personality differences, conflicting time schedules or for a variety of other reasons, you may wish to discontinue working with a particular patient. In these instances, consider requesting a consultation or referring your patient to another therapist for treatment.

This chapter will discuss some of the reasons for seeking consultation or referral and describe procedures which will facilitate the process and assure that the best interests of the patient are served.

LEARNING OBJECTIVES

By the time you complete this chapter, you should be able to do the following and apply the information to written case histories:

1. List and describe commonly encountered problems which may indicate the need for psychological consultation or referral.

2. Describe the steps and principles to follow when making a psychological consultation or referral.

INDICATIONS FOR PSYCHOLOGICAL REFERRAL

Occasionally while treating a patient you may find that he has problems which you cannot or do not wish to treat. Or you may feel that another therapist could deal more effectively with this patient. When this is the case, it is useful to recommend either a consultation (obtaining a second opinion from a specialist) or a referral (actually transferring the patient to the care of someone else). You can consult with or refer to a psychologist, psychiatrist, social worker, physician or marriage counselor depending upon which discipline is most appropriate for your patient. As the one who initiates the consultation or referral, it is important that you are familiar with the consultant's clinical experience, academic and clinical affiliations, certification and licensure by professional examining boards.

Now let us consider several common problem areas which may warrant a consultation and/or referral.

Diagnosis

Sometimes, despite a careful and detailed workup, the diagnosis may elude you. This can occur for various reasons including lack of clinical experience, incompatibility between you and the patient, or simply because the case is unusually complex. In such circumstances, consultation and/or referral would be indicated.

General Patient Management

Some patients present behaviors that may prove especially difficult to manage, for example, suicidal threats, overt seductiveness, persistent noncompliance or unremitting hostility expressed toward the therapist. Other patients may fail to improve despite all efforts at intervention, perhaps because particular therapeutic expertise is needed which the therapist does not possess. In such instances, to seek the help of a consultant of an appropriate discipline with whom to discuss the case and obtain some guidance may mean the difference between the therapy becoming "stalled" or progressing. Some examples of the typical specialists which may be needed are an adolescent or child therapist, a behaviorist, a psychoanalyst, a sex therapist or a marriage or vocational counselor.

Pharmacologic Therapy

When the use of psychotropic medications is being considered for your patient, it is often good practice to confer with a consultant who has had specialized medical or pharmacologic training. In this case, you might be interested in obtaining information about which drugs to use, advice about possible side effects and contraindications, the usual dosage and any follow-up laboratory tests which might be indicated. Eve the most experienced therapist will find it useful to occasionally consult an expert in psychopharmacology to receive an update on current information about psychotropic drugs. An experienced psychiatrist or a clinical pharmacist with special academic and hospital experience can provide the information.

Community Resources

Occasionally your patient may have problems other than psychological ones involving financial, legal, vocational, educational, military, or religious matters. It is best if these problems are handled concurrently with the psychological treatment if therapy is to be effective. Additional information, expert opinions, further testing, and specialized guidance may be essential in helping your patient get through trying periods or make important life decisions. In order to provide comprehensive patient care, you may often need the assistance of adjunctive services. Welfare, disability, day care agencies, sheltered workshops, home care services, community mental health programs, and medical clinics comprise a few of the services available as therapeutic resources. Most of these agencies provide a variety of informative booklets and literature along with listing their programs and locations. Placing a call to a social worker or medical case worker in an established psychiatric facility will yield information about community resources and referral procedures.

Limitations and Preferences of Referring Therapists

Certain limitations or preferences of the therapist may indicate the need for referral. Particular consideration should be shown to patients who come from a cultural background or language group that is completely alien to yours. Knowing very little or nothing about the traditions, mores and other aspects of a patient's culture may hinder your understanding and therapeutic effectiveness. Such cases require someone knowledgeable about the patient's ethnic background in addition to being professionally competent. Furthermore, many therapists have preferences about which kinds of problems that they prefer not to treat. Some therapists find persons with alcohol or drug-related problems unsatisfactory to work with; others find that patients with schizophrenia make them feel uncomfortable. It is important for you to acknowledge your personal preferences and refer to others those patients whom you find particularly disturbing.

Hospitalization

When symptoms are so severe as to warrant custodial care or inpatient treatment, you may want to refer your patient to a specialist. To this end, there are psychiatrists, psychologists, and social workers who have particular expertise in managing patients in a hospital setting and who possess staff privileges in psychiatric facilities.

Now complete Self-Assessment Exercise #1 beginning on the next page.

Self-Assessment Exercise #1

List and describe the problem areas outlined in the chapter which you might personally feel are indications for requesting a consultation and/or referral for your patients.

When you have completed this exercise to the best of your ability, check your answers with those on the following page.

Self-Assessment Exercise #1 - Feedback

You should have listed the following types of problems which may warrant a consultation and/or referral.

1. Diagnosis--when a working diagnosis cannot be definitively established.

2. General patient management--when patients manifest disruptive or dangerous behavior or fail to improve.

3. Pharmacologic Therapy--when the use of psychotropic drugs is contemplated.

4. Community resources--when the patient is needful of specialized home care, or a variety of community service programs which may include legal, financial, vocational, or other basically non-psychological-type advice or consuling.

5. Therapist preferences or limitations--personal preferences not to work with certain types of patients or problems and/or limited expertise in managing some types of cases.

6. Hospitalization--when specialized, in-patient treatment is indicated.

If your answers correspond closely with those above, continue reading. If not, please reread the preceding material.

PRINCIPLES OF EFFECTIVE CONSULTATION AND REFERRAL

Recommending a consultation and/or referral to your patient will be perceived by him as an act of considerable significance, and it deserves careful thought and tactfulness. The interaction between the two of you is unique in many ways, not the least of which is the intensity of feeling which he invests in the relationship. (For some patients, a change of therapist is likened to "changing horses in mid-stream.") However well intentioned your recommendations for referral, if the request for outside consultation is not skillfully handled, your patient likely will feel some combination of anger, rejection, fear and abandonment. Fortunately, there is much that you can do to facilitate the referral process and utilizing the following principles will help.

Explore your reasons and feelings about the consultation and/or referral. Define clearly in your mind the reasons and goals for the consultation, being sure that the added expense and time are justified for the well-being of your patient. If you have major reservations about the referral/consultation, try to analyze and resolve them. Otherwise it is likely that the patient will perceive your ambivalence, and his uncertainty and discomfort will be increased.

Describe the consultation/referral in positive terms. Your patient usually will need help in developing an attitude of positive expectancy about the consult or referral. To this end, try to convince your patient of the need and potential benefits of the referral. Point out the special expertise of the consultant and how he can be of help. It is important that your patient sense your personal concern for his welfare and that the referral is not because you are disappointed in him, that his case is hopeless or awesomely unique. For these reasons, statements such as, "It is not clear to me what may be causing your difficulty, and I think another opinion could be of help." or "I believe that your improvement would proceed faster if you were to work with someone who has specialized training in dealing with those problems." The preceding statements are preferable to, "I have never had a case like yours before." or "There is nothing more I can do." Your patient needs to feel that you are concerned with obtaining the best possible care available for him.

Help "educate" your patient about the consultation/referral. Be direct. Be positive. Tell your patient how you view the problem, what you expect the consultation to accomplish and what he can expect from the consultant. As a general rule, it is more effective to word the patient's problems in terms of behavior, not diagnostic labels which can be confusing or imply unpleasant connotations.

In this vein, help your patient feel positively about the consultant without making unrealistic promises. There is no guarantee that your patient will receive sensitive care or that the consultant will be able to deliver all that your patient hopes for. Certainly do not oversell the consultant or portray him as "the last word." Be sure to discuss the likely cost involved and, if there is a money problem, attempt to work out the difficulty between your patient and consultant in advance. Whenever possible, include your patient's relatives in the referral process. Providing reassurance and answers to their questions will go a long way toward developing cooperation with the treatment goals.

Closely assess your patient's response to the recommendation for consultation/referral. Most patients worry about reasons behind a referral and that it may mean that they are beyond hope or that you are no longer concerned about them. Therefore, listen carefully to their questions and statements monitoring them for indications of fear, resentment or rejection. Encourage your patient to express all that may be bothering him. In this way, any misconceptions, unfounded fears and fantasies can be corrected. An additional benefit from allowing your patient time to ventilate about the referral process is that he will see this extra consideration for his feelings as a measure of your concern.

Select a consultant. It is your responsibility to obtain for your patient the most competent consultant available. To this end, confer with colleagues, appropriate organizations or agencies, and/or directories to select the best qualified consultant. Once he is chosen, obtain your client's permission in writing to contact the specialist in order to relay information which you possess and indicate the purpose of the referral.

Contact the consultant. As a rule, it is advantageous for your patient to personally make the initial contact with the consultant. But if he has difficulty in doing so, call the consultant yourself. Don't depend on the patient's "getting to it sometime later."

As the referer, be prepared to supply the consultant with a concise history of the patient's problem, what you hope the specialist to accomplish, the nature of previous treatments and other relevant information. At the same time you can obtain information about fees, appointment times, his particular referral requirements, etc. Be sure to have your patient sign a release form so that you can discuss and/or forward written information about the case.

Follow-up on the consultation/referral. Ask your patient to call you when his first appointment was completed to make sure that it was satisfactory. Try to assess his feelings and ideas about the consultation -- you may be able to help if problems or uncertainties develop. If a comp transfer of the patient care is involved, it is appropriate to call periodically and ask how the patient is coming along. Should your patient contact you after the referral to discuss therapy or ask your advice about a particular problem, be sure to contact the consultant and apprise him of the matter.

<u>Abide by your patient's decision about the consultation/referral.</u> If your patient refuses your recommendation about the referral, does not follow through, or later prefers to return to your care, do not insist that he do otherwise. It is rarely advisable to apply strong pressure or insist on patient compliance. Hopefully, in time your patient may reconsider. Except for exceptional circumstances, each patient is the final judge of determining who he will accept for a therapist. Express your understanding, if not agreement, with his decision, and continue to provide the best therapy that you can. However, be sure to document thoroughly in your records the recommendations made and the patient's subsequent refusal to follow them.

When a consultation and/or referral has been done skillfully in accordance with the above principles, patients feel that they are being helped and not abandoned, that the therapist has a personal interest in them and that a more positive outcome is possible.

Now complete Self-Assessment Exercise #2 beginning on the following page.

Self-Assessment Exercise #2

Read the following case history and then answer the questions that follow:

> Susan Ranson is a 28-year-old married woman who has one child. Because of marital problems, she has experienced recurrent episodes of severe depression at which times she drank heavily and neglected her home and family. She has threatened and attempted suicide on two occasions by taking an overdose of pills. Her husband drinks excessively and, when angered by her depressive symptoms, has physically assaulted her. During family crises in the past, their son's performance in school deteriorated markedly
> you have been working with Susan for
> months, marital problems again cause her to become very depressed and she speaks of wanting to die.

1. List Susan's personal and family problems which warrant therapeutic intervention.

2. Assume that Susan may need hospitalization for self-protection and that you would like consultation with an expert about the matter. Briefly list the steps which you should take in arranging the consultation.

Self-Assessment Exercise #2 (Continued)

3. a. What type of consultant would be most appropriate?

b. What steps would you take to locate a well-qualified specialist?

4. How should you deal with Susan's husband with respect to your recommendation for a consultation/referral?

5. What should you say to Susan and her husband about the referral?

Self-Assessment Exercise #2 (Continued)

6. Upon hearing your recommendation for a referral, both Susan and her husband are reluctant to accept it. How should you deal with their reluctance?

7. Susan and her husband reluctantly agree to make an appointment with the specialist, and seem hesitant about setting a definite time when they will do so. What action should you take?

When you have completed this exercise to the best of your ability, check your answers with those on the following page.

Self-Assessment Exercise #2 - Feedback

1. Susan's personal and family problems which may warrant therapeutic intervention are:

   recurrent marital problems
   recurrent depressive episodes
   she is presently talking of suicide
   her husband drinks excessively
   her child is having problems in school

2. Steps for you to follow in arranging a consultation are:

   a. make sure in your own mind that the consultation is justified
   b. approach the consultation using optimistic terms
   c. help educate Susan and her husband about the prospect of referral
   d. deal with her response to the idea of referral
   e. select the consultant
   f. contact the consultant
   g. follow-up on the referral

3. Since Susan may need hospitalization, it is best to pick a person experienced in dealing with severely emotionally disturbed persons in a hospital setting. A psychiatrist having had medical training probably would be the best choice. If you personally don't have a specialist in mind, it would be a good idea to contact a family physician whom you know and get his recommendation. If that approach is not possible, then contact either a local medical society or mental health center for referral. Lacking these resources, the public library should have a directory of certified medical specialists in your area. And finally, you can turn to the Yellow Pages of the telephone directory. There are a number of psychologists and social workers who have hospital privileges. If you feel either of these professionals might be helpful, call the Psychological Association or Social Worker Association in your area for a referral.

4. Susan's husband should definitely be included in the decision about her hospitalization. Certainly he has played an important part in her distress and, as the other responsible adult in the family, has a great stake in the outcome of treatment. It is also important for you to assess whether he will be an asset or a liability with respect to her treatment. You also will be in a position to respond to any questions or doubts that he has about your recommendations.

Self-Assessment Exercise #2 - Feedback (Continued)

5. Properly preparing Susan and her husband for the referral is of vital importance. Present a brief summary in layman's terms of your findings and recommendations. Point out what the consultation would be like, its cost, if you know it, and what they might expect with regard to the personality and treatment approach of the consultant. They are likely to have many questions and misperceptions about the consultant process, so be sure to allow them an opportunity to state them.

6. When you detect in your patient or her family signs of reluctance to see a specialist, encouraging them to express their feelings, fears and fantasies will help alleviate the situation. Once their doubts are expressed openly you can help in dealing with them. Point out the disadvantages of not complying with your recommendation, but simultaneously convey your respect for their decision, if they decline to follow your suggestion. The disadvantages of their failing to comply should be made clear.

7. If after Susan and her husband agree to see a specialist but seem hesitant about initiating a call themselves, then you telephone the specialist while both are still in your office. Although it is usually desirable for patients to initiate their own appointment, it is sometimes necessary for the referring therapist to do so.

If your answers correspond closely with those above, please continue reading on the next page. If not, please reread the preceding material.

SUMMARY

It is not necessary, and probably not wise, for a therapist to treat every type of psychological problem and patient that comes for aid. Sooner or later, a patient will seek help whose therapeutic needs exceed the expertise of the therapist. It is well for the therapist to acknowledge the limitations of his capabilities and seek assistance from an additional source. Each therapist should take stock of his training, treatment preferences and skills and identify those patients and problem areas which should be referred to others. It is important for each therapist to cultivate those skills which will facilitate the process of referral.

REFERENCES

Bartemeier, L. H., "On Referring Patients to Other Physicians," Northwest Med., 56:312, 1957.

Binder, H. J., "Helping Your Patient Accept Psychiatric Referral," J. Okla, Med. Assn., 45:279, 1952.

Jaffee, M., "Psychiatric Referral," Rocky Mountain J., 60:26, 1963.

Mendel, W. M. and Solomon, P., The Psychiatric Consultation, New York: Grune and Stratton, 1968.

Pasnau, R. O., Consultation-Liaison Psychiatry, New York: Grune and Stratton, 1975.

Schwab, J. J., "Psychiatric Consultation: Problems with Referral," Dis. Nerv. Sys., 32:447-452, July 1971.

Schwab, J. J., et al, "Medical Patients' Reactions to Referring Physicians After Psychiatric Consultation," JAMA, 195:1120-1122, March 28, 1966.

Watters, T. A., "Certain Pitfalls and Perils in Psychiatric Referral," Am. Practit., 3:198, 1952.

Part II
Psychotherapeutics for Specific Disorders

CHAPTER 7. SCHIZOPHRENIC DISORDERS

The psychoses are severe psychopathologic conditions characterized by impaired reality testing (the ability to distinguish between personal motivations and the real world) and marked disturbances of affect, thinking and behavior. Psychotic disorders generally are classified into two distinct types -- the "organic" and "functional" psychoses. Organic psychoses result from a gross abnormality of brain tissue functioning due to trauma, infections, toxins, or other physiological alterations. The etiology of the functional psychoses is less well understood and the disorders can arise from psychological stress and/or subtle central nervous system disturbances, the presence of which is suspected but not yet proven by present diagnostic procedures. Delusions, hallucinations, impaired judgment and reality testing are common to both organic and functional psychoses. However, disorientation and disturbed memory and calculation ability are much more typical of organic psychoses -- an important point to remember when distinguishing between the two types of psychoses.

Schizophrenic disorders are classified among the functional psychoses because they do not have an identifiable physiological cause or show the typical findings of organic brain disorders. Schizophrenic disorders affect an estimated one percent of the general population and comprise the most common type of functional psychosis. The therapeutic management of patients with these disorders constitute a major health problem because they are often seriously incapacitated and require extensive treatment and rehabilitation. Before the advent of antipsychotic drugs, the principle form of treatment involved long-term hospitalization. Most of these patients now can be successfully managed on an outpatient basis, and sooner or later it is likely that you will be called upon to evaluate and treat them.

LEARNING OBJECTIVES

By the time you complete this chapter, you should be able to do the following and apply the information to written case histories:

1. Describe the current theories of etiology for schizophrenic disorders.
2. Describe the mental status examination findings typical of schizophrenic disorders.
3. Describe the early findings preceding the onset of schizophrenic psychosis.
4. Describe the major symptoms and findings of history which distinguish schizophreniform and schizophrenic disorders.
5. For each of the methods of therapeutic intervention listed below, describe the recommended treatment approach and provide a rationale for its use in the management of schizophrenic disorders:

   a. supportive psychotherapy
   b. behavioral therapy
   c. pharmacologic therapy
   d. consultation and referral

CHARACTERISTICS OF SCHIZOPHRENIC DISORDERS

Etiology

At the present time no single factor has been identified which causes all schizophrenic disorders. Present research strongly suggests that a group of schizophrenic disorders exist which share some findings in common but have differing etiologies, courses, combinations of symptoms and prognoses. Some schizophrenic disorders appear to result from a biochemical defect of the central nervous system that is either acquired or genetically inherited. Particular drugs including hallucinogens (for example, L.S.D., P.C.P.), central nervous system stimulants (amphetamines), and hormones (cortico steriods) have been implicated in the precipitation of schizophrenic symptoms. Other cases seem largely a response to devastating life circumstances. Many clinicians believe that schizophrenic disorders are multidetermined, that is, they arise from a combination of biological and sociologic factors which impact at a point in time. The interacting factors may include an emotionally traumatic childhood, disordered family relationships, intense life stresses and inherited and/or acquired biochemical defects of the central nervous system. Any therapeutic approach to schizophrenic disorders should attempt to identify and alleviate as many of the contributing factors as possible.

Mental Status Examination Findings

To make the diagnosis of a schizophrenic disorder, hallucinations and/or delusions and/or a disturbance of thinking should be detected at sometime during the course of the condition. No single finding of history or mental status examination (MSE) is characteristic of all persons with schizophrenic disorders, and the diagnosis is made by identifying a combination of signs and symptoms. MSE observations are important for establishing the diagnosis, but additional findings are necessary to further delineate the disorder and include: the absence of an Affective Disorder (a manic or depressive syndrome) prior to or during the onset of symptoms; the absence of findings which can be attributed to an Organic Mental Disorder; deterioration of former levels of functioning; and a tendency for symptoms to become chronic. MSE findings vary considerably from individual to individual and from time to time within the same patient. There frequently are "islands" of personality and intellectual intactness which exist simultaneously with symptoms of severe psychopathology. With this potential for symptom variation in mind, we will present the most characteristic findings of schizophrenic disorders. Diagnostic subtypes of schizophrenic disorders are distinguished according to the predominating symptoms (e.g., paranoid, catatonic), but here, we will focus only on helping you diagnose schizophrenic disorders as a broad class of psychopathology. Further information about the subtypes can be learned from the references listed at the end of this chapter.

Appearance. Personal appearance is usually in proportion to the severity of the schizophrenic disorder. If the condition is mild, then there may be few or no abnormal findings. However, if psychological symptoms become severe, then it is common to find evidence of personal neglect and highly eccentric or bizarre patterns of dress.

Behavior. Behavior patterns including facial expression, speech and bodily movements are often atypical, unpredictable and disorganized. Especially in schizophrenic disorders of an abrupt onset, patients may experience intense anxiety which is expressed by an apprehensive facial expression, generalized muscle tension, restlessness and rapid, disjointed speech. However, some patients show a bland, unresponsive facial expression, slowed body movements and speak with a dull, monotonous voice. Most patients with a schizophrenic disorder are distrustful of interpersonal relationships and may respond to you, their potential helper, with anxiety, suspiciousness or defensive hostility. Because they readily misinterpret your motives, these patients frequently are negativistic and uncooperative.

Mood and Affect. During the earliest stages of a schizophrenic disorder, your patients may complain of feeling persistent depression or apathy without an identifiable cause. Later, as the onset of psychosis becomes imminent, they may experience episodes of intense anxiety and unpredictable fluctuations of mood. Overt affect is often incongruous with thought content. For example, your patients may demonstrate inappropriate smiling while relating ideas which in normal persons would evoke feelings of sadness, apprehension or anger. It is difficult to anticipate just how such patients will respond emotionally, and sudden outbursts of anxiety or anger may occur for little apparent reason. In many patients, their overall emotional response seems "flat," "inappropriately bland," or "blunted." It is often difficult to empathize with persons experiencing a schizophrenic disorder and you may experience transient feelings of uneasiness when you talk with them.

Perception. Perceptual disturbances in the form of illusions and hallucinations are relatively common in persons with schizophrenic disorders. Auditory hallucinations are more common than visual ones and typically are harassing or persecutory in nature. Hallucinations involving touch, smell or taste are less frequently encountered.

Thinking. In schizophrenic disorders, both the thought content and sequential relatedness of ideas are abnormal. Except in instances when your patient's mental disorganization is severe, alertness, orientation, memory and calculation ability are minimally affected. However, concentration, psychological insight and judgment for day-to-day living activities generally are decreased. Abstract thinking frequently shows impairment as evidenced by literal or highly personalized interpretations of common proverbs. Thought content almost invariably will reveal some abnormality in the form of delusional beliefs, impaired reality testing, highly eccentric or bizarre ideation and occasionally homicidal or suicidal ideas. Delusions highly characteristic of this disorder include patient beliefs that actions and thinking is being controlled by others; that the thoughts of others are being inserted in the patient's mind; or that his thoughts are being broadcast and made known to others. Obsessive thinking and feelings of depersonalization (and derealization) are common. An associational disturbance is almost always present and may be mild or so severe that meaningful communication is difficult.

Now complete Self-Assessment Exercise #1 beginning on the following page.

Self-Assessment Exercise #1

1. Indicate whether the following statements about the etiology of schizophrenic disorders are true (T) or false (F):

_______ a. head trauma commonly causes schizophrenic symptoms

_______ b. schizophrenic symptoms are often the result of an interaction of multiple factors

_______ c. all schizophrenic disorders share a common etiology

_______ d. certain drugs/medications can precipitate a schizophrenic disorder

_______ e. some schizophrenic disorders may result from an inherited biochemical defect

_______ f. some schizophrenic disorders can be precipitated by a traumatic life event

2. Indicate whether the following statements about the MSE findings of schizophrenic disorders are true (T) or false (F):

_______ a. the presence of either delusions or hallucinations indicates the presence of a schizophrenic disorder

_______ b. most of these patients show impairment of orientation and recent memory

_______ c. islands of intellectual intactness may exist alongside symptoms of psychopathology

_______ d. most of these patients relate openly with their therapist

_______ e. auditory hallucinations are more common than visual ones

_______ f. it is usually easy to empathize with a person with a schizophrenic disorder

_______ g. reality testing and judgment for routine activities is frequently impaired

_______ h. some degree of an associational disturbance is typically present

_______ i. thought content is generally unusual or strange.

Self-Assessment Exercise #1 (Continued)

3. In the spaces provided, briefly characterize the MSE findings of an individual with a schizophrenic disorder:

APPEARANCE	
BEHAVIOR	
AFFECT/MOOD	
PERCEPTION	
THINKING	

When you have completed this exercise to the best of your ability, check your answers with those on the following page.

Self-Assessment Exercise #1 - Feedback

1. Statements are true (T) or false (F).

__F__ a. head trauma commonly causes schizophrenic symptoms

__T__ b. schizophrenic symptoms are often the result of an interaction of multiple factors

__F__ c. all schizophrenic disorders share a common etiology

__T__ d. certain drugs/medications can precipitate a schizophrenic disorder

__T__ e. some schizophrenic disorders may result from an inherited, biochemical defect

__T__ f. some schizophrenic disorders can be precipitated by a traumatic life event

2. Statements are true (T) or false (F).

__F__ a. the presence of either delusions or hallucinations indicates the presence of a schizophrenic disorder

__F__ b. most of these patients show impairment of orientation and recent memory

__T__ c. islands of intellectual intactness may exist alongside symptoms of psychopathology

__F__ d. most of these patients relate openly with their therapist

__T__ e. auditory hallucinations are more common than visual ones

__F__ f. it is usually easy to empathize with a person with a schizophrenic disorder

__T__ g. reality testing and judgment for routine activities is frequently impaired

__T__ h. some degree of an associational disturbance is typically present

__T__ i. thought content is generally unusual or strange

Self-Assessment Exercise #1 - Feedback (Continued)

3. Mental Status Findings of a Schizophrenic Disorder

APPEARANCE	Variable according to severity, but typically disheveled, eccentric or bizarre.
BEHAVIOR	Generally atypical or strange. Body movements--erratic, tense or slowed. Facial expression-apprehensive or atypically bland. Speech--rapid and intense or dull, slow, monotone. Therapist-patient relationship--emotional distance; distrust; negativistic; uncooperative.
AFFECT/MOOD	Variable. May range from intense anxiety or hostility to persistent blandness or "blunting." Often inappropriate to thought content.
PERCEPTION	Illusions and/or hallucinations often present. Auditory more frequent than visual hallucinations. Hallucinations are usually critical or persecutory.
THINKING	Alertness, orientation, memory usually intact. Reality testing, judgment typically impaired. Delusions, phobias, depersonalization often present. Ideas are eccentric or bizarre. Associational disturbance almost always present.

If your answers correspond closely with those above, please continue reading on the next page. If not, please reread the preceding material.

CHARACTERISTICS OF SCHIZOPHRENIC DISORDERS (Continued)

Course and Early Symptoms

It is difficult to make reliable predictions about the prognosis for any particular individual who develops a schizophrenic disorder, and in that regard, each case must be considered separately. However, there are findings which suggest persons who are at special risk or are developing an impending psychosis. Early detection and treatment of an incipient psychosis may help to avert it or lessen its severity.

Many of the psychological symptoms common to normal development are similar to those of an early schizophrenic disorder. Typically, the first psychotic episode occurs during the late teens or early adult years. During those years, young persons are struggling to cope with major life events such as developing a sexual and personal identity, becoming emotionally and financially independent from their families and selecting a vocation. At that time of life, most normal persons experience some degree of anxiety and depression and have difficulty with interpersonal relationships. Moodiness, irritability, and bodily preoccupations are common experiences. But these emotional ups and downs usually are transient, do not progress in severity, and rarely interfere with daily functioning. In schizophrenic disorders, the symptoms usually become progressively severe and incapacitating.

Some findings of history help to determine persons at special risk for developing a schizophrenic disorder at some future time. Evaluate closely those individuals who have not been able to gain satisfaction from friendships, scholastic or social activities. Usually these individuals are painfully shy and never have formed close and lasting personal relationships. They typically are "loners" who rarely participate in peer activities. In school or work they often are underachievers. Also, be alert to persons who have performed satisfactorily in the past, but currently are demonstrating a progressive withdrawal from social contacts and a steady deterioration of work or school performance.

A schizophrenic psychosis may take as little as a few weeks or as long as several years to develop. In the early phase disturbances of affect, thinking and behavior are apparent. Typically, there are multiple psychological and physical symptoms which fluctuate widely, worsen steadily and do not respond significantly to supportive measures, anti-anxiety medication or reduction of environmental stresses. Personal relationships and performance of routine activities falter. Irritability, moodiness and decreased concentration are frequent findings. Your patients may describe mood swings which encompass euphoria, depression, apathy and intense anxiety -- or they may complain of an inability to feel strongly about anything. Patients on the verge of a psychosis are frequently troubled by a combination of symptoms including bodily preoccupations, phobias and obsessional thinking. Many of these individuals are intensely aware of their failing coping abilities and describe fears of losing their sanity. Many patients describe an increasing suspiciousness about the motives of others. Although they do not yet have definitive delusions, they are often preoccupied with eccentric beliefs or become fanatical devotees of unusual philosophies, religions or political groups. Frequently, these persons have difficulty in communicating their ideas and may exhibit signs of an associational disturbance. From a physical standpoint, sleep and appetite patterns are disrupted and many patients complain of easy fatigibility. They may lose the capacity for enjoyment and pleasure, stating that "nothing seems good to me." In an attempt to lessen their feelings of anxiety and helplessness, many resort to compulsive drinking or reliance on various medications. If definitive therapeutic intervention is not initiated, symptoms of a full-blown psychosis including delusions, hallucinations and marked associational disturbances will follow.

Schizophreniform and Schizophrenic Disorders

Many clinicians feel that it is possible to distinguish schizophrenic conditions which have a relatively good prognosis from those with a more unfavorable outcome. We shall use the term "schizophreniform disorders" to refer to conditions which have a shorter course and a better prognosis, and "schizophrenic disorder" to refer to symptoms which are more chronic and refractory to therapy.

The term "schizophreniform disorder" is synonymous in the psychiatric literature with "reactive schizophrenia" or nonprocess schizophrenia. In this condition, the life adjustment pattern prior to the onset of symptoms is characterized by stable interpersonal relationships and satisfactory performance at work and school. There is no significant increased incidence of this disorder in close family members. Symptoms usually develop abruptly, last one week but less than 6 months, and frequently are related to an identifiable life trauma. During the early phase of this disorder, patients are likely to show intense affect in the form of anxiety, depression or hostility. The symptoms of psychosis are typically quite dramatic with prominent delusions, hallucinations and mental disorganization. In many cases, the MSE findings in schizophreniform and schizophrenic disorders are indistinguishable. Patient response is good to medications and active therapeutic intervention.

Schizophrenic disorders often have been called "true schizophrenia," "nonreactive schizophrenia," or "process schizophrenia." Premorbid adjustment is typified by longstanding problems with interpersonal relationships, shyness and marginal school and work performance. There seems to be a greater incidence of schizophrenic disorders among immediate family members than in the general population. In this disorder, symptoms are usually insidious in onset, taking months to years to develop, and are difficult to correlate with any actual life problems.

Symptoms last six months or longer. Affective tone generally is dulled or blunted and when the patient is evaluated, initial mental and behavioral disorganization is less dramatic. Therapeutic improvement tends to be slow, recovery incomplete, and relapses which necessitate repeated hospitalizations are common.

For this diagnosis to be assigned, symptoms must be continuously present for six months or longer at some time during the patient's lifetime and some residual pathology is present at the time of examination.

Now complete Self-Assessment Exercise #2 beginning on the following page.

Self-Assessment Exercise #2

1. For each of the following categories, briefly characterize the findings typical of an impending schizophrenic disorder.

   a. social behavior/general performance

   b. mood/affect

   c. thought content

   d. physiological status (sleep, appetite, etc.)

2. Compare schizophreniform and schizophrenic disorders by indicating whether the findings are "Present" or "Absent."

	Schizophreniform Disorders	Schizophrenic Disorders
a. rapid onset		
b. precipitating life stress often present		
c. good life adjustment prior to onset		
d. presence of intense anxiety/affect		
e. presence of emotional "blunting"		
f. increased familial incidence of schizophrenic disorders		
g. good long-term prognosis		
h. symptoms present over six months		

When you have completed this exercise to the best of your ability, check your answers with those on the following page.

Self-Assessment Exercise #2 - Feedback

1. The findings typical of an impending schizophrenic disorder are:

   a. social behavior/general performance

      Progressive social withdrawal and decreased performance at work/school.

   b. mood/affect

      Moodiness and irritability are typical.
      Mood swings from depression through euphoria.
      Often intense anxiety.
      Sometimes an inability to feel.
      Loss of capacity for pleasure.

   c. thought content

      Usually eccentric, but no definite delusions.
      Multiple phobias, obsessions, bodily concerns.
      Suspiciousness about the motives of others.
      Fears of impending insanity.
      Associational disturbance may be present.

   d. physiological status

      Decreased sleep, appetite, energy.

2.

	Schizophreniform Disorders	Schizophrenic Disorders
a. rapid onset	Present	Absent
b. precipitating life stress often present	Present	Absent
c. good life adjustment prior to onset	Present	Absent
d. presence of intense anxiety/affect	Present	Absent
e. presence of emotional "blunting"	Absent	Present
f. increased familial incidence of schizophrenic disorders	Absent	Present
g. good long-term prognosis	Present	Absent
h. symptoms present over six months	Absent	Present

If your answers correspond closely with those above, continue reading on the next page. If not, please reread the preceding section.

THERAPEUTIC INTERVENTIONS

Supportive Psychotherapy

Prior to the development of antipsychotic drugs, the treatment of schizophrenic disorders was a long and uncertain process consisting of hospitalization, prescribed sedatives, electroconvulsive therapy, and recreational or occupational therapy. Many patients required hospital treatment which lasted many months or longer, and it was difficult for them to function on an outpatient basis. Medications and treatment options are now available which greatly accelerate symptom improvement and enable most patients to manage outside of a hospital setting.

A discussion of several supportive psychotherapy techniques useful in the treatment of schizophrenia now follows.

Directive guidance. Many persons experiencing a schizophrenic disorder have problems in assessing reality and directing their day-to-day activities. They can become so emotionally disabled that they literally must depend upon others to provide even the basic necessities for living. In such cases, you must supply the reality orientation and guidance which your patients cannot provide for themselves.

You should convey a sense of authoritativeness and confidence to counteract the helplessness and confusion which your patients experience. When it is necessary, assume the responsibility for their total physical, social and emotional care. Therapy includes overseeing the treatment regimen, prescribing medications and therapeutic experiences, arranging for consultations and so forth. It may be necessary, at times, for you to recommend treatment which will not be popular. For example, if your patient is unable to care for himself and refuses help, then you should undertake his commitment to a psychiatric hospital. You must take the initiative and supply the judgment which he lacks.

Even when not hospitalized, your patients will need ongoing guidance. Your assistance will be needed to plan and carry out a daily routine and attend therapy or educational programs. Help patients make major decisions and set personal goals which are in keeping with their capabilities. As the psychosis subsides, encourage their taking increasing self-responsibility and, accordingly, decrease your direct involvement.

Education. Patient education should be an integral part of the treatment regimen. During the acute phase of a schizophrenic disorder, your patients will likely be overwhelmed by their symptoms and probably cannot benefit from any educational experience which requires concentration. That approach will have to wait until emotional equilibrium has been reestablished. Even though they may appear too disturbed to attend to your statements, inform your patients about each aspect of treatment. Describe the reasons for hospitalization and therapy. Tell them about the medications which they will receive including side effects. Make every effort to keep your explanations clear and simple -- avoid using technical terms which may be confusing or frightening.

Later, when your patients are better able to benefit from a definitive educational approach, instruct them about their disorder. If possible, help them identify the sources of stress which contributed to their difficulty and then teach methods for coping more effectively with these stresses. Your patients should be taught to recognize the early signs of a recurrence of their condition, namely an awareness of progressive anxiety, a persistent sleep disturbance, a return of disordered thinking, social withdrawal, decreased concentration and irritability. Emphasize the importance of seeking early help if these symptoms occur.

Most of your patients with schizophrenic disorders will need medication for an indefinite period so be sure to supply them with information about the dosage schedule, possible side effects and complications. Reinforce your verbal recommendations by writing them out. It is easy for your patients to misinterpret or forget your advice, so periodically review with them the important aspects of therapy.

Patients' families, too, should be fully informed about the details of treatment so that they can respond appropriately if complications arise. Be sure to spend time with them and encourage their questions. Discuss openly their feelings about the patient's prognosis and treatment.

Environmental intervention. Actively shape the environment to achieve an optimum therapeutic milieu. Severely disturbed persons usually need the around-the-clock support which only hospitalization can offer and, hopefully, your patients will agree to inpatient therapy. However, if they are incapable of managing their own affairs or are an imminent danger to themselves or others and refuse voluntary hospitalization, then arrange involuntary commitment.

But whether your patients receive treatment in or outside of a hospital, make sure that their environment is appropriately structured and offers therapeutic relationships and experiences. Even the amount of sensory stimuli should be thoughtfully prescribed. If patients are anxious, tense or hyperactive, then a less stimulating, quiet environment is indicated. Conversely, if your patients are withdrawn and self-preoccupied, efforts should be made to keep them involved with appropriate activities and social contacts.

It is countertherapeutic for patients to remain socially isolated or to dwell at length on feelings or eccentric ideas which interfere with daily living. Instead, they should be directed to activities and experiences which are structured, focused on reality and are adaptive. Examples of reality-oriented activities are participating in therapeutic work projects, maintaining personal grooming and attending social and therapy meetings. Their treatment regimen should include adequate physical exercise, recreational outlets and a nutritious diet. Arrange for your patients to receive a comprehensive physical examination to determine if intercurrent illnesses are present which need treatment.

If your patients are being treated outside of a hospital setting and need a structured milieu, recommend that they participate in a psychiatric day care center or sheltered workshop. Evaluate the environment with respect to its physical setting and the availability of supportive relationships and therapeutic activities. Help provide a structured daily routine. In instances when the patient's adjustment is marginal and stable resources and supervision are not available, arrange for a visiting nurse or a regular attendant to help establish a daily routine.

Diversion. Persons with schizophrenic disorders are adversely affected by intense emotions or dwelling upon disturbing thoughts. It is important for you to direct the patient's attention away from feelings and experiences which are potentially disruptive to those which are not. Kindly, but firmly, interrupt preoccupations with eccentric ideas or maladaptive behaviors by changing the subject and/or activities. Correspondingly, when meeting with an intensely disturbed patient, avoid exploring fantasies, dreams, remote childhood experiences or traumatic life events. In your dealings with the patient, focus on the "here and now" and tangible, reality-oriented activities. Talk about what he has been doing rather than what he is feeling -- selectively emphasize inner resources and successful coping behaviors rather than symptoms or inadequacies. Always commend behavior which demonstrates good judgment and is adaptive. It is generally a good policy to discourage patients from reading "psychology" books about their condition. Rather, encourage coming to you for answers about symptoms, treatment, etc.

Reassurance. The onset of a schizophrenic disorder is an awesome experience and evokes feelings of fear and helplessness. Affected persons feel terribly alone and incapable of emotionally sustaining themselves. Unfortunately, many patients also are suspicious and fearful of closeness with others and find it difficult to establish a trusting relationship with their therapist. Therapeutic reassurance should be given in a way which respects both their desperate need for help and simultaneous fear of relying on others. Because of their uneasiness about closeness, keep somewhat physically and emotionally distant. As a general rule, avoid sitting too close or touching patients.

It is your presence and ongoing concern which provides the greatest source of reassurance for your patients. They should sense by your words and actions that you are interested in their welfare and will "see them through" their present difficulty. They need to feel that you are "in control" of the situation and can provide whatever help is needed.

On occasion, that may mean your prescribing hospitalization or physical restraints to assure behavioral control. It is reassuring for patients to realize that you will not permit actions which in some way would be harmful.

Attend carefully to physical needs and, when possible, grant personal preferences about therapeutic activities, recreation, etc. Your dependability is particularly important. Schedule regular therapy sessions which are frequent (at least daily) and brief (15 to 20 minutes in length). Periodically make empathic comments about patient's feelings and distress -- this will convey that you are aware of their feelings and anxieties. Let them know that you have worked with others who have had similar problems and who went on to lead productive lives. Maintain a therapeutic optimism by commenting on signs of progress. Talk in terms of "when" not "if" your patients will recover and be able to resume their former activities. Finally, take time to meet with family members to reassure them about various aspects of treatment. Instruct them about ways that they, too, can provide support and reassurance.

Behavioral Therapy

Principles of behavioral therapy can be used for favorably modifying selected symptoms of schizophrenic disorders. Rewards in the form of praise, special recognition and privileges can be given to improve patient behaviors like personal grooming, participation in social activities and compliance with treatment recommendations. Actions which are clearly self-defeating, harmful or jeopardize others should firmly and promptly be discouraged. In rare instances, in order to control destructive or assaultive actions it may be necessary to temporarily seclude or apply physical restraints. However, punitive or adversive therapy is not an appropriate treatment approach.

For well-motivated patients who can tolerate stress, desensitization techniques can be introduced to improve their self-assertiveness, participation in social groups or exploring new educational activities. As a general principle, reinforce all behaviors which are adaptive and indicate progress.

Now complete Self-Assessment Exercise #3 beginning on the following page.

Self-Assessment Exercise #3

Read the following case history and then answer the questions which follow:

> Ms. Rita Enders, a 23-year-old secretary, was brought for consultation by her family because of inappropriate behavior and thinking. For three days she had refused to eat because of fears that her food was poisoned. Ms. Enders related in a disjointed fashion that for two months "the communists" had been trying to brainwash her thinking by beaming radar waves at her. Ms. Ender's family barely had been able to prevent her fleeing to Mexico because she believed she would be safe from harassment. Her history and findings were consistent with a diagnosis of a schizophrenic disorder. Ms. Enders was offered but refused hospitalization and psychiatric treatment.

1. In working with most persons who have a schizophrenic disorder, it is best to adopt a guidance approach which is directive/nondirective (circle one).

   In view of your answer, what would you do regarding her decision to go to Mexico and decline hospitalization?

   Assume that Ms. Enders was admitted for hospital treatment and placed on appropriate antipsychotic medications. When left alone, Ms. Enders wandered aimlessly about the ward and was observed to talk to herself, presumably in response to auditory hallucinations. She seemed fearful of social contacts and tried to avoid group therapy sessions. During her meeting with you she tended to talk about her eccentric ideas.

2. What therapeutic interventions would you make with respect to:

   educating her

   environmental intervention

   diversion

Self-Assessment Exercise #3 (Continued)

3. Briefly outline how you would attempt to reassure Ms. Enders.

4. Circle the following activities which would be most therapeutic for a withdrawn, disorganized and hallucinating patient.

   a. reading science fiction

   b. listening to classical music alone

   c. washing dishes and preparing meals

   d. participating in a Bingo game

   e. discussing the meaning of a recent dream

   f. painting abstract impressions of depressive feelings

   g. sculpting a vase

   h. folding linens

   i. planting flowers

   j. reading about various emotional disorders

5. For each of the following treatment goals, indicate whether behavior therapy techniques are (A) appropriate or (I) inappropriate:

_____a. to decrease feelings of depression

_____b. maintain personal grooming

_____c. increase attendance at recreational therapy sessions

_____d. decrease inhibitions about speaking up in group meetings

_____e. maintaining a regular schedule for taking medications

_____f. to stop hallucinations

When you have completed this exercise to the best of your ability, check your answers with those on the following page.

Self-Assessment Exercise #3 - Feedback

1. A directive approach is indicated with most patients with a schizophrenic disorder. You should prevent her trip to Mexico and insist on hospitalization.

2. educating her:

   describe treatment procedures using clear terms; inform her about her medication

   environmental intervention:

   direct her to structured and reality-oriented activities; make sure that she has a regular schedule of therapeutic activities and social contacts

   diversion:

   redirect her thinking and activities away from self-preoccupations to more tangible and reality-oriented topics

3. You should attempt to reassure her by:

   arranging for regular, brief therapy meetings
   being available for consultations
   preventing behavior which may be harmful
   attending to her physical comfort
   maintaining therapeutic optimism
   commenting favorably on her progress

4. Reality-oriented and structured activities are most therapeutic, therefore, prescribe:

   c. washing dishes and preparing meals

   d. participating in a Bingo game

   g. sculpting a vase

   h. folding linens

   i. planting flowers

Self-Assessment Exercise #3 - Feedback (Continued)

5. Behavior therapy techniques are (A) appropriate or (I) inappropriate for the following:

 I a. to decrease feelings of depression

 A b. maintain personal grooming

 A c. increase attendance at recreational therapy sessions

 A d. decrease inhibitions about speaking up in group meetings

 A e. maintaining a regular schedule for taking medications

 I f. to stop hallucinations

If your answers correspond closely with those above, continue your reading on the next page. If not, please reread the preceding section.

THERAPEUTIC INTERVENTIONS (Continued)

Pharmacologic Therapy

The following information about antipsychotic medications is an abbreviated version of that contained in the chapter on "Psychopharmacology." Because of the importance and complexities involved in prescribing psychotropic medications, we recommend that you carefully review the complete section on antipsychotic drugs in that chapter.

Antipsychotic medications are not curative, but they are very effective in alleviating many of the psychological and behavioral symptoms associated with schizophrenic disorders. Target symptoms which are particularly amenable to antipsychotic drugs are: intense anxiety, restlessness, belligerence, hypo- and hyperactivity, impulsive behavior associational disturbances, emotional lability, acute delusions and hallucinations. After the administration of an antipsychotic drug, symptoms of hyperactivity, hostility and intense anxiety often subside within a few hours or days. However, other findings such as associational disturbances, delusions and hallucinations may take one to several weeks or longer to diminish significantly. Some symptoms may never completely subside.

The medications appearing in Table I are equally effective in reducing many symptoms of schizophrenic disorders. However, each drug has special properties which deserve your consideration before prescribing them. There is no proven advantage to mixing antipsychotic drugs either to achieve a greater effect or to minimize undesirable side effects. Of the drugs listed, chlorpromazine has a tendency to produce more sedation episodes of low blood pressure, but rarely brings about extrapyramidal symptoms. Fluphenazine, thiothixene or haloperidol, on the other hand, are more likely to cause extrapyramidal symptoms, but not a fall in blood pressure or sedation side effects. Be prepared to treat extrapyramidal symptoms with oral or IM diphenhydramine (Benadryl), benztropine (Cogentin) or trihexyphenidyl (Artane Patients who require, but inconsistently take, antipsychotic medications can be given a long-acting fluphenazine decanoate by injection once or twice a month.

Now complete Self-Assessment Exercise #4 which follows Table I.

TABLE I

MEDICATIONS USEFUL
IN TREATING SCHIZOPHRENIC DISORDERS

ANTIPSYCHOTICS:

	Starting Oral Dose	I.M. Dose	Dose Range (in mg/day)
CHLORPROMAZINE (Thorazine, Chlor P-Z)	50-100 mg tid-qid	25 mg	100-1000
FLUPHENAZINE (Prolixin, Permitil)	2.5-5 mg bid-qid	2-5 mg	5-30
FLUPHENAZINE DECANOATE		½-1 cc (25 mg/cc)	----
THIOTHIXENE (Navane)	2-5 mg bid-qid	2-5 mg	5-30
HALOPERIDOL (Haldol)	2.5-5 mg bid-qid	2-5 mg	5-30

EXTRAPYRAMIDAL SYMPTOM DRUGS:

	Oral Dose	I.M. Dose
DIPHENHYDRAMINE (Benadryl)	25-50 mg bid-tid	25-50 mg (or I.V.)
BENZTROPINE (Cogentin)	1-2 mg bid	1-2 mg (or I.V.)
TRIHEXYPHENIDYL (Artane)	2 mg bid-tid	not available in injectable form

Self-Assessment Exercise #4

1. List 6 or more "target symptoms" which usually respond favorably to antipsychotic medications.

2. What medically related information should you obtain from your patient before prescribing antipsychotic medications?

3. For each of the patient vignettes below, list all of the following drugs which would be appropriate to prescribe.

chlorpromazine	thiothixene	benztropine
fluphenazine decanoate	haloperidol	trihexphenidyl

____________________ a. A 26-year-old psychotic patient is extremely agitated and needs a drug with sedating properties.

____________________ b. A middle-aged patient with a severe schizophrenic disorder needs to take antipsychotic medication regularly to control her psychotic symptoms but often "forgets" to do so.

____________________ c. A young man with a chronic schizophrenic disorder is known to develop marked extrapyramidal symptoms; select the antipsychotic drug least likely to bring about those symptoms.

____________________ d. A middle-aged man with high blood pressure has recurrent schizophrenic episodes; what antipsychotic medication(s) would be least likely to cause a fall in his blood pressure.

Self-Assessment Exercise #4 (Continued)

3.

____________________ e. Four days after being placed on haloperidol, a young woman develops increased muscle rigidity, a mask-like facial expression and shuffling gait.

4. Indicate the correct dosage and route of administration for at least two medications to treat the symptoms described in the following patient vignettes.

   a. After receiving fluphenazine, 2 mg tid for 5 days, the young woman developed an abrupt onset of muscular spasms of her neck, tongue and jaw muscles.

      (1)

      (2)

   b. Shortly after admission to a psychiatric hospital, the patient became restless, verbally threatening and began throwing books and furniture about the room.

      (1)

      (2)

   c. A 32-year-old woman was admitted to a psychiatric hospital because of a progressive social withdrawal, auditory hallucinations and paranoid delusions. She was diagnosed as having a schizophrenic disorder. She was in good physical health and had no history of prior psychological problems. What antipsychotic medications and starting dosage would be appropriate for her?

      (1)

      (2)

When you have completed this exercise to the best of your ability, check your answers with those on the following page.

Self-Assessment Exercise #4 - Feedback

1. "Target symptoms" which usually respond favorably to antipsychotic medications are:

   anxiety
   restlessness
   delusions
   hallucinations
   impulsive behavior
   belligerence
   hypo- and hyperactivity
   emotional lability
   associational disturbance

2. Before prescribing antipsychotic medications, you should inquire about:

   a. what, if any, antipsychotic drugs have been used before and their side effects and effectiveness

   b. what, if any, other medications are presently being used

   c. the presence of any current medical conditions, especially cardiovascular disease

3. The following drugs are most appropriate for the vignettes below.

chlorpromazine a. A 26-year-old psychotic patient is extremely agitated and needs a drug with sedating properties.

fluphenazine decanoate b. A middle-aged patient with a severe schizophrenic disorder needs to take antipsychotic medication regularly to control her psychotic symptoms but often "forgets" to do so.

chlorpromazine c. A young man with a chronic schizophrenic disorder is known to develop marked extrapyramidal symptoms; select the antipsychotic drug <u>least</u> likely to bring about those symptoms.

haloperidol thiothixene d. A middle-aged man with high blood pressure has recurrent schizophrenic episodes; what antipsychotic medication(s) would be <u>least</u> likely to cause a fall in his blood pressure.

Self-Assessment Exercise #4 - Feedback (Continued)

3.

trihexphenidyl
benztropine ______ e. Four days after being placed on haloperidol, a young woman develops increased muscle rigidity, a mask-like facial expression and shuffling gait.

4. For the following patient vignettes, the correct dosage and route of administration of medications to treat the symptoms are:

a. After receiving fluphenazine, 2 mg tid for 5 days, the young woman developed an abrupt onset of muscular spasms of her neck, tongue and jaw muscles.

The patient is experiencing an acute dystonic reaction, which can be quite frightening. It usually can be terminated by giving:

diphenhydramine, 25 mg I.M./I.V.
or
benztropine, 1-2 mg I.M./I.V.

b. Shortly after admission to a psychiatric hospital, the patient became restless, verbally threatening and began throwing books and furniture about the room.

This patient has lost behavioral control and needs to be medicated rapidly. Any of the following medications should be administed I.M.:

chlorpromazine	25 mg I.M.
haloperidol	2-5 mg I.M.
thiothixene	2-5 mg I.M.
fluphenazine	2-5 mg I.M.

Self-Assessment Exercise #4 - Feedback (Continued)

4. c. A 32-year-old woman was admitted to a psychiatric hospital because of a progressive social withdrawal, auditory hallucinations and paranoid delusions. She was diagnosed as having a schizophrenic disorder. She was in good physical health and had no history of prior psychological problems. What antipsychotic medications and starting dosage would be appropriate for her?

Because of her response to antipsychotic medications is unknown, it is best to start with a low dose of the following in divided doses:

haloperidol	2 mg bid-qid
or	
thiothixene	2 mg bid-qid
or	
fluphenazine	2 mg bid-qid
or	
chlorpromazine	50 mg bid-qid

If your answers correspond closely with those above, continue reading. If not, please reread the preceding section.

THERAPEUTIC INTERVENTIONS (Continued)

Consultation and Referral

Because of the many problems inherent in treating persons with a schizophrenic disorder, it is good practice to seek consultation with psychiatric specialists and make full use of the mental health resources which are available in your community. Certainly when your patient's behavior is sufficiently disturbed to require hospitalization or a special treatment approach, the help of a psychiatrist is in order. Other indications for referral or consultation are lack of response to treatment, difficulty in establishing a diagnosis, poor patient compliance, or potential legal complications such as the need for hospital commitment. Your patient and/or his family may benefit from referral to one or more community agencies which specialize in providing psychotherapy, prescribing medications, or can assist with vocational training or financial problems. Make it a point to become familiar with the mental health resources in your community.

For a variety of personal reasons, many therapists prefer not to treat patients who have a schizophrenic disorder. Such a disinclination is an appropriate reason for referring patients to a specialist. Special preparation of your patients is needed if you refer them to someone else for therapy.

Now complete Self-Assessment Exercise #5 beginning on the following page.

Self-Assessment Exercise #5

Assume that you are asked to evaluate a man in his early 20's with a "nervous" problem. At the time of your evaluation it is clear that he has a schizophrenic disorder. List the possible reasons that *you* would request consultation/referral for him.

When you have completed this exercise to the best of your ability, check your answers with those on the following page.

Self-Assessment Exercise #5 - Feedback

Any of the following may be reasons for seeking consultation/ referral for your patient evaluated as having a schizophrenic disorder:

personal preference for not treating serious emotional disorders
need for hospitalization
questions about diagnosis
lack of response to therapy
poor compliance
lack of progress
legal problems regarding his symptoms
seeking help from community agencies for medication, day care, vocational, financial and educational assistance

If your answers correspond closely with those above, continue reading. If not, please reread the preceding section.

SUMMARY

Schizophrenic disorders are commonly encountered psychopathologic conditions which constitute a major health problem in our country. Patients with these disorders are troubled by marked impairment of reality testing, thinking, affect and behavior. They require active and ongoing therapy for an indefinite period of time. A majority of patients with schizophrenic disorders can be satisfactorily managed without hospitalization, if appropriate supportive techniques and antipsychotic medications are prescribed.

REFERENCES

Anderson, W., Keuhnle, J. and Catanzano, D., "Rapid Treatment of Acute Psychosis," Am. J. Psychiatry, 133:1076-1078, 1976.

Bowden, C. and Giffen, M., Psychopharmacology for Primary Care Physicians, Baltimore: Williams & Wilkins Co., 1978.

Imboden, J. and Urbaitis, J., Practical Psychiatry in Medicine, New York: Appleton-Century-Crofts, 1978.

Mendel, W., Supportive Care, Los Angeles: Mara Books, 1975.

Shader, R. I., Manual of Psychiatric Therapeutics, Boston: Little, Brown & Co., 1975.

CHAPTER 8. AFFECTIVE DISORDERS

Although it is frequently said that we live in the age of anxiety, in terms of psychopathology, affective (mood) disorders actually are more prevalent and debilitating syndromes. By "affective disorders" we mean the group of psychopathologic conditions characterized by marked deviations in mood (a sustained affective state) and energy ranging from depression and underactivity at one end of a spectrum to mania and hyperactivity at the other. Disturbances of all other feelings such as anxiety or anger are classified under other headings. Psychologically normal persons experience emotional "highs" and "lows" from time to time, and the term affective disorder is reserved for the pathological exaggeration of these feelings to a degree which impairs adaptive functioning.

In recent years there have been developed new ways to conceptualize and treat affective disorders which will help you to deal with your troubled patients. In this chapter we will discuss affective disorders in terms of their typical findings, theories of etiology, diagnostic subtypes and therapeutic interventions.

LEARNING OBJECTIVES

By the time you complete this chapter, you should be able to do the following and apply the information to written case histories.

1. Briefly describe three etiologic factors which may be involved in affective disorders.

2. Describe the physical and mental status examination findings typical to depression and mania.

3. Correctly define and apply the following terms:

Major Affective Disorder	Bipolar Disorder
Major Depression	Organic Affective Syndrome

4. List three or more indications for hospitalizing depressed or manic patients.

5. For each of the methods of therapeutic intervention listed below, describe the recommended treatment approach and provide a rationale for its use in the management of affective disorders (both depression and mania):

   (a) supportive psychotherapy
   (b) behavioral therapy
   (c) pharmacologic therapy and electroconvulsive therapy
   (d) consultation and referral

ETIOLOGY OF AFFECTIVE DISORDERS

A viewpoint which is important for you to maintain throughout this chapter is that affective disorders comprise a heterogenous group of conditions each of which warrants an individualized treatment approach. Although two individuals may initially experience similar symptoms, such as the psychological and physical findings associated with depression, the causes and course of the respective conditions may be quite different. For example, one person in response to the death of a loved one may develop depressive symptoms from which he can be expected to fully recover within a few months time. Another individual initially may show comparable clinical findings, which are due to an inherited disorder and the patient may be subject to recurrent depressive attacks throughout his lifetime. Although the initial symptoms of depression are similar, the prognosis and treatment approach for each patient can be very different.

One or a combination of three factors, i.e., psychological, physical and hereditary, can give rise to symptoms of depression and/or mania. Look for and treat elements of all three factors in each of your patients having an affective disorder. Examples of psychological factors which can precipitate a depressive disorder are a loss of a key relationship, a fall in self-esteem or intense guilt about some wrongdoing.

Question carefully about physical factors such as illness and the use of drugs. A depressive syndrome may result in susceptible individuals who take medication such as anti-hypertensives, analgesics, hormones or sedatives. Manic behavior, likewise, may be brought about in individuals using central nervous system stimulants such as amphetamines or "street drugs" such as LSD or PCP. Depressive or manic behavior can accompany a variety of medical illnesses including hyper- and hypothyroidism, adrenal abnormalities, viral infections and others. Manic or depressive reactions clearly due to physical factors are called organic affective syndromes.

Hereditary factors also play an important part in some affective disorders. Research has shown that family members of individuals with recurrent affective disorders are much more likely than the general population to have psychological problems. In this regard, be sure to inquire of your patients if they have close relatives who have been troubled by alcoholism, depression or manic behavior.

Now complete Self-Assessment Exercise #1 beginning on the following page.

Self-Assessment Exercise #1

1. List and give examples of three etiological factors which are important to evaluate in all patients with affective disorders:

2. List three or more types of medical illnesses and drugs which may evoke symptoms of an affective disorder in your patients:

ILLNESSES	DRUGS

3. Indicate whether the following statements are true (T) or false (F).

_____ a. It is a sound policy to prescribe a similar treatment regimen for depressed patients as long as their initial M.S.E. findings are comparable.

_____ b. Persons who are closely related to individuals with diagnosed affective disorders are more likely than the general population to develop psychological problems.

When you have completed this exercise to the best of your ability, check your answers with those on the following page.

Self-Assessment Exercise #1 - Feedback

1. The three etiological factors which should be evaluated in all patients with an affective disorder are:

   psychological (psychological stress, etc.)
   biochemical (medical illness, drugs, etc.)
   hereditary (familial incidence of psychopathology)

2. Medical illnesses or drugs which may cause symptoms of an affective disorder are:

ILLNESSES	DRUGS
hyper-thyroidism	sedatives
hypo-thyroidism	hormones
adrenal disorders	anti-hypertensives
viral infections	central nervous system stimulants
	amphetamines (street drugs)

3.

False a. Although many depressed patients may have similar presenting symptoms, the etiology, cause and treatment approach may be quite different; an individualized therapy regimen must be determined for each case.

True b. Hereditary factors seem to be involved in many cases of affective disorders; be sure to take a careful family history from your patients having affective disorders.

If your answers correspond closely with those above, please continue your reading on the following page. If not, please reread the material in the preceding section until you are confident you know it.

PHYSICAL SYMPTOMS ACCOMPANYING AFFECTIVE DISORDERS

Becoming familiar with the typical physical and psychological findings of affective disorders will enable you to diagnose these conditions early in their development. There are several physical findings which are characteristic to depression and mania, and if your patients don't spontaneously mention them, inquire about them. Detecting the presence of these symptoms may help to establish a diagnosis.

In the case of depression, a disturbance of sleep and appetite is almost invariably present. Typically, patients complain of loss of sleep, appetite and weight, but occasionally, the reverse is true and they may eat and sleep excessively. They often describe easy fatigability, generalized weakness and recurrent pains in their back, head, stomach or chest for which no physical cause can be found. Constipation and a decline in sexual interest are commonly reported.

Patients experiencing mania also may have insomnia and a decreased appetite. Whereas depressed persons are unable to sleep or eat because of sadness and worry, manic patients possess such exuberance and abundance of energy that they just don't want to take the time to eat or sleep. Speech and physical movements typically are accelerated and continuous. These patients are likely to show signs of restlessness, pacing and talkativeness. Hypersexuality is often present. Without appropriate therapeutic intervention, persons with mania can overextend themselves to the point of physical exhaustion.

MENTAL STATUS EXAMINATION FINDINGS OF AFFECTIVE DISORDERS

During a full-blown manic or depressive episode, abnormal mental status examination (M.S.E.) findings are so prominent that a diagnosis of an affective disorder can be established easily. However, keep in mind that the M.S.E. findings of affective disorders can appear in varied combinations and intensities. The signs of mania and depression will be discussed separately and follow the outline presented in the chapter on "The Mental Status Examination."

M.S.E. Findings in Depression

The physical appearance of depressed patients generally corresponds to the severity of the condition. If the depression is mild, appearance may not be remarkable. In more severe cases, however, patients are likely to neglect personal care and appear unkempt. They may seem fatigued or physically ill, in part, due to loss of sleep, decreased appetite and lowered physical energy.

In terms of overall behavior, depressed persons frequently portray the picture of being dejected, overburdened and fatigued. Facial expression may be bland and unresponsive or prominently lined with a downturned mouth and furrowed brow. Patients are likely to sit with a slumped posture and demonstrate slowing of movement, speech and thought (psychomotor retardation). Occasionally, signs of increased emotional tension and anxiety appear as restlessness, pacing and agitation. Speech usually is decreased in quantity and amplitude. Although mild to moderately depressed patients will cooperate by providing history about themselves, those who are intensely depressed may be too preoccupied to respond fully to your questions.

Depressed patients express feelings of sadness, apathy and hopelessness which are appropriate to their thought content. Irritability and hostility may be evoked if they feel pressed by questions. The feelings of persons with affective disorders are often contagious, and you may briefly experience a sense of depression or fatigue while interviewing them. Prominent among the feeling described is an inability to experience pleasure.

Although illusions may be present, hallucinations are relatively rare. When present, the theme of auditory hallucinations often consists of accusations of guilt, sinfulness and personal inadequacy.

Alertness, memory, orientation, abstract thinking and intellectual functioning are not usually impaired unless psychomotor retardation and intense self-preoccupation are present. However, insight, judgment and the ability to concentrate are often compromised. Thought content typically reflects some combination of helplessness, hopelessness, apathy and self-recriminations. Patients usually describe worries about their future, finances and physical health. Suicidal ideation is frequently present and it is important that you thoroughly assess the potential for self-harm. If patients are disturbed to a psychotic degree, delusions can be present which reflect exaggerated personal guilt, hypochondriasis or paranoia. An associational disturbance is not usually present, but the normal flow of thinking may be markedly slowed and interrupted by extended pauses.

M.S.E. Findings in Mania

A triad of M.S.E. findings are typical to mania and consist of a euphoric mood, increased physical activity and rapid, continuous speech. Patients' general appearance varies according to their emotional state and ranges from being appropriately groomed to appearing disheveled and unkempt.

A prominent finding in most manic patients is their persistent need to talk (pressure of speech). They often pace restlessly about the room and use emphatic gestures to punctuate their loud speech. Puns, irrelevancies and sarcastic remarks are frequent. Their facial expression and movements usually are animated and dramatic. It is difficult for these patients to provide a sequential history because they are so easily distracted by their feelings and extraneous stimuli. In general, manic patients respond to others in a domineering fashion and, by their wit and forcefulness, may take control of the interview.

The feeling tone of manic patients generally is characterized by euphoria, optimism and high enthusiasm for pursuing personal projects and interests. Tolerance for frustration is low, however, and their elated mood may abruptly change to hostility if their wishes are frustrated. Affect usually corresponds closely with thought content. It is easy to identify emotionally with their humor, quick wit and enthusiasm.

Perceptual abnormalities are infrequent but if patients are severely disturbed, they may experience illusions and/or hallucinations. The theme of these abnormal perceptions are consistent with their affect and typically are grandiose in nature.

Manic patients are unusually sensitive to environmental stimuli and are easily distracted by them. Orientation, memory and calculation ability are intact, but they may have difficulty in completing intellectual tasks because of their distractibility. Judgment typically is impaired and patients may act impulsively, pursuing grandiose plans and projects without regard to future consequences. Insight is usually absent and it is likely that manic patients will disclaim having any significant psychological problems. There may be grandiose ideas, plans and delusions. These delusions usually express themes of personal power, ability or wealth. An associational disturbance generally is present in which patient thinking rapidly jumps from topic to topic.

Now complete Self-Assessment Exercise #2 beginning on the following page.

Self-Assessment Exercise #2

1. A middle-aged man comes to you with complaints suggestive of a mode severe depression. List the physical findings about which you should i

2. A 45-year-old woman was diagnosed as having "manic" behavior. Indi whether her findings in the following areas typically would be increase or decreased:

_______________ general physical activity

_______________ weight

_______________ speech rate

_______________ sexual interest

3. Describe the M.S.E. findings typical to moderately severe depression and mania:

	DEPRESSION	MANIA
BEHAVIOR		
Rate and amplitude of speech		
Rate of physical activity		
FEELING (mood/affect)		
Predominant affect		
Appropriateness to thought content		
PERCEPTION		
Incidence of hallucinations		
THINKING		
State of memory and orientation		
State of insight and judgment		
Presence of suicidal ideation		
Presence of an associational disturbance		

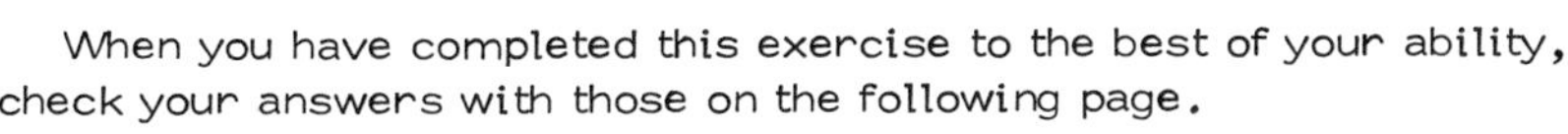

When you have completed this exercise to the best of your ability, check your answers with those on the following page.

Self-Assessment Exercise #2 - Feedback

1. The physical complaints common to a moderately severe depressive reaction and about which you should inquire are:

   insomnia
   loss of appetite
   loss of weight
   easy fatigability
   generalized weakness
   constipation
   decreased sexual desire
   aches and pains of the head, back, chest, legs

2. In a typical manic patient general physical activity, speech rate and sexual interest are increased. Because of extensive physical activity and being "too busy to eat" weight is usually lost. (Some manic patients may overeat and rapidly gain weight.)

	DEPRESSION	MANIA
BEHAVIOR		
Rate and amplitude of speech	decreased	increased
Rate of physical activity	decreased	increased
FEELING (mood/affect)	depression	elation
Predominant affect	sadness	euphoria
Appropriateness to thought content	appropriate	appropriate
PERCEPTION		
Incidence of hallucinations	rare	relatively rare
THINKING		
State of memory and orientation	intact	intact
State of insight and judgment	impaired	impaired
Presence of suicidal ideation	present	absent
Presence of an associational disturbance	absent	present

TABLE I

A Comparison of Diagnostic Terms

DSM-III	DSM-II
AFFECTIVE DISORDERS	MAJOR AFFECTIVE DISORDERS
A. MAJOR AFFECTIVE DISORDERS	
Bipolar Disorder	Manic-Depressive Illness
mixed	Manic-Depressive Illness, circular type
manic	Manic-Depressive Illness, manic type
depressed	Manic-Depressive Illness, depressive type
Major Depression	Involutional Melancholia
single episode	Psychotic Depressive Reaction (reactive depressive psychosis)
recurrent	Manic-Depressive Illness, depressed type
B. OTHER SPECIFIC AFFECTIVE DISORDERS	
Cyclothymic Disorder	Cyclothymic Personality
Dysthymic Disorder (or depressive neurosis)	Depressive Neurosis

CLASSIFICATION OF AFFECTIVE DISORDERS

Affective Disorders are among the most common syndromes of psychopathology, but because of their diverse etiologies, course and treatment response, no entirely satisfactory system of classifying them has yet been developed. In this chapter, we will adopt the terminology presented in the Diagnostic and Statistical Manual of Mental Disorders, Third Edition (DSM-III). Effective treatment depends on accurate diagnosis. Therefore, manic and depressive syndromes which are associated with drug use, illness, grief reactions or schizophrenic disorders, are not included here as Affective Disorders (see DSM-III for specific criteria). The various subtypes of Affective Disorders, which will be discussed in this chapter, are defined and distinguished below (see Table I for comparison of DSM-III and previously used diagnoses).

The Major Affective Disorders are conditions typified by episodes of manic and/or depressive syndromes which persist for at least one week. The episodes of pathological mood are separated by intervals of normal functioning which can last from weeks to years. Symptoms are severe enough to cause significant impairment in daily functioning and delusions and/or hallucinations may occur in severe cases.

The subtypes of Major Affective Disorders include Bipolar Disorders* and Major Depression**. A Bipolar Disorder usually begins before the age of 30 and is characterized by episodes of a manic syndrome alternating with depression. Assigning this diagnosis implies that episodes of both mania and depression will occur sometime during the course of the condition. A manic syndrome typically includes pressure of speech, an elevated mood and hyperactivity. A Major Depression is manifested by a depressive syndrome of severe proportions that is not associated with simple bereavement. Major Depression can occur as a single episode or be recurrent. A major life stress or personal loss is frequently involved in causing single episodes of depression, whereas recurrent depressions may often have a biochemical basis.

For patients who demonstrate significant mood changes but do not meet the criteria for a Major Affective Disorder, assigning the diagnosis

---

* Terms indicating "polarity" are widely used for classifying affective disorders. The term "unipolar" signifies a condition characterized by a single affect, i.e., depression. Whereas, a bipolar disorder refers to a condition which includes episodes of both mania and depression.

** Major Depressive Disorders encompass a variety of conditions which were formally diagnosed separately as Psychotic Depressive Reaction, Involutional Melancholia, and Manic Depressive Illness, Depressive Type.

of either a Cyclothymic Disorder or Dysthymic Disorder (depressive neurosis) may be indicated. For both of these conditions the symptoms occur earlier in life, are of milder intensity, but are much more persistent (they are present two years or longer) than is the case with Major Affective Disorders. No delusions or hallucinations occur in these conditions, and daily functioning is not markedly impaired.
A Cyclothymic Disorder is typified by recurrent and alternating episodes of mild depression and manic-like behavior. A Dysthymic Disorder (depressive neurosis) is a syndrome consisting of persistent depression which seems excessively severe or prolonged relative to the precipitating cause.

Now complete Self-Assessment Exercise #3 beginning on the following page.

Self-Assessment Exercise #3

Classify each case vignette below using one of the following diagnostic terms:

Major Affective Disorder
Organic Affective Syndrome
Cyclothymic Disorder
Dysthymic Disorder (depressive neurosis)

If you determine the presence of a Major Affective Disorder, further refine the diagnosis by applying one of the following terms:

Bipolar Disorder
Major Depression

1. A 42-year-old woman experienced her third severe depression in six years; none of the depressive episodes were associated with an identifiable life stress, illness or medication; each episode ended after a few weeks and she functioned normally between attacks.

   ____

2. Over a 10-year period, a 38-year-old merchant had two episodes of hyperactive behavior and elated affect which lasted several weeks; he also experienced intermittent depression associated with psychomotor retardation, insomnia and weight loss; only one of the depressive attacks could be related to a life stress; his father had experienced similar symptoms.

   ____

3. After taking large doses of an unknown type of central nervous system stimulant for several weeks, the young woman became hyperactive, spoke rapidly in a disjointed fashion and had an elated affect. She had not previously had similar symptoms.

   ____

Self-Assessment Exercise #3 (Continued)

4. A middle-aged woman developed tearfulness, depression and loss of appetite after her youngest child left home for college. Her symptoms increased in severity over the following several months and she became progressively withdrawn and apathetic. She showed signs of psychomotor retardation and described suicidal ideation. Neither she nor any relative had required previous psychological treatment.

____

5. A woman in her mid-20's sought consultation for her persistent depressive symptoms of at least five years duration. She complained that she easily became tearful and felt sad "most of the time" but could not attribute her symptoms to any particular cause. She had received various psychotropic medications without any appreciable improvement in her symptoms.

____

6. While recovering from viral pneumonia, the college student complained of feeling depressed; he became easily tearful, was troubled by insomnia and feelings of apathy toward activities which he formerly enjoyed; he had not previously experienced similar attacks of depression or hyperactive behavior.

____

When you have completed this exercise to the best of your ability, check your answers with those on the following page.

Self-Assessment Exercise #3 - Feedback

1. A 42-year-old woman experienced her third severe depression in six years; none of the depressive episodes were associated with an identifiable life stress, illness or medication; each episode ended after a few weeks and she functioned normally between attacks.

   Major Affective Disorder; Major Depression

2. Over a 10-year period, a 38-year-old merchant had two episodes of hyperactive behavior and elated affect which lasted several weeks; he also experienced intermittent depression associated with psychomotor retardation, insomnia and weight loss; only one of the depressive attacks could be related to a life stress; his father had experienced similar symptoms.

   Major Affective Disorder; Bipolar Disorder

3. After taking large doses of an unknown type of central nervous system stimulant for several weeks, the young woman became hyperactive, spoke rapidly in a disjointed fashion and had an elated affect. She had not previously had similar symptoms.

   Organic Affective Syndrome

4. A middle-aged woman developed tearfulness, depression and loss of appetite after her youngest child left home for college. Her symptoms increased in severity over the following several months and she became progressively withdrawn and apathetic. She showed signs of psychomotor retardation and described suicidal ideation. Neither she nor any relative had required previous psychological treatment.

   Major Affective Disorder; Major Depression

5. A woman in her mid-20's sought consultation for her persistent depressive symptoms of at least five years duration. She complained that she easily became tearful and felt sad "most of the time" but could not attribute her symptoms to any particular cause. She had received various psychotropic medications without any appreciable improvement in her symptoms.

   Dysthymic Disorder (depressive neurosis)

Self-Assessment Exercise #3 - Feedback (Continued)

6. While recovering from viral pneumonia, the college student complained of feeling depressed; he became easily tearful, was troubled by insomnia and feelings of apathy toward activities which he formerly enjoyed; he had not previously experienced similar attacks of depression or hyperactive behavior.

    Organic Affective Syndrome

If your answers correspond closely with those above, please continue reading on the next page. If not, please reread the preceding material.

THERAPEUTIC INTERVENTIONS

Supportive Psychotherapy

The mental distress which accompanies an affective disorder can be considerable. Depressed persons usually are unhappy, unproductive in their daily life and present a potential risk for self-harm. Similarly, the impaired judgment and grandiosity associated with mania can lead patients to take on unrealistic financial and social commitments which later prove embarrassing and costly. Your therapeutic intervention can go a long way toward alleviating and shortening the course of most affective disorders and thereby reduce much suffering for your patients and their families.

Because many principles of supportive psychotherapy already have been presented in the chapter on "Supportive Psychotherapy" and "Schizophrenic Disorders," we will present here only a summary of them. We recommend that you review those chapters for a more comprehensive discussion. The following principles of therapy can be appliec equally well to symptoms of depression and mania.

Directive guidance. As with other psychopathologic conditions in whic faltering coping mechanisms and impaired judgment are present, it is important that you adopt a directive guidance approach with respect to treatment. Provide active direction and authoritative advice. Oversee as many aspects of treatment and daily routine as possible. If your patients represent a potential danger to themselves or others, recommen and, if necessary, insist that they are hospitalized. As their symptoms improve, allow a gradual resumption of their self-determination.

Environmental intervention. An important method of helping your patients reestablish their adaptive capacities is to reduce sources of environmental stress and simultaneously provide therapeutic experiences Some patients having an affective disorder will need the around-the-clock supervision and care which only a hospital can supply. But whether your patients are treated in or outside of a hospital, make sure that the enviro ment provides therapeutic relationships and activities, a balanced diet an adequate recreational outlets.

Hospitalization usually is indicated for depressed patients who show signs of marked psychomotor retardation, delusions, agitation or express feelings of hopelessness or serious suicidal ideas. Hospitalization is als recommended for persons whose symptoms have failed to respond to othe forms of anti-depressant treatment. Inpatient treatment should be considered for manic individuals if they show persistent hyperactivity, sever impaired judgment or evidence of physical exhaustion.

Education. Keep patients and their families well informed about all aspects of treatment including the details about any medications which have been prescribed. Get the point across that, however disruptive and distressing the symptoms presently are, their condition is time-limited and will improve with appropriate treatment.

Help patients with a recurrent affective disorder understand that their condition likely can be controlled if they faithfully adhere to an appropriate medical regimen and will contact you at the first sign of a recurrence. Periodically review your treatment plans and the reasons for them with patients and their families.

Ventilation. Whether you allow your patients to discuss their feelings and problems at length or actively divert them to less emotionally charged topics will depend upon their mental state. It can be therapeutic for depressed patients to share their sadness and hopelessness with others -- they will feel less alone with their problems. However, for those who are obsessively preoccupied with their problems or remain socially withdrawn and underactive, it is important to divert their thinking into areas which have a greater therapeutic potential. Such patients should be involved in structured work projects, watching television, visiting with staff and relatives, and group activities. Manic patients, too, need assistance in directing their grandiose ideas and hyperactivity into constructive channels such as recreational outlets and productive projects.

Reassurance. Most patients derive feelings of reassurance from their therapist's ongoing concern and presence. Therefore, meet with your patients regularly, even if their depression and preoccupation is so severe that they show little acknowledgment of your presence. Strive to convey a feeling of therapeutic optimism and confidence. Brief (ten to fifteen minutes) daily sessions work best with additional meetings scheduled as needed. If your patients are treated outside of a hospital, make arrangements to keep in close touch by phone. Setting firm behavioral limits will reassure patients who cannot restrain their impulses to harm themselves or others. Remember, too, to provide reassurance for your patient's family.

Now complete Self-Assessment Exercise #4 beginning on the following page.

Self-Assessment Exercise #4

1. Circle the patient characteristics and behaviors which usually indicate the need for hospitalization:

    insomnia

    agitation

    5 lbs. weight loss

    delusional thinking

    marked psychomotor retardation

    expressions of hopelessness

    expressions of depressive feelings

    failure of response to supporti psychotherapy/medications

    occasional, vague suicidal ide

    physical debility caused by anorexia and sleeplessness

    persistent hyperactivity

    overspending based on grandio ideas

2. Assume that you plan to treat a patient with a bipolar disorder who presently is very depressed. Briefly answer each of the following questions about supportive psychotherapy.

    Would you use a directive or non-directive guidance approach? Why?

    What would you "educate" your patient about relative to his affective disorder?

    What would you do if your patient preferred to stay by himself and spoke only about his feeling of depression and guilt?

    How would you handle the frequency and duration of your meetings with him?

When you have completed this exercise to the best of your ability, check your answers with those on the following page.

Self-Assessment Exercise #4 - Feedback

1. The following patient characteristics and behaviors usually indicate the need for hospitalization:

   agitation

   delusional thinking

   marked psychomotor retardation

   expressions of hopelessness

   failure of response to supportive psychotherapy/medications

   physical debility caused by anorexia and sleeplessness

   persistent hyperactivity

   overspending based on grandio ideas

2. Would you use a directive or non-directive guidance approach? Why?

   A directive guidance approach should be used for persons suffering from an affective disorder. These patients usually have significant impairment of their insight and judgment and need help in making decisions, arranging therapeutic experiences, and require close supervision and direction.

   What would you "educate" your patient about relative to his affective disorder?

   Patients with a bipolar disorder should be told that their condition is time-limited, but may recur. It can be controlled if they are conscientious about taking their medications and seek help at the early signs of a recurrence. They should be familiar with their prescribed medications.

   What would you do if your patient preferred to stay by himself and spoke only about his feeling of depression and guilt?

   Patients who are socially withdrawn and/or dwell endlessly on their symptoms should be diverted to more therapeutic activities and social relationships.

   How would you handle the frequency and duration of your meetings with him?

   Brief, daily visits work best with depressed patients.

If your answers correspond closely with those above, continue reading on the next page. If not, please reread the preceding material.

THERAPEUTIC INTERVENTIONS (CONTINUED)

Behavioral Therapy

Interventions involving behavioral modification are not usually effective in the treatment of affective disorders.

Pharmacologic Therapy and Electroconvulsive Therapy

There is growing evidence that recurrent affective disorders are caused by a biochemical imbalance of the central nervous system. In many cases, the imbalance can be successfully treated by drugs or electroconvulsive therapy. Only a brief review of the pharmacology relating to affective disorders will be presented here, and we recommend that you read the more complete discussion which appears in the chapter on "Pharmacologic Therapy." Medications for depressive and manic disorders will be described separately. A brief presentation about electroconvulsive therapy (ECT) will be included in this section, because it is widely used and quite effective in the treatment of depressive symptoms.

The treatment of depression. We believe that tricyclic anti-depressants (TCA's) are the most reliable and effective medications for the treatment of selected depressive syndromes. We do not recommend the use of monoamine oxidase inhibitors (MAOI) or central nervous system stimulants such as amphetamines.

At the present time it is difficult to predict accurately which patients will respond to tricyclic anti-depressant medications. However, a positive therapeutic outcome is more likely for persons whose depressive symptoms have lasted several weeks or longer, not responded to conventional supportive therapy, lack a well-defined precipitating cause, and include prominent physical findings such as insomnia, anorexia, fatigability and constipation.

There is growing evidence that TCA's are indicated when treating depressive symptoms associated with major depression and bipolar disorders, but are relatively ineffective in persons having an uncomplicated grief reaction or a chronic depressive disorder.

The TCA's which we will discuss are imipramine, amytriptyline and doxepin. These medications are widely used and are quite comparable in effect, dosage, time required for onset of action and other characteristics. Before prescribing any TCA's, first determine that your patients are suitable candidates for treatment with respect to depressive symptoms and medical findings. Special caution should be used when prescribing anti-depressants for patients who are elderly, debilitated or have cardiovascular disease or increased intraocular pressure (glaucoma). If not medical contraindications exist, prescribe one of the TCA's at a dosage of 25 mgs. TID for five to seven days. At the end of a week's time, there should be enough medication accumulated in the body to allow administration as a single bedtime dose. After the initial five to seven days, the dosage can be increased by increments of 25 mgs. each three to four days until the total daily dosage of 150 mgs. is achieved. Keep in mind that TCA's usually take ten to fourteen days to produce a therapeutic response. If no significant improvement or undesirable side effects occur at 150 mgs. per day after three to four weeks, the total daily amount can be raised to 200 mgs.

Routinely inform your patients to expect side effects of drowsiness, dry mouth, and blurring of vision, but that most of these symptoms will subside after a few days. You should also tell them not to take other medications without advance medical approval and avoid alcoholic beverages. Instruct them to contact you at the first sign of <u>any</u> unusual physical complaints. Keep in mind that TCA's are potentially lethal drugs. If your patient is a potential suicidal risk, make sure that the TCA's and all other medications are kept and dispensed by a responsible family member.

Electroconvulsive therapy (ECT) or electroshock therapy (EST), as it is sometimes called, is a safe and effective treatment for rapidly improving symptoms of depression. Because of its awesome sounding name and complications which occurred during the early years of its development, ECT has been regarded with fear and misunderstanding by laypersons and professionals alike. In actuality, the troublesome side effects which formerly characterized ECT have been reduced almost to the vanishing point by incorporating muscle relaxants and general anesthetics into the treatment regimen. Usual side effects following present day treatment consist only of a mild headache and transient impairment of mental functioning. The temporary impairment of mental functioning and memory which accompany ECT is proportional to the number and spacing of the treatments. Memory deficits for the few minutes immediately before and after each ECT treatment will persist, but the capacity for intellectual functioning and memory rapidly returns to normal following the last treatment. Permanent residual effects of any kind are very rare. Furthermore, with the exception of increased intracranial pressure, there are essentially no medical contraindications to the use of ECT. It can be given safely to pregnant women, persons with a previous heart attack or high blood pressure, the elderly and others with serious medical disorders. ECT is a remarkably safe form of therapy with only four or five deaths reported per 200,000 treatments. The potential for death by suicide in undertreated depressed patients is many times greater.

ECT is especially recommended for persons who present a serious and imminent suicidal risk, are markedly debilitated due to prolonged depression, who have not responded to other treatment methods (TCA's, psychotherapy, etc.) or who are psychotically depressed, agitated or delusional. ECT generally is most effective for depressive symptoms associated with major depressive and bipolar affective disorders. It is not recommended for persons with chronic affective disorders.

ECT is a specialized treatment and should be administered only in a medical facility by trained experts. Each patient prior to treatment should undergo thorough physical and laboratory examinations to assess their state of health. The usual sequence of an ECT treatment is as follows: the patient is first fully anesthethized by the administration of an intravenous barbiturate. Next, a medication (succinyl choline) is given which produces total muscle relaxation within a few minutes. A small amount of electrical current is briefly administered through electrodes placed on the patient's temples and a grand-mal seizure is produced. Because of the muscle relaxant, only a slight general tensing of the body musculature can be observed at the time of the seizure. The mechanism by which ECT causes improvement is not fully understood, however, studies have shown that a seizure must be produced to achieve maximum therapeutic benefits. The patient will spontaneously awaken within a few minutes after the treatment, and following a rest in bed for half an hour or so, can walk about with assistance. In most cases, the patient can fully participate in ward activities within an hour or two following treatment. A course of three to eight ECT treatments usually results in significant improvement for most depressed persons.

The treatment of mania. Lithium carbonate is very effective for treating the acute symptoms of mania or bipolar disorders. The symptoms of mania including hyperactivity, elated affect, pressured speech and grandiosity begin to subside within a few days after optimal blood levels are achieved. This drug also has prophylactic value and reduces the incidence of recurrent episodes of mania and depression in bipolar disorders. However, lithium carbonate is less effective than TCA's in treating acute depressive symptoms. Since lithium carbonate takes several days to produce a therapeutic effect, it is often helpful to initially prescribe an anti-psychotic drug such as haloperidol or chlorpromazine to control manic behavior.

In order to reduce the incidence of medical complications, a thorough physical and laboratory examination should be performed before administering lithium carbonate. Excluding serious medical emergencies, there are no absolute contraindications to the use of lithium. However, special care should be taken in patients with kidney disease, liver or cardiovascular problems, diabetes or hypothyroid conditions. After medical clearance has been obtained, lithium carbonate can be administered, 300 mgs. after each meal, until the maintenance blood level of 0.6 to 1.2 milli-equivalents per liter is obtained. Side effects common to lithium are gastro-intestinal upsets (nausea, diarrhea, loss of appetite, and abdominal cramping), weakness and a fine tremor of the hands. If lithium carbonate reaches toxic levels, symptoms of mental confusion, drowsiness, and unsteady gait and seizures or coma may occur.

Consultation and Referral

Many persons with mild affective disorders can be managed as outpatients and without the need of special consultation. In more severe cases, however, treatment issues can arise which deserve consultation. Consultation with a mental health expert is indicated for patients who do not respond to usual therapeutic regimens, need hospitalization, or otherwise present special management problems. Persons who develop medical problems or present a risk of suicide warrant psychiatric consultation. Manic patients need special evaluation if their behavior leads to physical exhaustion or involvement in activities which later may cause serious social or financial consequences. The medications frequently prescribed for persons with affective disorders are potent and should be administered only by experienced therapists who are prepared to deal with any medical complications which arise.

Community agencies offer a variety of services which can provide support for your patients. Regional mental health centers can supply and monitor psychotropic medications and provide supportive psychotherapy on a regular basis. Vocational rehabilitation programs, day treatment centers, general medical clinics, welfare agencies and self-help groups are other facilities which can augment treatment.

Now complete Self-Assessment Exercise #5 beginning on the following page.

Self-Assessment Exercise #5

1. A middle-aged man asks you to recommend a medication to alleviate his symptoms of depression. Name four areas of history about which to inquire to determine whether TCA's may be effective.

2. Indicate whether the following statements about psychotropic medicatio are true (T) or false (F).

_____ a. Central nervous system stimulants are recommended for treating major depressive disorders.

_____ b. TCA's may be contraindicated for persons with cardiovascular disease.

_____ c. The total dosage for TCA's should not exceed 200 mg./day for outpatients.

_____ d. The most common side effects of TCA's are drowsiness, dry mouth and blurred vision.

_____ e. Lithium carbonate may be contraindicated for patients with renal or heart failure.

_____ f. The optimal blood level for lithium maintenance is 1.5 to 2.0 mi. eq./liter.

_____ g. Signs of lithium carbonate toxicity include mental confusion, drowsiness, and an unsteady gait.

Self-Assessment Exercise #5 (Continued)

3. Mr. John Roberts, a 68-year-old man, developed progressively severe depressive symptoms following the death of his wife. He made a serious suicide attempt and was hospitalized. Mr. Roberts refused to eat and could sleep only if sedated. After psychiatric evaluation, a course of ECT was recommended. The family was quite apprehensive about the treatment. What authoritative information could you provide regarding:

   (a) what short-term side effects to expect

   (b) residual side effects to expect

   (c) the nature of the treatment

   (d) the safety of the treatment for elderly patients

4. List four or more indications for psychiatric consultation for patients with mania or serious depression.

When you have completed this exercise to the best of your ability, check your answers with those on the following page.

Self-Assessment Exercise #5 - Feedback

1. Four areas of history about which to inquire to determine whether or not TCA's may be effective are:

   (a) the presence of physical symptoms (sleep, appetite, energy, etc.)

   (b) the duration of depressive symptoms (longer than 3 - 4 weeks)

   (c) responsiveness to supportive measures

   (d) the presence of a precipitating cause

2.

False a. Central nervous system stimulants are recommended for treating major depressive disorders.

True b. TCA's may be contraindicated for persons with cardiovascular disease.

True c. The total dosage for TCA's should not exceed 200 mg./day for outpatients.

True d. The most common side effects of TCA's are drowsiness, dry mouth and blurred vision.

True e. Lithium carbonate may be contraindicated for patients with renal or heart failure.

False f. The optimal blood level for lithium maintenance is 1.5 to 2.0 mi. eq./liter.

True g. Signs of lithium carbonate toxicity include mental confusion, drowsiness, and an unsteady gait.

3. With regards to ECT for Mr. Roberts:

   (a) Short-term side effects are a headache and transient intellectual and memory impairment.

   (b) Residual side effects -- memory impairment for the few minutes immediately before, during and after the ECT.

Self-Assessment Exercise #5 - Feedback (Continued)

3. (c) The nature of the treatment includes medications which will render him unconscious and totally relaxed. A small amount of electrical current is applied to his temples and a seizure results. Because of the medication, only generalized muscle tension occurs. After resting in bed for 30 minutes, Mr. Roberts can freely move about.

   (d) The treatment is very safe, even for elderly patients who are in reasonably good health.

4. Psychiatric consultation should be sought for patients with mania or depression who:

   (a) need hospitalization (voluntary or involuntary)

   (b) have not responded to other therapy

   (c) are suicidal

   (d) need special medications

   (e) are physically ill

If your answers correspond closely with those above, continue reading on the next page. If not, please reread the preceding material.

SUMMARY

Affective disorders are common pathologic conditions which are characterized by the psychological and physical findings of depression or mania. Careful evaluation is needed for each case to determine the appropriate diagnosis and treatment approach. Therapeutic intervention includes the use of supportive psychotherapy techniques, psychotropic medications, hospitalization and ECT. Appropriate treatment can greatly alleviate patient suffering and shorten the duration of affective disorders.

REFERENCES

Barchas, J., Berger, P., Ciaranello, R., and Elliott, G., Psychopharmacology, From Theory to Practice, New York: Oxford University Press, 1977.

Bowden, C. and Griffin, M., Psychopharmacology for Primary Care Physicians, Baltimore: The Williams and Wilkins Co., 1978.

Diagnostic and Statistical Manual of Mental Disorders, Third Edition, Washington, D.C.: American Psychiatric Association, 1979.

Goodwin, D. and Guze, S., Psychiatric Diagnosis, New York: Oxford University Press, 1979.

Imboden, J. and Urbatis, J., Practical Psychiatry in Medicine, New York: Appleton-Century-Crofts, 1978.

Shader, R. I., Manual of Psychiatric Therapeutics, Boston: Little, Brown and Co., 1975.

CHAPTER 9. ORGANIC MENTAL DISORDERS

Organic mental disorders (OMD's) comprise a group of psychopathologic conditions which result from dysfunction of the brain. For this diagnosis to be applied, brain dysfunction should be documented by laboratory and physical examination (e.g., electroencephalograms, x-rays, etc.) and/or by a history which indicates that an organic factor (i.e., drugs or head trauma) are involved. Many persons erroneously believe that OMD's are conditions generally restricted to elderly or drug intoxicated patients. But, in actuality, brain dysfunction also occurs in connection with many physical illnesses, and indeed, can be the first sign of a developing medical problem. Because of the high incidence and medical significance of these disorders, it is important that you develop expertise in diagnosing and treating them.

LEARNING OBJECTIVES

By the time you complete this chapter, you should be able to do the following and apply the information to written case histories.

1. List the mental status findings typical of an organic mental disorder.

2. Using the criteria described, characterize and distinguish between the following organic brain syndromes:

   a. delirium
   b. dementia
   c. intoxication
   d. drug withdrawal

3. List five classes of physical disorders that can give rise to an organic brain syndrome.

4. List six factors which may predispose one to developing an organic brain syndrome.

5. For each of the methods of therapeutic intervention listed below, describe the recommended approach and provide a rationale for its use in the management of an organic brain syndrome:

   a. supportive psychotherapy
   b. behavioral therapy
   c. pharmacologic therapy
   d. consultation and referral

GENERAL DIAGNOSTIC CONSIDERATIONS

The brain dysfunction basic to OMD's may be temporary or permanent, mild or marked and variously affects patient behavior, emotions, and intellectual functioning. OMD's are further classified into subgroups, that is, organic brain syndromes which are named according to the nature of the brain dysfunction, clinical course, and predominant symptoms. Generally, organic brain syndromes are characterized by global impairment of higher intellectual functioning, orientation, memory, and abstract thinking. However, the predominant symptoms of some organic syndromes consist primarily of impaired memory or abnormalities of affect, or perceptual dysfunction, or personality and behavioral disturbances in the absence of significant intellectual impairment. These latter syndromes are less common and we will confine our discussion to those which you are more likely to encounter (i.e., delirium, dementia, intoxication, and withdrawal).

There is growing evidence that some of the so-called "functional" psychoses (i.e., schizophrenic and major affective disorders) also may be due to a subtle brain dysfunction and therefore are "organic" in nature. Although brain dysfunction may be involved in both classes of disorders, it appears that the underlying abnormalities are significantly different and, for the foreseeable future, that diagnostic differentiation should be continued.

MENTAL STATUS EXAMINATION FINDINGS

Although the types of organic brain syndromes (OBS's) which we will discuss can vary considerably with respect to etiology, course, and outcome, most have similar mental status examination (MSE) findings. A thorough mental status examination generally provides a rapid and reliable means for establishing the diagnosis of an organic brain syndrome. To further aid your diagnostic efforts, keep in mind that the findings of these syndromes can wax and wane considerably over time and characteristically worsen at night and improve during the day.

The intensity and rate of progression of symptoms varies widely and depends upon the cause of the disorder. For example, symptoms of a dementia can be mild and take years to develop in the case of cerebral arteriosclerosis in which narrowing of small blood vessels gradually impairs blood circulation to the brain. A full-blown delirium may develop in a few hours if caused by drugs or ingested poisons. In some organic brain syndromes such as those due to alcohol intoxication or mild concussion, the symptoms may disappear in a matter of a few hours, while those caused by severe head injury may last indefinitely.

A MSE will help determine the presence of an organic brain syndrome, but cannot discriminate diagnostically between different etiological factors (i.e., whether an injury or drug ingestion were causative). However, MSE observations provide information about the overall status of the central nervous system, and if it is generally excited or depressed. Therefore, if drug use is suspected, it may be impossible to infer from patient behaviors whether the substance taken was a central nervous stimulant or depressant. We will now describe the MSE findings typical of most organic brain syndromes and later point out findings which help discriminate between delirium, dementia, intoxication and withdrawal syndromes.

Appearance. The greater the impairment of brain functioning, the greater the likelihood that self-care and personal grooming will be neglected. An unkempt appearance, disheveled clothing, uncleanness, unshavenness or lack of attention to makeup are common findings. If a serious medical problem is present or a drug withdrawal syndrome is in progress, there may be signs of physical illness in the form of chills, nausea, vomiting, pallor or weight loss.

Behavior. Patients with an organic brain syndrome commonly show an abnormality of movement such as decreased or excessive activity, tremulousness, discoordination, an unsteady walk, and impulsive, purposeless movements. Facial expression corresponds with the predominant affect being experienced, be it elation, depression, apprehension or irritability. Speech is often atypical in quality and quantity, and may be indistinct, slurred, or range from loud talkativeness to a soft slow monotone.

Feeling (Mood/Affect). Patients may demonstrate a variety of feelings. For example, if drugs were taken which depress the central nervous system (i.e., barbiturates, alcohol, or heroin) then the patients are likely to experience lethargy, melancholy or irritability. Conversely central nervous system stimulants typically cause feelings of euphoria, grandiosity or irritability and belligerence. Generally, the affect shown is consistent with the thought content being expressed but is often labile and can change rapidly.

Perception. Perceptual disturbances in the form of illusions and auditory or visual hallucinations are common, especially in individuals with a delirium, a dementia, or who have taken a hallucinogenic drug. Hallucinations experienced as pure sounds, vivid colors, geometric patterns, animals or insects usually are indicative of a chemical or toxic effect on the central nervous system.

Thinking. Alterations of thinking can be found in almost all persons with an organic brain syndrome, although the degree and type of impairment varies widely. Early signs of impairment occur as fluctuating levels of consciousness, decreased ability to concentrate, and distractibility. If the central nervous system functioning is depressed from any cause, your patients may become lethargic or stuporous. Delirious patients or those intoxicated with stimulating drugs often seem hyperalert and become easily startled by minor stimuli. In persons with a significant degree of organic brain syndrome, orientation, recent memory, concentration, and general intellectual functioning are impaired. Disorientation successively affects awareness of time, place and person. The sequence is reversed as patients improve. Reasoning and judgment are also compromised. Delusions can occur and frequently are paranoid in nature. An associational disturbance of some degree is present with many organic brain syndromes.

PHYSICAL FINDINGS SUGGESTING DRUG INTOXICATION OR WITHDRAWAL

Because you are likely to encounter patients intoxicated or withdrawing from drugs, we are including a brief discussion of physical findings which are associated with those conditions.

Your patient's eyes can provide diagnostic information. If the pupils are unusually constricted, dilated or unresponsive to light, a drug reaction might be responsible. Similarly, signs of horizontal or vertical jerking eye movements (nystagmus) indicate possible intoxication.

Blood pressure and heart rate are directly influenced by the state of the central nervous system, and if these functions are noticeably increased or decreased from normal levels, the deviation may be drug related.

Close observation of the body musculature also will yield important information. Signs of generalized restlessness, increased or decreased tendon reflexes, spasmodic muscle twitches, purposeless movements, or marked startled response to minor stimuli may indicate drug intoxication or withdrawal.

The skin also should be closely noted. Especially look for needle marks, "tracks," or infections on the inner aspects of the arm about the elbow, a common sight for injecting drugs. Goose flesh or generalized chills also are prominent in persons during a withdrawal syndrome.

Other symptoms which may indicate a drug withdrawal syndrome are fever, cramping abdominal pains, nausea, vomiting, excessive tearing, a stuffy nose, unusual sweating, or repeated yawning and sneezing.

Common Organic Brain Syndromes

We will now describe four common organic brain syndromes; namely delirium, dementia, intoxication and withdrawal.

Delirium. A delirium is a profound mental disorder arising from generalized brain dysfunction such as might result from a high fever, head injury, severe infection, drug withdrawal or similar toxic condition. Typically, the syndrome develops within a relatively short period of time -- hours to a few days. Early in the course of a delirium, patients have difficulty maintaining their concentration and attention, and may show fluctuating levels of alertness. They are easily distracted by unimportant stimuli. Increasing restlessness, irritability, apprehension, and insomnia with frightening nightmares follow. Patients often lose the ability to discriminate between things which are similar, but non-identical, and may confuse strangers with relatives or friends. Reality testing is markedly impaired and delusions with vivid hallucinations develop. Patients typically are disoriented to time, place and person, and retain little capacity for abstract thinking or recent memory. Thinking patterns are fragmented and patients often become totally incoherent. In most cases, the intensity and duration of a delirium parallels the course of the underlying medical problem; and as the illness subsides, so does the organic brain syndrome. A delirium implies the presence of an underlying medical disorder which always warrants prompt evaluation and treatment. In summary, a delirium is characterized by a rapid onset and fluctuating symptoms. Foremost among the mental status findings are a disturbance of attention which impairs goal-directed thinking and behavior, disordered memory and orientation, either decreased or increased psychomotor activity, hallucinations, delusions, and lethargy or insomnia. The presence of brain dysfunction usually can be demonstrated by means of history or laboratory findings.

Dementia. The diagnosis of dementia is applied to persons who show gradual and marked deterioration of former levels of intellectual functioning. Typically, the course of a dementia is gradual and may take months or many years to develop. The most significant findings include evidence of severe impairment in the area of thinking, in particular, with respect to abstract thinking, problem-solving skills, judgment, orientation, and recent memory. Intellectual deterioration and disordered behavior reach severe proportions and eventually, such patients are unable to handle even routine decisions of daily living. Persons with dementia occasionally experience hallucinations, and impaired reality testing with delusions are common. Judgment is impaired and these persons are likely to overact emotionally to minor incidents. Dementias result from severe dysfunction of brain cells as might be caused by tumors, infections, and blood vessel or degenerative diseases. Demented persons are predisposed to the development of a secondary delirium which can be precipitated by medical illness or various medications. Little can be done to restore intellectual functioning lost in the course of a dementia, and treatment consists primarily of providing custodial and supportive care. A dementia, then, is characterized by deterioration of previously acquired intellectual abilities including the capacity for memory, abstract thinking, orientation, impulse control, and problem-solving abilities. These individuals usually undergo a personality change. It is usually possible to detect abnormal brain functioning by laboratory and other findings.

Intoxication. This organic brain syndrome is defined as maladaptive behavior arising from drugs (chemicals) taken to alter central nervous system functioning. Basic to this diagnosis is the requirement that behavior is present which interferes with regular occupational or social functioning (i.e., impaired judgment, impulsivity, fighting or other disorderly conduct). As defined here, this diagnostic term does not apply to the usual intoxication by alcohol or other "recreational" drugs unless accompanied by maladaptive behavior. During non-pathologic intoxication, sleepiness or talkativeness, discoorindation, an unsteady walk, slurred speech, and slowed thinking can be observed -- but not maladaptive behavior. Intoxication can result from a number of drugs or chemicals and patient behavior generally coincides with the effect which the chemical has on the central nervous system. Central nervous system depressants such as barbiturates, heroin, and psychotropic drugs usually cause slowed thinking and movement, slurred speech, discoordination, and feelings of depression. Respiration and blood pressure are likewise reduced. The reverse is true for drugs which stimulate the central nervous system. Cocaine, amphetamines, and methylphenidate may result in hyperactive behavior, pressured speech, restlessness, and elevated blood pressure and pulse rate. Usually, this type of organic brain syndrome lasts for a few hours but may be extended in duration to several days. Associated medical complications may arise according to the amount and type of drug taken. For example, in the instance of central nervous system depressants, respiratory distress or arrest may occur. It is usually possible to identify the drug causing the intoxication by taking a history or examining the patient's blood or urine. Intoxication, then, is an organic brain syndrome which develops soon after taking a drug. The particular behavioral and psychological response depends upon the nature of the drug taken. In addition to the usual finding of intoxication, evidence of maladaptive behavior during the waking state of the patient must be present.

Withdrawal. This organic brain syndrome results from reducing or stopping the intake of a drug upon which patients had become physically dependent to some degree. These drugs are generally used because of their intoxicating effects upon the central nervous system, and were taken often enough to produce a tolerance and physical dependency (see the chapter on "Substance Use Disorders" for details). The symptoms of withdrawal result as the body readjusts to a decreased level of the drug taken. Substances which can cause a withdrawal response include tobacco, alcohol, opiates, and various sedatives. Most withdrawal symptoms have in common symptoms of insomnia, distractibility, restlessness, anxiety, irritability, nausea, vomiting, tremulousness and others described earlier in this chapter. Usually a withdrawal response is limited to a few days. If marked physical dependency upon alcohol or sedatives has occurred, withdrawal can result in a delirium and produce serious medical complications. The clinical picture is highly varied with respect to physical and mental status findings, and depends upon the drug taken, the degree of physical dependency, and the speed with which the medication has been decreased.

Now complete Self-Assessment Exercise #1 beginning on the next page.

Self-Assessment Exercise #1

Read the following case history and answer the questions that follow.

Case History

Consultation was requested for Mr. George Lee, a post-surgical patient in the intensive care unit at a local general hospital. At the time of his interview, Mr. Lee appeared to be a man in his late 50's, lying in bed restlessly pulling at the soft restraints which tied each of his extremities. He was mumbling incoherently and staring intently at the ceiling. He seemed apprehensive, easily distracted and it was difficult to obtain a relevant history from him. His answers to questions were brief and incomplete. When asked what he was staring at on the ceiling, Mr. Lee described seeing spiders and bugs dropping onto his bed. Despite the obvious nature of his surroundings, he denied having any medical problems and insisted that he was in a St. Louis hotel. He remembered nothing of his recent surgery and was at a loss to explain the various medical apparatus which surrounded him. Mr. Lee was unable to state correctly the month or year.

1. List the significant MSE findings in the spaces provided:

BEHAVIOR	
FEELING (Affect/Mood)	
PERCEPTION	
THINKING	

Self-Assessment Exercise #1 (Continued)

2. Circle the correct diagnosis for Mr. Lee's condition.

   a. dementia
   b. delirium
   c. intoxication
   d. withdrawal

3. Characterize each of the following syndromes by "yes" or "no" answers.

	INTOXICATION (secondary to alcohol)	DELIRIUM	DEMENTIA
usually reversible			
rapid onset (minutes to hours)			
typically associated with current medical problems			
disorientation present			
recent memory impaired			
vivid hallucinations (usually visual) present			
markedly impaired intellectual functioning			

When you have completed this exercise to the best of your ability, check your answers with those on the following page.

Self-Assessment Exercise #1 - Feedback

1. Mr. Lee's MSE findings are:

BEHAVIOR	restlessness mumbling staring at the ceiling
FEELING (Affect/Mood)	tense and apprehensive appropriate to thought content
PERCEPTION	described visual hallucinations (illusions)
THINKING	decreased attention span (distractible) disorientation to time and place recent memory impaired impaired insight into his present problems and environment somewhat incoherent (assocational disturbance)

2. The diagnosis of Mr. Lee's condition is:

   a. delirium -- which is characterized by a rapid onset, restlessness, disorientation, decreased attention span and intellectual functioning, impaired recent memory and hallucinations

Self-Assessment Exercise #1 - Feedback (Continued)

3. The following syndromes can be characterized as follows:

	INTOXICATION (secondary to alcohol)	DELIRIUM	DEMENTIA
usually reversible	yes	yes	no
rapid onset (minutes to hours)	yes	yes	no
typically associated with current medical problems	no	yes	no
disorientation present	no	yes	yes
recent memory impaired	no	yes	yes
vivid hallucinations (usually visual) present	no	yes	no
markedly impaired intellectual functioning	no	yes	yes

If your answers correspond closely with those above, continue reading on the next page. If not, please reread the preceding material.

PREDISPOSING FACTORS OF ORGANIC BRAIN SYNDROMES

Patients are predisposed toward developing an organic brain syndrome by factors which can be anticipated and often counteracted. Prolonged physical inactivity due to bed confinement or immobilization because of casts, traction or restraints may lead to an organic brain syndrome. Extremes of sensory input either sensory deprivation or over stimulation, sleep deprivation and intense anxiety are predisposing factors. Pre-existing brain damage of any type, prolonged or excessive alcohol or drug abuse, and being over 50 years of age are other contributing factors.

PHYSICAL CAUSES OF ORGANIC BRAIN SYNDROMES

Physical factors cause brain dysfunction and result in an organic brain syndrome including primary disease of the brain and many conditions which secondarily impair brain functioning. Keeping in mind the following classes of causes will help establish a diagnosis:

1. central nervous system intoxication by drugs, medications or exposure to toxic substances is the most common etiology of organic brain syndromes. Intoxication may result from prescribed drugs, street drugs, hormones and various chemicals and noxious fumes or gases (including anesthetic agents)

2. endocrine (glandular) disorders can give rise to signs and symptoms of an organic brain syndrome. Under this heading are glandular dysfunction of the pituitary, adrenal, thyroid (both under- and over-active thyroid states) and the pancreas

3. metabolic and nutritional disorders are often sources implicated in brain dysfunction. Drug withdrawal, severe vitamin deficiency (pellagra), blood chemical imbalances (acidosis, etc.), liver and kidney disease which secondarily cause the build up of certain body waste products in the blood are examples

4. severe infections which result in high fever or a general toxic state interfere with normal brain functioning and include pneumonia, thyphoid fever, malaria, rheumatic fever, and others

5. intracranial conditions which can cause an organic brain syndrome are cerebral arteriosclerosis, cerebral vascular disorders (such as thrombosis or hemorrhage), epilepsy, brain degeneration, tumors and infections and trauma

Now complete Self-Assessment Exercise #2 beginning on the following page.

Self-Assessment Exercise #2

Read the following case history and then answer the questions which follow it.

Case History

Consultation was requested for 28-year-old Jane Bryant who had been involved in an automobile accident. She had been drinking heavily before the accident and relatives state that "for years" she had regularly consumed large amounts of alcoholic beverages. As a result of the accident, Mrs. Bryant sustained a brain concussion and fractured pelvis and leg. During surgery for her injuries, she was placed in a body cast and traction was applied. After spending an hour in the post-surgical recovery room, she was moved to a private room. Four hours later, Mrs. Bryant was observed by the nurse to be restless, mentally confused and speaking incoherently. Believing that she was in her home, Mrs. Bryant tried to leave her bed and had to be forcibly detained.

1. The likely diagnosis is an organic brain syndrome (delirium). If she were given a thorough mental status examination, circle the <u>other</u> findings below which you would expect her to demonstrate:

    a. impaired recent memory

    b. a euphoric mood

    c. compulsive behavior

    d. impaired abstract thinking

    e. impaired calculation ability

    f. disorientation to time

2. Circle the classes of medical disorders which may have contributed to her organic brain syndrome (more than one answer may be used).

    a. central nervous system intoxication

    b. an endocrine disorder

Self-Assessment Exercise #2 (Continued)

2. c. a metabolic-nutritional disturbance

   d. an infectious process

   e. an intracranial condition

3. What factors were present which predisposed Mrs. Bryant to develop an organic brain disorder?

4. Was her age a significant predisposing factor?

5. What are the advantages and disadvantages about placing physical restraints on Mrs. Bryant to make sure that she stays in bed?

When you have completed this exercise to the best of your ability, check your answers with those on the following page.

Self-Assessment Exercise #2 - Feedback

1. If Mrs. Bryant does have an organic brain syndrome, in addition to being confused and disoriented to place, she would demonstrate:

    a. impaired recent memory

    d. impaired abstract thinking

    e. impaired calculation ability

    f. disorientation to time

2. The classes of medical disorders which might apply to her case are:

    a. central nervous system intoxication (due to her recent alcohol ingestion and the surgical anesthesia)

    e. intracranial condition (brain concussion)

3. Factors which may have predisposed Mrs. Bryant to developing an organic brain disorder are:

    a. history of alcohol abuse

    b. a head injury

    c. bodily restraint (the body cast and traction)

    d. isolation (being placed in a private room)

    e. surgical anesthesia

4. Mrs. Bryant was under 50, and it is not likely that her age was a predisposing factor.

5. Physical restraints are useful and necessary for keeping Mrs. Bryant in bed and making possible definitive medical care. On the other hand, body immobilization predisposes a person towards developing an organic brain syndrome.

If your answers correspond closely with those above, continue reading on the next page. If not, please reread the preceding material.

THERAPEUTIC INTERVENTION

Although the therapeutic approach should be individualized to each case, the principles listed below are suitable for treating most persons with an organic brain syndrome.

First and foremost, evaluate and treat any medical conditions which may contribute to the disorder. Prompt intervention often can improve the prognosis. Undertake a thorough medical evaluation whenever you suspect that an organic brain syndrome is present.

Supportive Psychotherapy

Techniques of supportive psychotherapy are useful for treating organic brain syndromes.

Directive guidance. Judgment and problem-solving abilities are almost always impaired in patients with an organic brain syndrome and it will be necessary for you to provide guidance and support which they cannot supply themselves. In general, your task is to prescribe structured daily routine which meets their basic needs. For delirious or demented patients, it may be necessary that you oversee their total psychological and physical care. Make yourself readily available to these patients and actively guide their decision making. Offer specific suggestions for solving problems, mobilizing therapeutic resources, and conducting their daily living.

Environmental intervention. The environment of patients with an organic brain syndrome can either be a source of comfort or great distress and it is important that you thoughtfully attend to their milieu. Many individuals with a mild organic brain syndrome can be successfully managed as outpatients if their day-to-day activities, eating and sleeping habits, and personal care can be monitored by responsible persons. More disturbed patients will need hospitalization and professional supervision. Consider carefully your patients' living environment, physical activity and social contacts. Sensory deprivation or overload are undesirable. If stimulation in one sensory organ (eyes, ears) is impaired, help the patient compensate for the loss by increasing the sensory input in others. For example, if patients' ability to see is decreased, make sure that they receive increased stimulation by sound (via a radio) and touch (frequent reassuring pats by the staff). Environmental characteristics greatly influence the behavior and feeling of persons with an organic brain syndrome. This is particularly evident for persons admitted to intensive care units which are designed more for maintaining life than attending to the emotional needs of patients. In these units, the sights, sounds and sense of timelessness inadvertently promote patient anxiety and confusion. For this reason, patients should be relocated in less stressful surroundings as soon as it is medically appropriate to do so. As a general principle, patient mobility should be encouraged and restraints of any kind should be avoided. Patients do better if their surroundings include familiar objects such as pictures of family members and other personal articles. Frequent but brief visits with relatives and friends are therapeutic. The selected use of television and radio programs and occupational therapy projects are additional resources for creating a therapeutic milieu. Finally, a small light left on will help maintain their orientation during the night.

Reassurance. Patients with organic brain syndromes lack inner stability and feel insecure when dealing with the problems of everyday living. Their uncertainty and anxiety can be counteracted somewhat by reassurances from you and others caring for them. Brief, regular consultations with you provide a stabilizing influence and help maintain a sense of continuity and predictability to their life. Touching patients, speaking kindly and softly while maintaining a friendly facial expression are other ways to convey reassurance. Your voice intonation may be as calming as what you say, but specific words of reassurance are effective, too. For bed fast patients, attending to their basic physical care by providing water and assuring good bed positioning are important methods for providing tangible reassurance.

Education. In spite of the fact that their intellectual capabilities are impaired, many patients will benefit from a limited educational program about their condition. Repetition is important. Explanations about treatment procedures or anticipated changes should be repeated often and stated in simple terms. Frequent spoken reminders of the day, date, and location can help patients maintain their orientation. It is useful to instruct family members and other care providers about the patient's condition and appropriate treatment approach.

Behavioral Therapy

Behavioral techniques are useful for selected patients if their mental disorder is stabilized and not too severe. You can assist these patients by instituting simplified behavioral modification programs which reinforce adaptive behavior such as maintaining proper grooming, attending meals, and participating in group activities. Aversive techniques, modeling techniques, or complex contractual agreements are not suited for patients with organic brain syndromes.

Pharmacologic Therapy

Psychotropic medications can cause complications in many patients with an organic mental disorder and should be used judiciously. Psychotropic medications should be reserved for problems such as recurrent insomnia, intense restlessness or anxiety, aggressive behavior, and disruptive psychotic symptoms. (See the chapter on "Pharmacologic Therapy" for details about dosage, side effects, etc.).

A few words of caution are in order when prescribing medications for persons with organic brain syndromes. Psychotropic drugs are not a substitute for treating the underlying cause of brain dysfunction, and you should make every effort to alleviate the medical problem. Do not prescribe psychotropic medications for patients showing signs of central nervous system depression (e.g., stupor, lethargy, or reduced respiration, heart rate and blood pressure). In these cases, brain functioning already is impaired and psychotropic medications are likely to further accentuate the difficulty. Organic brain syndromes are often associated with serious medical conditions and psychotropic drugs may interact adversely with other prescribed medications or aggrevate the disease itself. However, if you determine that medications must be administered, in spite of the risks involved, initially use the least potent drug in the smallest dose necessary to achieve the desired effect. Even then, closely and regularly monitor your patient's progress. Be sure to reduce the customary dosage for elderly or debilitated patients.

For patients who demonstrate persistent or intense symptoms of restlessness, anxiety, insomnia or belligerence, use diazepam, 2 to 10 mgs. BID to TID. Commonly prescribed sedatives and hypnotics such as barbiturates typically worsen symptoms or cause over-sedation and confusion.

If a quicker onset of drug effect is desired, diazepam, 2 to 5 mgs. can be cautiously administered IV q2 to 4h to control symptoms of marked agitation or disruptive behavior. Diazepam also possesses anti-convulsant properties and is particularly useful for treatment of drug and/or alcohol withdrawal states during which seizures occur. Specific anti-convulsant medications such as diphenylhydantoin (Dilantin) are indicated if seizures become problematic. During some acute organic brain syndromes, it may be necessary to apply physical restraints to keep patients in bed or facilitate medical treatment. The restraints should be kept in place only so long as is absolutely necessary.

Because of the increased likelihood of complications, the major tranquilizers (neuroleptics, antipsychotics) are not recommended for controling the usual symptoms associated with organic brain syndromes. The major tranquilizers may be indicated, however, for patients who demonstrate delusions, hallucinations, agitation or belligerence. Haloperidol, 1 to 3 mgs. given BID to TID p.o. generally will control most of these symptoms. Special care should be taken when prescribing neuroleptics for elderly or debilitated patients.

Consultation and Referral

Consultation with other health care professionals about your patients may prove very beneficial. As mentioned earlier, patients with symptoms suggestive of an organic brain syndrome of recent onset always warrant immediate medical attention. Similarly, persons with a dementia should be periodically examined by a physician to evaluate their physical status.

Psychiatric consultation is indicated for patients who develop behavioral disturbances, psychosis, or need a specialized treatment approach. For patients needing residential care, financial aid, rehabilitation services or daily supervision, consultation should be requested from appropriate social agencies.

Now complete Self-Assessment Exercise #3 beginning on the following page.

Self-Assessment Exercise #3

1. Read the following case history and then answer the related questions.

   a. A 70-year-old man, Mr. Roberts, was admitted to a hospital for eye surgery. The surgeon explained that both of Mr. Roberts' eyes would be bandaged for several days after the operation. For each of the following areas of supportive psychological intervention, describe measures which could be done to reduce the likelihood of an organic brain syndrome.

      (1) environmental intervention

      (2) reassurance

      (3) education

   b. If Mr. Roberts developed persistent insomnia, prescribing a hypnotic medication may be indicated. Comment briefly on the appropriateness of prescribing each of the following for him.

      (1) phenobarbital, 60 mg. PO HS

      (2) diazepam, 2 mg. HS

      (3) secobarbital, 100 mg. HS

Self-Assessment Exercise #3 (Continued)

2. Each of the patients described below has an organic brain syndrome. Match each patient with the best medication prescription based on their symptoms. Each item may be used more than once or not at all.

   a. give no medication
   b. give chlorpromazine, 25 mg. IM
   c. give diazepam, 2 mg. PO
   d. give diazepam, 5 mg. IV
   e. apply physical restraints

_______(1) the patient took an overdose of barbiturates; she rarely shows spontaneous movements and seems lethargic; her respiratory rate is slowed

_______(2) the young man is intoxicated with alcohol; he demonstrates impaired coordination, slurred speech and an unsteady gait; his speech is loud but he is cooperative

_______(3) a woman sought your advise about her elderly father with whom she lived; she stated that he was troubled by persistent insomnia, confusion and restlessness at night; he was mildly forgetful during the day but was not otherwise difficult to manage

_______(4) while withdrawing from alcohol, the middle-aged man developed the delirium tremens; he became tremulous, agitated and anxious; he experienced visual hallucinations and began to convulse

3. For each of the patients listed below, briefly describe the type of consultation/referral needed.

   a. following a head injury, the young man became mentally confused and disoriented

Self-Assessment Exercise #3 (Continued)

3. b. an elderly woman with high blood pressure and heart problems develops assaultive behavior which is associated with a chronic brain syndrome

c. a young man is brought for evaluation of symptoms of an organic brain syndrome which followed his ingestion of an unknown type of street drug

d. a middle-aged woman with a chronic organic brain syndrome caused by alcohol can no longer care for herself

When you have completed this exercise to the best of your ability, check your answers with those on the following page.

Self-Assessment Exercise #3 - Feedback

1. a. The following measures may lessen the likelihood of Mr. Roberts developing an organic brain sydrome.

   (1) environmental intervention -- since Mr. Roberts' vision will be impaired, he would likely do better if his exposure to sound and tactile sensations were increased (e.g., a radio or T.V. in his room would be of help); similarly, a room with another patient would be preferable to his having a private room; helping him get acquainted with his surroundings and room prior to the surgery would be of value; frequent brief visitations with the staff and family should be encouraged; frequent discussions and reorienting him to his surroundings will help; ambulation with assistance as soon as is possible should be encouraged

   (2) reassurance -- verbal reassurance in the form of encouragement about his progress is important; he should have ready access and frequent visits with the staff and others; attentive physical care will provide an element of reassurance as well

   (3) education -- it is important for Mr. Roberts and his family to know what to expect about his surgery and treatment; the purpose of any medical procedures, bandages, medications, etc. should be simply and clearly explained; he should be told what to expect regarding ambulation privileges, his course of treatment, etc.

   b. (1) phenobarbital, 60 mg. -- this medication may cause a paradoxical effect in elderly patients resulting in confusion, restlessness, etc. and should not be prescribed

   (2) diazepam, 2 mg. -- both the medication and the dosage are appropriate

   (3) secobarbital, 100 mg. -- this medication should not be prescribed for the same reasons as was given in (1) above with respect to phenobarbital

Self-Assessment Exercise #3 - Feedback (Continued)

2.

__a__ (1) this patient shows evidence of central nervous system depression as evidenced by lethargy, decreased movements and decreased respiratory rate -- no medication for her organic brain syndrome should be given

__a__ (2) the young man shows all the signs of mild to moderate intoxication which is reversible and his behavior is not a significant problem -- no medication is needed

__c__ (3) diazepam may help sleep and to reduce restlessness

__d__ (4) in the presence of convulsions, agitation and anxiety due to alcohol withdrawal, diazepam, 5 mg. IV is appropriate

3. a. consultation with a physician should be requested immediately; the recent onset of symptoms of an OBS warrants medical evaluation

b. medical and/or psychiatric consultation should be sought; she will likely need medication, and her medical problems require careful evaluation before prescribing any drugs

c. medical/psychiatric consultation is needed to establish a correct diagnosis and treatment regimen

d. consult social agencies to arrange for custodial care

If your answers correspond closely with the above, continue reading on the next page. If not, please reread the preceding material.

SUMMARY

Organic brain syndromes are commonly encountered among individuals who are hospitalized with medical problems or who are over fifty. Typical mental status findings include generalized intellectual impairment, disorientation and recent memory deficits. Early diagnosis, along with prompt medical and psychological intervention will help to alleviate or reverse this disorder.

REFERENCES

Engle, G. and Romano, J., "Delirium: A Syndrome of Cerebral Insufficiency," Journal of Chronic Disorders, 9:260, 1959.

Freedman, A., Kaplan, H., and Sadock, B., Modern Synopsis of Comprehensive Psychiatry, Textbook II, Baltimore: Williams and Wilkins, 1976.

Morse, R. and Litin, E., "The Anatomy of a Delirium," American Journal of Psychiatry, 128:111, 1971.

Wells, C., "Dementia Reconsidered," Arch. General Psychiatry, 26-385, 1972.

CHAPTER 10. ANXIETY DISORDERS

Anxiety disorders comprise a group of psychological conditions in which anxiety is either felt directly or covertly present, but kept from overt expression by special mental coping mechanisms (e.g., compulsions, phobias, etc.). Complaints of anxiety are commonplace, and more prescriptions are written in the United States for anti-anxiety drugs than any other medications. Symptoms of anxiety result from many different causes and take varied forms. Many patients seek consultations because of physical symptoms which actually are secondary to underlying anxiety. Because anxiety disorders are common and manifested differently, it is important that you are thoroughly familiar with the varied findings of this syndrome. In this chapter we will discuss the diagnosis and general treatment approach of four subtypes of anxiety disorders, i.e., phobic, obsessive/compulsive, panic and generalized anxiety disorders.

LEARNING OBJECTIVES

By the time you complete this chapter, you should be able to do the following and apply the information to written case histories:

1. Describe the Mental Status Examination (M.S.E.) findings typical of anxiety disorders.

2. Describe the physical findings associated with tension and anxiety disorders.

3. Describe and distinguish between the following types of anxiety disorders:

   a. panic disorder (or anxiety neurosis)
   b. generalized anxiety disorder (or anxiety neurosis)
   c. phobic disorder (or phobic neurosis)
   d. obsessive/compulsive disorder (or obsessive/compulsive neurosis)

4. List three or more diseases and drugs which can cause symptoms of anxiety.

5. For each of the methods of therapeutic intervention listed below, describe the recommended approach and provide a rationale for its use in the management of anxiety disorders:

   a. supportive psychotherapy
   b. behavioral therapy
   c. pharmacologic therapy
   d. consultation and referral

GENERAL DIAGNOSTIC CONSIDERATIONS

Overview

Laypersons use the term "anxiety" when speaking about a wide-range of symptoms relating to nervousness and tension. However, for purposes of accurate diagnosis and treatment, a more precise definition is needed. Except in one aspect, anxiety duplicates the response experienced during intense fear. When confronted with an external danger or threatening situation, most persons develop feelings of apprehension, tension, and a variety of physical symptoms. In the case of a fear reaction, the cause can be identified and corrective action taken -- be it "flight or fight." With anxiety, however, the threat is psychological in nature and out of conscious awareness. Patients experience apprehension and disturbing physical symptoms but are unable to identify the cause or relieve their distress. The anxiety is therefore compounded by a marked sense of helplessness. Symptoms of anxiety can be acute or chronic, of varying intensity and are manifested in a variety of forms. Many persons during their lifetime experience episodes of anxiety which do not justify a psychiatric diagnosis. But when anxiety is persistent, intense enough to cause significant distress or interferes with daily functioning, then the diagnosis of an anxiety disorder is warranted.

Symptoms of anxiety can result from one or a combination of factors including an intense psychological conflict, a major life stress, and particular medical illnesses or drugs. However, the term "anxiety disorder" is reserved for conditions which meet specific criteria and are not a part of other psychopathologic conditions or caused by physical or environmental problems.

Medical conditions which can give rise to anxiety symptoms include hyperthyroidism, an abnormally low blood sugar level, and withdrawal from drugs or alcohol. Hallucinogens (L.S.D. and P.C.P.), central nervous system stimulants (e.g., amphetamines), or caffeinism (arising from excessive coffee or tea intake), all are capable of producing the physical and emotional findings characteristic of anxiety. Symptoms of anxiety also accompany other types of psychopathology such as acute schizophrenia, organic brain and affective disorders. The presence of any of these medical or psychological conditions preclude assigning the diagnosis of an anxiety disorder.

Physical Findings Associated with Anxiety Disorders

Bodily changes accompany all intense emotional states. Anxiety caused physical symptoms such as shortness of breath, dizziness, rapid heart rate, and others may prompt some persons to seek medical evaluation. The physical findings which accompany anxiety vary in type and intensity and are those which one would expect when the body is mobilized to meet a threat.

Several of these physical findings can be objectively demonstrated, including an elevation of blood pressure, pulse rate and respiration. Muscle tension and reflexes are increased, and there is usually evidence of restlessness and tremulousness, particularly of the hands. Pupils are often dilated and the skin appears either pale or flushed and may feel cold and clammy to touch.

The subjective physical complaints are many. Anxious individuals commonly describe feeling light-headed, dizzy or nauseated. They may experience muscular tension or pain in the chest, head and extremities. They may have sensations of air hunger or suffocation and breath rapidly. Prolonged over-breathing is termed "hyperventilation" and results in decreased blood levels of carbon dioxide which, in turn, gives rise to light-headedness, sensations of numbness and tingling about the face, mouth and upper extremities. These unpleasant sensations often further accentuate patient fears. A rapid and pounding heartbeat regularly accompanies anxiety and may cause worry that a "heart attack" is imminent. Patients also may complain of a dry mouth and urinary or bowel frequency.

The Mental Status Examination (M.S.E.)

An appraisal of M.S.E. findings will help indicate the severity and type of anxiety disorder present. Remember that the diagnosis of an anxiety disorder is not made if findings indicative of other major psychopathologic disorders are present.

Appearance. Unless symptoms are severe and lead to self-neglect, the appearance of individuals with anxiety is unremarkable. A possible exception are persons experiencing a panic disorder in which they may show signs of dilated pupils, rapid respiration, and an unkempt general physical appearance.

Behavior. The overall behavior of persons with anxiety is consistent with that feeling. Facial expression usually portrays apprehension and tenseness, perhaps with a furrowed brow. Speech is likely to be rapid, pressured, and often possesses a quavering quality. Physical behavior is typified by generalized restlessness and tremulousness. In contrast to many other psychopathologic conditions, patients usually seek out the therapist's help and insist on his immediate presence. Patient apprehension is often contagious and may evoke in the therapist transient feelings of tension.

Mood/Affect. Patient affect is characterized by pervasive fear, apprehension and worry, and also may show elements of helplessness, irritability or depression. The affect is appropriate to the thought content.

Perception. In anxiety disorders, illusions may be present, but hallucinations do not occur. If hallucinations are present, another type of psychopathology such as a functional psychosis or an organic brain disorder is likely.

Thinking. Persons experiencing anxiety are usually fully alert, often to the point of being hypervigilant and easily distractible by environmental stimuli. Intellectual functioning basically is intact, but if patients are particularly preoccupied, they may show an impaired ability for calculation, abstract thinking and recent memory. Orientation usually is within normal limits. Judgment for day-to-day living activities is satisfactory, but patients rarely possess more than superficial insight into the nature and causes of their emotional problems. Thought content typically reflects themes of apprehension and fear of impending personal catastrophe such as sudden death, insanity or losing emotional control. Various combinations of phobias, obsessions, and compulsions may be described, but no delusions are present. Many patients complain of experiencing depersonalization and a sense of marked helplessness. A transient associational disturbance may occur if anxiety is sufficiently intense.

Now complete Self-Assessment Exercise #1 beginning on the next page.

Self-Assessment Exercise #1

Indicate whether the following statements are true (T) or false (F).

_____ 1. Intensely anxious persons may evoke transient feelings of tension in their therapist.

_____ 2. Symptoms of anxiety regularly occur in a variety of psychopathologic disorders.

_____ 3. Many patients seek medical consultation primarily for physical symptoms which are secondary to anxiety.

_____ 4. The physical manifestations of intense fear and anxiety are identical.

_____ 5. The term "anxiety disorder" can be appropriately applied to symptoms of anxiety due to hyperthyroidism or the use of central nervous system stimulants.

_____ 6. Circle all of the following conditions in which symptoms of anxiety may be prominent.

a. during the acute stage of a functional psychosis

b. following the use of a central nervous system stimulant

c. a depression characterized by psychomotor retardation

d. an overdose of insulin which results in a low blood sugar level

e. a life threatening experience

f. an organic brain disorder associated with alcohol withdrawal

Self-Assessment Exercise #1 (Continued)

7. Circle the M.S.E. findings which are typical of anxiety disorders.

   a. psychomotor retardation

   b. auditory hallucinations

   c. an affect of fear/apprehension

   d. disorientation to time and place

   e. recurring unwanted thoughts

   f. a transient associational disturbance

   g. increased muscular activity, fidgetiness

   h. slowed, deliberate speech

   i. a dependent relationship towards the therapist

8. For each of the physiological processes listed below, indicate whether their response to intense anxiety will increase (I) or decrease (D).

   _____ a. pupil size

   _____ b. respiration rate

   _____ c. muscle tone

   _____ d. pulse rate

   _____ e. blood pressure

   _____ f. perspiration

When you have completed this exercise to the best of your ability, check your answers with those on the following page.

Self-Assessment Exercise #1 - Feedback

__T__ 1. Intensely anxious persons may evoke transient feelings of tension in their therapist.

__T__ 2. Symptoms of anxiety regularly occur in a variety of psychopathologic disorders.

__T__ 3. Many patients seek medical consultation primarily for physical symptoms which are secondary to anxiety.

__T__ 4. The physical manifestations of intense fear and anxiety are identical.

__F__ 5. The term "anxiety disorder" can be appropriately applied to symptoms of anxiety due to hyperthyroidism or the use of central nervous system stimulants.

6. The following conditions all may have prominent symptoms of anxiety:

   a. during the acute stage of a functional psychosis

   b. following the use of a central nervous system stimulant

   d. an overdose of insulin which results in a low blood sugar level

   e. a life threatening experience

   f. an organic brain disorder associated with alcohol withdrawal

7. The M.S.E. findings which are typical of anxiety disorders are:

   c. an affect of fear/apprehension

   e. recurring unwanted thoughts

   f. a transient associational disturbance

   g. increased muscular activity, fidgetiness

   i. a dependent relationship towards the therapist

Self-Assessment Exercise #1 - Feedback (Continued)

8. In the presence of intense anxiety, all of the following are increased:

   a. pupil size

   b. respiration rate

   c. muscle tone

   d. pulse rate

   e. blood pressure

   f. perspiration

If your answers correspond closely with those above, continue your reading on the following page; if not, please reread the material in the preceding section until you are confident you know it.

SUBTYPES OF ANXIETY DISORDERS

We will now discuss four subtypes of anxiety disorders, each of which is named according to unique clinical features, i.e., panic disorders, generalized anxiety disorders, phobic disorders, and obsessive/compulsive disorders. These disorders share in common the presence of anxiety -- either overtly experienced or released when certain conditions occur such as sudden confrontation with a feared situation. Formerly, these disorders were classified as neuroses or psychoneuroses. To help relate former with present DSM-III classification, the neurotic terminology will be presented in parenthesis.

Panic Disorders (or Anxiety Neurosis)

Panic disorders consist of recurring episodes of intense anxiety which are limited in duration from a few minutes to several hours. The emotional and physical findings associated with panic disorders reflect the findings expected in persons who are overwhelmed by extreme fear.

The onset of a panic disorder usually begins abruptly and patients experience rapidly escalating feelings of anxiety and apprehension, along with the equally disturbing physical symptoms described earlier. These persons commonly describe their experience as a sense of impending personal catastrophe in the form of a heart attack, suffocation, impending death, loss of emotional control or insantiy. Although the attacks are usually of short duration, the distress experienced is so disturbing that patients dread a recurrence. These episodes occur unpredictably and without a cause identifiable by most patients. Thus, to the frightening emotional and physical symptoms is added an element of helplessness. Patients are unable to anticipate the attacks or take corrective action because the precipitating factors cannot be identified. They can neither fight nor escape from the frightening feelings. Persons with a panic disorder may be symptom free between attacks, but more often are chronically subject to fluctuating degrees of mild anxiety. Other conditions can give rise to single episodes of anxiety and warrant the diagnosis of a panic disorder. Several episodes of intense anxiety should occur which are not associated with environmental stress or medically related conditions. In most instances, anxiety symptoms abruptly begin; rapidly reach a plateau and then gradually subside. Patients are left feeling physically exhausted and fearful of a subsequent attack.

Generalized Anxiety Disorders (or Anxiety Neurosis)

A generalized anxiety disorder is characterized by milder, but more persistent feelings of apprehension and physical symptoms than is the case of a panic reaction. The symptoms of anxiety wax and wane in intensity but patients are troubled by almost continuous emotional tension and related physical complaints over a several month period. Persons with generalized anxiety disorders can develop episodic panic attacks. This diagnosis is assigned only when no other psychopathologic condition or physical disorder is present.

Phobic Disorders (or Phobic Neurosis)

A phobic disorder is diagnosed when patients experience a persistent, unrealistic fear of an object, situation or activity which they will avoid as much as possible. Such individuals may be relatively free from anxiety symptoms until confronted with the object of their phobia. When such a confrontation occurs, patients will respond as if they were in danger and develop escalating anxiety. Patients usually acknowledge that their fear is excessive and "irrational," but are powerless to change their response. Phobias are common phenomena in children and are present in mild forms among many, otherwise normal adults. Only when a phobia significantly interferes with daily functioning, or is the source of marked personal distress should it be classified as a disorder.

Phobias take varied forms. A common phobia is agoraphobia, the fear of open places. Persons with agoraphobia usually fear leaving a place which is secure and familiar. They often experience anxiety if left alone or when traveling away from home unless accompanied by a close friend or relative. Agoraphobia can be so severe that patients literally become house-bound and functionally incapacitated. A related condition is a social phobia in which persons fear attending a social gathering or performing in public some activity (e.g., speaking or eating) from which could come criticism or embarrassment. Finally, many individuals suffer from a simple or specific phobia, i.e., the fear of a well-defined situation (being in a crowded place), object (dog or furry animals), or activity (riding in an elevator). Phobias like other symptoms of anxiety can occur in association with psychosis, organic brain disorders, and other emotional disturbances.

Obsessive/Compulsive Disorders (or Obsessive/Compulsive Neurosis)

The diagnosis of an obsessive/compulsive disorder is made when the most prominent symptoms consist of obsessions and/or compulsions which are not a manifestation of other types of psychopathology. As was described in the chapter on "The Mental Status Examination," obsessions are recurring, unwanted ideas or feelings which cannot be suppressed or put out of mind. Obsessions frequently involve impulses to perform some socially unacceptable behavior such as assaulting a respected person or yelling profanities in a public place. Persons with obsessions generally are fearful of acting upon their impulses. Most obsessed individuals have great difficulty in diverting their attention from the repetitious, unpleasant thoughts.

A compulsion is a behavior or ritualistic activity which must be performed in order to avoid feelings of anxiety. Common compulsions include an aversion to touching things believed to be unclean, counting particular objects, and the need to repeatedly wash personal belonging or hands to assure cleanliness. If the individuals are prevented from enacting their compulsive behavior, they will experience mounting tension and anxiety.

Obsessive and compulsive symptoms often appear simultaneously and can become so distracting and pervasive as to seriously interfere with daily functioning. When the symptoms reach that severity, they are classified as a disorder. Most patients realize that their obsessions and/or compulsions are inappropriate and undesirable but they, nevertheless, are unable to stop them.

Now complete Self-Assessment Exercise #2 beginning on the next page.

Self-Assessment Exercise #2

1. Select the letter indicating the anxiety disorder which most closely corresponds to the case description below:

   a. panic disorder (or anxiety neurosis)
   b. generalized anxiety disorder (or anxiety neurosis)
   c. phobic disorder (or phobic neurosis)
   d. obsessive/compulsive disorder (or obsessive/compulsive neurosis)

_____ (A) A young man sought medical attention because of an abrupt onset of marked apprehension, rapid pulse, and profuse sweating; he described fears of "going crazy" and complained of being unable to get enough air to breathe.

_____ (B) A musician complained of the need to wash his hands six times after touching anyone.

_____ (C) A woman experienced feelings of marked fear when asked to attend large social gatherings; she felt relatively relaxed when she was with family or friends.

_____ (D) A middle-aged man developed recurrent thoughts of striking his work supervisor; he was unable to rid himself of the aggressive impulses which frightened him.

_____ (E) A married woman sought consultation because of feeling chronically tense and "nervous" for over a year; she was troubled by loud noises, tended to become irritable, and felt persistently "uneasy and restless."

2. For each of the case vignettes on the next page, indicate the most appropriate diagnosis from the following:

   a. panic disorder
   b. generalized anxiety disorder
   c. phobic disorder
   d. obsessive/compulsive disorder
   e. symptoms of anxiety due to conditions <u>other</u> <u>than</u> an anxiety disorder

Self-Assessment Exercise #2 (Continued)

2.

_____ (A) A 20-year-old college student was brought for evaluation after developing symptoms of restlessness, insomnia, rapid heartbeat, tremulousness and feelings of an impending personal catastrophe. The symptoms began one hour after taking a large dose of a central nervous system stimulant (amphetamine).

_____ (B) Brenda Jones, a 37-year-old housewife, was brought for consultation by her husband. He stated that since the birth of their second child 3 months earlier, his wife had become socially withdrawn and acted strangely. She insisted on washing her infant 7 times a day to "ward off infection coming from atomic radiations in Russia," and became agitated if prevented from carrying out the baths. For similar reasons, she refused to shake hands or touch anyone. Mrs. Jones insisted on wearing rubber gloves throughout the day. M.S.E. findings showed that Mrs. Jones was fully oriented. She admitted hearing "voices" when no one else was around.

_____ (C) Ben Iverson, a successful insurance man turned down a promotion because it would require him to fly to yearly meetings at a distant city. He described becoming "intensely nervous" even when thinking of being in a plane, much less getting into one. He acknowledged that his fears were unfounded but could not overcome them.

_____ (D) Following an argument with her husband, a young woman developed symptoms of increasing physical tension, restlessness, dizziness and fears that she was going to faint. She appeared pale, tremulous and was gasping for breath. A physical examination was essentially normal, except for a slightly elevated blood pressure and heart rate. The woman related that she had experienced seven similar episodes within the past 4 months. She took no medication.

When you have completed this exercise to the best of your ability, check your answers with those on the following page.

Self-Assessment Exercise #2 - Feedback

1. The following are the correct diagnoses:

   __a__ (A) (panic disorder)

   __d__ (B) (obsessive/compulsive disorder)

   __c__ (C) (phobic disorder)

   __d__ (D) (obsessive/compulsive disorder)

   __b__ (E) (generalized anxiety disorder)

2. The following are the correct diagnoses:

   __e__ (A) The symptoms of anxiety were secondary to a drug and, hence, cannot be classified as a panic (anxiety) disorder.

   __e__ (B) Mrs. Jones' compulsive behavior occurs in association with a functional psychosis and cannot be classified as an obsessive/compulsive (anxiety) disorder.

   __c__ (C) (phobic disorder)

   __a__ (D) (panic disorder)

If your answers correspond closely with those above, continue your reading on the following page; if not, please reread the material in the preceding section until you are confident you know it.

THERAPEUTIC INTERVENTIONS

Supportive Psychotherapy

Many principles presented in the chapter on "Supportive Psychotherapy" can be successfully applied to anxiety disorders, but keep in mind that treatment should be individualized and based on the type and intensity of symptoms.

Directive guidance. In most cases, you should take a directive approach with anxious patients, particularly during a panic attack. At such times, they seek an authoritative person who can assist with important decisions and act as a stabilizing influence. Encourage patients to depend upon you until their anxiety subsides and they can manage without your support.

Ventiliation. It is therapeutic for anxious persons to express their thoughts, feelings and fears. Their symptoms are frightening, and most patients are helpless to deal with them. Putting feelings into words serves as an outlet for tension and simultaneously helps them to feel less isolated. Friends and relatives rarely know how to deal with anxiety in others, and tend to discourage patients from talking about their complaints. As patients tell their story, listen carefully so that you can identify factors which brought about the symptoms. Listen especially for changes or stress in interpersonal relationships, finances, or health, and problems at work or home. If patients appear very restless, initially allow them to smoke, stand or even pace about the room. It will help to discharge their tension. Later, suggest that they speak more slowly, sit down and deliberately relax their muscles. Speak unhurriedly and calmly, yourself. Such behavior on your part will have a calming effect. Only if patients show signs of escalating anxiety while talking about specific topics should you direct them to more neutral ones.

Education. If patient symptoms are severe, it will be difficult for them to focus attention on anything other than their anxiety. But after the symptoms subside, it may be possible to help them gain understanding about the origins and nature of their disorder. For example, explain that the attacks are time-limited and can be brought under control by therapy and medications. Help patients understand the anxiety and that however unbearable it may presently seem, the unpleasant feelings will always subside. Learning that the symptoms will decrease after a short time will enable them to tolerate future attacks. Make the point that symptoms are related to specific life events which can be identified and action taken to correct them. Teach patients to look for life events which aggrevate the symptoms and help develop more adaptive ways to cope with those circumstances.

Inform patients that they will experience emotional tension and various physical complaints from time to time, but that these symptom do not indicate serious disease or other psychopathology. Answer ques tions about their condition in clear and simple terms and keep them fully apprized about prescribed treatment and medications.

Teach your patients to cope with the physical accompaniments of anxiety. For example, if they are troubled by recurring episodes of hyperventilation, demonstrate how to breathe into a paperbag to reduce the symptoms caused by over-breathing. Provide simple muscle relax ing techniques which can be used at times of mounting tension. Similar ly, raise resistance to stress by making sure that patients include in their daily schedule adequate time for physical exercise, social and recreational interests, and sufficient sleep. Recommend that the intake of stimulants such as caffein in the form of coffee, tea or coke be kept low.

Environmental intervention. The symptoms of anxiety can be precipitated by specific factors and/or an accumulation of tension from many sources. Identify as many of the sources of stress as you can, and systematically work to alleviate them. Investigate especially patients' home and work environment. Patients who are flooded with anxiety have trouble functioning and may need relief from their usual responsibilities. Recommending absences from school or work or arranging for temporary help in the home can be of benefit. It is generally not helpful for persons with an anxiety disorder to be without a structured routine or left just to think about their problems. Hospitalization is rarely indicated, but these persons need help to devise a daily routine which includes therapeutic activities -- ones that do not require a great deal of concentration or precision, and yet are productive. Repetitive obsessions and compulsions can be alleviated by encouraging patients to engage in physical activities such as washing the car, cleaning out closets and gardening. Physical exercise such as jogging, gardening, scrubbing floors provides an excellent means to reduce physical and emotional tension, and should be encouraged in your patient's daily routine. Be sure that the patient's environment provides the right combination of social interactions, physical activities and rest.

Reassurance. Patient feelings of anxiety and helplessness will lesser if your words and actions convey a sense of confidence and authority. Move and speak deliberately and in an unhurried fashion; give direct assurance and emotional support when needed. Don't promise that whic you can't deliver; such as a quick cure, but convey a feeling of therapeu optimism.

Persons with anxiety disorders feel greatly reassured by your presence and knowing that they can depend upon you for ongoing support.

Reinforce your availability by assuring patients easy access to you by telephone, and schedule appointments at a frequency based upon their emotional needs. If your patients are experiencing recurring anxiety episodes, arrange to meet with them for brief periods (10 to 15 minutes), at frequent intervals (daily or semi-weekly) until the symptoms improve. Gradually extend the time between consultations as the complaints subside. Some patients feel less helpless about their condition if they develop insight about the factors which influence their symptoms. Whenever possible, offer explanations which help them identify and cope with the anxiety provoking events. Many patients will need specific reassurance that their emotional and physical complaints do not indicate serious medical illness or impending insanity.

Now complete Self-Assessment Exercise #3 beginning on the next page.

Self-Assessment Exercise #3

Answer the questions which follow this case vignette.

1. A distraught college student is brought to you for evaluation. He is markedly tense, restless and paces about the consultation room. He appears fearful and describes worries that he is losing his mind. The student's speech is rapid and has a quavering quality. He appeals to you for help.

   A. Briefly characterize the guidance approach which should be used in dealing with him.

   B. Should you carefully structure the interview or allow him to talk fully with minimal intervention? Why?

   After 20 minutes the intensity of his symptoms subsides and he describes feeling calmer but physically fatigued. He relates that he has had almost daily attacks of anxiety of increasing severity for the past two weeks. You agree to meet with him and provide supportive therapy.

   C. What criteria would you follow in determining how frequently you should schedule consultations?

   D. He lives by himself and spends most of his time studying. What recommendations about his schedule could you make that may help to reduce his anxiety and physical tension?

When you have completed this exercise to the best of your ability, check your answers with those on the following page.

Self-Assessment Exercise #3 - Feedback

1. A. In dealing with persons who are severely anxious, your demeanor should be calm, deliberate and authoritative.

   B. It is usually therapeutic for anxious persons to freely ventilate their thoughts, feelings and fears. This helps them to release emotional tension and feel less isolated from others because of their problems.

   C. You should schedule the frequency of consultations in accordance with the patient's emotional needs. If he is very anxious and experiences frequent attacks, see him often, daily if necessary. Reduce the consultations as his symptoms subside in severity.

   D. The student's current daily routine seems overly isolated and focused only on study. Suggest that he study less, socialize more and include daily vigorous physical activity to discharge some of his tension and anxiety.

If your answers correspond closely with those above, continue your reading on the following page; if not, please reread the material in the preceding section until you are confident you know it.

THERAPEUTIC INTERVENTIONS (CONTINUED)

Behavioral Therapy

Patients with phobias may respond favorably to behavior modification (see the chapter on "Behavioral Therapy"). After carefully evaluating the characteristics of the phobic behavior, a therapy which utilizes systematic desensitization can be implemented. Such a program is exemplified by the following situation: assume that an individual has a strong aversion to riding elevators and wants to overcome his fear. A therapy program can be designed which encourages the patient to use the elevator in gradually increasing amounts. The patient begins by first standing in an unmoving elevator. As he is able to overcome the feelings of anxiety which arise from being in the elevator, he then should be encouraged to ride a single floor. As he becomes comfortable in doing that, he then can be asked to ride a second floor and so on. Behavior modification is a more complex process than is represented here, but the basic approach is comparable. Behavioral therapy generally is less successful in patients who lack motivation, have multiple phobias, or other psychological symptoms.

Behavior therapy which emphasizes muscle relaxation techniques or biofeedback have been successfully used in reducing physical and psychological symptoms associated with anxiety. Research has shown that feelings of anxiety are relatively incompatible with a state of physical relaxation. In this therapy form, patients are first taught to physically relax. They then are asked to imagine being in the situation which evokes anxiety, e.g., giving a public speech, flying, using an elevator, etc. As they fantasize being present in the dreaded situation, the physical and psychological responses of anxiety develop. The patients then are instructed to relax their muscles as trained, breathe slowly and focus on calm thoughts. The anxiety and physical tension usually will subside. After this procedure has been sufficiently practiced, patients will be able to fantasize in the aversive situation with little or no anxiety. This newly learned response can then be applied to an actual life circumstance.

Patients also can be taught to control symptoms of tension and anxiety by using the biofeedback techniques described in the chapter on "Behavioral Therapy."

Pharmacologic Therapy

As mentioned earlier, medications such as diazepam and chlordiazepoxide are over-prescribed for symptoms of anxiety and should be given judiciously. The target symptoms most susceptible to drugs are the psychological and physical manifestations of panic and generalized anxiety disorder. Diazepam and chlordiazepoxide have limited success in treating phobic and obsessive/compulsive disorders.

Unfortunately, many therapists erroneously believe that prescribed medications are the most important elements of their therapy. In actuality, it is the therapist's unhurried attentiveness and reassuring presence which is more beneficial. It is almost always possible to "talk a patient down" from feelings of intense anxiety. It is tempting to respond to the patient's urgent need to do something by administering a drug, but prescribing medication has its drawbacks -- not the least of which are physical side effects and the prospect of developing psychological dependency.

For individuals who insist on medication or are so anxious that they require medicinal relief, diazepam or chlordiazepoxide in doses of 5 to 10 mgs. TID or 25 mgs. TID respectively, are suitable. These medications lose their effectiveness and may cause dependency if taken longer than two or three weeks. However, they cause fewer complications than sedatives (such as barbiturates) which are still prescribed for symptoms of anxiety. It is best to prescribe anti-anxiety drugs sparingly and only for acute, severe symptoms. As a rule, administer these medications orally rather than by injection. Anti-anxiety drugs given I.M. are not well absorbed, and I.V. administration carries the risk of an adverse physical response. Anti-psychotic drugs (the major tranquilizers) should be prescribed only in cases of severe anxiety which does not respond to diazepam or chlordiazepoxide or where there is a special risk of developing dependency.

Referral/Consultation

By using the treatment methods outlined above, most patients with anxiety disorders can be successfully treated without referral, but some may need specialized care or evaluation for reasons which we will now outline.

Referral to a mental health specialist should be considered for patients whose symptoms worsen or do not respond to usual supportive measures and medication. Patients with long-standing; obsessive/compulsive disorders frequently are refractory to supportive treatment alone and may require intensive therapy which only specially-trained psychotherapists can provide. Psychiatric consultation is indicated when anxiety, phobias or obsessive/compulsive behavior are symptomatic of more severe underlying pathology such as psychosis. Referral to a specialist for behavioral modification may be helpful for treating persistent phobias. If you suspect that symptoms of anxiety are disease related, request evaluation by a competent physician. Finally, some persons may wish to develop a deeper understanding of their emotional problems and it is appropriate to refer them to a well-trained psychotherapist. Be sure to prepare your patients for the referral by explaining what they can expect from the consultant in terms of treatment, cost and time.

Now complete Self-Assessment Exercise #4 beginning on the next page.

Self-Assessment Exercise #4

Answer the questions which follow the case vignettes.

1. A young man sought therapy because of a long-standing fear of furry animals. When near dogs or cats he would develop feelings of intense anxiety, rapid breathing, dizziness, and a sensation that he was about to "pass out." He did not have symptoms of other psychopathology. Comment on the appropriateness of the following treatment approaches.

   A. Prescribing an anti-anxiety drug for his symptoms.

   B. Tell him to "Pull yourself together. The animals won't hurt you."

   C. Refer him to a behavioral therapist for systematic desensitization.

Self-Assessment Exercise #4 (Continued)

2. A man of 28 complained of increasing anxiety and the need to wash his hands and feet many times a day because of the belief that "someone is out to contaminate me with germs and viruses." He steadfastly maintained this belief despite reassurances to the contrary. He also felt that strangers on the street were talking about him and could read his mind. Comment on the appropriateness of the following treatment approaches to the patient.

   A. Refer the patient to an experienced psychotherapist for further evaluation and/or treatment.

   B. Prescribe an anti-anxiety medication such as diazepam for his symptoms.

When you have completed this exercise to the best of your ability, check your answers with those on the following page.

Self-Assessment Exercise #4 - Feedback

1. A. The patient has a chronic phobic disorder and experiences anxiety only when confronted with furry animals. Anti-anxiety drugs are indicated for alleviating acute symptoms of anxiety. These medications provide little benefit for a phobic disorder.

   B. Appealing to his willpower or superficial reassurances that no actual danger exists will not benefit this patient. His phobia is an automatic response to a psychological threat and quite beyond his control.

   C. His phobia is a single and specific one. He appears motivated for help and systematic desensitization is an appropriate treatment option.

2. A. This patient shows evidence of serious psychopathology (i.e., psychosis) in addition to his obsessive/compulsive symptoms. He should be referred to a psychiatrist for further evaluation.

   B. The patient demonstrates delusional thinking, along with anxiety. Anti-anxiety medications, including diazepam, are not usually effective for treating psychotic symptoms and, therefore, are not recommended. Antipsychotic medications such as haloperidol or thiothixene are more appropriate for reducing this patient's anxiety.

If your answers correspond closely with those above, continue your reading on the following page; if not, please reread the material in the preceding section until you are confident you know it.

SUMMARY

The psychological and physical manifestation of anxiety are common and may occur in association with a variety of medical, situational and psychopathologic conditions. However, the term "anxiety disorder" is reserved for conditions in which manifestations of anxiety are directly or indirectly expressed, interfere with daily functioning, and are not related to other psychiatric syndromes. In this chapter four subtypes of disorders are defined according to whether anxiety is intense and episodic (panic), chronic and persistent (generalized) or is manifested indirectly through mental mechanisms, such as phobias, obsessions and/or compulsions. Despite the wide-spread practice of prescribing psychotropic drugs for psychological and physical tension, these medications are not recommended for the long-term management of anxiety disorders. Supportive psychotherapy and behavior modification techniques are useful for alleviating symptoms of anxiety disorders.

REFERENCES

American Psychiatric Association, *Diagnostic and Statistical Manual of Mental Disorders*, 3rd Ed., Washington, D.C., 1978.

Cadoret, R. and King, L., *Psychiatry in Primary Care*, St. Louis: C. V. Mosby Co., 1974.

Feighner, J., Robins, E., et al, "Diagnostic Criteria for Use in Psychiatric Research," *Arch. Gen. Psychiatry*, 26:57, 1972.

Freedman, A., Kaplan, H. and Sadock, B., *Modern Synopsis of Comprehensive Textbook of Psychiatry*, 2nd Ed., Baltimore: Williams & Wilkins Co., 1976.

Woodruff, R., Goodwin, D. and Guze, S., *Psychiatric Diagnosis*, New York: University Press, 1979.

CHAPTER 11. SUBSTANCE USE DISORDERS

Man's interest in taking intoxicants to induce pleasurable feelings goes back thousands of years, but with the possible exception of alcohol, drug abuse did not constitute a significant health problem for most western countries prior to World War II. Since the 1950's, however, the situation has dramatically changed. The "liberalization" of social attitudes and advertising campaigns by manufacturers exhorting the public to take vitamins, aspirin, sleep aids and other chemicals to "feel good" or reduce tension has resulted in a generation which looks to medication to solve many of their life problems. These, plus other social factors, have lead to unprecedented drug experimentation and usage among teenagers and young adults. Drug and alcohol dependency now constitutes a major health problem because the chemical intoxicants so widely used often cause serious psychological, social and physical problems.

At the present time, literally dozens of chemical substances are taken by mouth, injected or inhaled to alter central nervous system functioning and bring about changes in mood, behavior and perception. Unfortunately, an ever increasing number of persons are developing serious social, health and psychological consequences because of drugs; they are diagnosed as having substance use disorders. In this chapter we will present basic information about terminology relating to substance use disorders, typical behavioral patterns associated with drug dependency, and a review of the characteristics of drugs commonly used. A description of the medical management of persons with substance use disorders is beyond the scope of this chapter, but we will discuss general principles of therapeutic management which will enable you to work more effectively with patients who are drug dependent.

LEARNING OBJECTIVES

By the time you complete this chapter, you should be able to do the following and apply the information to written case histories:

1. Correctly describe and use the following terms:

    a. substance use disorder
    b. psychological (psychic) dependence
    c. physical dependence
    d. withdrawal (abstinence) syndrome/tolerance
    e. substance dependence

2. Describe four etiologic factors important in the development of a substance abuse disorder.

3. List the personality traits common to individuals susceptible to developing a substance abuse disorder and finding of history which suggest a worsening of the disorder.

4. For each of the types of classes of drugs listed below, indicate the potential for causing:

    a. actual physical (body organ) disease
    b. psychological dependency
    c. physical dependency and a withdrawal syndrome

    Substances:

    a. alcohol
    b. barbiturates/sedatives and hypnotics
    c. opiates
    d. cocaine
    e. amphetamines and related C.N.S. stimulants
    f. cannabis
    g. hallucinogens (L.S.D., P.C.P., etc.)
    h. inhaled solvents

5. For each of the methods of therapeutic intervention listed below, describe the recommended approach and provide a rationale for its use in the management of persons with substance abuse disorders.

    a. supportive psychotherapy
    b. behavioral therapy
    c. pharmacologic therapy
    d. consultation and referral

TERMINOLOGY

When communicating about substance use disorders, it is important that the meaning of the terms used are clearly understood. In this chapter, the term "substance" refers to any chemical (including alcohol, opiates, amphetamines, etc.), which is taken to produce changes of mood, perception or behavior. We will use "chemical substance", "drug", and "intoxicants" interchangeably. The diagnosis "substance use disorder" is applied to individuals who persistently use alcohol and/or drugs in ways which are detrimental to themselves or others. More will be said later about this diagnostic category. This diagnosis refers to patterns of drug-taking behavior, but does not include the effects and mental responses resulting from the drugs. The latter findings are classified as organic mental disorders and are described in this chapter.

In recent years the words addiction and habituation mistakenly have been used interchangeably when describing patient responses to drugs. In order to clarify communication, both words have been replaced by the broader term "drug dependency" which is defined as an individual's continued psychological and physical need for intoxicating chemicals.

It is useful for treatment purposes to have terms which indicate the special physical and psychological effects caused by some chemical intoxicants. Psychological (psychic) dependency is the compelling emotional need and desire to repeatedly take a chemical substance to achieve a feeling of well-being and/or reduce emotional tension. Psychological dependency usually implies that the patient is unable by self-control alone to reduce consumption of the drug.

Tolerance, physical dependency, and a withdrawal (abstinence) syndrome are interrelated terms and conditions. The body frequently undergoes significant physiological alterations as it attempts to accommodate to the presence of some drugs. Repeated use of certain substances such as alcohol, sedatives or opiates results in physical changes which cause a tolerance to the drugs, that is, an ever-increasing amount of the drug is necessary to produce the same effect formerly brought about by smaller doses. In most instances, when tolerance develops, the body's metabolism has been modified in a way which requires the presence of the drug if regular functioning is to continue without disruption. A state of physical dependence then exists. If after physical dependence has been established the drug is abruptly decreased below a critical level, the body must then dramatically readjust its functioning. During the process of readjustment, various physical signs and symptoms occur which comprise a withdrawal (abstinence) syndrome. Every body organ system is involved to some degree during a withdrawal syndrome, and the resultant psychological and physical manifestations depend on the chemical action and duration of the drug taken, the dosage used, and the patient's state of health. Withdrawal symptoms can be mild and require little intervention or they can be life threatening, and necessitate hospitalization along with vigorous medical treatment. Common manifestations of a withdrawal syndrome are headache, tremulousness, nausea and vomitting, tension, depression, and irritability.

Some chemical substances (i.e., hallucinogens) can be taken regularly over extended periods without development of tolerance and physical dependence, while other drugs such as opiates (e.g., heroin) are capable of causing physical dependency after use for only a few days. More will be said later about which drugs cause physical dependency.

CRITERIA FOR DIAGNOSING SUBSTANCE USE DISORDERS

In our society the moderate use of some chemical intoxicants (e.g., alcohol, tobacco, and caffein) is sanctioned for normal or so-called "recreational" purposes. Taking certain drugs (e.g., heroin) or the excessive consumption of some intoxicants (e.g., alcohol) is considered illegal and/or pathological. In this chapter we will present criteria which help to discriminate between the normal use of drugs and when a pathologic condition (i.e., a substance use disorder) is present.

Before the diagnosis of a substance use disorder can be applied, specific criteria must be met with respect to the duration and type of problematic behavior which a patient demonstrates. Drug use should constitute a problem for longer than one month. In other words, the diagnosis of a substance use disorder defines a pattern of behavior extending over time, and by definition, excludes brief or isolated incidents of intoxication. This criteria distinguishes between occasional drug use and actual dependency upon it. Furthermore, to warrant the diagnosis of a substance use disorder, persistent drug use should result in serious consequences to the patient's life in the form of impaired relationships, health or routine functioning. Discretely question your patient about several key areas of his life with respect to drug use. Inquire especially about any disruption of important relationships such as marital separation and divorce. Legal difficulties such as multiple arrests because of drug-related accidents and intoxication or the development of recurrent or serious physical illness (e.g., infections and liver abnormalities) which are attributable to drugs, strongly suggesting the presence of a substance use disorder. Of equal significance is impairment of daily functioning, such as faltering performance at work or a loss of a job. Finding indications of psychological and/or physical dependence on drugs or alcohol usually indicates the presence of a substance use disorder. If one or more of these findings occur, then the limits of normal "recreational use" of an intoxicating substance has been exceeded and it is likely that a substance use disorder is present. According to the newly developed definitions (DSM-III), an individual is diagnosed as "substance dependent" if he shows the findings just described and, in addition, is physically dependent upon the drug he has used. A substance use disorder can accompany any type of psychopathology including personality disorders, schizophrenic disorders, affective disorders and others.

Now complete Self-Assessment Exercise #1 beginning on the next page.

Self-Assessment Exercise #1

1. For each of the case vignettes below, correctly apply one (or more) of the following terms:

   a. tolerance development
   b. psychological dependency
   c. physical dependency
   d. withdrawal (abstinence) syndrome
   e. a substance use disorder is present
   f. a substance use disorder is not present

_______ (1) A 37-year-old man found it necessary to take ever increasing amounts of alcohol over several months to function at work and control symptoms of tremulousness and nausea.

_______ (2) A 22-year-old housewife described a need to regularly smoke marijuana in order "to feel good"; she disclaimed any increase in her consumption of the drug or that it interfered in any way with her daily functioning.

_______ (3) A college student occasionally uses PCP (phencyclidine) on weekends to "get high."

_______ (4) A middle-aged woman seeks consultation requesting a prescription for aspirin compound with codeine; she related that four months earlier she started taking the medication once or twice a day because of "migraine" headaches; she stated that she now must take 6 to 8 tablets a day to achieve the same effect and if she omits the medication she feels "shaky", irritable and nauseated.

2. George Martin sought consultation at the insistence of his wife because of an alleged "drinking problem." Mr. Martin emphatically disclaimed that he drinks excessively. List 3 or more areas of his life about which you should inquire to determine if he indeed has a substance use disorder.

When you have completed this exercise to the best of your ability, check your answers with those on the following page.

Self-Assessment Exercise #1 - Feedback

1.

a,b,c,e (1) The 37-year-old man needed increasing amounts of alcohol to function at work and avoid more severe symptoms of withdrawal. He has developed a tolerance to alcohol and is psychologically and physically dependent upon it. He qualifies for a diagnosis of a substance use disorder.

b,f (2) The young housewife is psychologically dependent upon marijuana. However, since using the drug apparently has not caused her problem in health or daily living she does not have a substance use disorder.

f (3) Occasional use of PCP does not meet the criteria for diagnosing a substance use disorder and no tolerance or dependency is described.

a,b,c,d,e (4) The woman has developed a tolerance to codeine and is physically and psychologically dependent upon the drug. She has used the medication for longer than 9 months and therefore meets the criteria for having a substance use disorder.

2. To help determine whether Mr. Martin is alcohol dependent and has a substance use disorder, inquire if alcohol use has caused:

disruptions in important relationships, legal problems, serious medical illnesses (liver problems, pancreatitis, etc.), impairment of daily/work activities, psychological or physical dependence.

If your answers correspond closely with those above, continue your reading on the following page; if not, please reread the material in the preceding section until you are confident you know it.

ETIOLOGIC FACTORS

Substance use disorders occur in persons from all socioeconomic, ethnic and racial groups, although the incidence of drug-related problems within these groups varies considerably. For example, alcoholism is much more common among Irish-Americans than the general population and less frequent among Jews and first generation Asians. No single hypothesis satisfactorily explains the etiology of substance use disorders in all cases, and many investigators believe that a combination of conditioned learning, genetic, psychological and socio-environmental factors are implicated. We will briefly review some of these theories of etiology.

There is evidence that drug dependency is learned behavior which is perpetuated according to principles of conditioning. Soon after taking a drug or alcohol, an individual experiences relief from emotional "pain" such as anxiety or depression, and develops instead a feeling of well-being and relaxation. These pleasurable feelings act strongly to reinforce the drug-taking behavior which caused them. Research findings suggest that in some cases the development of drug dependency may be influenced by genetic factors. Alcoholism, for instance, tends to run in families and some in-bred ethnic groups such as the American-Indian. It is hypothesized that these individuals inherit genetic defects which impair their ability to metabolize alcohol or that they possess an unusual physical sensitivity which leads to an intense psychological craving for intoxication.

Psychological factors are also important. Many individuals with substance use disorders describe a history of long-standing psychological problems and frequently are diagnosed as having anti-social or dependent personality disorders. They usually are troubled by chronic feelings of low self-esteem, insecurity and persistent anxiety and depression. These individuals generally are excessively dependent on others for emotional support and direction. They often lack self-assertiveness and do poorly in interpersonal relationships. Such persons have little capacity for delaying gratification and when frustrated, tend to act impulsively with little thought for long-term consequences.

Socio-environmental factors, too, play a significant role in the causation of substance use disorders. Studies have shown that the early family environment of drug dependent individuals often is emotionally and financially impoverished and unstable. Substandard housing, separation or divource are frequent findings among drug-dependent adults, and there is a greater incidence of emotional and drug-related problems among their parents. Many of these patients describe feeling that they lacked consistent discipline and affection and did not have an adequate opportunity for constructive pursuits or recreation. An unstable home environment which is depressing and oppressing frequently leads teenagers to turn elsewhere for support and many were introduced to drug use during their teen years largely as a result of peer pressure to "join the gang."

Signs of Worsening Drug/Alcohol Dependence

Several findings may signal that an individual's drug dependency may be worsening. Listen especially for statements which indicate that your patient is using drugs or alcohol more frequently and/or in larger amounts. It is likewise significant when drug-taking behavior assumes a place of increasing importance in your patient's daily life -- that he is spending more time thinking and talking about "getting high" than formerly was the case. Your patient may drop hints that controlling the frequency and amount of drugs that he is using is difficult -- whereas drug-taking was restricted before to weekend, "recreational use", it now has become a regular means to escape an ever expanding variety of life problems. Signs of impaired work performance or trouble with interpersonal relationships, likewise may signify increasing drug use. Unfortunately, as your patient's drug consumption increases, so does his tendency to minimize and deny the adverse consequences which it is having upon his life.

DRUG CHARACTERISTICS

In order to formulate an appropriate treatment plan, it is important that you are familiar with the characteristics of the drug which your patient has used. We will review several classes of commonly taken drugs in terms of their effect on the central nervous system, typical behavioral manifestations, and potential for developing physical dependence, and causing actual body organ disease.

It is useful to evaluate your patient's behavioral response to the chemical substance which he has taken. Noting whether your patient is behaviorally over- or under-active may help to determine the general class of the drug which was taken. A word of caution is needed when attempting to identify the cause of your patient's unusual behavior because a number of other types of legitimately prescribed medications and/or medical conditions can either excite or depress the central nervous system. As a general rule, alcohol, barbiturates, other sedatives and opiates react to depress the functions of the central nervous system, whereas cocaine, amphetamines, and benzedrine act as central nervous system stimulants. In this section we will discuss the following chemical substances: ethyl alcohol, barbiturates, and related sedatives, opiates, amphetamines, cannabis, hallucinogens, and inhaled solvents.

Central Nervous System Depressants

Ethyl alcohol. Ethyl alcohol is the most widely used intoxicant for all age groups. Although alcohol is socially sanctioned and often portrayed as the intoxicant of sophistication, more personal disability and economic loss occurs yearly from its use than all other drugs combined. The pathological use of alcohol now constitutes the most serious drug problem among teenagers and adults, far surpassing that of all other drugs including sedatives, L.S.D., P.C.P., heroin and others.

Alcohol is rapidly absorbed from the gastrointestinal tract, and its early effects cause emotional disinhibition, excitability, and mild euphoria. Nevertheless, alcohol acts primarily as a central nervous system depressant, and within several minutes will produce a slowing of speech, thinking, and reaction time. The effects of alcohol are dose related and range from mild intoxication to stupor, respiratory depression and death.

Psychological dependency to alcohol is readily established and tolerance occurs. Physical dependence develops when alcohol is injested in large quantities over a period of several weeks. If alcohol consumption is then dramatically decreased, a withdrawal syndrome characterized by psychological and physical reactions will begin within 24 to 72 hours. The most severe form of the alcohol withdrawal syndrome is the delirium tremens (the DT's), a toxic condition manifested by mental confusion, delusions, hallucinations, and serious medical complications. Without prompt and expert medical treatment, the delirium tremens may cause death in approximately 10% of cases. The pathological effect of alcohol upon the central nervous system is greatly increased by the simultaneous use of many other prescribed and illicit drugs.

In contrast to many other intoxicants which are in common use, persistent and excessive alcohol consumption usually results in irreversible tissue damage in the brain, digestive tract, liver and heart. Coronary artery disease, cirrhosis of the liver, gastritis, pancreatitis, malnutrition, and organic brain disorders are diseases frequently associated with prolonged, excessive alcohol intake. The medical effect of alcohol abuse in our country is enormous, and alcohol related disease now ranks among the top ten causes of death in adults.

Sedatives and hypnotics. Barbiturates (phenobarbitol, secobarbitol, etc.) and most other sedatives and hypnotics (e.g., chloralhydrate, ethchlorvynol (Placidyl), methaqualone (Quaalude) also act as central nervous system depressants. Consequently, these drugs are considered "downers," that is, they cause muscle and body relaxation, sleepiness, a diminution of instinctual drives, and psychological and physiological depression. Psychological dependence on sedatives is often marked and development of tolerance and physical dependency begins after a few days of moderate use. If a substantial physical dependency has been established, and the intake of drugs is abruptly reduced, a severe withdrawal syndrome characterized by delirium, mental confusion and seizures may result. An overdose (OD) of any of these substances can lead to coma, respiratory arrest and death. The risk of serious medical complications arising from sedatives is increased dramatically when they are combined with alcohol.

Opiates. The opiates (narcotics and analgesics) which include substances such as morphine, meperidine (Demerol), heroin, codeine, and others also exert a depressant effect on the central nervous system and produce feelings of calm, euphoria, drowsiness, and generalized relaxation. The repeated use of these drugs causes a rapid development of tolerance and psychological and physical dependence. After physical dependence has occurred, a withdrawal syndrome follows an abrupt reduction of the drug. The withdrawal process is an unpleasant and stressful experience, but usually does not bring about the serious medical complications which are associated with withdrawal from alcohol or sedatives. Like other central nervous system depressants, an overdose can lead to respiratory depression and death. Because the IV route of administration of opiates is frequently selected, many drug dependent persons are at risk to develop diseases such as serum hepatitis, and infections of the heart and blood vessels the result of using improperly sterilized needles and equipment.

Now complete Self-Assessment Exercise #2 beginning on the next page.

Self-Assessment Exercise #2

1. David Jordan was referred by his supervisor for psychological evaluation because of repeated absence from work. His supervisor suspected that the excessive use of alcohol might be involved. Assume that Mr. Jordan has characteristics "typical" of most alcohol dependent persons.

    a. Briefly describe the psychological and personality traits that you would expect him to show.

    b. What is the rationale for routinely inquiring of alcohol dependent persons whether family members have had drinking problems?

    c. List three or more areas of his life into which you should inquire to determine if his alcohol dependency is worsening.

Self-Assessment Exercise #2 (Continued)

2. Correctly indicate whether the following statements are:

T = true F = false

_____ a. The persistent and excessive use of any central nervous system depressants (alcohol, sedatives, opiates) usually results in the development of a tolerance and physical dependency.

_____ b. Alcohol dependency is the most common "drug problem" among teenagers.

_____ c. Persistent and excessive consumption of alcohol characteristically results in actual disease of major body organs, e.g., heart stomach and liver.

_____ d. The depressant effects of sedatives are "cancelled out" by the simultaneous ingestion of alcohol.

_____ e. Even after tolerance and physical dependency are established, abrupt withdrawal from alcohol or sedatives rarely cause any serious medical consequences.

_____ f. Development of physical dependency on sedatives or opiates usually takes several weeks or longer.

_____ g. Singly or in combination an overdose of alcohol, sedatives or opiates may lead to respiratory arrest and death.

When you have completed this exercise to the best of your ability, check your answers with those on the following page.

Self-Assessment Exercise #2 - Feedback

1. a. The personality and psychological traits typically associated with drug dependency include:

   emotional immaturity, insecurity, marked dependency, chronic tension and depression, poor interpersonal relationships, decreased capacity to tolerate frustration, and impulsive reactions to stress.

   b. Some forms of alcoholism are caused by an inherited genetic defect. The diagnosis and treatment may be facilitated by knowing whether family members of the patient have similar problems.

   c. To determine if alcohol (drug) dependency is worsening, inquire to see if your patient is experiencing:

   (1) increased and/or more frequent consumption
   (2) increased preoccupation with getting high
   (3) impaired work performance
   (4) " interpersonal relationships
   (5) difficulty controlling intake

2.

__T__ a. The persistent and excessive use of any central nervous system depressants (alcohol, sedatives, opiates) usually result in the development of a tolerance and physical dependency.

__T__ b. Alcohol dependency is the most common "drug problem" among teenagers.

__T__ c. Persistent and excessive consumption of alcohol characteristically results in actual disease of major body organs, e.g., heart, stomach and liver.

__F__ d. The depressant effects of sedatives are "cancelled out" by the simultaneous ingestion of alcohol.

__F__ e. Even after tolerance and physical dependency are established, abrupt withdrawal from alcohol or sedatives rarely cause any serious medical consequences.

Self-Assessment Exercise #2 - Feedback (Continued)

2.

__F__ f. Development of physical dependency on sedatives or opiates usually takes several weeks or longer.

__T__ g. Singly or in combination an overdose of alcohol, sedatives or opiates may lead to respiratory arrest and death.

If your answers correspond closely with those above, continue your reading on the following page; if not, please reread the material in the preceding section until you are confident you know it.

Central Nervous System Stimulants

Chemicals which stimulate the central nervous system, so-called "uppers," evoke feelings of well being, a "high," along with a sense of increased energy and mental capability. As one might expect, these drugs reduce feelings of fatigue and bring about significant physical changes, and cause an increase of muscular tension, blood pressure and heart rate. Marked insomnia and loss of appetite are common side effects. Drugs which usually react as central nervous system stimulants are cocaine, amphetamine, methylphenidate hydrochloride (Ritalin).

Cocaine. This substance primarily acts as a central nervous system stimulant, and produces a "high" characterized by feelings of euphoria, exhilaration, and enhanced self-confidence. In comparison with other stimulant drugs, the duration of action of cocaine is brief, rarely lasting longer than one to two hours. As the effect of cocaine wears off, the patient is left feeling morose, restless, weak and irritable. This drug tends to heighten sexual and aggressive drives and produces a strong psychological dependence because of its pleasurably stimulating effects. No significant tolerance, physical dependence, or withdrawal syndrome develops, however. Repeated use of cocaine can lead to a paranoid psychosis manifested by unpredictable and belligerent behavior. It is usually taken by sniffing or injection.

Amphetamine and Methylphenidate. Amphetamine and methylphenidate (Ritalin) cause much the same psychological and physical effects as cocaine but have a longer duration of action. Psychological dependence and tolerance occurs, but no significant physical dependency or withdrawal syndrome develops even after prolonged use. However, a state of depression and physical exhaustion, a "crash," generally follows prolonged and excessive use when the drug is abruptly decreased. A psychosis clinically indistinguishable from paranoid schizophrenia, high blood pressure and cardiac arrythmias are medical complications associated with chronic amphetamine use. Amphetamines usually are taken orally or injected IV.

Hallucinogens. Hallucinogens include a variety of chemical substances which have in common the ability to markedly alter perception, thinking and feeling. These drugs generally are taken to produce transient psychotic symptoms including vivid hallucinations, feelings of depersonalization, perceptual distortions, and intense affective states. Usual thinking processes are disrupted and the user may become preoccupied with topics of a mystical or religious nature. Delusions of a grandiose or a paranoid type are common but usually are temporary phenomena.

Included among hallucinogens are LSD (lysergic acid diethamide), mescaline, PCP (phencyclidine), and others. These drugs are derived from such divergent sources as mushrooms, morning glory seeds, cactus or chemically synthesized in simple "kitchen laboratories." Psychological dependence upon these substances is variable and depends upon the emotional needs of the user. There is no significant development of tolerance, physical dependence or withdrawal syndrome even if the drug is regularly taken and abruptly stopped. Behavioral responses to hallucinogens are often unpredictable and extreme hyperactivity, social withdrawal and changes of mood are commonplace.

Although many hallucinogens cause findings which are suggestive of intoxication associated with organic brain disorders, patient responses are sometimes difficult to distinguish from acute schizophrenic disorders. Users of hallucinogens run the risk of experiencing "bad trips," when instead of drug-taking being a pleasurable experience, it becomes a disruptive and frightening one. During a bad trip, panic or intense depression can be associated with frightening delusions and hallucinatory experiences. "Flashbacks" or recurring bad trips may spontaneously begin weeks to months after any hallucinogens have been used. In some instances, irreversible functional psychosis may be precipitated by hallucinogens.

Cannabis. Cannabis sativa is the botanical name for the hemp plant from which hashish and marijuana are derived. In contrast to most other drugs, inhalation by smlking is the usual route of administration of this chemical. The psychoactive substance, tetrahydrocannabinal (THC) is found in varying concentrations within the plant. Hashish, the more potent form of the drug is made from the flowering tops of the plant, and the milder marijuana consists of a mixture of small stems and leaves. Smoking cannabis generally results in a feeling of euphoria, muscular relaxation, increased perçeptual sensitivity, and mild depersonalization. Taking cannabis regularly produces a moderate degree of psychological dependence, but no tolerance or physical dependence develops even after prolonged use. Psychotic symptoms and panic states occasionally may be precipitated by smoking cannabis and persistent use may cause mild memory impairment and generalized apathy.

Inhaled solvents. The inhalation of solvents such as airplane glue, hairspray, gasoline, acetone, and others produces a "high" which is found pleasurable by some teenagers. The psychological response is equivalent to the intoxication produced by alcohol or sedatives. Varying degrees of psychological dependence to the inhaled substance may occur, but no physical dependence has been noted. These solvents are highly toxic to major body organs including the brain, heart, liver and kidneys. Pathological and often irreversible organic brain disorders and neurological disease are frequently found in persons who persistently inhale solvents.

Now complete Self-Assessment Exercise #3 beginning on the next page.

Self-Assessment Exercise #3

1. For each of the following drugs, indicate if it produces:

a = tolerance and physical dependency
b = psychological dependency only

_____ a. amphetamines

_____ b. marijuana

_____ c. alcohol

_____ d. barbiturates (sedatives)

_____ e. cocaine

_____ f. inhaled solvents

_____ g. phencyclidine (P.C.P.)

_____ h. heroin (and other opiates)

2. For each of the brief cases below and on the following page, indicate which drugs are most likely to cause the finding. More than one drug can be used for each vignette.

a = alcohol
b = cocaine
c = phenobarbitol
d = inhaled gasoline
e = marijuana
f = methylphenidate or amphetamine
g = P.C.P.
h = L.S.D.
i = heroin

_______ (1) an abstinence syndrome characterized by tremulousness, nausea, decreased coordination

_______ (2) marked slowing of respiration, psychomotor retardation, lethargy

_______ (3) hyperactivity, elevated blood pressure, rapid speech, grandiosity in the absence of hallucinations

Self-Assessment Exercise #3 (Continued)

2.

________ (4) hallucinations not associated with a withdrawal syndrome

________ (5) pathological changes or disease in the brain, liver or kidneys

________ (6) paranoid delusions, hallucinations, aggressive behavior not associated with a withdrawal syndrome

________ (7) irreversible brain damage, memory impairment, mental confusion and neurological pathology

________ (8) the onset of hallucinations, impaired reality testing, anxiety, and depersonalization four weeks after taking drugs

When you have completed this exercise to the best of your ability, check your answers with those on the following page.

Self-Assessment Exercise #3 - Feedback

1. The following drugs may produce:

a = tolerance and physical dependency
b = psychological dependency only

b a. amphetamines

b b. marijuana

a c. alcohol

a d. barbiturates (sedatives)

b e. cocaine

b f. inhaled solvents

b g. phencyclidine (P.C.P.)

a h. heroin (and other opiates)

2. The following drugs can cause the findings below:

a = alcohol
b = cocaine
c = phenobarbitol
d = inhaled gasoline
e = marijuana
f = methylphenidate or amphetamine
g = P.C.P.
h = L.S.D.
i = heroin

a,c,i (1) an abstinence syndrome characterized by tremulousness, nausea, decreased coordination

a,c,i (2) marked slowing of respiration, psychomotor retardation, lethargy

b,f (3) hyperactivity, elevated blood pressure, rapid speech, grandiosity in the absence of hallucinations

g,h (4) hallucinations not associated with a withdrawal syndrome

Self-Assessment Exercise #3 - Feedback (Continued)

2.

a,d (5) pathological changes or disease in the brain, liver or kidneys

b,f,g,h (6) paranoid delusions, hallucinations, aggressive behavior not associated with a withdrawal syndrome

a,d (7) irreversible brain damage, memory impairment, mental confusion and neurological pathology

h (8) the onset of hallucinations, impaired reality testing, anxiety, and depersonalization four weeks after taking drugs

If your answers correspond closely with those above, continue your reading on the following page; if not, please reread the material in the preceding section until you are confident you know it.

THERAPEUTIC INTERVENTIONS

Substance use disorders result from a combination of psychological, behavioral, physical and environmental problems, and any therapeutic program should deal with as many of these factors as possible. Many of the principles of supportive psychotherapy and behavioral therapy which we will now present are not applicable to persons who are markedly intoxicated. Appropriate treatment for intoxicated persons is outlined in the chapter on "Organic Brain Disorders."

The maintenance of persons with substance use disorders usually is a long process in which the quality of the therapist-patient relationship assumes great importance. This relationship deserves special comment because of the negative feelings which frequently surface in therapists and adversely effect treatment. Many health professionals covertly feel resentment towards individuals having substance use disorders, viewing that behavior as the epitomy of self-indulgence which brings about needless suffering for the patient and others close to him. The therapist's feelings arise from the fact that he has invested long years of training learning to help others overcome suffering and find it difficult to show patience towards persons who create health problems because of lack of willpower. The education of health care professionals demands considerable self-discipline and self-denial -- and the seeming lack of these traits in drug users is hard to accept. So in two basic ways, therapist and patient personality traits are diametrically opposed to one another. But, however antagonistic the therapist's feelings, he should make every effort to hold them in check. Most persons with substance use disorders already feel inadequate and guilty, and criticism from the therapist will only worsen the situation. For similar reasons, it is generally not wise to refer to your patients as "addicts," "alcoholics" or similar names which have a negative connotation. Furthermore, the goals and standards of the therapist must be imposed upon the patient. If the therapist becomes overly zealous rapport may be lost.

Supportive Psychotherapy

Most individuals with substance use disorders are troubled with long-standing personality disorders, depression and anxiety. As a group they tend to be emotionally immature, dependent, and suffer from chronic feelings of personal inadequacy and insecurity. These characterologic traits should be considered as you design a therapeutic regimen for them.

Directive guidance. Your role as therapist should encompass elements of both directive and non-directive guidance. You should become involved in helping your patients to solve problems of living by supplying advice and direction, and yet, leave to them the responsibility for dealing with their drug-taking behavior. You can be of greatest help in the role of an interested, authoritative counselor who supplies emotional support and a stable point of reference -- a ready listener who accepts but does not encourage their drug dependency.

Patients with substance use disorders often become demanding and manipulative, especially when under emotional pressure. Be alert for various ploys which they may use to undermine your therapeutic stance. Their tolerance for psychological "pain" is typically quite low, and when a life problem appears they may demand medication or special concessions from you to relieve their distress. Your response should include a calm, but firm "no," and a statement which acknowledges their discomfort and provides an alternative method for dealing with them. In such an instance you might say, "I can see that you're hurting right now, but I think it would be better for you if we were to talk about your feeling rather than have me give you drugs. Occasionally, a patient may test your therapeutic "staying power" by persistently pressing you to relent saying, "If you don't give me the drug I need, I'll get it on the streets." Point out as often as is necessary that you will help him only in ways which are consistent with good principles of treatment and that ultimately decisions about drug abstinence are his. Other patients may attempt to use guilt to gain concessions by saying something like, "I can't stand the tension, if you *really* are interested in me you will give me the drug I asked for." A suitable response to this ploy is to affirm your interest in the patient's well being and acknowledge his discomfort, but steadfastly refuse to participate in action which in the long run is contrary to treatment goals.

As the therapist you should be directive but not authoritarian, emotionally support your patient during times of distress, and help him set realistic and graduated treatment goals. He should not expect to overcome his drug dependency without help or considerable self sacrifice.

Reassurance. Users of chemical intoxicants typically feel helpless, dependent and unloved. As a consequence, many crave attention and have what seems to be an insatiable need for reassurance. Even after a positive relationship has formed, your patient may develop fears that you eventually will lose interest in him as have so many others in his life. He may then test your "real interest" in him by episodically backsliding into drug use, call you while intoxicated, skip appointments, or make excessive requests for your time. In each instance, set reasonable limits for his behavior but reassure him that you will continue as his therapist for as long as he is willing to work at his problem. Your task is to encourage your patient's progress and maintain modest therapeutic optimism even when he is not abstinent. Your availability and non-judgmental attitude, tempered with steadfast therapeutic optimism will be very reassuring to him.

Ventilation. It is therapeutic for patients with substance use disorders to express their feelings to an interested and empathic listener. Your patient should be encouraged to talk about any and all things regarding his drug dependency, life experiences and frustrations. Open expression of his ideas and emotions usually will decrease his psychological tension and sense of emotional isolation and helps build the trust and rapport needed for maintaining therapeutic motivation.

Education. Most drug dependent individuals are all too familiar with the medical facts about their condition. They usually have been thoroughly "lectured and educated" by well-meaning others about the dangerous effects which alcohol and drugs can have on their health and emotional well being. These threats of loss of health rarely are successful in reducing drug-taking behavior. However, it is important that patients receive in a clear and matter-of-fact way up-to-date information about the consequence which drug-taking has upon their health. First, find out what your patient already knows about his condition and correct any misconceptions which he may have. Inform, but don't threaten. If your patient's disorder possibly is inherited or due to an illness, as may be the case with alcoholism, make this point, adding that it is a condition which can be controlled if not cured. Such information can relieve inappropriate guilt which your patient may have about his condition. Help him develop insight and understanding about life events which improve or aggrevate his drug dependency. This insight can help him to seek positive experiences and avoid situations which are detrimental. Spouse and family members can play a very important role in the treatment process, and for this reason, educate the family about current concepts regarding the etiology and treatment of substance use disorders.

Environmental intervention. Any comprehensive treatment program for individuals with substance use disorders should include attention to environmental factors. The life setting of the drug dependent person needs evaluation to determine if sub-standard housing, employment problems, inadequate recreational outlets, or lack of supportive relationships contribute to his problem. A detailed evaluation of your patient's social interactions and daily routine can be very revealing in this regard. Drug dependent persons often belong to a subculture in which the main focus of daily activity and relationships center upon acquiring and using intoxicants. Drug peer groups provide a degree of mutual emotional support, but at the cost of perpetuating drug dependency. Eventually, they should be replaced with relationships and pursuits which interrupt drug-taking behavior -- not reinforce it. Giving up a known life style for a new one, however beneficial it may be, can be a trying experience for one who already feels insecure and socially inadequate. It will be up to you to take the lead by helping to arrange an optimal living environment, new social contacts and constructive activities. Encourage your patient to attend therapy and self-help groups such as Alcoholics Anonymous. Help him enroll in suitable educational or vocational training programs and begin new recreational interests. Athletic and physical conditioning programs provide excellent outlets for emotional tensions and enhance feelings of well being.

A residential treatment center or "half-way house" may be appropriate for drug dependent patients who need a consistent therapeutic milieu, structured activities and supportive relationships. In instances when your patient's drug dependency is intractible, you are concerned that a drug withdrawal syndrome may occur or he has medical problems, hospitalization is indicated. Many drug dependent patients will need to be gradually weened (detoxified) from drugs they have been using. Careful medical monitoring in a hospital is appropriate.

Behavioral Therapy

Principles of behavioral therapy have been used successfully in the treatment of substance use disorders. For some patients, establishing behavioral contracts has proved an effective treatment approach. In return for actively participating in drug therapy programs or reducing their use of intoxicants, patients are rewarded with special privileges, permission to live in special residential treatment centers, or receive a reduction in parole. These contracts should clearly state behavioral expectations, rewards for compliance, and punishment for lack of it. Some patients will test the contractual limits (and your therapeutic consistency) by failing to comply fully with their agreement and offer "reasons" for not doing so. It is important that the agreed upon penalty for noncompliance be enforced firmly and consistently, but not punitively.

Special aversive conditioning techniques have been developed to treat substance use disorders. In this form of treatment, immediately after taking his "drug of choice," the patient is given a painful electroshock or medication which causes nausea, vomiting or similarly disagreeable effects. Drug-taking behavior which formerly brought pleasure, then, becomes psychologically associated with a strongly undesirable experience. After one or more training sessions, the desire to use the drug evokes more aversion than pleasurable expectation. This type of conditioning treatment requires considerable motivation on the part of the patient and periodic "refresher" sessions may often be needed for the aversive feelings to continue.

Now complete Self-Assessment Exercise #4 beginning on the next page.

Self-Assessment Exercise #4

Mrs. Doris Peters requested consultation because of symptoms of depression, irritability and marital problems of at least three years duration. She somewhat reluctantly admitted to the persistent use of sedatives for sleep and alcohol to calm her nerves and was finding that she had to take ever increasing amounts to achieve a feeling of calm. At times, she was unable to adequately attend to her housework because of being intoxicated. Laboratory tests indicated the presence of early liver disease -- likely caused by alcohol.

1. Does she meet the criteria for a substance use disorder? Why?

2. Comment on the appropriateness of making the following statement to Mrs. Peters after you have established that she has a drinking problem.

   "Mrs. Peters, you have been drinking too much and are on your way to developing serious liver disease. I want you to get a hold of yourself and stop drinking."

Self-Assessment Exercise #4 (Continued)

3. Mrs. Peters elects to work with you on her drug related problems. What therapeutic approach should you take about:

   a. episodic recurrences of intoxication

   b. her wish to talk about her family and marital problems

   c. participating in a social group which actively promotes alcohol consumption

When you have completed this exercise to the best of your ability, check your answers with those on the following page.

Self-Assessment Exercise #4 - Feedback

1. Mrs. Peters qualifies for the diagnosis of a substance use disorder because she has been troubled by drinking and drug use for over one month, shows signs of physical dependency, impairment of daily functioning and related health problems.

2. The statement may be factually correct but relies on scare tactics and is much too directive. A better course of action would be to point out the psychological and laboratory findings which "suggest" the diagnosis of an alcohol related problem. Then ask Mrs. Peters what (if anything) she would like to do about her condition.

3. a. Episodic recurrences of intoxication should be treated matter of factly. They are a common phenomenon and Mrs. Peters should not be penalized when they occur. Maintaining therapeutic optimism and a non-judgmental attitude usually works best. Focus therapy more on her successes than her failures.

   b. Patients generally should be encouraged to talk about their personal and emotional problems. This builds rapport and helps relieve emotional tension.

   c. Continued participation in groups or with relationships that may be detrimental to treatment should be discouraged. But actively help her to find new and more therapeutic outlets, relationships and activities.

If your answers correspond closely with those above, continue your reading on the following page; if not, please reread the material in the preceding section until you are confident you know it.

THERAPEUTIC INTERVENTIONS (CONTINUED)

Pharmacologic Therapy

As mentioned earlier, the use of intoxicating chemicals can profoundly effect body physiology -- sometimes to a degree that can result in serious medical consequences. The treatment of patients who are markedly intoxicated or are in the midst of a withdrawal syndrome is primarily a medical matter and one which requires considerable expertise. Therapeutic management can be further complicated by other illnesses which co-exist with substance use disorders and treatment in a hospital setting frequently is indicated. Good medical care dictates that the treatment regimen be tailored to the particular drugs used. To outline in detail the therapy indicated for even the major drug categories presented in this chapter is beyond the scope of this book, however, we will discuss some general principles of management which can be applied to most persons with substance use disorders.

If your work with patients involves dispensing medications, be cautious of prescribing any for individuals who especially request medications such as sedatives or analgesics for symptoms which are chronic atypical or vague in nature. They may be drug dependent. Keep in mind that the medical history given by these persons may be unreliable -- that their symptoms may be overstated and their drug use understated.

It is well to assess the life style of patients who may need medications which have the potential to cause drug dependency. Patients who are emotionally immautre, impulsive, excessively dependent, or who have a low tolerance for pain or frustration are at risk to develop substance use disorders.

As a general rule, you should not routinely prescribe drugs for persons with substance use disorders and there are sound reasons for not doing so. A prime treatment goal for most persons with these disorders is to eliminate their inclination to take chemical substances for alleviating physical or emotional discomfort. An approach which incorporates taking any drug (even if prescribed by the therapist) to relieve emotional distress reinforces and perpetuates drug-taking behavior. At times, it may be necessary to compromise this principle and prescribe psychotropic drugs for selected patients -- those experiencing a withdrawal syndrome, who have symptoms of psychosis, intense anxiety, depression, or whose behavior cannot otherwise be controlled.

Another reason for withholding psychotropic drugs is because they can interreact adversely with other chemical substances already taken by the patient. Many psychotropic drugs increase the effect of alcohol, sedatives, and analgesics, thereby worsening his medical status. The risk for precipitating adverse reactions is especially great if your patient shows obvious signs of intoxication such as lethargy, discoordination, etc., and serious and even fatal medical complications can occur with hallucinogens (P.C.P., L.S.D., S.T.P.). A possible exception to the policy of not prescribing neuroleptics for treating substance use disorders is psychosis due to amphetamines. Symptoms of amphetamine psychosis usually respond favorably to chlorpromazine. But bear in mind that it is difficult to determine with certainty which drug your patient actually has been taking. Street drugs are notoriously adulterated and may not contain what the patient believes.

Whether or not you prescribe medications for treating markedly intoxicated patients, order bed rest, placement in a quiet, well-lighted room, and around-the-clock supervision by an experienced nurse. If your patient becomes belligerent or over-active, order physical restraints until his disorganized behavior subsides.

Occasionally, it will be necessary to administer medications to achieve behavioral control. When such is the case, prescribe a drug which is least likely to cause adverse problems and use the smallest dose necessary to alleviate disordered behavior. Many neuroleptics of the phenothiazine class (chlorpromazine, fluphenazine, etc.) are contraindicated because of their tendency to react adversely with many street drugs. A more suitable choice is haloperidol given in amounts of 2 to 5 mgs. IM. A still safer but less potent medication is diazepam which can be administered 5 to 10 mgs. orally or 5 mgs. IV every two to four hours. Haloperidol or diazepam will help to reduce restlessness, emotional tension and promote sound sleep. But use these drugs cautiously -- each is capable of precipitating serious medical complications. Whenever you prescribe any psychotropic medication for someone already under the influence of drugs, monitor his vital signs (blood pressure, pulse, respiration, and state of consciousness) at hourly intervals. Keep him under the close scrutiny of an experienced health professional.

Patients with substance use disorders suffer from chronic symptoms and are susceptible to becoming psychologically dependent on many psychotropic drugs which are prescribed for them. Therefore, it is best to prescribe such medications only during crises and only on a short-term basis. This guideline can be set aside for persons who are unalterably dependent upon opiates (usually heroin) and for whom there is little likelihood that they can achieve total abstinence. For such persons, methadone, a narcotic similar to heroin but which causes milder physical and psychological side effects can be substituted. Some communities have methadone maintenance clinics which supply patients with controlled doses of methadone on a daily basis and closely monitor the patient's mental and medical status.

Alcohol dependent patients may benefit by treatment with disulfiram (Antabuse), an oral medication which is taken daily. This medication interferes with alcohol metabolism in the body and results in a buildup of toxic by-products which may cause symptoms of nausea, vomiting, palpitations, and in some cases, serious cardiovascular problems. Once a patient has been started on disulfiram he cannot consume even small amounts of alcohol without experiencing a toxic response. Disulfiram is metabolized slowly in the body and its effect may last up to two weeks after the last dose is taken, thus preventing impulsive drinking. Side effects and contraindication to disulfiram therapy generally are few. Patients considered for disulfiram therapy must be thoroughly counseled not to take alcohol in any form. Proper motivation and compliance are necessary for this form of treatment.

Consultation and Referral

Because patients with substance use disorders often are troubled with a combination of problems , the services of several health professionals and agencies may be needed to provide a sufficiently comprehensive treatment program.

Medical evaluation should routinely be carried out for all individuals with substance use disorders because of the increased incidence of associated physical problems. Medical evaluations are particularly important for individuals who are presently intoxicated or have administered drugs to themselves by injection, and may have contracted diseases from using unsterilized needles and equipment. Medical examinations are also indicated for patients who need detoxification or have used drugs capable of causing a withdrawal syndrome.

Referral to a psychiatrist is important if your patient shows evidence of serious psychopathology such as an organic brain disorder, psychosis, or severe depression. Psychiatric consultation is appropriate if your patient does not respond to supportive treatment, needs special medications, or is persistently non-compliant with your therapeutic regimen.

Consider referring your patient to suitable community agencies which can assist him arrange for housing, financial aid, family counseling, and job placement or training. Referral to a residential treatment facility is indicated for patients who do not need full-time hospitalization, but can use a supervised living arrangement and supportive relationships. Encourage your patient to seek reputable self-help groups such as Alcoholics Anonymous which offer psychological counseling, education programs, and group support.

Now complete Self-Assessment Exercise #5 beginning on the next page.

Self-Assessment Exercise #5

1. A man in his early 20's was brought to you for consultation by the police who found him wandering about the streets wearing disheveled, dirty clothing. The man was unable to give a coherent history but related that he had been getting high on "street drugs." He described paranoid delusions, was actively hallucinating and hyperactive, and spoke continuously at a rapid rate. Without provocation he suddenly became argumentative and belligerent.

   a. Assuming that his symptoms were due to an overdose of drugs (but not a withdrawal syndrome) circle all of the possible intoxicants which most likely could have caused his findings:

phenobarbitol	alcohol
phencyclidine (P.C.P.)	marijuana
amphetamines	cocaine

   b. Would you treat him as an in- or outpatient? Why?

   c. Comment briefly on the appropriateness for prescribing the following:

      (1) chlorpromazine, 50 mg. I.M., stat

      (2) bed rest and restraints as needed

      (3) placement in a private room with a special nurse in attendance

      (4) psychiatric consultation

Self-Assessment Exercise #5 (Continued)

1. d. After his acute symptoms have subsided, should you maintain him on psychotropic drugs? Why?

When you have completed this exercise to the best of your ability, check your answers with those on the following page.

Self-Assessment Exercise #5 - Feedback

1. a. The findings of paranoid delusions, hallucinations, hyperactive and aggressive behavior are most commonly associated with:

   phencyclidine (P.C.P.)
   amphetamines
   cocaine

   b. The young man should be treated as an inpatient. He presently is psychotic, shows impaired judgment and may become a danger to others or himself. He requires close medical supervision and treatment.

   c. (1) Inspite of his hyperactive and belligerent behavior, administering chlorpromazine, 50 mgs. I.M. is hazardous. The drug causing his symptoms is not known and an adverse reaction to chlorpromazine may occur. If medication must be given, haloperidol, 5 mgs. I.M. or diazepam may be safer choices.

   (2) Placing the patient at bed rest and prescribing physical restraints as indicated is a satisfactory treatment approach. This approach will protect the patient from causing harm to himself or others, and allows medical monitoring.

   (3) Placement in a private room with a nurse in attendance is good treatment. Environmental stimuli should be optimal (not too exciting) and the nurse will be able to provide verbal reassurance, support, and orientation to the patient during his mental confusion.

   (4) Psychiatric consultation certainly should be requested to establish the diagnosis, prescribe medications, and evaluate the need for follow-up psychotherapy.

   d. As a general principle, one should <u>not</u> routinely prescribe maintenance psychotropic medication for persons with substance use disorders. The condition is chronic and substituting one medication for another tends to reinforce, not diminish drug-taking behavior. An exception to this policy exists if the patient has underlying psychopathology such as intense anxiety, depression, psychosis, etc. which requires medication for symptom relief.

If your answers correspond closely with those above, continue your reading on the following page; if not, please reread the material in the preceding section until you are confident you know it.

SUMMARY

Drug and alcohol dependency in this country constitutes a wide spread and serious health problem. Substance use disorders result from various psychological environmental and genetic factors which can be difficult to diagnose and treat. The therapeutic management of these disorders should be tailored to each patient and the drug upon which he is dependent. As a health professional, you should possess a general working knowledge about the typical characteristics of the drugs commonly used. Be especially alert to the potential medical and psychological problems which are frequently found in individuals with substance use disorders.

REFERENCES

Barchas, J., Berger P., et al, Psychopharmacology from Theory to Practice, New York: Oxford University Press, 1977.

Shader, R., Manual of Psychiatric Therapeutics, Boston: Little, Brown and Co., 1975.

Slaby, A., Lieb, J. and Tancredi, L., Handbook of Psychiatric Emergencies, Flushing: Medical Examination Publishing Co., 1975.

Westermeyer, J., A Primer on Chemical Dependency, Baltimore: Williams & Wilkins Co., 1976.

CHAPTER 12. SOMATOFORM DISORDERS

Somatoform Disorders are a unique group of psychopathologic conditions in which the major symptoms consist of bodily complaints that do not have a physical basis, but instead, are psychological in origin. Patients with these conditions mistakenly seek a medical remedy for their symptoms, and unless the true cause of their disorder is diagnosed, treatment may be prescribed which is costly, ineffective and frustrating. A specialized approach is needed for treating patients with Somatoform Disorders. In this chapter we will discuss the diagnostic characteristics and therapeutic management for the four subtypes of Somatoform Disorders -- Somatization Disorders, Conversion Disorders, Psychogenic Pain Disorder and Hypochondriasis. It is important from the outset to emphasize that these conditions represent a coping response to psychological stress which is involuntary and quite outside of patient awareness. These conditions should not be confused with malingering, in which patients intentionally manufacture bodily symptoms in order to achieve some personal gain.

LEARNING OBJECTIVES

By the time you complete this chapter, you should be able to do the following and apply the information to written case histories.

1. Describe the mental status examination (MSE) findings typical to Somatoform Disorders.

2. Define and characterize each of the following subtypes of Somatoform Disorders.

   (a) Somatization Disorder
   (b) Conversion Disorder
   (c) Psychogenic Pain Disorder
   (d) Hypochondriasis

3. Distinguish between the four subtypes of Somatoform Disorders in terms of:

   (a) time of onset, course and duration
   (b) the number of organ systems affected
   (c) the type of organ systems affected
   (d) response to supportive intervention and reassurance
   (e) whether or not actual function loss occurs.

4. For each of the methods of therapeutic intervention listed below, describe the recommended treatment approach and provide a rationale for its use in the management of Somatoform Disorders.

   (a) Supportive Psychotherapy
   (b) Behavioral Therapy
   (c) Pharmacologic Therapy
   (d) Consultation and/or Referral

MENTAL STATUS EXAMINATION (MSE) FINDINGS

In contrast to many psychopathologic conditions, Somatoform Disorders have a few mental status examination findings that point to the diagnosis. However, the presence of these disorders should be suspected when patient complaints consist primarily of physical symptoms in the absence of MSE findings indicative of other psychopathology (e.g., organic brain disorders). It should be noted, however, that preoccupation with somatic symptoms can occur in association with schizophrenic, major affective and organic brain disorders. But in the latter cases, abnormal physical preoccupations represent only one of several abnormal MSE findings.

With the possible exception of Conversion Disorders which can have some readily observable signs of pathology (such as impaired movement or speech), there are no findings of appearance, general physical behavior, speech or facial expression which are typical to Somatoform Disorders. There are no specific disturbances of affect or mood which are diagnostic, although many patients seem tense or worried. Perceptual abnormalities are not characteristic of Somatoform Disorders.

The findings that are most diagnostically specific occur in the MSE subcategory of "Thinking". However, there generally is no impairment of orientation, memory or intellectual functioning, and no associational disturbance is present. The findings most indicative of Somatoform Disorders are thinking and behavior. Some patients experience actual loss of function (e.g., blindness, paralysis), while others have only fears that they are sick. The complaints are often described in dramatic terms but, in many cases, are vague with respect to details of onset, causation and factors which influence the course of symptoms. With the possible exception of Conversion Disorders in which patients may appear unexpectedly indifferent to their loss of function, most persons with Somatoform Disorders are clearly distressed by their symptoms, pain, and impairment.

SUBTYPES OF SOMATOFORM DISORDERS

We will now describe and define the four major subtypes of Somatoform Disorders -- Somatization Disorders, Conversion Disorders, Psychogenic Pain Disorder, and Hypochondriasis. The management and treatment of these conditions will be discussed later in the chapter.

Somatization Disorder

A Somatization Disorder is a chronic, psychopathologic condition characterized by multiple physical complaints involving several body organ systems (e.g., gastro-intestinal, cardiovascular, musculoskeletal, etc.) for which no organic cause can be detected by physical or laboratory examinations. These patients are sufficiently troubled by their symptoms to seek relief by means of repeated medical consultations, prescribed medications and even surgery. Unfortunately, the course of this disorder is chronic and patients often become dependent upon drugs prescribed to help them.

The physical symptoms of Somatization Disorders can fluctuate considerably in kind and intensity. The most frequently reported complaints include chronic fatigue, dizziness, headache, generalized weakness, nausea, back, joint and extremity pains, abdominal discomfort, menstrual and sexual problems, shortness of breath, chest pain and palpitations. Persons with this disorder may experience numbness, tingling sensations, muscular weakness, visual difficulties and other findings suggestive of neurological disease. This list of bodily complaints is often accompanied by feelings of "nervous tension", anxiety and depression. Symptom description frequently takes on a dramatic and exaggerated style. For example, a patient might say, "I've had so much pain that I haven't slept for a month." or "I've vomitted every day of my life." In contrast to the dramatic portrayal of complaints, the remainder of the history may be notably vague with respect to details of symptoms such as the time of onset, and related life factors.

Somatization Disorders are more common in females than males, generally begin in the late teens or early twenties and persist throughout life. Patients with Somatization Disorders typically are suggestible and respond favorably to therapeutic enthusiasm, and new recommendations or medications. However, improvement is generally short lived and either the old symptoms recur or new ones appear. The multiplicity and varying course of symptoms can mimic physical diseases (e.g., multiple sclerosis or systemic lupas erythematosis) and a final diagnosis may have to be delayed weeks or months to see if actual organ pathology occurs. If the initial complaints improve and/or objective signs of physical illness such as fever, significant weight loss, progressive debility do not develop, then it is more likely that symptoms reflect a Somatization Disorder. It is important to remember that somatic complaints in the absence of modified physical findings also can be associated with other types of psychopathology including schizophrenic and affective disorders.

In summary, a Somatization Disorder is characterized by recurrent physical complaints involving many bodily organ systems for which no objective cause can be found. This chronic disorder is more common in females and usually begins before the age of 25.

Conversion Disorders (or Hysterical Neurosis, Conversion Type)

Conversion Disorders are characterized by impaired physical functioning (especially involving the sensory organs or voluntary musculature) in the absence of objective somatic disease. The symptoms of Conversion Disorders frequently simulate neurological disease which also are manifested by impaired functioning of sensory organs and voluntary body movements. Examples of typical symptoms include loss or impairment of speech, sight, smell or hearing, decreased or increased sensitivity of touch, muscle weakness, paralysis, and atypical body movements. Patient symptoms rarely match present-day knowledge about disease. For example, patients may develop a total paralysis of their legs but maintain normal muscle tone, reflexes and sensation -- findings which are inconsistent with current knowledge about the nervous system. Another illustration are patients who develop unilateral loss of sensation extending precisely to the mid-line of their body. While such symptoms seem reasonable to laypersons, in actuality there is considerable overlapping of the nerve distribution from each side of the body making a mid-line loss of feeling improbable. Conversion Disorders usually can be distinguished from neurological and medical disease by careful physical examination. The discrepancy between the patient findings and those expected if actual disease were present should not be interpreted that the symptoms are contrived. In Conversion Disorders symptom formation precedes automatically out of the conscious awareness of patients.

The onset of a Conversion Disorder is typically abrupt and generally can be related by an objective observer to an identifiable psychological conflict or traumatic life incident. Considering the sudden and often impressive symptomatology (e.g., blindness or paralysis), many patients do not seem as concerned about their impairment as one would expect. This seeming "indifference" to symptoms is characteristic but not invariably present.

Many clinicians believe that Conversion Disorders represent an attempt to deal with an intolerable psychological conflict by means of developing physical symptoms. Consider for example an individual who develops intense anger and an urge to physically strike the offending person. Simultaneous with the assaultive impulse is an opposing one originating from anticipated guilt or fear of retaliation. The patient's mind automatically "resolves" the conflicting feelings by producing arm weakness, and the assaultive act is blocked from completion -- but a symptom remains. The resolution of a conflict by symptom formation is termed "primary gain". As stated before, this entire process occurs automatically and is out of the patient's awareness and conscious control. Once established, the symptom can be perpetuated because of special attention or other benefits which are received because of the disability. (The gratifying or stress-reducing advantages which accrue from the presence of symptoms are called "secondary gain".) Conversion symptoms can serve to divert from underlying psychological problems at home, work, etc.

Conversion symptoms occasionally can be found in association with schizophrenic, affective and other psychopathologic disorders. In contrast to other Somatoform Disorders, conversion symptoms usually run a short course and often improve in response to positive suggestions and active interventions such as physical therapy and medications.

Although no actual disease is present at the outset of a Conversion Disorder, organic pathology may result if appropriate treatment is not given. This possibility is exemplified by an individual who develops a conversion paralysis of his legs and does not use them for an extended period of time. Due to prolonged disuse, the leg muscles may atrophy and joints may become arthritic. Thus, what started out as a purely psychological problem can develop into an actual physical disorder.

Now complete Self-Assessment Exercise #1 beginning on the following page.

Self-Assessment Exercise #1

A. Read through the following case vignette and then answer the questions which follow.

38-year-old, Mrs. Cummings, sought consultation because of symptoms of nausea, headache, indigestion and dizziness. A carefully-taken history revealed additional complaints of intermittent menstrual pain, shortness of breath, nervousness, and crying spells. Mrs. Cummings further stated that she was troubled by occasional joint pains and abdominal swelling. All of her symptoms were described in detail and Mrs. Cummings mentioned that in the past she had consulted several physicians and received numerous medications with little benefit. In view of her history and diagnosis, what would you expect with regards to:

1. The duration of her condition?

2. The short and long-term results of newly-prescribed medications, reassurance and suggestions that her symptoms would improve?

B. For each of the following items, indicate whether it is true (T) or false (F):

_____ 1. Symptoms suggestive of Somatoform Disorders rarely occur in combination with other psychopathologic conditions such as depression or schizophrenia.

_____ 2. Suggestion and reassurance are often effective in persons with Somatization Disorders and Conversion Disorders.

_____ 3. The MSE findings most characteristic of Somatoform Disorders are the presence of a depressive affect and atypical physical behavior.

_____ 4. Conversion Disorders typically have an abrupt and stress-related onset.

Self-Assessment Exercise #1 (Continued)

B.

_____ 5. Symptoms of Conversion Disorders often mimic findings of neurologic disease.

_____ 6. The symptoms of Somatization and Conversion Disorders are under a patient's volitional control and can be aborted if he chooses to do so.

When you have completed this exercise to the best of your ability, check your answers with those on the following page.

Self-Assessment Exercise #1 - Feedback

A. 1. The patient's history of chronic complaints involving multiple organ systems which have been unresponsive to treatment, suggest a diagnosis of a Somatization Disorder. While her specific symptoms may fluctuate in kind and intensity, the disorder itself is chronic and usually lasts a lifetime.

2. Patients with Somatization Disorders generally are quite suggestible and respond favorably to new and innovative treatments, reassurance and medications. Over the short-term, Mrs. Cummings likely will improve in response to any or a combination of these treatment measures. However, sooner or later her old symptoms likely will recur and/or new ones develop.

B.

False 1. Symptoms suggestive of Somatoform Disorders rarely occur in combination with other psychopathologic conditions such as depression or schizophrenia.

True 2. Suggestion and reassurance are often effective in persons with Somatization Disorders and Conversion Disorders.

False 3. The MSE findings most characteristic of Somatoform Disorders are the presence of a depressive affect and atypical physical behavior.

True 4. Conversion Disorders typically have an abrupt and stress-related onset.

True 5. Symptoms of Conversion Disorders often mimic findings of neurologic disease.

False 6. The symptoms of Somatization and Conversion Disorders are under a patient's volitional control and can be aborted if he chooses to do so.

If your answers correspond closely with those above, continue your reading on the following page; if not, please reread the material in the preceding section until you are confident you know it.

SUBTYPES OF SOMATOFORM DISORDERS (CONTINUED)

Psychogenic Pain Disorder

A Psychogenic Pain Disorder is a condition in which the predominant complaint is pain that cannot be explained by present medical knowledge or physical and laboratory examinations. The pain of a Psychogenic Pain Disorder may be experienced in a location, intensity or duration which is not consistent with verifiable disease processes. The pain is usually troublesome enough so that patients seek medical consultation and/or relief by means of anti-pain medications. Because a Psychogenic Pain Disorder is a chronic condition, many persons become dependent upon the drugs prescribed to relieve them.

A therapist usually can identify psychological problems which coincide with the onset or worsening of the pain. Patients may use pain as an excuse to avoid unpleasant responsibilities and receive special attention, and either result may reinforce the symptoms of pain (secondary gain). A Psychogenic Pain Disorder can begin at any age.

Due to lack of objective methods for measuring pain, you should assign the diagnosis of a Psychogenic Pain Disorder only after careful evaluation. The diagnosis can be made with relative certainty if the following criteria are met:

1. no organic basis for pain can be found after thorough evaluation
2. the pain appears associated with psychological factors and offers significant secondary gains for the patient
3. the nature of the pain (location, intensity, etc.) is atypical with respect to current knowledge about anatomy, physiology, and disease
4. pain is the patient's major complaint and symptom

The management of a Psychogenic Pain Disorder will be described later.

Hypochondriasis (or Hypochondriacal Neurosis)

The diagnosis of Hypochondriasis is assigned to patients who maintain a persistent fear that they are physically ill despite authoritative reassurance to the contrary. Patients with this condition are chronically worried that their physical symptoms signify serious and possibly fatal illness, and usually seek reassurance by means of repeated consultations with physicians, clinics and other health care agencies. Their persistent symptoms and demands that "something be done" too often are rewarded with a new round of examinations or medications. Favorable medical reports are met with skepticism and newly-prescribed medications, and treatments provide only short-term improvement. Not only do most patients with Hypochondriasis fail to improve in response to reassurance, they may react adversely to it.

For reasons out of their awareness, hypochondriacal patients tenaciously maintain their concerns about ill health, and in some cases, their hypochondriacal beliefs approach delusional intensity. The patients express a need for reassurance that they are healthy, but paradoxically are unable to accept it. By way of explanation, some clinicians believe that hypochondriasis is the overt manifestation of underlying psychopathology. These patients make medical treatment and telling others about their symptoms and suffering the center of their life. These expressed worries serve as an acceptable "excuse" for obtaining attention, eliciting dependency gratification, diverting patients from feelings of low self-esteem, loneliness, and depression. In most cases, these patients have little or no awareness of their psychological problems -- they are concerned only about their health. If this hypothesis about Hypochondriasis is correct, then it is apparent why these persons cling so tightly to their symptoms -- to di otherwise would require them to acknowledge problems more threatening than those presented by medical illness.

Hypochondriacal symptoms can begin at any age and often occur in association with affective and schizophrenic disorders and during normal adolescence. It is useful to distinguish transient (reactive) Hypochondrias from the more chronic type. Transient hypochondriacal episodes frequen occur in persons who have recently experienced a major medical illness, e.g., heart attack. In these instances, patients are especially sensitive to bodily sensations and may fear that any change in pulse rate or incident chest pain may signal a recurrence of their illness. Initially, such patier are very preoccupied with the workings of their bodies and persistently se reassurance from medical personnel. As time pases and no relapses occ most patients lose their excessive concern with bodily symptoms. Succes ful resolution of hypochondriacal worries is more likely if "secondary gai from their symptoms is kept to minimal levels.

The chronic form of Hypochondriasis is characterized by self-centere concerns about illness. With these persons, seeking medical attention an treatment becomes a way of life and gradually crowds out interest in other people and activities. By their endless recitation of symptoms, treatment and suffering, these patients drive away the very persons to whom they look for support and care. The chronic form of Hypochondriasis is very difficult to treat successfully.

Now complete Self-Assessment Exercise #2 beginning on the next page.

Self-Assessment Exercise #2

Indicate the most appropriate diagnostic category for each of the following case vignettes. List the findings which support your answer.

a. Somatization Disorder
b. Conversion Disorder
c. Psychogenic Pain Disorder
d. Hypochondriasis
e. Presence of an Actual Illness

____ 1. A 21-year-old navy man sought consultation because of a pain in his lower abdoman which became increasingly severe over a 36-hour period. He complained of nausea, intermittent vomiting and diarrhea. His abdomen was quite tender to touch and he had a fever of 101 degrees. Laboratory testing showed that the patient had an abnormally elevated white blood count. The serviceman incidentally related that the onset of his symptoms coincided with a duty assignment which he did not like.

____ 2. Harold Jones, a man in his late 50's, described a marked concern that he had cancer. He complained of chronic fatigue, nausea, and intermiitent abdominal cramping extending over five years. Mr. Jones was financially well-to-do and for several years had consulted numerous prestigious clinics and physicians for extensive medical evaluations. Although some minor physical changes consistent with his age were noted, there was no evidence of serious illness. Mr. Jones remained unconvinced by reassurances from reputable physicians. A variety of diets and medications had been prescribed to relieve his symptoms but none had brought lasting relief.

Self-Assessment Exercise #2 (Continued)

____3. Thirty-four year-old, Helen Black, sought consultation because of recurrent medical illness. She stated that, "I have been in poor health since I was a teenager and never had a week when I didn't feel sick with something. Just as I get well from one illness, I get something else." Mrs. Black complained of a variety of symptoms including indigestion, nausea, "migraine" type headaches, and joint and back pains. Mrs. Black related that she had experienced episodes of abdominal pain so severe that exploratory surgery only found a "normal appendix". She brought to the interview a paperbag containing fifteen different medications which had been prescribed for her through the years. She medicated herself according to which symptoms were most prominent. Further questioning reve led that Mrs. Black had recurrent marital problems and easily became tearful often without discernable reasons.

____4. Rhonda James, a 41-year-old homemaker, complained of headaches and intermittent neck and back pains of several years' duration. The pains appeared gradually over a several month period following a minor automobile accident and became increasingly severe. At the time of the accident, the patient had been thoroughly evaluated and was diagnosed as having a "mild whiplash injury". Physical therapy and mild pain medications were prescribed. Mrs. James stated that pain frequently caused her to stop housework and rest in bed. She regularly asked her husband to take over household duties including cooking the evening meals. A carefully-taken history revealed that Mrs. James was worried about her marriage and that her husband seemed lesss attentive stating that, "He just doesn't seem to care how I feel anymore." A physical and laboratory examination failed to show any significant pathology.

When you have completed this exercise to the best of your ability, check your answers with those on the following page.

Self-Assessment Exercise #2 - Feedback

__e__ 1. The seaman had actual physical illness. Although his physical symptoms seemed associated with an undesirable work assignment, fever, an elevated white blood count, and other physical findings indicated the presence of an actual physical disease.

__d__ 2. Mr. Jones is suffering from Hypochondriasis. This diagnosis is supported by his persistent and unfounded belief that he is physically ill. His worry was not relieved despite authoritative reassurances and normal laboratory findings.

__a__ 3. The most likely diagnosis is that of a Somatization Disorder. Mrs. Black presents a history of chronic and varied somatic symptoms beginning in her teen years. Her many symptoms and surgeries involve several different organ systems and, in addition, she is troubled by psychological problems of tension and depression. Her numerous visits to physicians and extensive use of prescribed medications further support this diagnosis.

__c__ 4. Mrs. James is suffering from a Psychogenic Pain Disorder. Her main symptoms consist of pain which is not supported by objective physical findings. Her symptoms appear related to underlying psychological (marital) difficulties. Secondary gain is evidenced by her neglecting household duties, and regularly requesting her husband to take over cooking.

If your answers correspond closely with those above, continue your reading on the following page; if not, please reread the material in the preceding section until you are confident you know it.

THERAPEUTIC INTERVENTIONS

Treating patients with Somatoform Disorders requires an approach which reckons with the unique characteristics of these conditions. Consider for a moment some of the inherent therapeutic dilemmas. Patients plead for relief of symptoms which on one hand are distressing them, and on the other are needed to maintain their psychological equilibrium. Complaints are expressed in terms of physical symptoms, but in actuality, psychological factors which are out of conscious awareness are the cause of difficulties. These circumstances make improvement hard to come by.

With the possible exception of Conversion Disorders which typically run a short course, most Somatoform Disorders are chronic and can last a lifetime. Treatment aimed to achieve a symptom "cure" is an unrealistic goal, and patients and therapists alike must be content with more modest goals, such as limiting additional medical evaluations and reducing reliance on drugs. Frustration and disappointment for both patients and therapists are common outcomes unless treatment is carefully planned. We will now discuss principles of supportive psychotherapy, behavioral therapy, pharmacologic therapy, and consultation and referral which can be effective with patients having Somatoform Disorders.

Supportive Psychotherapy

Directive guidance. Your therapeutic approach deserves thoughtful consideration. Most patients with Somatoform Disorders simply do not know what is best for them. Being unaware of the psychological determinants of their problems, they determinedly press for medical interventions for symptomatic relief -- a course of action which is generally unsuccessful. These patients need a therapist who is knowledgeable about their disorder, who patiently will listen to their complaints, will not yield to demands for additional evaluation and treatment, and yet will provide emotional support and directive guidance. They need assistance in developing alternative ways to handle personal problems and reduce stress in daily life. Anticipate that your determination to "hold the line" on prescribing new examinations or drugs will be vigorously challenged. But in spite of the patient challenges, convey your continued desire to help and optimism about the treatment outcome.

It is important that you continuously monitor your own feelings to avoid either responding with hostility or withdrawing into therapeutic indifference. Either reaction will evoke anxiety and a resurgence of symptoms.

Environmental intervention. It is appropriate to assist your patients to overcome environmental and other problems of living which contribute to their disorder. Help them deal realistically with financial, work and housing difficulties. If pending litigation may be perpetuating symptoms (as might be the case with a suit brought because of an accident or industrial injury), help facilitate a speedy settlement because it is difficult to relinquish symptoms if maintaining them will result in financial gain.

Education. It is best not to attempt to educate patients with Somatoform Disorders by discussion of the theoretical aspects of mind-body interactions, the working of unconscious psychological mechanisms, or similar abstractions. This approach serves only to confuse or upset them. For similar reasons, don't discuss their diagnosis using terms which may have unpleasant connotations, such as "hysteria", "hypochondriasis", or "atypical somatoform disorders". Patients are likely to be affronted by these terms or, on their own, consult medical books or friends about their condition. Simply explain that although the medical nature of their condition is not clear, no serious disease is present.

If you plan to prescribe medications or diagnostic tests, tell patients in simple terms what will be involved, being sure to prepare them for potential side effects which might arise. Keep your patients well informed about the results of all tests which are performed. Your silence about any medical matter may be mistakenly interpreted by them as "something too bad to talk about". Without sounding overly-pessimistic, let patients know that their symptoms will fluctuate from time to time and may persist for an indefinite period.

Few patients with Somatoform Disorders have any meaningful understanding of the psychological factors which influence their symptoms. In some cases, it is possible to gradually expand their self-awareness which then can lead to taking corrective action about problems. One way to educate such patients is to point out in a tentative fashion symptom changes which coincide with current life events. If patients are unable to accept your observations, do not press the issue, but try again later. However, if they are receptive to your insightful comments, you can help them develop new ways of handling problems, such as expressing feelings more openly, becoming assertive, etc.

It is well to help family members develop a constructive understanding of the difficulties involved. Teach them ways to show their concern without reinforcing the symptoms.

Ventilation. As a rule, it is therapeutic for patients to openly talk about their symptoms and worries with an authoritative, interested listener. Family members and friends soon weary of learning about symptoms and treatment. As a therapist you can space consultations and supply the objective attentive ear which is needed. However, you should balance the therapeutic gains which come from allowing patients to speak freely about their symptoms, against the drawbacks of symptom reinforcement which result when attention is paid to them. Balanced listening can be achieved by making empathic comments to enhance rapport and yet set reasonable time limits for consultations and not overreact to the symptoms described. Excessive ruminations about symptoms should firmly (but kindly) be discouraged and consultations limited to 10 - 20 minutes in length. Similarly, unscheduled "drop in" appointments or frequent telephone contact between consultations should be discouraged. Over the course of time, show increasing interest in the psychological aspects of your patient's history and proportionately less concern about their somatic symptoms. By using selective attention, you can help them focus on the causes of their symptoms.

Reassurance. Your patients will ask for authoritative reassurance regarding their physical complaints -- but not all of them will be able to accept it. For patients with a Somatization or Conversion Disorder, reassurance about prognosis and that their symptoms soon will subside may result in improvement. But for reasons described earlier, hypochondriacal patients respond abundantly to statements which imply that their symptoms will resolve. Some patients may pressure you for promises of rapid cure or guaranteed recovery. Convey a tentative hopefulness, but don't give superficial reasssurances or specific recovery dates to placate them. Their symptoms are chronic in nature, and the therapeutic relationship may be jeopardized if you are unable to deliver what you promised.

Because of its potential impact, reassurance should be worded carefully. If medical reports are normal, present these findings positively. For example, "Mrs. Jones, I am pleased to say that after thorough evaluation, no indications of a serious disease was found." There is a subtle but important difference between that statement and an announcement that, "No disease is found." or "There's nothing wrong with you." In the latter cases, your patients would be left without any way to justify their complaints either to themselves or others. Such a position would be unacceptable for many, and your appraisal might be discounted altogether. If your patients ask for a specific diagnosis, state that the exact cause of their condition is not clear, but add that no serious disorder is present. Convey the feeling that, even without a specific diagnosis, you want to help and will continue as therapist for as long as your services are needed. Most patients will feel better if they have tangible evidence that you will continue to see them, i.e., receiving a follow-up appointment at the end of each consultation. This dated guarantee of support is especially reassuring for patients who feel that without identified disease they could not justify continuing the relationship. Most patients with Somatoform Disorders fear losing the relationship with their therapist. Further reassure patients that although their symptoms may wax and wane, such fluctuations do not indicate a worsening of their condition. Help get the point across that they can live productive and active lives <u>in spite</u> of their symptoms.

Now complete Self-Assessment Exercise #3 beginning on the next page.

Self-Assessment Exercise #3

Read the case vignette and answer the questions which follow.

1. Mr. George Bosworth is a 49-year-old clerk who complains of a several year history of "nervousness", shortness of breath, slight dizziness, and intermittent palpitations with chest pain. The pain was described as "being very sharp," although it lasted only a few seconds and was unrelated to stress or exertion. Mr. Bosworth had undergone four complete physical examinations within the past three years seeking to remedy his symptoms. A cardiac specialist had performed a thorough medical evaluation by including an electrocardiogram, a treadmill exertion test, and various laboratory procedures. All tests were within normal limits. Despite reassurances to the contrary, Mr. Bosworth continued to express concerns that "something must be very seriously wrong with me." He described fears that he might have a heart attack and die at any moment.

   A. In addition to his other symptoms, Mr. Bosworth complained of feeling "nervous" and requested medication that would help him to relax. After considering the nature of his problems, what course of action would you take with regards to his request? Why?

   B. A review of his medical records and consultation with the heart specialist indicates that Mr. Bosworth is in good health and does not have organic heart disease. Later, Mr. Bosworth asks, "What's wrong with me?" How would you respond to his question?

   C. Mr. Bosworth seems very concerned about his symptoms and plaintively asks, "Am I going to get better? Can't you _do_ something for me?" What would you say in response?

Self-Assessment Exercise #3 (Continued)

D. You note a temporal relationship between the onset of Mr. Bosworth's pain and problems with his work supervisor. Briefly comment on the appropriateness of the following ways that you could handle the observation.

1. Say to Mr. Bosworth, "Did you note that the symptoms often began immediately after disagreements with your boss? I believe that this finding indicates that your symptoms are psychological in origin."

2. Reflect out loud, "On several occasions you described that the pain and shortness of breath began right after a disagreement with your work supervisor. What do you make of that?"

When you have completed this exercise to the best of your ability, check your answers with those on the following page.

Self-Assessment Exercise #3 - Feedback

1. A. Mr. Bosworth's history of worry about having heart trouble despite authoritative reassurances to the contrary, is consistent with a diagnosis of Hypochondriasis. Prescribing medications to relieve his "nervousness" is inadvisable on at least two counts: (1) persons with this condition psychologically "need" to be worried about their physical condition and no medications would likely remove his symptoms, (2) Hypochondriasis is a chronic disorder and attempting to deal with it via medication probably would lead to physical and/or psychological dependency on any prescribed medicines. For these reasons (which should not be stated to Mr. Bosworth), you should explain that drugs will not yield any lasting help, but that you will continue to meet and talk with him and perhaps, in time, discover more effective means to relieve his symptoms.

   B. In responding to Mr. Bosworth's question, "What's wrong with me?", you must proceed carefully. He needs you to reassure him that nothing serious is wrong with him, and yet acknowledge the presence of his physical complaints and worries. Of course, the diagnosis "hypochondriasis" should not be used. Some statement of fact and reassurance like the following one may be effective:

   > "It's not clear exactly what is causing your symptoms, Mr. Bosworth, but I can assure you that you do not have serious medical disease. Examinations have ruled out that possibility. But specific diagnosis or not, I will continue to be your therapist for as long as you want me to."

   C. Consciously, Mr. Bosworth is in distress and would like to be free of his symptoms. He's asking for reassurance. At a deeper psychological level, he probably cannot do without health worries. You should not promise that he will "get better", i.e., that he will be without symptoms. A response which acknowledges his feelings and provides reassurance which he can accept is as follows:

   > "I can see that you're pretty worried about your health. The cause of your condition is not yet identified -- but your physical health has been stable for some time now. We know that no serious disease is present. For the near future, if you agree, I'd like to meet for scheduled appointments to talk with you and learn more about the symptoms.

Self-Assessment Exercise #3 - Feedback (Continued)

C. I know that you'd like to have some specific treatment now, but I'd like to proceed slowly until I know more about how I can be of most help to you."

D. 1. Making a statement which so directly links psychological causation with physical symptoms probably won't work. Mr. Bosworth either won't "hear" your implications or might be affronted by your observations.

2. This is a better way to state your observation. It allows Mr. Bosworth to express his feelings without forcing the issue and becoming defensive. If he shows some capacity for insight, you can pursue the matter further now. If he belittles your observations, let the matter rest until a later time.

If your answers correspond closely with those above, continue your reading on the following page; if not, please reread the material in the preceding section until you are confident you know it.

THERAPEUTIC INTERVENTIONS (CONTINUED)

Behavioral Therapy

Developing symptoms of sickness offers the potential for special benefits (secondary gains), for example, a sanctioned excuse for avoiding work or responsibility and receiving attention from others. The principle of secondary gain is always operating in persons with Somatoform Disorders. As a rule, the more chronic the illness, the more likely that secondary gain will reinforce and perpetuate the symptoms. One important therapeutic task is to conduct therapy in a way which encourages adaptive behavior (e.g., the development of self-reliance) and discourages maladaptive behavior (such as excessive dependence on the therapist or medications). Because of these factors, principles of behavioral therapy are well suited for treating patients with Somatoform Disorders. Some specific guidelines will be given which will help to rehabilitate your patient.

1. Directly praise or otherwise "reward" your patients when they show signs of improvement, e.g., as they get along with fewer medications, become more socially oriented or develop insight.

2. Minimize the reinforcement of symptoms by not over-attending to them by prescribing additional tests or medications; order only those interventions which are essential to establish a diagnosis and treatment.

3. Comment empathically about patients' feelings of distress, but show less interest in their physical complaints.

4. Gradually reduce medication and other therapeutic interventions which reinforce the sick role.

5. Emphasize that you will continue as therapist as long as your help is needed.

Referral to behavior modification specialists in biofeedback and muscle relaxation technique may be indicated for patients with Psychalgia or pain caused by excessive muscle tension.

Pharmacologic Therapy

The complaints associated with Somatoform Disorders are chronic in nature and generally respond little, if at all, to psychotropic medications. Nevertheless, many patients persistently seek a pharmacologic remedy for their physical symptoms; and well-meaning therapists all-too-frequently go along with patient demands and prescribe medications which do little good and may cause harm.

Many of these patients go from doctor to doctor requesting new medications and omit telling successive physicians of the drugs which already have been prescribed. As a result, it is common for patients with a Somatization Disorder or Hypochondriasis to be taking several medications simultaneously, the side effects of which can aggrevate symptoms of weakness or physical debility. The potential is great for persons with Somatoform Disorders to become drug dependent.

The following principles will help you manage the issue of prescribing medications. As a rule, try to keep all medications to a minimum. If your patients already are taking drugs in excessive amounts, explain that their symptoms actually may be accentuated by the drugs. Your patients may resist giving up all medications at once, therefore, for the immediate term allow them to take those drugs which have the least potential for side effects. Prepare a schedule to gradually discontinue medications over several weeks or months, eliminating first those which cause physical side effects or have a high potential for habituation, (e.g., analgesics, sedatives and hypnotics). Anticipate a temporary resurgence of physical symptoms each time patients are asked to give up a medication. Their anxiety about giving up medications can be diminished if you provide an ongoing supportive relationship and regularly schedule appointments. It is important that you reward a diminishing dependence on drugs with words of encouragement. Occasionally, it will be necessary to prescribe drugs to relieve intense pain, tension or insomnia. (See the chapter on "Pharmacologic Therapy" for indications.) Before recommending a specific drug, inquire if they have taken it before and, if so, whether it was beneficial. If the medication is new, suggest, but don't promise symptomatic improvement. Do not prescribe any medication on a "let's try it and see if it will work" basis. This equivocal presentation will doom it to failure. Finally, make it clear that the medication is effective only over the short-term and should be taken for a limited time.

Consultation and Referral

Treating persons experiencing a Somatoform Disorder can be a difficult process, and under the circumstances described below, it may be advisable to ask for special consultation or refer your patients to other therapists for care.

One reason for requesting consultation is the development of intense feelings of frustration or discouragement within the therapeutic relationship which impair the patient motivations or your therapeutic objectivity. Similarly, a persistent lack of progress or continued non-compliance with your recommendations warrants seeking consultation. Because patients with Somatoform Disorders often present a complicated and ever changing medical history, it is best that they be treated by one therapist who is thoroughly acquainted with the vicissitudes of their condition. However, if patients emphatically request outside evaluation, it is best to comply with their wishes.

Referral to a psychiatrist is indicated if, in addition to somatic complaints, your patients develop signs of serious psychiatric problems such as schizophrenia or depression. Similarly, obtain medical consultation for patients who develop bonafide physical illness. Referral to a therapist for more extensive psychotherapy should be considered for persons who show a capacity for psychological insight into the nature of their problems. Referrals for psychotherapy require special tactfulness because of the patient sensitivity to any action which might imply their symptoms are "imaginary" or are "all in their head."

Now complete Self-Assessment Exercise #4 beginning on the next page.

Self-Assessment Exercise #4

Fifty-seven year-old, Matilda Altman, sought consultation because of intermittent abdominal pain associated with nausea, loss of appetite, and constipation. Her symptoms dated back at least five years to the death of her husband. Mrs. Altman also complained of feeling chronically tired and generally tense. She stated that she had taken special stomach medications, followed a bland diet, and regularly took "pain killers", and nerve medicines without benefit. Repeated medical evaluations, x-rays, and laboratory studies had been performed by a number of physicians. Despite her complaints, she remained physically active and her weight was stable. However, Mrs. Altman remained worried about her condition despite reassurances that there was no objective evidence of physical illness. Briefly answer the following questions about the management of Mrs. Altman:

(1) If she were to ask, "Don't you think we should repeat the x-rays?", what would you say to her request? Why?

(2) If Mrs. Altman asks the question, "What's really wrong wrong with me?", comment on the appropriateness of each of the following statements that you might make.

a. "There's nothing physically wrong with you."

b. "There's nothing seriously wrong with you."

c. "Your physical symptoms are essentially all due to psychological problems."

Self-Assessment Exercise #4 (Continued)

(3) The following represents some treatment goals for Mrs. Altman. Indicate for each objective whether it is more appropriately considered as:

a. a short-term goal (a few weeks)

b. a long-term goal (many months)

Briefly explain your answer.

_____ (a) Wean the patient from all medications.

_____ (b) Help her develop insight into the possible psychological origins of her physical problems.

_____ (c) Help her to overcome excessive emotional dependency upon you.

_____ (d) Discontinue medications which are interacting adversely with one another and are presently causing undesirable side effects.

When you have completed this exercise to the best of your ability, check your answers with those on the following page.

Self-Assessment Exercise #4 - Feedback

(1) Politely but firmly say "no" to her request for further radiologic testing. In the absence of new or worsening symptoms, there is no reason to believe that the x-ray will show anything new. She will not be assured by the results and will have been needlessly exposed to more radiation. Explain that you appreciate her worry, but there is no evidence of serious disease and for the time further x-ray evaluation is contraindicated. Reassure Mrs. Altman that you will continue to see her at regular intervals.

(2) a. Saying that "nothing is physically wrong with you" would miss the therapeutic mark. Mrs. Altman needs to believe that she has physical illness. She would likely respond to such a remark by discounting the statement -- or you.

b. A statement that "nothing seriously wrong" is more acceptable. It acknowledges the presence of physical symptoms but offers a note of reassurance against serious disease.

c. Implying that her symptoms are largely psychological in nature probably would be unacceptable to Mrs. Altman. She is unaware that psychological factors are related to her complaints, and such a statement would be without meaning and may be felt as an affront.

(3)

__b__ (a) Wean the patient from all medications.

It is hard for patients to give up medication which they are accustomed to. This is a long-term goal.

__b__ (b) Help her develop insight into the possible psychological origins of her physical problems.

Mrs. Altman believes her symptoms are physical in origin. Only gradually over time is she likely to understand her symptoms in psychological terms.

__b__ (c) Help her to overcome excessive emotional dependency upon you.

Most persons with Hypochondriasis are very dependent upon their therapist for emotional support. She will need a relationship with you indefinitely. Only gradually should you pull back.

Self-Assessment Exercise #4 - Feedback (Continued)

__a__ (d) Discontinue medications which are interacting adversely with one another and are presently causing undesirable side effects.

This is an appropriate short-term goal. Explain to Mrs. Altman that some of her present symptoms may be due to the medication she is taking. For the short-term, allow her to continue the less troublesome drugs.

If your answers correspond closely with those above, continue your reading on the following page; if not, please reread the material in the preceding section until you are confident you know it.

SUMMARY

Somatoform Disorders consist of an interesting group of condit in which psychological problems are expressed in terms of physical symptoms. The most characteristic findings are physical complain the origins of which cannot be substantiated by medical evaluation ar testing. These disorders often are present as puzzling medical prol lems which can be difficult to diagnose and equally difficult to succe fully treat if the psychological factors are not appreciated. Most Somatoform Disorders (except Conversion Disorders) run a chronic course and require the therapist to adopt modest treatment goals wi regards to symptom improvement. An individualized treatment appı is needed for each case, and psychotropic drugs are of questionable value. It is especially useful for health care professionals to be fan with the characteristic findings of these disorders.

REFERENCES

Bowden, C. and Burstein, A., Psychosocial Basis of Medical Pract Baltimore: Williams & Wilkins Co., 1974.

Dubovsky, S. and Weissberg, M., Clinical Psychiatry in Primary C Baltimore: Williams & Wilkins Co., 1978.

Imboden, J. and Urbaitis, J., Practical Psychiatry in Medicine, New York: Appleton-Century Crofts, 1978.

Mayerson, E., Putting the Ill at Ease, New York: Harper & Row, 1

CHAPTER 13. MENTAL RETARDATION

There are between two and four million individuals in our country who are intellectually below normal because of mental retardation. Their limited intellectual capacity greatly influences the success of any medical, social or educational program which you might suggest. Therefore, it is important that you be able to assess the intelligence of each patient you treat and take special measures to assist those with mental retardation.

LEARNING OBJECTIVES

By the time you complete this chapter, you should be able to do the following and apply the information to written case histories.

1. Define mental retardation in terms of:

    a. intellectual functioning
    b. adaptive behavior
    c. age of onset

2. List the mental status findings associated with mental retardation.

3. List five common causes of mental retardation.

4. For each of the methods of therapeutic intervention listed below, describe the recommended treatment approach and provide a rationale for its use with mentally retarded patients.

   a. supportive psychotherapy
   b. behavioral therapy
   c. pharmacologic therapy
   d. consultation and referral

MENTAL RETARDATION DEFINED

The diagnosis of mental retardation is reserved for persons who demonstrate significantly sub-average general intelligence, which exists concurrently with deficiencies in adaptive behavior, and is first manifested during the developmental period of life. We shall now discuss these diagnostic criteria.

The general intelligence referred to in the definition is measured by performance on a standardized test of intelligence that has been individually administered. This involves determining I.Q. scores obtained on the Wechsler Adult Intelligence Scale (WAIS), the Wechsler Intelligence Scale for Children - Revised (WISC-R) or the Stanford-Binet.

An I.Q. of 100 is average. "Significantly sub-average" is defined as I.Q.'s of 68 or 70 or lower, depending upon the standard deviation of the test used. This sub-average category of intelligence can be further sub-typed as shown in Table I, which relates degrees of retardation with I.Q. ranges on the WISC-R or WAIS.

TABLE I

DEGREE OF MENTAL RETARDATION AND I.Q. RANGE

Degree of Retardation	I.Q. Range on WISC-R or WAIS
Mild	55 - 69
Moderate	40 - 54
Severe	25 - 39
Profound	0 - 24

Deficiencies in adaptive behavior are defined as problems in achieving those standards of personal care, independence and social responsibility which are expected of most persons of similar age and social group.

An assigned diagnosis of mental retardation does not rest solely on low scores on an intelligence test, but must include an assessment of the patient's ability to adapt to life, i.e., to work productively, handle money, form meaningful relationships, maintain personal grooming and manage the problems of daily living. If an individual with demonstrated "significantly sub-average" intelligence is able to handle these basic skills of living, it is inappropriate to classify him as mentally retarded.

Finally, before mental retardation can be officially diagnosed, symptoms of low intelligence and poor adaptive behavior must first appear during the developmental period -- the time during which major intellectual growth occurs, that is, from birth to 18 years of age. Low intellectual functioning and poor adaptive behavior which are the result of injuries or diseases occurring later in life, are not categorized as mental retardation.

In summary, then, the diagnosis of mental retardation cannot be made without all of the following criteria being met: sub-average intelligence, deficiencies in adaptive behavior, and an onset which is manifeste during the developmental period.

Now complete Self-Assessment Exercise #1 beginning on the following page.

Self-Assessment Exercise #1

1. Define mental retardation using the three criteria presented.

2. Is the diagnosis of mental retardation appropriate for the following case? Check yes or no and state the reasons below.

(a) Arthur Smith is an 11-year-old boy who scored 65 on the WISC-R. He was kept back in school for two years and is currently doing "D" work. His mother must drive him to school because he cannot make change or handle money, and has problems with bus travel. His mother also must help him dress each morning. When Arthur was born he suffered brain damage due to a temporary lack of oxygen.

Is Arthur mentally retarded? _____ yes _____ no

Why?

Self-Assessment Exercise #1 (Continued)

2. (b) Roberta Rogers, a secretary of 25, was severely injured in an automobile accident. Several months after the accident she remained disoriented to time, was unable to perform even simple arithmetic problems or manage her own funds. Psychological testing showed her I.Q. to be 55.

Is Roberta mentally retarded? _____ yes _____ no

Why?

When you have completed this exercise to the best of your ability, check your answers with those on the following page.

Self-Assessment Exercise #1 - Feedback

1. Mental retardation is significantly sub-average intelligence existing concurrently with deficits in adaptive behavior, and is first manifested during the developmental period.

2. (a) Yes. Arthur should be diagnosed as mentally retarded because:

    (1) he scores below 70 on the WISC-R
    (2) he has adaptive problems with money, dressing, bus and school
    (3) adaptive problems became apparent during his developmental years, i.e., since birth

   (b) No. Roberta does not qualify for the diagnosis of mental retardation. Although she is severely intellectually impaired and unable to manage her own affairs, the mental defect occurred after her developmental period of growth. She would more appropriately be assigned the diagnosis of an organic mental disorder.

If your answers correspond closely with those above, please continue reading on the next page. If not, please reread the preceding material.

CAUSES OF MENTAL RETARDATION

Mental retardation can be caused by a variety of infections, genetic, physiological or psychosocial factors. Indeed, over 200 different causes have been suggested to date. However, it is only when mental retardation reaches "severe" or "profound" intensity that specific causes can be identified with certainty. These cases are usually associated with brain disease, physical handicaps and neurological problems. For 80 to 90 percent of all cases, which include most mildly or moderately retarded persons, there are no distinguishing physical abnormalities and the causes of intellectual deficit cannot be determined with a high degree of confidence.

We will now briefly review some of the major types of causes of mental retardation. Pre- or Post-natal infections are regularly implicated in cases of mental retardation. For example, the virus caused rubella (german measles) occurring during the pre-natal period, produces mental retardation in 10 to 50% of the offspring of that pregnancy. Metabolic and nutritional disorders causing mental retardation include diseases such as hypothyroidism. In infants, hypothyroidism results in cretinism, a syndrome of stunted physical and intellectual growth which is caused by an insufficent supply of thyroid hormone in the developing infant. Down's syndrome (Mongolism) is representative of mental retardation arising from chromosomal abnormality, an inherited genetic defect. This condition is the most frequent cause of moderate to severe mental retardation. Research has shown that if pregnant women are poorly nourished or are exposed to various toxic substances or excessive amounts of alcohol and addictive drugs, a mentally retarded child may result. Mechanical trauma of the infant's brain or temporary lack of oxygen are other sources of intellectual impairment.

Interestingly, it has become clear that socio-economic and psychological deprivation also can lead to permanent mild intellectual deficits. The early months of development are critical to intellectual growth, and insufficient fondling, attention, physical affection and sensory stimulation can lead to mental retardation.

The causes of mental retardation are multiple and often obscure. But by means of genetic counseling, assuring good medical care for pregnant women and young infants, and attending to the emotional and intellectual needs of young infants, it is now possible to reduce the incidence and/or severity of mental retardation in many cases.

MENTAL STATUS FINDINGS

The mental status findings for mildly mentally retarded individuals usually do not differ substantially from persons of normal intelligence except in the area of thinking, and the condition often is not diagnosed until children reach school age -- a time when their intellectual performance becomes increasingly important. Their appearance, behavior, feelings and perception are generally affected because of mental retardation.

By the same token, mental retardation may exist in conjunction with other kinds of psychopathology including organic brain disorders, psychosis, affective disorders, and others. When such is the case, mentally retarded persons demonstrate hallucinations, unpredictable behavior, disordered appearance or mental confusion just as individuals of normal intelligence would who have similar disorders.

In persons with moderate to severe mental retardation, neurological and physiological abnormalities are more prevalent and are clearly reflected in mental status examination findings and the diagnosis is detectable at a much earlier age than in the instance of mild retardation. Their general appearance is often atypical, facial expression may be unresponsive, and speech monotonous and indistinct. Discoordination, problems with movement, and bland or labile affect are common. Persons with moderate to severe mental retardation are likely to behave in a very childlike, immature fashion and require constant supervision and care.

It is in the area of thinking that mentally retarded persons uniformly deviate from "normal" individuals. The degree to which their thinking is affected is proportionate to the severity of retardation. Most are alert and are oriented to person and place but not always to the day and date. The capacity for abstract and conceptual thinking is impaired and they are likely to respond to questions in a literal, highly personalized fashion. For example, when a mentally retarded person is asked what is meant by the proverb, "don't cry over spilled milk", he might say, "I cry when I spill my milk at home." Rather than interpreting the proverb abstractly to mean that it is inappropriate to dwell upon unchangeable past failures, mentally retarded persons generally respond with personal and literal explanations. The vocabulary of mentally retarded persons is noticeably simple and they are likely to speak in short phrases and talk about topics more typical to children than adults. Their ability to perform calculations, make decisions in complex situations and for their future is impaired. They often may confuse their wishes and fears with actual reality. They will often give incomplete answers to complex questions or give excuses for not knowing them. Also, it is not uncommon for mentally retarded individuals to demonstrate an associational disturbance.

Now complete Self-Assessment Exercise #2 beginning on the following page.

Self-Assessment Exercise #2

1. Circle the mental status findings which are basic to most persons with mental retardation. Omit those that could be associated with other mental disorders.

   a. labile affect

   b. unkempt appearance

   c. depersonalization

   d. delusions

   e. impaired abstract thinking ability

   f. impaired level of consciousness

   g. impaired calculation ability

   h. hallucinations

   i. concrete (literal) thinking

   j. impaired judgment

   k. depression

   l. blunted affect

2. Indicate whether the following statements are true (T) or false (F).

_____ (a) The M.S.E. findings of impaired orientation, calculation ability and abstract thinking are common to both mental retardation and an organic mental disorder.

_____ (b) The appearance and general behavior of persons with mild mental retardation is similar to that of individuals with normal intelligence.

_____ (c) The presence of mental retardation excludes the likelihood of other types of psychopathology.

Self-Assessment Exercise #2 (Continued)

3. List four or more types of causes of mental retardation and give a specific example of each.

When you have completed this exercise to the best of your ability, check your answers with those on the following page.

Self-Assessment Exercise #2 - Feedback

1. The mental status findings typically associated with mental retardation are:

    e. impaired abstract thinking ability

    g. impaired calculation ability

    i. concrete (literal) thinking

    j. impaired judgment

2.

True (a) The M.S.E. findings of impaired orientation, calculation ability and abstract thinking are common to both mental retardation and an organic mental disorder.

True (b) The appearance and general behavior of persons with mild mental retardation is similar to that of individuals with normal intelligence.

False (c) The presence of mental retardation excludes the likelihood of other types of psychopathology.

3. Common causes of mental retardation include:

    (1) chromosomal abnormalities - Down's syndrome (Mongolism)

    (2) pre- or post-natal infections - rubella

    (3) metabolic or nutritional disorders - hypothyroidism

    (4) trauma or lack of oxygen - birth trauma

    (5) psychosocial - sensory deprivation

If your answers correspond closely with those above, please continue reading on the next page. If not, please reread the preceding material.

THERAPEUTIC INTERVENTIONS

We will now discuss therapeutic approaches which you can apply to help patients who are mentally retarded.

Supportive Psychotherapy

The following interventions are most appropriate for patients with mild mental retardation, i.e., if their I.Q. is greater than 55. But in addition to I.Q. scores, you should base your therapeutic efforts upon each patient's ability to respond to a verbally oriented therapy program.

Keep in mind that your therapeutic interventions should emphasize other development of practical skills of living and personal care -- not intellectual insight. Retarded individuals are helped especially by providing an ongoing relationship which is supportive and nonjudgmental. Care should be exercised in your choice of words because technical jargon and terms may be confusing. Many feel too embarrassed by their lack of comprehension to ask for clarification of your statements or other questions which they may have. Make your explanations clear, concise and repeat them.

Directive guidance. Retarded patients may need considerable guidance in order to function satisfactorily in their daily life activities. Being a "good friend" and teacher summarizes the approach which is needed. Your ideas, suggestions and guidance are invaluable and you should actively give counsel about schooling, managing social relationships, personal grooming and educational training. It is likely that you will be called upon to provide basic advice on dating, parental relations, how to maintain friendships, sexual education, setting realistic personal goals, and similar topics.

Environmental intervention. Retarded patients constantly need environmental assistance in dealing with problems of school work, social relationships, authority figures, self-care, and economic matters. They tend to function best in familiar settings which have a predictable routine, do not require rapid decision making and provide emotional support. Until they reach 18, most can attend school in special education classes which are available in most cities. Thereafter, they can participate in sheltered workshops where in return for unskilled work they can earn money and gain worthwhile educational experiences.

If your patients are severely retarded, have marked behavioral or medical problems, placement in a residential treatment setting or hospital may be indicated. In those settings, specially trained personnel and facilities are available to help meet their particular emotional and intellectual needs. Most retarded persons adapt better to life when they can be productively occupied and participate fully in worthwhile activities and relationships. Make sure that the environment for your patient is pleasant, and conducive to ongoing intellectual stimulation and growth.

Education. For the majority of mentally retarded persons, the treatment approach of choice is a well-planned educational program. Mental retardation is not an emotional disorder and your patients will benefit most by learning to cope with inter-personal relationships, adapting to their environment (using public transportation) and managing their feelings. Learning takes place best in an atmosphere of mutual trust and respect and where they receive support and encouragement. As mentioned before, special education classes are mandated for mentally retarded children in most cities. In these classes, education is provided which emphasizes the learning of social and practical educational skills, i.e., how to make purchases, etiquette, grooming, etc. Sheltered workshops are also available where mentally retarded individuals can learn unskilled jobs and receive pay.

An excellent way to reinforce adaptive skills is to spend time with your patients in real life situations. Take them shopping and help them resolve potentially frustrating situations such as waiting in line, making purchase selections, etc. Explain basic problem-solving strategies for getting directions, etc. When your patients "succeed" in a task, reinforce their behavior with compliments and other rewards. If frustration develops, help them to moderate it and ask, "How could we have handled this better?" Do not assume that your patients cannot do minimally complicated tasks without letting them first try. Recent studies have shown that mentally retarded individuals thought to be only "trainable" actually can be educated to do more complex activities, i.e., custodial work, gardening, etc. Families should be educated about mental retardation and ways in which they, too, can reinforce the intellectual and emotional growth of the patient. They should be encourage to provide a variety of interesting and potentially educational experiences such as visits to parks, museums, movies, and vacations which expand their life experiences and learning.

Ventilation. Your retarded patients will need a place where they can express their feelings. Given a chance to do so, they will describe a sense of loneliness, frustration or worry about the future. They likely will have many questions about why it is so hard for them to learn and adjust in daily life or why they are subject to ridicule. Your patients should be allowed to freely discuss these feelings with you, but they may have problems modulating their emotions which sometimes can overwhel them. Be sure to teach your patients ways that they can vent their frustrations constructively, i.e., through physical activity, concentrating on more pleasant activities, etc.

Reassurance. Give supportive reassurance to your patients by means of scheduling regular visits, providing a stable and consistent relationship, and encouraging their efforts for self-improvement. They can easily become discouraged by their frustrations and "failures" and specific words of encouragement and rewards for their achievements help to build self-esteem. Convey a sense of therapeutic optimism about their potential to try and learn new experiences, but help them to set goals which are realistic in keeping with their intellectual abilities. Because their concepts of past and future are limited, make it a point to often remind them of their past achievements and potential for deriving satisfactions in the future.

Behavioral Therapy

Applying principles of behavioral therapy to institutionalized patients has achieved considerable success in improving their capacity for adaptation. Likewise, you may find that behavioral techniques can be useful for treating patients who live at home and are treated on an outpatient basis. A token reward system is often effective for reinforcing desirable behaviors. A few specified behaviors such as maintaining personal grooming and performing household chores, etc. should be selected for reward. Patients are then given script or tokens with which they may purchase candy, or other rewards such as going on outings when they have performed in the agreed upon way. Parents, friends and others can use this system to promote adaptive behavior. This type of reward and reinforcement system is quite therapeutic for improving behavior.

"Time-out" methods may be adopted for patients with problem behavior such as excessive aggressiveness or temper outbursts. Patients are advised in advance that such behavior is unacceptable and that specific disciplinary action will be taken if it is repeated. If the problematic behavior recurs, the patient is immediately placed in an isolated, quiet place for a minute or two. It is important that this disciplinary action be carried out consistently and immediately following the disapproved action. This type of discipline should not be administered in a punitive fashion. By using this method, retarded patients can learn to control behaviors which are unacceptable.

Aversive behavioral techniques are sometimes used in instances of recurring self-destructive or assaultive behaviors. In this form of treatment, patients are administered a painful stimulus such as a mild electroshock immediately following the problem behavior. This type of intervention should be used only in extreme circumstances and administered only by specially trained therapists.

Pharmacologic Therapy

The pharmacologic treatment of the mentally retarded is effective for modifying specific problematic behaviors such as agitation, hypersexuality, intense anxiety, agressiveness, psychosis or severe depression. No medications can improve the basic intellectual impairment, but they can reduce some symptoms which impair adaptation. Indeed, taking any psychotropic medication is likely to cause additional mental "dulling," a side effect which further compromises the patient's adaptive abilities. If a drug is prescribed, its administration should not be left to the patient, rather it should be given only by responsible relatives or friends.

For retarded patients who demonstrate intense anxiety or tension, anti-anxiety medications such as diazepam, 2 to 5 mgs. p.o. TID or chlordiazepoxide, 15 mgs. TID may be effective. Because of the potential for developing drug tolerance and dependence, these medications should be used only intermittently during periods of intense anxiety.

Occasionally, depressive symptoms may become sufficiently severe to warrant prescribing specific anti-depressant medications (e.g., imipramine, doxepin, etc.). The same criteria for prescribing tricyclic anti-depressants, selecting the dosage, etc. are used as for persons of normal intelligence. (See the chapter on "Pharmacologic Therapy" for details.) In the event that your patients develop severe agitation, become assaultive or demonstrate delusions or hallucinations, then consider administering an appropriate neuroleptic such as haloperidol, chlorpromazine or thiothixene. (See the chapter on "Pharmacologic Therapy" for details of dosage, side effects, etc.) Keep in mind that persons with moderate to severe mental retardation often have accompanying neurological disorders and that potent psychotropic medications may lower their threshold for seizures and other complications. Furthermore, special care should be taken to evaluate patients' medical status and whether they are taking other medications which may interact adversely with any psychotropic drugs prescribed.

Consultation and Referral

Appropriate consultation and referral should be considered an integral part of the therapeutic regimen for each mentally retarded person. It is important to firmly establish the diagnosis of mental retardation and to rule out a possible emotional basis for the intellectual impairment shown. In this regard, a psychologist should be consulted to administer appropriate diagnostic tests. Similarly, a neurologist, pediatrician or other medical specialist may be required for determining the final diagnosis and prescribing an appropriate management program. Behavioral therapists can be consulted for helping to design a therapeutic approach to deal with specific problematic behaviors such as unusual agressiveness refusal to cooperate with treatment, etc. Most school systems employ specialists who can assist with educational placement and arranging suitable classroom experiences for children who are mentally retarded. Social agencies specializing in treatment and/or placement are located in most large communities. Finally, medical centers and agencies can help you locate lay groups of family members and others interested in helping persons with mental retardation. These groups provide mutual support and are active in developing new approaches to helping the mentally retarded.

Now complete Self-Assessment Exercise #3 beginning on the following page.

Self-Assessment Exercise #3

Indicate whether the following statements are true (T) or false (F).

_____ 1. Techniques of supportive psychotherapy work best on patients whose I.Q. is greater than 55.

_____ 2. It is beneficial for most mentally retarded children to participate in such activities as attending school, visiting museums, etc.

_____ 3. Behavior modification therapy is more appropriate for helping the mentally retarded than an insight oriented treatment.

_____ 4. It is best not to let mentally retarded persons attempt activities at which they may fail.

_____ 5. Most persons with mental retardation prefer a constantly changing environment and making important decisions by themselves.

_____ 6. Aversive behavioral therapy should be applied to most retarded persons.

_____ 7. Most school districts now have educational facilities for mentally retarded children.

_____ 8. Most persons with mild mental retardation are sensitive about their intellectual deficit and try to conceal it.

_____ 9. A token reward system is not generally an effective approach to modifying behavior of persons with a low I.Q.

_____ 10. Diazepam should be routinely prescribed for most mentally retarded individuals.

_____ 11. Psychotropic drugs are likely to compromise intellectual functioning.

_____ 12. Prescribing psychotropic drugs present special medical risks for patients who are moderately or severely retarded.

_____ 13. Psychological testing is usually necessary to establish the diagnosis of mental retardation.

Self-Assessment Exercise #3 (Continued)

Read the following case and then answer the questions asked. Mr. and Mrs. Stevens request consultation with you regarding their 7-year-old son, Arthur. Arthur was suspected by his teacher as having mild mental retardation and was recommended for psychological testing.

14. His parents question the reason for the testing. What would you tell them?

15. They ask if Arthur should be allowed to attend sporting events and outings with other children in the neighborhood or kept at home. What advice would you give?

16. Arthur is described as eager to help his parents work in the yard, but repeatedly neglects his personal grooming. Briefly outline a behavior modification program which may help Arthur.

Self-Assessment Exercise #3 (Continued)

17. His parents state that Arthur seems "nervous" when exposed to new activities. They inquire about the possibility of obtaining some "nerve medicine" to help him. What would you advise?

When you have completed this exercise to the best of your ability, check your answers with those on the following page.

Self-Assessment Exercise #3 - Feedback

True 1. Techniques of supportive psychotherapy work best on patients whose I.Q. is greater than 55.

True 2. It is beneficial for most mentally retarded children to participate in such activities as attending school, visiting museums, etc.

True 3. Behavior modification therapy is more appropriate for helping the mentally retarded than an insight oriented treatment.

False 4. It is best not to let mentally retarded persons attempt activities at which they may fail.

False 5. Most persons with mental retardation prefer a constantly changing environment and making important decisions by themselves.

False 6. Aversive behavioral therapy should be applied to most retarded persons.

True 7. Most school districts now have educational facilities for mentally retarded children.

True 8. Most persons with mild mental retardation are sensitive about their intellectual deficit and try to conceal it.

False 9. A token reward system is not generally an effective approach to modifying behavior of persons with a low I.Q.

False 10. Diazepam should be routinely prescribed for most mentally retarded individuals.

True 11. Psychotropic drugs are likely to compromise intellectual functioning.

True 12. Prescribing psychotropic drugs present special medical risks for patients who are moderately or severely retarded.

True 13. Psychological testing is usually necessary to establish the diagnosis of mental retardation.

Self-Assessment Exercise #3 - Feedback (Continued)

14. The testing should be performed to help determine whether or not mental retardation is present. Psychological factors can sometimes cause impaired intellectual functioning. Also, the severity of the impairment should be determined.

15. Arthur should be encouraged to participate in all such outings and activities. Socialization with peers is important to his development and these activities may help expand his intellectual growth and adaptive ability.

16. Outline a token reward system to the parents. Arthur should be told about receiving a reward each time he maintains his grooming. The rewards should be immediate and consistently given. He should be regularly complimented about his improved appearance.

17. Inform the parents that transient "nervousness" in new situations is to be expected and that medications are not indicated unless the tension persists or worsens. Tell them that "nerve medications" cause side effects which may further compromise his intellectual functioning.

If your answers correspond closely with those above, please continue reading on the next page. If not, please reread the preceding material.

SUMMARY

In the United States over two million persons are mentally retarded, that is, they have a significantly sub-average intelligence and deficiencies of adaptive behavior which first become evident during their developmental years. Much study has been devoted in recent years to understanding the causes and developing a therapeutic approach for this mental condition. The therapeutic approach to persons with mental retardation includes supportive psychotherapy, behavioral modification, special education instructions, sheltered workshops, and the selective use of medications.

REFERENCES

Bijou, S. W., "The Mentally Retarded Child," Psychology Today, 2:47 - 51, June, 1968.

Farber, G., Mental Retardation: Its Social Context and Social Consequences, Boston: Houghton Mifflin, 1968.

Ingalls, Robert, Mental Retardation: The Changing Outlook, New York: John Wiley & Sons, Inc., 1978.

MacMillan, D. L., Mental Retardation in School and Society, Boston: Little, Brown & Company, 1977.

Maloney, M. P., Ward, M. P., Psychological Assessment: A Conceptual Approach, New York: Oxford University Press, 1976.

Maloney, M. P., Ward, M. P., Mental Retardation and Modern Society, New York: Oxford University Press, 1979.

Robinson, N. M., Robinson, H. B., The Mentally Retarded Child: A Psychological Approach (2nd Ed.), New York: McGraw-Hill, 1976.

Part III
Psychotherapeutics for Problems of Living

CHAPTER 14. PSYCHIATRIC EMERGENCIES

It is inevitable that you will be called upon to assist someone experiencing a psychiatric emergency. A "psychiatric emergency" can include many different types of psychological crises, but we will restrict our discussion to four representative ones which call for immediate intervention -- in particular, dealing with persons who are potentially assaultive, suicidal, intensely anxious or gravely disabled. By gravely disabled persons we mean those who are so mentally disturbed that they cannot appropriately care for themselves. To diagnose and manage these patients is a challenging and stressful task, but timely intervention can prevent unfortunate consequences. In this chapter we will outline methods and principles for assessing and managing patients during a psychiatric emergency.

LEARNING OBJECTIVES

By the time you complete this chapter, you should be able to do the following and apply the information to written case histories.

1. Characterize and identify patients who are potentially assaultive, suicidal, gravely disabled or intensely anxious in terms of: a) general behavior, b) MSE findings, c) nature of the patient-therapist relationship, and d) significant physical findings.

2. Briefly describe each of the three steps recommended for dealing with patients experiencing a psychiatric emergency.

3. Describe the techniques for "defusing" intense feelings which the patient may have.

4. Outline the four areas of information which should be explored during an emergency consultation.

5. Outline interviewing principles which are useful during an emergency consultation.

6. For each of the methods of therapeutic intervention listed, describe the recommended approach and provide a rationale for its use in the management of patients during a psychiatric emergency.

   a. supportive psychotherapy
   b. behavioral therapy
   c. pharmacologic therapy
   d. consultation and referral

DIAGNOSTIC FINDINGS

Patients experiencing a psychiatric emergency may have any of a variety of psychopathologic conditions, including an organic brain disorder (e.g., drug intoxication), a functional psychosis (such as schizophrenia) or intense depression or anxiety. It is important to be knowledgeable about the typical findings of these psychiatric syndromes so that you can establish a diagnosis by selective questioning and MSE observations. Determining the diagnosis will often provide an estimate of behavioral control because persons with impaired reality testing, an organic brain disorder, or who are overwhelmed by intense emotions, may act out their impulses and feelings.

However, it is not always possible to establish a definitive psychiatric diagnosis during an assessment under emergency conditions. Sufficient history and other diagnostic information just may not be available. Furthermore, prescribing interventions such as hospitalization or psychotropic medication is not necessarily based on diagnosis alone. Not everyone who is psychotic, depressed or anxious constitutes a psychiatric emergency -- only those persons who pose a significant threat to themselves or others. Rather, the severity of symptoms and patient behaviors are more influential in deciding which treatment approach is most appropriate. With these qualifications in mind, we will place special emphasis on assessment of patient behavior and estimating the potential for harmful actions.

Mental Status Findings

Often, only a sketchy history will be available and therapeutic interventions have to be based on observations of the patient's mental status and behavior. The Mental Status Examination (MSE) findings outlined below are particularly important for assessing patients in crisis.

Appearance. A patient's appearance can provide valuable clues about his mental and emotional state. Is anything remarkable about his clothing, grooming or physical appearance? Is there unusual pallor, sweating, bruises or other findings suggestive of illness or injury? Note pupil size, since atypical dilation or constriction of pupils may be caused by various drugs.

Behavior. When assessing patients, behavior is often more revealing than spoken words. Take special note of the facial expression and general physical activity because these findings often reflect inner emotional states. Patients who are intensely distressed or are about to lose behavioral control typically are hypervigilant, excitable, restless and show evidence of increased muscle tension such as clinched fists or tremulousness. During states of agitation and marked anxiety, respiration is frequently rapid and shallow.

Look for impaired coordination, slurred speech and an unsteady walk, findings which often indicate an organic brain disorder due to drug intoxication or physical illness. The intonation and speech patterns usually will reveal the affect which patients are experiencing. Mentally note the quality of the therapist-patient relationship and whether the patient is uncooperative, distant, threatening or unduly suspicious. If such is the case, compliance with treatment recommendations will be lessened.

Feelings. Since patient behaviors are greatly influenced by feelings, monitor the affective state closely and continuously. Determine if feeelings of anxiety, belligerence, depression, elation predominate or if the affect is uniquely blunted. Note whether feelings escalate or diminish in intensity during the interview and if they moderate in response to your interventions.

Perception. Observe carefully for hallucinations for they indicate the presence of psychosis and markedly impaired reality testing. If patients pause mid-sentence and stare intently at the ceiling or begin talking with themselves, they may be experiencing auditory or visual hallucinations. Ask about what is seen or heard.

Thinking. Systematic observations about a patient's thought content and patterns are very revealing because if thinking is impaired, impulsive behavior is more likely to occur. Fluctuating lapses of alertness, impaired orientation and recent memory suggest the presence of an organic brain disorder. Try to estimate the tendency for impulsive actions, judgment in daily living activities and capacity for cooperating with therapeutic recommendations. Identify the major themes of thought. If bizarre, delusional or eccentric ideas are expressed, they may signify a psychosis. Of particular significance are statements which indicate an intention to cause self-harm or assault others. When such ideas occur, special therapeutic intervention such as hospitalization may be needed. Finally, determine if an associational disturbance exists, since disorganized thinking often is related to impaired judgment and impulsive actions.

Significant Patient Characteristics

We will now summarize patient characteristics which help identify persons who are potentially assaultive, suicidal, gravely disabled or anxious. The diagnostic categories which are commonly associated with these behavioral descriptions are indicated. These findings represent generalizations and exceptions are common. The patient characteristics are outlined in terms of general behavior, key mental status findings, the patient-therapist relationship, and significant physical signs.

Potentially assaultive patients. The diagnostic categories which are often associated with belligerent behavior are manic and schizophrenic disorders (especially when accompanied by paranoid features), anti-social personality disorders, and organic brain disorders which are drug related. The general behavior of these patients is frequently characterized by hypervigilance, excitability, restlessness, emphatic speech and gesturing and belligerent actions. The MSE findings usually include some combination of the following: irritability or angry mood, suspiciousness, persecutory ideas, delusions and/or hallucinations and impaired reality testing and judgment. With regards to the relationship with the therapist, patients are often hostile, suspicious, distant, and guarded and tends to evoke fear or uneasiness in the therapist. Physical findings are typical to persons who are ready for "fight or flight," that is, dilated pupils, tremulousness, and an increase of pulse rate, respiration and muscle tension.

Potentially suicidal patients. The risk of suicidal behavior is greater among persons with major depressive disorders, organic brain disorders, schizophrenic disorders and alcohol or drug-dependent individuals. Typically, the general behavior of suicidal persons is slowed -- but occasionally tension or even agitation can be evident. The MSE findings usually include a depressed affect accompanied by psychomotor retardation, self-recriminations and ideational themes of helplessness, hopelessness and intent for self-harm. If the affective disorder is prominent, patients can evoke in the therapist transient feelings of sadness and perhaps an urgent concern about imminent suicidal actions. There are no specific physical findings associated with depression.

Gravely disabled patients. Persons who are gravely disabled are unable to provide for their basic needs because of a severe organic brain disorder or functional psychosis. Their general behavior varies according to the type of underlying pathology and, can range from lethargy to hyperactivity with pacing and agitation. Behavior often is ineffectual and lacks purposefulness and goal-directedness. The MSE findings characteristic of gravely disabled persons usually show marked abnormalities in appearance, reality testing, judgment and problem-solving ability. If an organic brain disorder is present, findings will include impairment of intellectual functioning, orientation, recent memory, alertness and concentration. If a severe functional psychosis is the basis for the disability an associational disturbance, eccentric/bizarre ideation and/or delusions and hallucinations are commonly observed. The patient-therapist relationship usually is such that the therapist may feel "confused" or perplexed and unable to follow the patient's thinking patterns. There are no specific physical findings characteristic of persons who are gravely disabled. However, many of these persons neglect their health, personal hygiene, and may appear ill and move unsteadily.

Panic-anxiety reactions. Symptoms of intense anxiety can occur in association with a non-psychotic anxiety disorder, a situational disturbance, functional psychosis or an organic brain disorder which is caused by drugs or alcohol. The general behavior of panic-stricken individuals is usually characterized by restlessness, tension and rapid movements and speech. The MSE findings typical of this condition include a prominent affect of anxiety which often is expressed as fears of an impending personal catastrophe such as insanity, fainting or loss of emotional control. Patients often express concerns about physical symptoms such as rapid heartbeat, shortness of breath, chest pain, dizziness and generalized tension. The patient-therapist relationship differs from those mentioned previously in that the patient usually reacts in a helpless, dependent manner and often pleads for help to alleviate his emotional distress. The physical findings coincide with those of many persons who are intensely frightened, that is, skin pallor, dilated pupils, sweating, rapid heartbeat and respiration, tremulousness and increased reflexes.

Now complete Self-Assessment Exercise #1 beginning on the following page.

Self-Assessment Exercise #1

1. In the spaces provided briefly list the typical patient findings according to whether they are suicidal, assaultive or are intensely anxious.

	Suicidal	Assaultive	Anxiety State
General Behavior			
MSE Findings Predominant Feelings Thought Content			
Associated Physical Findings			

Self-Assessment Exercise #1 (Continued)

2. Circle the patient findings which increase the potential for assaultive behavior or self-harm.

   a. disorientation to time and place
   b. auditory hallucinations directing his behavior
   c. a history of drug or alcohol dependency
   d. presence of mild, chronic anxiety
   e. beliefs that others are poisoning his food
   f. a history of aggressive or impulsive actions
   g. rambling, disorganized thinking

3. You have been asked to evaluate a young man described as "tense, rapid talking, and restlessly pacing about the consultation room". Briefly describe what you would expect regarding his response to you if his increased activity represents a manifestation of:

   a. an intense anxiety reaction

   b. potentially assaultive behavior

4. Based on the findings described, determine if the following patients are more likely to be: (There may be more than one correct answer to each case.)

   a = an imminent danger to others
   b = a suicidal risk
   c = gravely disabled
   d = intensely anxious

_____ a. An old man was found wandering in the streets and unable to give his name or address.

_____ b. A young woman described having marked fears that she was going to die; she seemed frightened, tense, and restless and was breathing deeply.

_____ c. A middle-aged woman sat slumped in the chair carrying on a conversation with unseen persons; she appeared malnourished, unkempt and barefooted; she lives alone.

Self-Assessment Exercise #1 (Continued)

4.

_______ d. A patient frowned and showed signs of increasing restlessness, clinched fists and loud, explosive speech; he demanded compliance with his wishes.

_______ e. A patient's behavior evoked feelings of apprehension and uneasiness in the interviewer.

_______ f. A well-dressed woman stared at the floor, murmuring over and over in a barely audible voice, "All is lost, all is lost."

When you have completed this exercise to the best of your ability, check your answers with those on the following pages.

Self-Assessment Exercise #1 - Feedback

1. The following are the findings typical of persons who are suicidal, assaultive or are intensely anxious.

	Suicidal	Assaultive	Anxiety State
General Behavior	decreased slowed few gestures slowed speech	increased restlessness pacing rapid speech	increased restlessness rapid speech
MSE Findings			
Predominant Feelings	depression sadness	anger hostility	apprehension fear worry
Thought Content	themes of: helplessness hopelessness guilt self-recrimi-nations self-harm	themes of: suspiciousness revenge physical harm to others	fear of: impend-ing calamity insanity fainting "loss of control" concern about physical symp-toms -- plea for help
Associated Physical Findings	none typical	increased: muscle tension respiration heart rate pupil size	increased: muscle tension respiration heart rate pupil size sweating pallor

Self-Assessment Exercise #1 - Feedback (Continued)

2. The following findings increase the likelihood of a patient translating his feelings into action in order to harm himself or others.

   a. disorientation to time and place
   b. auditory hallucinations directing his behavior
   c. a history of drug or alcohol dependency
   e. beliefs that others are poisoning his food
   f. a history of aggressive or impulsive actions
   g. rambling, disorganized thinking

3. The patient is tense, talkative and restless. His response to you would vary according to the basic diagnosis.

   a. an intense anxiety reaction -- This patient likely will approach you seeking help for his anxiety and physical symptoms.

   b. potentially assaultive behavior -- This patient is more likely to be emotionally distant, suspicious, evasive and hostile or threatening; he is likely to evoke fear or uneasiness.

4. Based on the findings described, the patient most likely is:

   a = an imminent danger to others
   b = a suicidal risk
   c = gravely disabled
   d = intensely anxious

__c__ a. An old man was found wandering in the streets and unable to give his name or address.

__d__ b. A young woman described marked fears that she was going to die; she seemed frightened, tense, and restless and was breathing deeply.

__c__ c. A middle-aged woman sat slumped in the chair carrying on a conversation with unseen persons; she appeared malnourished, unkempt and barefooted; she lives alone.

__a__ d. A patient frowned and showed signs of increasing restlessness, clinched fists and loud, explosive speech; he demanded compliance with his wishes.

<u>Self-Assessment Exercise #1 - Feedback (Continued)</u>

4.

<u>a, b</u> e. A patient's behavior evoked feelings of apprehension and uneasiness in the interviewer.

<u>b</u> f. A well-dressed woman stared at the floor, murmuring over and over in a barely audible voice, "All is lost, all is lost."

If your answers correspond closely with those above, continue reading. If not, please reread the preceding section.

PRINCIPLES OF THERAPEUTIC MANAGEMENT

We recommend that you routinely follow a three-step procedure when dealing with psychiatric emergencies. The steps are: assure safety, defuse intense emotions, and collect pertinent information.

Assure Safety

Since you cannot predict how patients will behave, proceed as if each were potentially assaultive. Therefore, the first step in the evaluation process is to assure safety for yourself, the patient and any bystanders. A basic rule is never to approach any emergency situation alone. Only if no other staff are available and the situation requires immediate intervention, should you attempt to handle an acute problem alone. Wait for other staff support. Ideally, the interview should be conducted in a setting where specially trained personnel, psychotropic medications and restraints are available for immediate use.

Obtain as much information as possible about patients prior to beginning the interview. Before entering the interviewing room, look over patients for suspicious bulges which might indicate a concealed weapon or other dangerous objects. Inspect any carried belonging such as packages and handbags for similar reasons. Be sure to "disarm" patients before proceeding further with the consultation. If you suspect that they may be potentially assultive, conduct the interview with the door left open, making sure that sufficient staff are readily available if you need them. If patients are already out of behavioral control, keep attendants with you throughout the evaluation.

Conduct the interview in a room which has been made safe prior to the meeting. The consultation room should not be lockable from the inside or contain objects such as chairs, ashtrays or lamps which could be used as weapons. Arrange the chairs so that you neither block patient access to the door nor sit too closely. Many patients become uneasy if they feel "hemmed in" or are located too close to the interviewer. Do not sit down if patients remain standing. To do so, would place you at a physical disadvantage if they become assaultive.

Defuse Emotions

After appropriate safety precautions have been taken, begin to "defuse" any intense emotional feelings which may interfere with obtaining the history. Intense feelings of anger, sadness or anxiety generally can be reduced by one of these approaches: encouraging their open expression, diverting the theme of thought to more neutral topics or imposing firmer controls in order to actively suppress them. Begin by encouraging the patients to verbally express their feelings. The outpouring of feelings should subside after a few minutes with a noticeable relief of tension and a greater willingness for cooperation. However, if during the interview patients show signs of escalating emotional tension which further disorganizes thinking and behavior, divert the discussion to more neutral topics. This can be done by interrupting and asking patients to supply data about their street address, date of birth or place of employment. A similar tack is to ask questions about recent and inconsequential events such as, "Was it a long ride to get here?". To answer these questions, patients must change their line of thought to a less emotionally charged topic. Most persons will respond positively to this approach.

If attempts at diversion are unsuccessful, a firm authoritative approach may be needed to reestablish emotional control. You may have to take a firm stand and emphatically say something like, "If you continue making physical threats, it will be necessary to restrain you. Now I want you to sit down". Occasionally, a threat of force may be indicated to control patient behavior, but we do not suggest that course of action unless you are immediately prepared to carry it out. Ultimatums make further negotiations difficult and can provoke some patients to assaultive behavior. This technique should be used only as a last resort. For similar reasons, do not try to humor or belittle patients into compliance.

Collect Information

If patients respond positively to the defusing procedures, the next step is to obtain a pertinent history. Keep in mind that your time may be limited for obtaining a history and arriving at a therapeutic disposition. At any moment the patient may become uncooperative, uncommunicative or otherwise disrupt the history-taking process. For these reasons, you should focus especially on obtaining information which is vital for your evaluation objectives. In particular, you should determine by findings of observation and history the following:

(a) Does a psychiatric emergency exist? That is, is the patient an imminent danger to himself or others, gravely disabled or otherwise troubled so as to require immediate psychiatric treatment?

(b) What psychological, physical and social factors have combined to cause the present symptoms? Are the factors such that they will immediately improve with intervention or will they require longer treatment?

(c) What resources (social, financial, therapeutic, and others) are available? Can these resources be mobilized immediately and are they sufficient to meet the patient's needs?

(d) What is the psychiatric diagnosis? Is it a problem which is acute or chronic, mild or severe?

Focus on gathering information about the chief complaints and present life history to determine if psychiatric intervention is needed. What are the presenting symptoms? Is there a theme of intended violence or self-harm? Is the patient capable of rational decisions about daily living and adequately providing for himself? Or is he literally overwhelmed by mental confusion or feelings of depression, anxiety or anger?

Try to answer the question, "Why now?" with respect to the onset of symptoms. When did these symptoms begin and what seems to alleviate or worsen them? What family, work, health or other factors may have played a part in the present difficulties? Determine if it is possible to make interventions which will achieve immediate relief or if more extended treatment is needed. Be sure to get the patient's ideas about what would be helpful to him. Frequently, a patient can state precisely what is needed to relieve his distress. Inquire about the presence of any current illness and use of medications, prescribed or otherwise. Sickness and drugs can adversely effect behavior and emotions. Question whether there have been previous emotional difficulties and psychiatric treatment.

Gather what information you can about the patient's present living arrangements and other resources. Final decisions about treatment may hinge upon the availability of a concerned family or friends and adequate finances.

Finally, supplement the history with information from family, friends, police and any others who can add to your understanding.

You will find it useful to now review the general interviewing principles outlined in the chapter, "Abbreviated Psychological Assessment." Most patients are under considerable emotional stress in crisis situations and close attention should be paid in managing their overt and covert feelings. The following principles will help you guide the interview in accordance with their emotional state.

Begin the consultation by introducing yourself and stating the purpose of the interview -- to identify the cause of the patient's trouble and what can be done to help. Carefully observe your patient. If he appears particularly troubled by any emotion, be it depression, anxiety, anger or others, phrase your next comments in a way to openly explore the feeling. For example, "By your facial expression you seem to be pretty angry (depressed...frightened, etc.) about something. What's the trouble?". Such an empathic comment conveys interest in the patient's immediate distress and provides a chance to discuss it openly. Your willingness to talk first about what is troublesome to the patient goes a long way toward building rapport. Try to put the patient at ease by attending to his physical comfort -- offer a comfortable chair, to light his cigarettes, and other amenities.

Continue the interview by asking general, open-ended questions which encourage elaboration. For example, "What's been bothering you?".

This question directs the interview towards current problems and yet allows the patient to select the specific areas of distress. You will learn more about a patient's thinking, behavior and history by listening than by talking. Therefore, during the initial part of the consultation make extensive use of open-ended questions and do not interrupt the patient's recitation for details. Demonstrate your interest by leaning forward, maintaining eye contact and making periodic emphatic comments. Do not take notes or read medical charts duri ng the interview.

After you have an overview of the problem, switch to using closed-ended questions for gathering specific details. Closed-ended questions also are helpful for providing directions for patients who ramble or are unable to follow an idea through to its logical conclusion. Be sure to fully explore the areas of information listed above.

Silence can be a useful interviewing technique. When you are quiet, subtle pressure is generated within the patient to speak. However, this technique should be used judiciously because repeated or prolonged periods of silence can generate excessive tension in very anxious or disorganized patients.

It is good practice to periodically summarize important themes which come to light during the patient's narrative. These statements indicate your understanding of his circumstances and also define subjects important for further discussion. Examples of summarizing comments are, "From what you've said over the past few minutes, I guess the loss of the relationship with your wife made you feel depressed." or "Three times you've mentioned problems at work which have effected your sleep and appetite. It sounds as if you're worried about your job."

Sometimes suppressed but intense feelings can interfere with a patient's ability to relate a relevant history. The situation can be remedied by deliberately focusing on the intrusive feelings. Simply describe the prominent nonverbal behavior and speculate out loud what you think the associated feelings may be. Examples of such responses are, "By the way you are clinching your fists and scowling, I guess you must be feeling pretty angry." or "I notice that when I ask you questions about your marriage, your voice quivers as if you were sad. Is that so?" These behavioral descriptions usually will cause the suppressed feelings to surface so that they can be discussed openly and resolved.

Finally after you have established a diagnosis and treatment plan, explain your findings and recommendations concisely and give the patient an opportunity to respond to them. Be sure to deal with his feelings about your conclusions.

Now complete Self-Assessment Exercise #2 beginning on the following page.

Self-Assessment Exercise #2

Read the following case vignettes and answer the questions.

Case #1

A distressed mother calls requesting you to evaluate her son. He was described as "acting irrationally" and broke furniture in his home after allegedly smoking PCP. You have the option of evaluating the patient in his home, your office, or the emergency room of a local hospital. Which would be the most appropriate location for the interview? Why?

Case #2

A middle-aged man was brought in by police after assaulting two strangers on the street. The patient asserted that the strangers actually were "communist agents out to get me." The patient agreed to an interview but insisted on talking with you alone with the consultation room door closed. Would you comply with his offer? Why?

Case #3

After allowing a psychotic patient to ventilate his feelings about his mother, you observe that he is becoming increasingly restless, tense, and angry. He abruptly stands up and begins yelling profanities. What are two other "defusing" procedures which you can follow which might help him to regain his emotional control?

Self-Assessment Exercise #2 (Continued)

Case #4

A middle-aged man is referred for emergency evaluation after taking an overdose of heart medicine in a suicide attempt. He states he is depressed and wants to die. Assuming that you have only 20 minutes to complete a history, what general and specific areas of information would you pursue?

Case #5

An agitated patient talks rapidly and continuously in a disjointed fashion. Comment briefly on the methods of approach which are consistent with good management of the interview.

a. Would you elect to use more open- or closed-ended questions? Why?

b. Would you take detailed notes during the interview to promote your recall of the details which he relates? Why?

c. When talking with this patient, would it be best to remain silent or become verbally active in directing the interview? Why?

When you have completed this exercise to the best of your ability, check your answers with those on the following page.

Self-Assessment Exercise #2 - Feedback

Case #1

A distressed mother calls requesting you to evaluate her son. He was described as "acting irrationally" and broke furniture in his home after allegedly smoking PCP. You have the option of evaluating the patient in his home, your office, or the emergency room of a local hospital.

If possible, this patient should be seen in an emergency room setting. With the history of breaking furniture and "irrational" behavior, he may need to be physically restrained and hosptalized. You likely would need support from others to control him. Furthermore, there may be medical complications from the drugs which he took and treatment facilities are immediately available in an emergency room.

Case #2

A middle-aged man was brought in by police after assaulting two strangers on the street. The patient asserted that the strangers actually were "communist agents out to get me." The patient agreed to an interview but insisted on talking with you alone with the consultation room door closed.

You should not comply with his request. The patient is delusional (psychotic) and already has been assaultive. He should be interviewed either with others present or the consultation door left open and "help" immediately available.

Case #3

After allowing a psychotic patient to ventilate his feelings about his mother, you observe that he is becoming increasingly restless, tense, and angry. He abruptly stands up and begins yelling profanities.

To help this patient regain emotional control, you should attempt to divert him to more neutral topics. If this approach does not succeed, then firm behavioral guidelines can be used, i.e., insisting that he stop yelling and sit down.

Self-Assessment Exercise #2 - Feedback (Continued)

Case #4

A middle-aged man is referred for emergency evaluation after taking an overdose of heart medicine in a suicide attempt. He states he is depressed and wants to die.

During the brief time available to interview him you should attempt to get information about the following areas:

(1) What psychological, social and physical factors are contributing to his depression now?

(2) What personal and social resources are available to help him?

(3) His psychiatric diagnosis (MSE findings).

(4) Present medical problems and medications.

(5) History of prior psychological problems and treatment.

Case #5

An agitated patient talks rapidly and continuously in a disjointed fashion.

a. Would you elect to use more open- or closed-ended questions?

Closed-ended questions would be more appropriate. They help provide structure to the patient and tend to limit the length of his replies.

b. Would you take detailed notes during the interview to promote your recall of the details which he relates?

Your full attention should be directed to listening and observing the patient. Do not take notes during an evaluation interview.

c. In interviewing this patient, would it be best to remain silent or become more verbally active in directing the interview?

Silence would encourage his rambling. The behavior of this type of patient requires you to be active, directive and verbal.

If your answers correspond closely with those above, continue reading. If not, please reread the preceding section.

THERAPEUTIC INTERVENTIONS

After you have completed the interview and established a working diagnosis, the next step is to develop an individualized treatment plan. This section will outline guidelines for treating patients in terms of supportive psychotherapy, behavioral therapy, consultation/referral and psychotropic medications. The treatment plan should be based upon careful assessment of patients' present behavior, MSE findings, psychiatric diagnosis, medical condition, available resources, and data from significant others. All interventions imposed upon patients including restraints, medications, hospitalization, etc. should be administered in compliance with legal decisions designed to protect patient's civil rights.

Therapeutic options should be selected according to patient needs and may call for psychotropic medications, hospitalization, supportive psychotherapy, medical treatment, and/or referral to mental health specialists or various community resources. Occasionally, symptoms will subside in response to the assessment process itself and need nothing more. But many persons will require more definitive care. In all cases, direct your therapeutic efforts toward alleviating the basic problems and disturbing symptoms and feelings.

Supportive Psychotherapy

Dealing with patients in crisis can be a stressful experience. Far-reaching decisions often must be made rapidly with limited information upon which to base them. Therapist and patient typically are strangers to one another with the consequence that their working alliance is tenuous. Emergency patients are emotionally distraught and often are unpredictable and uncooperative.

The central element of the emergency interview is the therapist-patient relationship. Your attitude and behavior will greatly influence the outcom Many patients feel threatened by the evaluation procedure and will watch you closely for clues about your intentions and what the situation may hold for them. At times, you will feel uncertain and even anxious when approac ing new patients, particularly if they have a history of threatening behavior But if you respond by becoming markedly authoritarian, fearful or indecisive, their emotional distress will escalate and complicate the evaluation process. If you feel too uncomfortable about working in emergency circumstances, arrange for a consultant either to assist or replace you. It is neither necessary nor expected that you treat all patients who come seeking help, but it is your responsibility to find for them someone who can. It is important that you know and respect your therapeutic abilities and limitations -- especially when dealing with emergencies.

Directive guidance. Because of their distraught emotional state, most patients during psychiatric crises respond in a confused and ineffectual fashion. To counteract their disorganization use a directive guidance approach. Your therapeutic approach should be firm and authoritative, supplying reassurance to counteract anxiety, structure for disorganized thinking, and behavioral limits for patients who cannot control their impulses.

Speak in a calm but authoritative voice. The feelings of decisiveness which you convey is as calming as what you say. Set behavioral limits and make it clear that the patient can say whatever they like, but that harmful behavior will not be permitted. Attempt to gain his cooperation but stand ready to implement appropriate therapy whether or not he is able or willing to comply with your recommendation.

Environmental intervention. Many patients brought for emergency treatment are overwhelmed by a variety of problems which can be remedied by effective environmental intervention. In this regard, you may find it useful to make a mental list of problems in order to systematically alleviate them. The two-fold aim of this treatment approach is to reduce sources of environmental stress and simultaneously provide a milieu which is conducive to reestablishing emotional equilibrium.

For patients who are potentially suicidal, assaultive or are unable to provide adequately for themselves, some form of inpatient treatment is a viable option. Psychiatric hospitalization can be used to supply supervised care on an around-the-clock basis and/or separate patients from a stressful environment. Hospitalization is also indicated for persons who lack sufficient social resources or need definitive medical care. Therapeutic activities should be developed which provide for emotional support, social interaction, and firm behavioral control. Inpatient care also serves to provide a needed respite for overstressed family members.

Other types of environmental interventions which may be appropriate are arranging for placement in a supervised nursing home, board and care home, suggesting time off from stressful work, or referral to a day treatment center. But whether patients are treated in or outside of the hospital, make sure that their environment is optimal and offers good physical care, therapeutic relationships and activities. Be sure to evaluate financial, transportation, welfare, and other pertinent data to ensure that your plans can succeed.

Since you may have to impose inpatient treatment on unwilling patients, be thoroughly familiar with the criteria and procedures dictated by law for doing so. Keep detailed notes which substantiate your diagnosis and treatment recommendations as well as the rationale for your decisions.

Education. The treatment focus for psychiatric emergencies is resolving acute problems, and educational efforts usually are limited to keeping patients informed about diagnostic findings and treatment. If they have a condition which warrants definitive treatment, say so. Keep in mind that it is difficult for persons experiencing intense emotions to comprehend complex explanations or terminology. Make your statements clear, simple and concise. Because your patients may be confused or preoccupied, repeat your explanations. Finally, family members should be fully informed about your findings and recommendations. Often the family can be of help in planning and decision making and should be involved in all levels of treatment.

Reassurance. Reassurance should be an integral part of any treatment regimen which involves acutely disturbed individuals. The form by which reassurance is given may vary, but the message is the same -- there is hope and concerned others will help.

Without making unrealistic promises, try to convey a sense of therapeutic optimism. It is useful to inform patients that however disturbing their plight might seem, it is a time-limited crisis and likely will improve with treatment. Establishing and enforcing firm guidelines for behavior can be quite reassuring for patients who fear loss of control. It is important for disturbed patients to understand that potentially harmful behavior will not be permitted and medications, physical restraints or hospitalization will be used if necessary. Confused patients feel reassured by a firm approach which helps them structure their world and make decisions which they could not do by themselves. Depressed or anxious persons usually take comfort from words of direct assurance and anti-anxiety medications.

Behavioral Therapy

Because of the intensity of symptoms and limited time available for treatment during an emergency evaluation, most behavioral modification therapies are not effective or appropriate.

Pharmacologic Therapy

A variety of psychotropic drugs are available which can alleviate many of the psychological and behavior symptoms associated with psychiatric emergencies. Occasionally, a medical illness or other medications will cause symptoms which will be aggrevated by drugs which you prescribe. For that reason, a thorough evaluation of the history and physical status of patients should precede administering any medications. In cases where you suspect the symptoms are drug related (especially if sedatives or "street" drugs were taken) arrange for a laboratory examination of blood and urine. This should be done to establish your diagnosis even when the test results won't be available until after a preliminary disposition of the case is made.

Especially during emergency situations and when working with new patients, it is vital that you are thoroughly familiar with the contraindications, potential side effects and complications for any medication which is prescribed. (We recommend that you review the chapter on "Pharmacologic Therapy" for details.) If patients are belligerent or otherwise unmanageable, it may be expedient to administer a calming drug even at the risk of causing some undesirable side effects. But proceed cautiously, and give the least amount of medication necessary to produce an optimal result. As a rule, psychotropic drugs given orally are less likely to cause complications than those given by injection. Administration of medications by the IM or IV route should be reserved for instances when a rapid onset of effect is indicated or when patients refuse drugs by mouth. After giving any psychotropic medication to new patients, closely monitor their mental state, behavior and vital signs including blood pressure, pulse, respiration rate and general alertness. Have the medical means immediately available to treat any complications which may arise.

Most patients in crisis will comply with recommendations which are tactfully and authoritatively given. However, some individuals are too emotionally distraught or confused to cooperate even with recommendations that are clearly in their best interest; and for them, more decisive intervention is needed. A quiet show of force is usually all that is necessary to induce patients to accept hospitalization, medication or behavioral controls. Calmly, but firmly state the reasons for the treatment and it will be carried out. Arrange for several attendants to quietly and slowly surround the patient (attendants should be specially trained for dealing with such circumstances). Continue to give reassurance that no harm is intended but that the treatment is needed and will be given. Most patients will concede to this show of force and begrudgingly go along with your recommendations.

When it is necessary to give medications or apply restraints to combative patients, make sure that you have sufficient help. There should be one person assigned to restrain each extremity and a fifth to administer the medications and apply restraints. In some cases, it may be necessary to apply arm and leg restraints in order to give the medication. The restraints should be made of leather and in good repair. Psychotropic medications are effective in calming agitated, belligerent patients, but can take 1/2 hour or longer to achieve a therapeutic result, even when given intramuscularly. Therefore, if restraints have been applied because of uncontrollable behavior, do not remove them until you are certain that the medication has produced the desired calming effect. All restrained patients should be positioned near a nursing station or similar facility where they can be continuously monitored.

For nonpsychotic patients with marked anxiety and related physical symptoms such as restlessness, palpitations, hyperventilation and tremulousness, either diazepam or chlordiazepoxide are appropriate. Diazepam, 5 mg. p.o. or chlordiazepoxide, 25 mg. p.o. can be given. These are relatively safe drugs and unlikely to cause side effects other than drowsiness or decreased coordination. Diazepam can be given 5 to 10 mg. slowly IV to control intense anxiety or panic states, when a rapid relief of symptoms is desired or if a gastro-intestinal disturbance precludes taking oral medication. Unfortunately, no rapid acting medication is available for the treatment of depressive symptoms, and therefore, prescribing tricyclic or other anti-depressants in order to resolve depressive symptoms is not appropriate.

Any of the previously described anti-psychotic drugs (chlorpromazine, haloperidol, thiothixene or fluphenizine) in oral or IM form may be suitable for patients with intense symptoms of agitation, belligerence, psychosis and hallucinations or delusions. These potent medications, more than the anxiety drugs, are likely to cause side effects and interact adversely with other medications which the patient may have taken. The overall effectiveness and incidence of side effects among these anti-psychotic drugs are comparable. With one possible exception, chlorpromazine given IM is more likely to cause a significant drop of blood pressure, and for that reason, should not be administered IM particularly to elderly persons or those with known cardiovascular disease. The starting doses for the anti-psychotic and anti-anxiety drugs mentioned are summarized in Table I.

Consultation and Referral

With the possible exception of persons who are suffering from a mild disorder and respond quickly to minimal intervention, most patients qualifying as a psychiatric emergency will need consultation with a psychiatrist, physician or one of a variety of specialists in community agencies. Psychiatric consultation certainly should be sought for all who are a potential danger to themselves or others or are gravely disabled. Persons who are brought for evaluation and have intercurrent physical problems should receive a thorough physical and laboratory examination. For patients with environmental difficulties, referral to a family service agency, mental health clinic or welfare agency is appropriate.

Now complete Self-Assessment Exercise #3 beginning on the following page.

Self-Assessment Exercise #3

1. A man in his early 30's is brought in handcuffs by police for evaluation. He gives a rambling and disjointed history of taking various kinds of "street drugs" over the past two years. Four hours before being picked up by the police, he took some unknown drug and developed unpredictable and belligerent behavior. At the time you see him, he is shouting profanities and demanding that the handcuffs be removed or he will "sue everyone within two miles."

   a. Would you remove his handcuffs at this point? Why?

   b. A nurse asks if she should give the patient an injection of haloperidol to "quiet him down a bit." What would you tell her to do? Why?

2. A woman in her 40's is brought for evaluation by her concerned family because she spoke of committing suicide. The family had to stay with her around-the-clock for the past 72 hours because of repeated efforts to take pills, cut her wrists, or in other ways harm herself. The woman had experienced severe insomnia and loss of appetite for two weeks. Evaluation showed her to be very tense, restless and depressed. She expressed feelings that she had committed the "greatest sin in the world and deserved to die." She felt hopeless and helpless and felt that the world would soon come to an end.

   a. Would you recommend in- or outpatient treatment for this patient? Why?

Self-Assessment Exercise #3 (Continued)

2. b. The patient insisted on being allowed to return to her home so she could "die in peace" and stated that you had no right to detain her. Her family seemed uncertain about what course of action to take. In what way could you reassure and educate the patient and her family about her condition and need for treatment?

c. Her family suggested that you administer a drug which would rapidly resolve her depressed symptoms and suicidal ideation. What would you tell them about such a medication?

3. Indicate whether the following questions are true (T) or false (F). Briefly substantiate your answers.

______ a. A directive and authoritative approach should be used only as a last resort when dealing with patients in crisis.

______ b. Patients who are out of behavioral control may feel less anxious if their physical actions are firmly (or even forcibly) limited.

______ c. It is good policy to remove restraints within 10 minutes after an injection of haloperidol is given to calm an assaultive patient.

______ d. Ordering diazepam, 5 mg. IM is an appropriate prescription for an agitated patient who is combative and hallucinatory.

______ e. Chlorpromazine more than haloperidol is likely to cause an abrupt drop in blood pressure when given by injection.

______ f. Intense anxiety may be a manifestation of both psychotic and nonpsychotic disorders.

When you have completed this exercise to the best of your ability, check your answers with those on the following page.

Self-Assessment Exercise #3 - Feedback

1. A man in his early 30's is brought in handcuffs by police for evaluation. He gives a rambling and disjointed history of taking various kinds of "street drugs" over the past two years. Four hours before being picked up by the police, he took some unknown drug and developed unpredictable and belligerent behavior. At the time you see him, he is shouting profanities and demanding that the handcuffs be removed or he will "sue everyone within two miles."

   a. His handcuffs should not be removed unless they are immediately replaced by leather restraints. He recently has been belligerent and obviously is still out of emotional control. Only after he has become and remains calm should the restraints be removed.

   b. Tell the nurse not to give any medication until you have further evaluated the patient. He may have taken drugs which would interact adversely with the one you prescribe.

2. A woman in her 40's is brought for evaluation by her concerned family because she spoke of committing suicide. The family had to stay with her around-the-clock for the past 72 hours because she had made repeated efforts to take pills, cut her wrists, or in some other way harm herself. The woman had experienced severe insomnia and loss of appetite for two weeks. Evaluation showed her to be very tense, restless and deprssed. She expressed feelings that she had committed the "greatest sin in the world and deserved to die". She felt hopeless and helpless and felt that the world would soon come to an end.

   a. The patient is agitated, depressed and delusional. She has made suicide attempts and is still at risk. She needs the close monitoring and support which only a hospital can provide.

   b. In response to the patient's insistance to return home, tell her and the family that although she feels very troubled now the condition is time limited and likely will respond favorably to inpatient treatment. Make it clear that in her present state she is potentially suicidal and that hospitalization is indicated and the treatment of choice.

Self-Assessment Exercise #3 - Feedback (Continued)

2. c. Her family asked about medication which you could give her to bring about quick relief for her depressive symptoms.

Inform the family that no rapid-acting antidepressant presently exists. She may however benefit from drugs that would reduce her tension and restlessness.

3. Indicate whether the following questions are true (T) or false (F).

False a. A directive and authoritative approach should be used only as a last resort when dealing with patients in crisis?

In most emergency situations, a firm and directive approach is needed to handle the patient's anxiety and impaired judgment.

True b. Patients who are out of behavioral control may feel less anxious if their physical actions are firmly (or even forcibly) limited?

It is reassuring for most patients to feel that they will be prevented from committing harmful or unacceptable acts.

False c. It is good policy to remove restraints within 10 minutes after an injection of haloperidol is given to calm an assaultive patient?

It usually takes 30 minutes or longer for IM medication to take effect.

False d. Ordering diazepam, 5 mg. IM is an appropriate prescription for an agitated patient who is combative and hallucinatory?

Anti-anxiety drugs are not recommended for treating psychotic patients.

True e. Chlorpromazine more than haloperidol is likely to cause an abrupt drop in blood pressure when given by injection?

Chlorpromazine given by injection is more likely than haloperidol to cause a fall in blood pressure.

Self-Assessment Exercise #3 - Feedback (Continued)

3.

True f. Intense anxiety may be a manifestation of both psychotic and nonpsychotic disorders?

Intense anxiety may be experienced by nonpsychotic and prepsychotic and overtly psychotic patients.

If your answers correspond closely with those above, continue reading. If not, please reread the preceding section.

SUMMARY

The proper management of patients experiencing a psychiatric emergency requires special skills in interviewing, rapidly formulating a working diagnosis and prescribing an appropriate treatment plan. It is particularly important for you to identify patients who are a danger to themselves or others or who are gravely disabled. Therapists dealing with emergency patients should be thoroughly knowledgeable about the clinical indications for hospitalization, prescribing psychotropic drugs and the various mental health resources in the community.

REFERENCES

Dubovsky, S. and Weissberg, M., Clinical Psychiatry in Primary Care, Baltimore: Williams & Wilkins, 1978.

Resnik, U. and Ruben, H., Emergency Psychiatric Care, Bowie: Charles Press Publishers, 1975.

Rosenbaum, P. and Beebe, J., Psychiatric Treatment Crisis Clinic Consultation, New York: McGraw-Hill, 1975.

Slaby, A., Lieb, J. and Tancredi, L., Handbook of Psychiatric Emergencies, Flushing, New York: Medical Examination Publishing Co., 1975.

CHAPTER 15. HOSPITALIZATION AND CRITICAL CARE

Most persons take their good health, like life and liberty, for granted -- assuming that it will always be there. They expect that a pain-free and physically unrestricted way of life will be theirs and that serious illness happens only to someone else. Consequently when a major illness comes, few persons are adequately prepared to deal with it. Serious physical illness is perceived as a threat to one's very existence and always evokes feelings of fear, uncertainty and helplessness. While such feelings are expected, excessively intense emotions can delay recovery and worsen a patient's physical status. By understanding the particular fears which an illness evokes and counteracting them by using modern principles of therapeutic intervention, you can promote healing and alleviate suffering. This chapter describes the fears commonly associated with serious illness, typical patient responses to these fears, and principles for therapeutic intervention.

LEARNING OBJECTIVES

By the time you complete this chapter, you should be able to do the following and apply the information to written case histories.

1. List and briefly discuss the common fears caused by physical illness and hospitalization.

2. List and describe typical patient responses to major illness and hospitalization.

3. Describe sources of emotional stress often caused by hospitalization.

4. For each of the therapeutic interventions listed below, describe the recommended approach and provide a rationale for its use in the management of physically ill and/or hospitalized patients:

    a. supportive psychotherapy
    b. behavioral therapy
    c. pharmacologic therapy
    d. consultation and referral

COMMON FEARS RELATING TO ILLNESS

Some of the most difficult problems encountered in medicine are helping patients to cope effectively with illness. Far too many men needlessly have become cardiac cripples following a minor heart attack, and far too many women have developed incapacitating depression following an uncomplicated hysterectomy. As a health care professional, you regularly will be called upon to help persons who already are ill or are anticipating medical treatment. It will be important for you to identify their fears and therapeutically intervene to counteract them.

The way in which individuals respond to significant life events, including physical illness, depends greatly on the meaning which these incidents have for them. Previous experience with illness and physicians, learned family attitudes towards pain and sickness, the nature of the illness itself and expectations about recovery are but a few of the variables which influence patients' reactions. One or a combination of the fears now to be discussed will be present in all patients. Look for the fears, they will be present even if they are not openly mentioned.

The Fear of Pain, Debility and Death

The onset of illness serves as a forcible reminder of physical vulnerability. During good health it is possible to set aside thoughts of vulnerability to pain, debility or death. But sickness stirs up fantasies and fears about these possibilities which are difficult to suppress. Rare is the ill person who does not wonder: "Can I stand the pain?", "Will I fully recover?", or even "Will I survive?". These and related fears are invariably present when sickness comes and deserve your thoughtful intervention.

Fear of the Unknown

What your patients know about their illness can cause worry, but the prospect of having to deal with the unknowns relating to disease is even more disturbing. Very few persons possess even a basic understanding about the workings of their bodies. Therefore, when sickness comes they often are made anxious because of misconceptions about disease. And what patients don't know about their illness really does hurt them, because uncertainty evokes feelings of helplessness and worry. Only to the degree that patients can define the unknown can they begin to mobilize coping abilities.

Common questions which patients have but may hesitate to ask are: "Is the illness serious?", "Will there be pain?", "What will the treatment be like?", "How much will it cost?", and so forth. Of course, many questions about their sickness and treatment cannot be fully answered at a particular point in time. But to the degree which uncertainty is replaced by information, your patients likely will feel less helpless and frightened.

Fear of Helplessness and Dependency

For many, one of the most disturbing aspects of illness is the feeling of helplessness which it causes. Pain and physical weakness frequently transform independent, self-determining individuals into persons who must passively depend on others to meet such basic needs as food preparation, assistance in walking and body care. The sense of helplessness is greatest in persons who are hospitalized, undergoing anesthesia or experiencing a catastrophic illness such as a "stroke" or paralysis. The inability to control one's own bodily functions or physical activity often result in feelings of shame, a drastic fall in self-esteem, anxiety and depression.

Fears of Change and Self-Image

Some illnesses may adversely affect your patients' self-image, i.e., the way they view themselves physically, emotionally and as persons in general. Some examples may help to illustrate this concept.

> Mrs. Roberts, a woman in her mid-thirties, was advised to undergo surgical removal of her breast because of suspected cancer. At the prospect of surgery, she experienced marked fear and anxiety which, in part, was due to the anticipated change in her self-image. Not only was she confronted with an actual change in her physical body, but she must also cope with a loss of a highly valued organ which is closely associated with her sense of femininity and sexuality.

> Another example is that of 52-year-old, Mr. John Roberts, who took considerable satisfaction in being the conscientious worker and responsible provider for his family. His work required a great deal of physical activity, and while on the job he received a crushing injury to his legs. Even after extensive rehabilitation efforts, his mobility will be restricted; he will walk with a noticeable limp and will be unable to resume his former work. Mr. Roberts' physical appearance, ability to ambulate and his role as a provider have abruptly changed. He now must adapt to a dramatic change in his self-image.

Self-image is a part of one's personality which is highly valued and tenaciously maintained. Any medical condition or treatment which significantly disrupts a patient's conception about their bodily configuration, sexual identity, physical attractiveness or social or vocational roles will be felt as a threat to personal identity and will be strongly resisted.

There are several medical conditions which are especially likely to threaten a patient's self-image. Keep these conditions in mind so that you can anticipate and deal with the fears which they may evoke. Illnesses are especially threatening which:

change body appearance -- it is emotionally painful to feel physically different from others especially if the differences are disfiguring or easily noticed by others; skin lesions, facial scaring, amputations and bone deformities are examples.

affect sexual identity -- conditions which directly or indirectly influence an individual's sexual performance or role will be felt as a major threat, for example, a hysterectomy, a breast removal or sterilization procedures for women, or a prostatectomy, illness-related impotency or sterilization for men.

affect self-esteem -- when your patient is unable to perform physically, socially, or vocationally up to standards which he expects, his self-image may falter; sickness which impairs physical activity, socializing or productive work are exemplified by severe heart or lung disease, severe arthritis and cancer.

Fear of Disturbed Relationships

Your patients often develop worries that illness will interefere in key relationships with family, friends, or co-workers -- that others will come to regard them with fear, pity, or even disgust. Many debilitated patients harbor fears that their medical condition will result in a major role change for them within their family constellation or business, and that they will be relegated to an invalid status. Another common concern expressed by patients who must depend upon others for their physical care is that their family and friends will come to resent caring for them. A frequent worry of patients whose physical appearance has been markedly altered by surgery, e.g., a mastectomy or colostomy, is that they no longer will be sexually attractive or esteemed by their loved ones.

Many of these fears are exaggerated or unfounded. However, in instances when interpersonal relationships within the family already are problematic, illness is likely to cause even further stress. It is important that you explore the effect which illness has upon the key relationships of your patients.

Fear of Economic Problems

Not the least of worries that accompanies sickness is the expense. Specialized outpatient treatment or a short-stay hospitalization is costly enough, but major surgery, prolonged treatment or hospitalization can mean a severe financial hardship. Add to the medical expense income lost because of not working, and the reason for concern becomes evident. Patients often experience guilt feelings if the cost of their treatment deprives other family members of things which they want or need.

Now complete Self-Assessment Exercise #1 beginning on the following page.

Self-Assessment Exercise #1

1. List the six major categories of fears that a patient may experience during illness and treatment.

   a.

   b.

   c.

   d.

   e.

   f.

2. List the major fears which each of the patients may be experiencing in the case vignettes which follow.

   A 5-year-old boy soon will undergo a tonsillectomy. He asks many questions about the hospital, when he will get to go home, "if it will hurt," what the anesthetic will smell like.

   He likely is expressing fears about: ______________________________

3. A middle-aged physician responded to brief hospitalization for a broken shoulder by insisting that he read his X-rays and chart. It was difficult to get him to comply with routine orders for bed rest.

   He is likely responding to fears of: ______________________________
   ____

4. A 35-year-old mother of three children received severe burns to her face, neck and arms as a result of a gasoline explosion. Extensive surgery and therapy will be necessary in order to rehabilitate her.

   What types of fears would you expect her to experience? __________
   ____

Self-Assessment Exercise #1 (Continued)

5. A prominent 56-year-old attorney was hospitalized in the cardiac care center after experiencing an acute coronary thrombosis (heart attack). Initially after hospitalization he lay in bed as if afraid to move and asked many questions about his treatment, the electrical apparatus and frequently requested explanations about "what was going to happen next."

   What were his initial fears about? ______________________________

   ____

When you have completed this exercise to the best of your ability, check your answers with those on the following page.

Self-Assessment Exercise #1 - Feedback

1. The six major categories of fears that a patient may experience during illness and treatment are:

   a. pain, debility, death

   b. the unknown

   c. helplessness

   d. change in self-image

   e. disturbed relationships

   f. economic problems

2. The 5-year-old boy soon to undergo a tonsillectomy is likely expressing fears about the unknown and pain.

3. The middle-aged physician briefly hospitalized for a broken shoulder is likely responding to fears of the unknown, helplessness and change in self-image.

4. The 34-year-old mother of three children hospitalized due to severe burns to her face, neck and arms would likely experience fears of pain, the unknown and change in self-image.

5. The prominent 56-year-old attorney hospitalized in the cardiac care center after experiencing an acute coronary thrombosis (heart attack) would likely experience initial fears about the unknown.

If your answers correspond closely with those above, continue reading. If not, please reread the preceding material.

PATIENT RESPONSES TO ILLNESS

Anticipate that illness and medical treatment always will be regarded as a potential threat by your patients. But the nature of the threat will vary depending on their previous experience with sickness and its present and future meaning. For example, a broken leg may mean little more than six or eight weeks of discomfort and inconvenience to a teacher whose livelihood is not dependent upon mobility. However, the same condition may cause considerable financial worry for a house painter whose income depends upon an ability to climb ladders and easily move about. Similarly, the separation from family which occurs as a consequence of hospitalization can be handled reasonably well by most adults, but stirs up great anxiety in young children who feel insecure without the presence of their mother.

Patients react to illness by using the same coping mechanisms which they have called upon to deal with previous life stresses. They often are unable to verbalize their feelings, and instead, may express them through behavior which is difficult to understand. Therefore, be alert for the subtle behaviors which indirectly reflect their distress. Most patients have worries about pain, possible debility, helplessness, death and uncertainty about the future. Whether or not these fears are verbalized, watch for physical evidence of anxiety such as rapid heartbeat and breathing, tremulousness, restlessness, muscle tension and a frightened facial expression. Patients' fears also can be indirectly manifested by their asking endless questions about their condition, avoiding the topic altogether, making jokes about the illness or becoming unusually compliant. Don't be misled. Act on the premise that all patients are frightened about some aspect of their illness, whether or not the feelings are openly displayed.

Depression

Symptoms of depression frequently occur in sick patients. The depression may result from the loss of income, physical mobility or waning self-confidence because of having to depend upon others for care. Depression often accompanies illnesses that are associated with social stigma such as cancer, skin disease or scaring. Insomnia, restricted physical activity and many prescribed medications can also intensify depressive symptoms.

Anger and Irritability

The treatment of illness regularly involves discomfort, fear, and frustration, and many patients respond with some form of anger. Although no person in actuality is responsible for their sickness, patients regularly vent angry feelings on you, the hospital staff or their family. Patients often "displace" resentments onto persons whom they feel are unlikely to retaliate. For instance, if some of your patients are uneasy about criticizing you, they may vent their feelings on family members.

Anger can be expressed in a variety of intensities and forms ranging from icy silence, indirect criticisms, non-compliance with treatment, to shouts of rage. Seemingly trivial incidents can set off an explosive tirade.

Try not to personalize or become unduly defensive about the anger which may be directed towards you from time to time -- the feelings generally represent an indirect expression of frustration and fear.

Regression

When subjected to the emotional stresses of illness, patients may show signs of regression, which means behaving in a more childlike and immature fashion than is usually the case. During regression, mature methods of coping with stress give way to those typical of earlier levels of development. Regression occurs to some degree in all sick persons and takes various forms. Persons who are usually independent and easy going can become excessively dependent and demanding. They may respond impulsively, become stubborn or react with outbursts of tearfulness or irritation. These regressive behaviors can be quite dramatic, but generally disappear as the illness improves and psychological stress decreases.

Denial

Denial is a response to an unpleasant reality in which the affected person acts intellectually and emotionally as if nothing is wrong -- that no threat exists.

Most people occasionally use denial to deal with stressful life events, but an overuse of this coping mechanism can be self-defeating. An impressive example of denial at work is a recent study which showed that one-forth of all patients who had a "heart attack" requiring intensive care treatment for several days, later disclaimed that they had any heart disease. As might be expected, they did not comply with prescribed diets and recommendations. Approach your patients who use denial excessively by reducing their stress and providing ample emotional support. Only gradually confront them with the unpleasant facts about their illness.

Projection

Projection is the process of attributing to another one's own unacceptable (or threatening) feelings, thoughts and motivations. Projection is used occasionally by everyone, and is pathological only if it becomes a major method of coping with stress. Persons who generally are suspicious and distrustful of others are likely to overuse projection. Hostile, aggressive and sexual feelings are those most likely to be projected on others.

If some of your patients excessively use projection, try offering an alternative explanation to their misinterpretation of reality. But don't engage in arguments because such actions on your part will only serve to accentuate distress and mistrust. Instead, approach the situation with a firm, matter-of-fact attitude. Keep your patients well informed of all treatment procedures by giving clear and factual explanations and avoid giving superficial reassurances which, if they are not realized, may increase suspiciousness.

STRESS CAUSED BY HOSPITALIZATION

Most persons regard the prospect of inpatient treatment with mixed feelings, viewing hospitals both with hopeful expectancy and a sense of awe and uncertainty. Many of the unpleasant restrictions and regimentations are necessary for maintaining orderliness and efficiency, but keep alert for ways that you can make inpatient treatment less traumatic.

Hospitalization may be a source of patient distress for one or more of the following reasons.

Loss of Personal Identity

Hospitalization requires patients to relinquish many of the personal belongings and routines which contribute to their unique identity. For a variety of legitimate reasons, patients are asked to give up their purses, wallets, clothing and many personal prerogatives. Of considerable importance to identity is the temporary loss of family life, work and interpersonal relationships. Familiar surroundings and the daily activities which play such an integral part in maintaining each person's identity are left outside upon entering the hospital.

Loss of Autonomy

Hospital care may compound your patients' distress by reducing their sense of self-determination. In the interest of maintaining a smoothly run hospital which must consider the needs of many individuals, patients must give up a large measure of personal autonomy. Inpatients cannot freely come and go as they would in their own home. They generally must eat, sleep and follow routines dictated by others. Illness, pain and treatment may further constrict the range of choices which patients have concerning their physical activity and meetings with friends and family.

The Hospital Environment

The hospital setting itself is regarded as a mixed blessing by most patients. Those who are gravely ill appreciate the hospital milieu which provides medical care and attention on a 24-hour basis. All others quickly come to realize the disadvantages of their inpatient environment. Personal privacy is greatly compromised and hospital sights, smells and sounds are difficult to adjust to.

The environmental differences between home and hospital is dramatically exemplified by the intensive care centers (cardiac and intensive medical care units). These areas are specifically designed to handle life-saving emergencies, provide intensive monitoring and simultaneously manage several patients.

The beds in intensive care units usually are located close together, making inescapable the sounds and sights of other patients and dramatic treatment procedures. The awesome appearing electronic monitoring and treatment apparatus is often a source of patient anxiety. Only rarely do critical care areas have windows with views or other reminders of the outside world and changes in time, and without such perceptual feedback many patients become disoriented and mentally confused. Staff activity is medically focused and relatively impersonal. The staff are preoccupied with supporting life systems and there is little time for providing emotional support. Patient contact with family and friends typically is restricted to five minutes of each hour. Few areas of medical care are capable of illiciting such a sense of helplessness and anxiety as the intensive treatment units.

Now complete Self-Assessment Exercise #2 beginning on the following page.

Self-Assessment Exercise #2

Indicate whether the patients described primarily are responding to their illness with:

anxiety
regression
denial
projection
depression

1. Prior to receiving a general anesthesia, a teenaged girl complained of her "heart pounding," was noted to be restless, tremulous, and appeared somewhat wide-eyed.

   She is likely showing the physical concomitants of what feeling?

   ____

2. Twenty-four hours after being informed that he had inoperable cancer, the 63-year-old man became progressively quiet and socially withdrawn. He ate and slept little and maintained a very solemn facial expression.

   He is likely experiencing feelings of ______________________

3. After being hospitalized for six days, an eight year-old boy became intermittently tearful and demanding. On two occasions he wet his bed although he had not previously done so for three years.

   His behavior is indicative of ______________________

4. Five days after experiencing a moderately severe "stroke," a middle-aged woman seemed surprisingly unaffected by her hospitalization and symptoms. She cheerfully stated "all that is the matter with me is that I need a little rest" and minimized the obvious weakness in her arm.

   The woman is demonstrating ______________________ in response to her anxiety about her physical status.

5. Following the birth of an unwanted child, the young mother began behaving in a strange manner. She refused to let the nurse take the child from her saying "she doesn't like my baby and she plans to hurt it if I give her a chance."

   The mother is using ______________________ to deal with her own unacceptable feelings.

Self-Assessment Exercise #2 (Continued)

6. Describe the characteristics of intensive care units which may (a) be reassuring and (b) anxiety provoking to patients assigned to them.

   a.

   b.

7. A 39-year-old business executive is admitted to the hospital for exploratory surgery and evaluation. Describe aspects of hospitalization which may effect his sense of personal identity and autonomy.

   a.

   b.

When you have completed this exercise to the best of your ability, check your answers with those on the following page.

Self-Assessment Exercise #2 - Feedback

1. Prior to receiving a general anesthesia, a teenaged girl complained of her "heart pounding," was noted to be restless, tremulous and appeared somewhat wide-eyed.

   She is likely showing the physical concomitants of anxiety, fear and/or apprehension.

2. Twenty-four hours after being informed that he had inoperable cancer, the 63-year-old man became progressively quiet and socially withdrawn. He ate and slept little and maintained a very solemn facial expression.

   He is likely experiencing feelings of depression.

3. After being hospitalized for six days, an eight year-old boy became intermittently tearful and demanding. On two occasions he wet his bed although he had not previously done so for three years.

   His behavior is indicative of regression.

4. Five days after experiencing a moderately severe "stroke," a middle-aged woman seemed surprisingly unaffected by her hospitalization and symptoms. She cheerfully stated "all that is the matter with me is that I need a little rest" and minimized the obvious weakness in her arm.

   The woman is demonstrating denial in response to her anxiety about her physical status.

5. Following the birth of an unwanted child, the young mother began behaving in a strange manner. She refused to let the nurse take the child from her saying "she doesn't like my baby and she plans to hurt it if I give her a chance."

   The mother is using projection to deal with her own unacceptable feelings.

Self-Assessment Exercise #2 - Feedback (Continued)

6. The following characterisitcs of intensive care units which may (a) be reassuring and (b) anxiety provoking to patients are:

   a. surrounded by lifesaving apparatus and personnel; close monitoring

   b. awesome sights, sounds apparatus; sense of helplessness; few contacts with family; difficulty in maintaining orientation

7. A 39-year-old business executive is admitted to the hospital for exploratory surgery and evaluation. The aspects of hospitalization which may effect his sense of personal identity and autonomy are:

   a. loss of personal identity -- separation from family, work, usual routines; change in role from "executive" to "patient"

   b. loss of autonomy -- must follow hospital routine: for sleeping, eating, activities; increased dependency on others

If your answers correspond closely with those above, continue reading. If not, please reread the preceding material.

THERAPEUTIC INTERVENTIONS

Supportive Psychotherapy

Early in this chapter we described several factors which may adversely affect patient responses to illness and treatment. Your therapeutic approach will more likely succeed if it is designed to counteract as many of these factors as possible. The application of principles of supportive psychotherapy to patient problems will now be discussed.

Directive and nondirective guidance. How successfully a patient copes with illness and complies with treatment recommendations depends largely upon the therapeutic relationship. Therefore, the decision to adopt either a relatively directive or nondirective treatment approach is an important one.

If your patient seems intellectually disorganized, mentally confused, unduly anxious or otherwise overwhelmed by feelings, then use a directive approach. Supply structure and actively help with decision making. Give unequivocal advice and, at least temporarily, "take over" for the patient. But emphasize that your interventions are only temporary and to expect to resume self-determination as soon as possible. Your actions should refelct firmness and authority without conveying the feeling of condescension or disappointment that the patient can't manage effectively. Even after implementing a directive stance, encourage the patient's participation in decision making. For example, after determining that an injection is necessary, ask the patient if he would rather have it in the arm or the buttocks. If a treatment procedure is indicated, let the patient decide whether it will be done immediately or in ten minutes. As a rule, cooperation and compliance are more likely when a patient participates in medical decision making, however minor the role.

A suspicious or overtly psychotic patient usually responds better if you deal with them in a matter-of-fact, authoritative (but not authoritarian) way. Treatment recommendations to such individuals should be clear, concise and factual.

A nondirective approach is usually preferable for patients who are intellectually intact and emotionally stable, or who strongly react against situations in which they feel dependent or helpless. Keep your patients fully apprised about their medical status and your recommendations. When major decisions are needed, outline the options open and their consequences. Allow your patients to make the final decision about what to do. Encourage questions and discussion, but don't compromise your authoritative opinion. Your patients need your expertise and guidance. Help them deal with their natural reluctance to face an unpleasant reality such as surgery or hospitalization. It is best not to use "scare tactics" or attempt to coerce patients in order to gain their compliance.

Environmental intervention. If your patients are quite incapacitated you should intervene actively to assure an optimum environment. If hospitalization is indicated, consider whether a private or semi-private room is better and make the necessary arrangement. Determine which visitors should be allowed for the length of their stay. For the elderly and children, arrange frequent family visits, and place in view personal belongings and pictures. Prescribe optimal physical comfort and sensory imput. Because of the potentially disturbing environment of intensive care units, minimize patient stays in them as much as possible.

Become familiar with the home and work environment of your patient. Find out what, if any, environmental changes are needed to reduce sources of stress. At times, it may be appropriate for you to prescribe an absence from stressful work or school environment, and that adequate physical care, nutrition and activity are regularly provided. If home confinement is indicated, educate family members as to what they can do to improve the living milieu. Consider arranging for a visiting nurse if special treatments are needed.

Ventilation. You may have noticed that sick persons repeatedly tell the story of their illness and treatment to whomever will listen. By means of these recitations they somehow feel relieved and better able to manage their distress. They relive their experience and fears through words, and gradually desensitize themselves to the emotional impact of their condition. Also describing their fears to an empathic listener helps them to feel less alone with their problems. It is important that you encourage your patients to talk with you and others about that which is troubling.

The following techniques will facilitate patient ventilation. Set aside enough time for unhurried listening and by behavior and speech convey attentiveness. Assure privacy and delay note taking or chart reading until after the interview is completed. Actively encourage your patients to ask questions and describe their fears and fantasies about their medical problems and treatment. It is often surprising to hear the misconceptions and unrealistic expectations which otherwise intelligent persons have about illness and therapy.

It may take several meetings for your patients to fully verbalize their feelings and questions. Regularly scheduled brief meetings, say five to ten minutes in length, may work better with patients who are quite ill and have a diminished capacity for expressing themselves.

It is important that patients ventilate their feelings however inappropriate or unrealistic they may be. Hold your comments until the feelings have been expressed fully before offering an alternative viewpoint. Many patients hesitate to verbalize their feelings, fearing that they may sound "childish" or that criticism of the caregivers may result in retaliation. Encourage these individuals to speak out. Pay special attention to patients who in the face of major illness or surgery become withdrawn or ask few questions. Although they may appear to be coping well, their need to talk and receive support is as great as those who are more outspoken. If your patient becomes markedly upset while discussing his symptoms, it is best to divert him to more neutral topics. Please review the chapter on "Abbreviated Psychological Assessment" for other principles which will help to facilitate ventilation by your patient.

Now complete Self-Assessment Exercise #3 beginning on the following page.

Self-Assessment Exercise #3

1. Based on the information describing the patients below, indicate by either a (D) or (N) which general treatment approach you would use.

   (D) = Directive Guidance and/or maximum environmental intervention.
   (N) = Nondirective Guidance and/or minimal environmental intervention.

   ______ a. Following surgery the patient shows signs of restlessness, mental confusion and disorientation.

   ______ b. A 72-year-old man lives alone, does his own shopping and cooking.

   ______ c. A 35-year-old woman teacher asks your advice regarding whether she should have a sterilization procedure performed.

   ______ d. A hospitalized woman becomes emotionally upset following each visit by her family but feels unable to tell them not to come.

2. Indicate whether the following statements about patient ventilation of their feelings is true or false.

   ______ a. Patients who ask very few questions about their medical conditions are probably less worried than those who ask many.

   ______ b. Patients who are seriously ill respond best to extended periods devoted to talking about their illness.

   ______ c. Most patients feel worse after talking at length about their medical problems.

   ______ d. To demonstrate interest in your patient, it helps to write down key points as they state them.

   ______ e. It is therapeutic to correct patient misinterpretation immediately after they are stated.

When you have completed this exercise to the best of your ability, check your answers with those on the following page.

Self-Assessment Exercise #3 - Feedback

1. Based on the information describing the patients below, you should have indicated the following:

   (D) = Directive Guidance and/or maximum environmental intervention.
   (N) = Nondirective Guidance and/or minimal environmental intervention.

D a. Following surgery the patient shows signs of restlessness, mental confusion and disorientation.

N b. A 72-year-old man lives alone, does his own shopping and cooking.

N c. A 35-year-old woman teacher asks your advice regarding whether she should have a sterilization procedure performed.

D d. A hospitalized woman becomes emotionally upset following each visit by her family but feels unable to tell them not to come.

2. The following statements about patient ventilation of their feelings should have been marked true or false:

False a. Patients who ask very few questions about their medical conditions are probably less worried than those who ask many.

False b. Patients who are seriously ill respond better to extended periods devoted to talking about their illness.

False c. Most patients feel worse after talking at length about their medical problems.

False d. To demonstrate interest in your patient, it helps to write down key points as they state them.

False e. It is therapeutic to correct patient misinterpretation immediately after they are stated.

If your answers correspond closely with those above, continue reading. If not, please reread the preceding material.

Reassurance. As mentioned earlier physical illness and medical treatment usually evokes patient feelings of insecurity and fear which warrant reassurance. Reassurance directed toward specific fears are more therapeutic than global statements such as "Don't worry." or "Everything will be okay." Whenever possible, reassurance should be tangible and specific. Therefore, develop an understanding of what in particular your patients need reassurance about. You can learn this by listening carefully for the themes of worries and the nature of questions about treatment and prognosis. But if it is not clear to you what is so troubling, ask. Also, ask what would help them feel better.

Address yourself directly to the sources of distress. For example, if a patient expresses fears about a treatment procedure which he doesn't understand, explain in simple terms what is involved. Similarly, if he is anxious about experiencing pain, give reassurance that appropriate medications will be readily available. If worries about a permanent disability are present, introduce plans for rehabilitation which emphasize the development of remaining capabilities. To help reassure your patient about autonomy, encourage his participation in making decisions. Incorporate some element of hope with each patient contact. This does not mean that you should make unrealistic promises, but rather that your attitude should reflect optimism and concern. You can ease the news of a serious illness by following it with an outline of helpful treatment. If your patient will lose an important function because of surgery, prior to the operation emphasize the capacities that he will retain post-surgery.

Sometimes it will be difficult to provide reassurance. For terminally ill patients or those with a grave illness, reassurance directed toward personalized concern rather than achieving a "cure" is indicated. In those instances, conveying that you will "see the patient through", that he will be comfortable and not abandoned is all that you can deliver.

Some patients because of misconceptions or medical experiences may be difficult to reassure. But don't give up. Repeat the reassurances pointing out signs of progress whenever you can. If you have good news -- make it explicit. If you have bad news -- frame it in a way to hold out some element of hope -- if not for long life, then a painfree existence; if not debility free, then emphasize capabilities that remain.

Pay special attention to all aspects of your patient's physical comfort. This concern conveys your interest at a very basic and personal level and is very reassuring. A reassuring touch or pat provides a degree of support and closeness that cannot be expressed by words alone. Physical reassurance of this kind is particularly supporting to children and those who are gravely ill or mentally confused.

Your presence and attention are immensely reassuring to patients. Assess the needs for support of your patient's close friends and family members. Sometimes the most effective way of helping patients is to provide emotional support for those upon whom they depend.

Education. In spite of living in an enlightened age when medical topics are openly discussed in newspapers and television, most persons have little understanding about disease or medical treatment. Unfortunately, too few health care professionals take time to sufficiently educate patients about illness, erroneously believing that they "wouldn't understand" or that open discussion of such matters promotes rather than reduces anxiety. With only limited knowledge and past experience to go on, most patients greatly fear medical treatment. Appropriate education of patients should be an integral part of any treatment program.

Making sure that your patients are well informed will positively influence treatment. Patients generally are less fearful when they know what to expect about their medical condition and treatment. A recent study shows that patient compliance with physician recommendations typically is a dismal 50%. This striking statistic, in part, may be due to inadequate patient education because without understanding the reason for treatment, many patients just will not follow advice.

First find out what your patients already know about their condition. Ask about their understanding of what is wrong and what therapy entails. This will allow you to skip over details which are known already to focus on supplying information that is needed. The information which you provide should be clear, concise and worded in layman's terms. Even if the illness is common such as a peptic ulcer or appendicitis or a "heart attack," don't assume that your patients really know what is wrong with them. Studies have shown that persons from low income groups and little formal education are least likely to understand their medical problems. But assume that all patients will need specific information. Usually your patients will feel better if they know the common name (diagnosis) of their illness; but don't stop there. In layman's terms explain the expected outcome, medical recommendations, possible complications and treatment. Help them prepare for things such as anesthesia, medical costs and hospitalization. Anticipate that they likely will consult the public library and friends about their medical status, so encourage questions to avoid misunderstandings.

Keep in mind that most patients remember only a small portion of what they have been told during the consultation. They will retain even less information if they are intellectually impaired or emotionally distressed, so offer explanations in graduated doses according to their receptivity and capacity to comprehend. Regularly ask for restatements of their understanding of the illness and treatment. You can reinforce verbal instruction by using visual representations in the form of diagrams and pictures. Some patients may benefit from a visit to a hospital or treatment facility. This procedure has been successfully used with children and expectant mothers. Many excellent books and pamphlets describing hospital facilities, common diseases and their treatment are available from various medical and health care organizations. They can greatly enhance your educational efforts. Be sure to extend your educational program to include family members. A spouse or friend who is well informed can be an important asset.

Some patients with catastrophic illnesses (e.g., cancer, hemophilia) or who have undergone disfiguring surgical procedures (e.g., colostomy, mastectomy) have formed volunteer societies with the purpose of helping and educating others with similar conditions. Upon request, these societies will send a member to visit with your patient either in the hospital or at home to discuss their personal experiences in adjusting to their condition. This personalized sharing and education by one with the disorder can be very beneficial. Most of these self-help groups can be contacted through a local medical association or public health nurse.

Education, like treatment, is an ongoing process. Through each step of therapy keep your patient informed.

Now complete Self-Assessment Exercise #4 beginning on the following page.

Self-Assessment Exercise #4

1. Following an automobile accident your patient is placed in an intensive care unit for observation. She is alert, but appears quite apprehensive and is too confused to ask questions. What measures could you take to help provide reassurance for her?

2. Describe the principles involved in providing reassurance to a terminally ill patient.

3. Outline the general steps you could take to help educate a young woman who is pregnant with her first child.

When you have completed this exercise to the best of your ability, check your answers with those on the following page.

Self-Assessment Exercise #4 - Feedback

1. Following an automobile accident your patient is placed in an intensive care unit for observation. She is alert, but appears quite apprehensive and is too confused to ask questions. The measures you could take to help provide reassurance for her are:

   explain treatment and testing procedures
   frequent, brief contacts
   make her physically comfortable
   give reassuring touches
   help keep her oriented

2. Some principles involved in reassuring a terminally ill patient are:

   allow ample time for questions and discussion
   assure physical comfort
   assure adequate pain medication
   give reassuring touches
   provide frequent meetings with you, family, friends

3. Steps you could take to help educate a young woman who is pregnant with her first child are as follows:

   find out what she already knows about birth, natal care, etc.
   using pictures, diagrams, etc. explain the birth process in layman's terms
   periodically ask her to describe in her own words her understanding of what you have presented
   supply her with appropriate books, pamphlets, etc. about birth, child care, etc.
   consider having her attend an introductory visit to the hospital
   include her husband in the education
   encourage questions

If your answers correspond closely with those above, continue reading. If not, please reread the preceding material.

THERAPEUTIC INTERVENTIONS (CONTINUED)

Behavioral Therapy

Principles of behavioral therapy can be applied with benefit to medical problems which call for changes in specific behaviors -- for instance, reducing the intake of food following a prescribed medication regimen or exercise schedule. As outlined in the chapter on "Behavioral Therapy," the desired behavior first should be defined and performance goals established. Patients should keep a record of their progress and appropriate rewards given if the goals are achieved. It is important that the major responsibility for attaining the behavioral objectives rests clearly with the patients.

Some of the biofeedback techniques mentioned in the chapter on "Behavioral Therapy" can be adapted to the treatment of selected medical problems, i.e., elevated blood pressure, muscle tension and heart rate. However, special training and apparatus usually is required to achieve a good result. If you decide on this therapeutic approach, a biofeedback specialist should be consulted.

Pharmacologic Therapy

Some degree of tension and anxiety accompanies most illnesses. Only if these symptoms become intense, should you consider prescribing medications.

Symptoms of tension and anxiety often subside following the administration of an anti-anxiety drug such as chlordiazepoxide, 10 to 20 mg. BID to TID or diazepam, 2 to 10 mg. BID to TID. Special care should be taken when prescribing these medications for persons who are elderly, debilitated or are taking other pharmacologic agents. (See the chapter on "Pharmacologic Therapy" for details of prescribing instruction, potential side effects, etc.). Antipsychotic drugs are rarely indicated for reducing medically related anxiety and can cause side effects which will further complicate treatment.

Antidepressant medications usually will not decrease depressive symptoms resulting primarily from medical illness. Unless the symptoms persist over many weeks and include insomnia, fatigability, weight loss and constipation. A trial dose of imipramine, doxepin or amitriptyline can be administered, 25 mg. TID p.o. (See the chapter on "Pharmacologic Therapy" for details.). Avoid prescribing antidepressant medications to patients with a history of heart disease or increased ocular pressure.

The insomnia which often accompanies sickness is usually mild and transient, and prescribing special medications to counteract it is rarely indicated. However, persons who are troubled by intense or persistent insomnia may respond favorably to flurazepam, 15 to 30 mg. p. o. HS or diazepam, 5 to 10 mg. HS. Generally, barbiturates and comparable hypnotics are not recommended. These medications often impair sound sleep, are potentially habituating and can interact adversely with other drugs and alcohol.

Consultation and Referral

Some indications for seeking consultation and/or referring your patient for medical or psychological evaluation and care are: an inability to establish a working diagnosis, an unsatisfactory response to therapy, deterioration of the patient-therapist relationship, patient noncompliance or the appearance of marked behavioral pathological symptoms.

Now complete Self-Assessment Exercise #5 beginning on the following page.

Self-Assessment Exercise #5

Read the following case history and answer the questions that follow.

Case History

George Robbins was admitted to the coronary care unit of the local hospital following a "heart attack." Although he seemingly had been in good health prior to his admission, he was forty pounds overweight and was a chain smoker. He had been known to work long hours and rarely take time off for either relaxation or physical exercise.

A few hours after his admission he became markedly restless and apprehensive. In general, he found it difficult to adjust to "being a patient" and complained that he was unable to sleep soundly for several nights.

1. After his physical recovery and assuming his cooperation, which of his described behaviors might be amenable to a behavior modification program?

2. If you elected to treat his restlessness and anxiety by medication, which of the following would be appropriate? (More than one answer may be correct.)

   a. chlordiazepoxide, 20 mg. TID
   b. diazepam, 5 mg. TID
   c. chlorpromazine, 50 mg. QID
   d. imipramine, 25 mg. TID

3. Which one of the following medications would be most appropriate to prescribe for his insomnia?

   a. flurazepam, 15 to 30 mg. HS
   b. chlorpromazine, 100 mg. HS
   c. imipramine, 75 mg. HS
   d. phenobarbitol, 100 HS

Self-Assessment Exercise #5 (Continued)

4. A few days after being told that he would require extensive time away from his work for rehabilitation, Mr. Robbins was noted to become increasingly apathetic, socially withdrawn and stated on one occasion "there is no use for me to go on living anymore." These findings are consistent with a severe depressive reaction. Briefly describe what you would do for Mr. Robbins relative to:

   (a) prescribing antidepressant drugs

   (b) psychological referral/consultation

When you have completed this exercise to the best of your ability, check your answers with those on the following page.

Self-Assessment Exercise #5 – Feedback

1. After his physical recovery and assuming his cooperation, the following behaviors might be amenable to a behavior modification program:

   overweight
   smoking
   lack of adequate exercise

2. If you elected to treat his restlessness and anxiety by means of a medication, the following would be appropriate:

   a. chlordiazepoxide, 20 mg. TID
   b. diazepam, 5 mg. TID

3. The following medication would be most appropriate to prescribe for his insomnia:

   a. flurazepam, 15 to 30 mg. HS

4. A few days after being told that he would require extensive time away from his work during rehabilitation, Mr. Robbins was noted to become increasingly apathetic, socially withdrawn and stated on one occasion "there is no use for me to go on living anymore." These findings are consistent with a severe depressive reaction. The following should be done for Mr. Robbins:

   a. Regarding prescribing antidepressant drugs

      Don't prescribe them -- they are usually contraindicated for patients with heart disease.

   b. Regarding psychological referral/consultation

      The patient is depressed and expressing thoughts of suicide. If you don't have the time, expertise or inclination to treat a patient with such symptoms, request a psychiatric consultation. Transfer of the patient's care to a psychiatrist may be indicated if the symptoms persist or intensify.

If your answers correspond closely with those above, continue reading. If not, please reread the preceding material.

SUMMARY

Few other life events cause as intense an emotional response as medical illness and treatment. As a health care professional you can offer invaluable support to your sick patients by first identifying the sources of their anxiety and then applying the therapeutic principles outlined in this chapter.

REFERENCES

Blum, R. H., The Management of the Doctor-Patient Relationship, New York: McGraw-Hill, 1960.

Cassem, N., and Hackett, T., "Psychiatric Consultation in a Coronary Care Unit", Ann. Intern Med., 75:9-14, 1971.

Enelow, A., and Swisher, S., Interviewing and Patient Care, New York: Oxford University Press, 1972.

Freeman, A., Sack, R., et al, Psychiatry for the Primary Care Physician, Baltimore: Williams & Wilkins Company, 1979.

Kiely, W., "Psychiatric Syndromes in Critically Ill Patients, J. Amer. Med. Assn., Vol. 235, No. 20, June 1976.

Mayerson, E. W., Putting the Ill at Ease, New York: Harper and Row, 1976.

Shontz, F., The Psychological Aspects of Physical Illness and Disability, New York: MacMillan, 1975.

CHAPTER 16. SUICIDE

It comes as a surprise to many that suicidal behavior constitutes a major health problem in our country. In 1975 almost 27,000 documented suicides occurred in the United States, making it the 10th leading cause of death among the general population, and the second most common cause of death for teenagers and young adults. Suicidologists believe that for each documented suicide, a comparable number of persons die as a result of actions which likely were intended to be self-destructive but couldn't be proven so, for example, an "accidental" overdose of medication or taking needless chances while driving. Furthermore, for each of the 27,000 individuals who killed themselves, it is estimated that an additional 10 times that number attempted suicide but survived. On the basis of sheer numbers alone, it is inevitable that you will be involved directly with persons who are potentially suicidal. Early recognition and therapeutic intervention may mean the difference between life and death for some patients. This chapter provides basic information that will aid you in identifying and managing patients who have recently attempted or are considering suicide.

LEARNING OBJECTIVES

By the time you complete this chapter, you should be able to do the following and apply the information to written case histories.

1. List six findings which indicate the need for evaluation of suicidal risk.

2. List six physical symptoms typical of an individual who is depressed.

3. Describe the mental status findings typical of an individual who is potentially suicidal.

4. For each of the following categories, describe the characteristics of patients with increased risk for suicide:

   a. demographic factors
   b. physiological status
   c. past and present psychological status
   d. suicidal ideation

5. For each of the methods of therapeutic intervention listed below, describe the recommended approach and provide a rationale for its use in the management of potentially suicidal patients:

   a. supportive psychotherapy
   b. behavioral therapy
   c. pharmacologic therapy
   d. consultation and referral

INDICATIONS FOR A CAREFUL EVALUATION

As a health care professional, it is important to be ever alert to changes in the behavior of your patients and this statement is particularly pertinent for persons who are suicidal. For depressed individuals suicide represents a final solution to a series of disappointments, frustrations and losses. But despite their mental pain, such individuals rarely seek help or openly announce their need for therapy. The hesitancy to seek aid may be due to guilt and the social stigma which is directed toward self-destructive behavior. Many people find it difficult to seek assistance for emotional and personal problems -- they perceive such acting as a blow to their self-esteem, and an indicator of their "failure" in life. Thus, their appeals for help are likely to be indirect, subtle and often overlooked. Studies have shown that at least one-half of those individuals committing suicide had sought medical consultation six months prior to their death. It may be that many had sought help from their physician about their distress, but their communications were unclear or unheeded.

Any of the following findings suggest the need for closer evaluation in depressed persons. Determine if patients have experienced only major personal losses such as failing health, financial reverses, loss of an important job or meaningful relationship. Listen for complaints of loss of satisfaction in activities which were formerly enjoyed such as sex, hobbies or work. Patients may make statements suggesting marked depression such as "life doesn't seem to have much meaning anymore for me," or "it's getting harder and harder for me to cope with life." Evaluate any information from patients or their family which indicates decreased productivity at work, self-neglect, increased consumption of alcohol or sedatives, social withdrawal, or atypical changes in lifestyle. Finally, be alert to symptoms suggestive of depression.

If you suspect that your patients may be harboring suicidal ideas -- ask about them. Contrary to popular beliefs, to inquire about suicidal thoughts will not put them into another's mind. Rather, it is likely that the idea for self-harm has been there for some time and the opportunity to talk about these feelings with you will be welcomed.

Confronting a patient with their suicidal thoughts can be accomplished without undue discomfort. Here are some examples of ways to broach the topic:

Therapist: "You seem pretty discouraged about things. I wonder if you ever have any thoughts about harming yourself?"

Patient: "Yes -- sometimes."

Therapist: "Could you tell me more about the ideas you have?"

or

"Do you sometimes feel that life is not worth living?"

or

Therapist: "Do you ever have the feeling that you would rather not go on living?"

If the answer is affirmative, encourage your patient to explore in detail what his thoughts and feelings are. It is vital that you determine whether the thoughts are occasional and vague or are persistent, well planned and lethal. The section to follow provides information about areas to investigate when assessing suicidal risk.

Typical physical findings of depression. Physical symptoms are prominent in many patients who become depressed and often are the first complaints described. The most common symptoms are easy fatigability and disturbances of appetite, weight and sleep, findings which frequently accompany actual physical illnesses. Most patients complain of loss of appetite and sleep but some eat and sleep excessively. Depressed persons regularly describe feeling chronically tired and "worn out." Interestingly, the lack of energy is generally unrelieved by rest, but tends to improve as the day progresses. One would expect the reverse to be true in instances of medical illness. Other common complaints are constipation and decreased sexual desire and performance. Bodily aches and pains, especially involving the head, back, chest and extremities are frequent accompaniments of depression.

In spite of the association of physical complaints with depression, you should not assume that all bodily symptoms are caused only by emotional factors. Similar symptoms occur with a variety of medical illnesses including diabetes, infections, glandular disorders, heart problems and others. Furthermore, many commonly prescribed medications including sedatives, anti-hypertensive drugs, hormones, and others may bring about depressive symptoms. For these reasons, it is essential that a thorough medical evaluation be performed on persons who are persistently or markedly depressed.

Now complete Self-Assessment Exercise #2 beginning on the following page.

Self-Assessment Exercise #1

1. List three or more types of personal losses which are associated with depression.

2. Mr. Robert George, age 55, was referred for psychological evaluation by his supervisor because of increased alcohol intake, absenteeism and steadily deteriorating work performance. Mr. George stated that until six months ago, he had maintained an excellent work record. For several months he had been troubled by persistent insomnia, weight loss and fatigability. Assuming that his difficulty is due to psychological depression, what other behavioral changes would you expect to find?

3. For each of the following physical findings, indicate whether it is more likely to be increased (I) or decreased (D) in the presence of a moderately severe depression.

______ energy level	______ weight
______ body and muscle pains	______ sexual interest
______ appetite	______ constipation

4. Four months following the death of her mother, Mrs. Georgia Reynolds sought consultation because of persistent depression and tearfulness. She described a loss of appetite and weight and feeling "tired all of the time." Her psychotherapist thought that Mrs. Reynolds' symptoms probably were related to the death of her mother, but recommended that a thorough medical examination be performed. Why was this recommendation a good idea?

When you have completed this exercise to the best of your ability, check your answers with those on the following page.

Self-Assessment Exercise #1 - Feedback

1. A depressive reaction is a typical response to personal losses in the following areas: health, finances, employment, important interpersonal relationships.

2. In addition to Mr. George's productivity at work, increased alcohol intake and physical complaints (insomnia, weight loss and fatigability) one would look for: mental status examination findings consistent with depression, possible statements suggesting depression, social withdrawal, signs of self-neglect.

3. In the presence of a moderately severe depression, the following physical findings are: (I = increased, D = decreased)

D	energy level	D	weight
I	body and muscle pains	D	sexual interest
D	appetite	I	constipation

4. The physical symptoms of depression are very similar to those which accompany medical illness. If a patient has persistent physical complaints, a medical evaluation is indicated to rule out organic disease.

If your answers correspond closely with those above, continue reading. If not, please reread the preceding section.

MENTAL STATUS EXAMINATION FINDINGS OF DEPRESSION

Most potentially suicidal patients reveal their distress during the mental status examination (MSE). For that reason, it is important that you are thoroughly familiar with MSE findings typical to depressed persons. Depressive symptoms vary in type and intensity and may occur in association with a variety of psychopathological conditions including schizophrenia and organic brain disorders, bipolar affective disorders, and others.

Some combination of the following MSE findings are likely to be present in most depressed patients.

Appearance

A patient's attention to personal grooming and appearance often depends on his emotional state. Indications of self-neglect which represent a change from usual grooming habits may be diagnostically significant. Accordingly, individuals who are depressed and preoccupied may show signs of personal neglect, perhaps in the form of disheveled hair, lack of makeup, unkempt clothing, or being unshaven. Occasionally, a depressed patient may demonstrate no significant change in appearance.

Behavior

Depressed individuals typically behave in ways which convey the feeling that they are emotionally and physically overburdened, fatigued and apathetic. Facial expression is blank or suggests sadness. Their movements are slowed, posture is usually slumped and use of gestures decreased. Speech is likely to be decreased in quantity, of low amplitude and either depressed or monotone in quality. To the degree that they are able, depressed patients usually are cooperative in answering questions. However, profoundly depressed persons may be unresponsive to questions. Signs of restlessness and agitation associated with depression often indicate serious psychopathology and an increased suicidal risk.

Feeling (Mood and Affect)

Although individuals who are mildly depressed may show variation in feeling, the affect of those who are more severely disturbed is that of unchanging sadness, hopelessness and helplessness. Feeling responses may be noticeably dulled or convey marked depression. Some patients describe feeling "empty" and devoid of feeling. The feelings of depressed persons usually are contagious and may evoke similar, but transient feelings in you.

Perception

Illusions may occur, but hallucinations are relatively rare. When hallucinations occur, they typically are auditory in nature, self-deprecatory, and indicate an increased risk for suicidal behavior.

Thinking

Patient thinking and intellectual functioning are affected roughly in proportion to the intensity of their mental pain and self-preoccupation. In most nonpsychotic depressions, mental responses may be slowed but usually there is no significant impairment of alertness, intellectual functioning, orientation, memory or judgment. Depressed patients typically describe feeling apathetic about activities or work which they formerly enjoyed. Their thought content may reveal a sense of hopelessness, helplessness, guilt, sadness or self-doubt. Ideas of self-harm may be present.

In profound depressive disorders and/or when psychosis is present, intellectual functions may show considerable impairment. Alertness, abstract thinking, orientation, memory and judgment all may be disordered. At such times, the impairment may be so great that it is difficult to distinguish symptoms of a marked depression from those of an organic brain disorder. The impairment is not caused by an actual disorder of brain functioning, but rather intense self-preoccupation, decreased concentration and a loss of interest in the environment. If patients are able to verbalize, they likely will mention feelings of profound hopelessness, despair and helplessness. Delusions about bodily functions, personal wrongdoing and nihilistic ideas about the "end of the world" may be described. Associational disturbances occur as marked slowing of speech and thought patterns and mid-sentence interruptions of thinking (blocking).

Now complete Self-Assessment Exercise #2 beginning on the following page.

Self-Assessment Exercise #2

1. Using the MSE chart below, describe the findings which typify a depressed and/or suicidal person.

MSE CATEGORIES	TYPICAL FINDINGS
APPEARANCE	
BEHAVIOR	
FEELING (Affect & Mood)	
PERCEPTION	
THINKING	

2. Briefly describe the MSE findings which indicate the presence of a profound depressive disorder with psychosis.

When you have completed this exercise to the best of your ability, check your answers with those on the following page.

Self-Assessment Exercise #2 - Feedback

1. The following MSE findings typify a depressed and/or suicidal person:

MSE CATEGORIES	TYPICAL FINDINGS
APPEARANCE	signs of self-neglect; poor grooming; clothing disheveled
BEHAVIOR	generally cooperative with therapist; posture slumped; facial expression is blank or depressed
FEELING (Affect & Mood)	persistent depressive feeling
PERCEPTION	illusions may occur; hallucinations rare
THINKING	rarely actual impairment of intellectual functioning, memory, orientation, etc.; thoughts of sadness, helplessness, hopelessness, self-doubt, self-harm; slowing of thinking

2. MSE findings which indicate the presence of a profound depressive disorder with psychosis are:

    impairment of some intellectual functioning
    delusional beliefs
    auditory hallucinations
    agitation
    profound self-preoccupation
    marked slowing of thinking

If your answers correspond closely with those above, continue reading. If not, please reread the preceding section.

THE ASSESSMENT OF SUICIDAL RISK

When determining whether or not patients are a suicidal risk, it is useful to collect information about them in five areas: relevant demographic factors, physiological status, past and present psychological states, and suicidal ideation.

The following discussion concerns the information which is important to obtain and suggests a way that it can be organized to estimate the degree of suicide risk.

Demographic Factors

Demographic data often provides useful prognostic information about suicidal potential. The risk of suicide is greater among persons who live alone, are divorced, widowed or separated. Limited financial and/or social resources, unemployment, and being over 50 further increases the risk. Your estimate of the level of risk may be indicated on the rating scale provided.

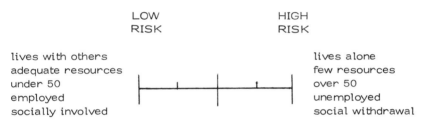

LOW RISK — HIGH RISK

lives with others adequate resources under 50 employed socially involved	|—|—|—|—|	lives alone few resources over 50 unemployed social withdrawal

Physiological Status

An evaluation of physiological status is helpful in determining suicidal potential. The likelihood of suicidal behavior is increased in patients with chronic illness, especially if it interferes with highly valued activities or involves progressive debility or pain. Cancer, severe arthritis or a debilitating respiratory or heart disease are examples of "high risk" illnesses. Particularly significant is a history of drug or alcohol dependency. The presence and degree of insomnia, fatigability, and loss of weight and appetite often correlate with the severity of depression and, therefore, suicidal risk.

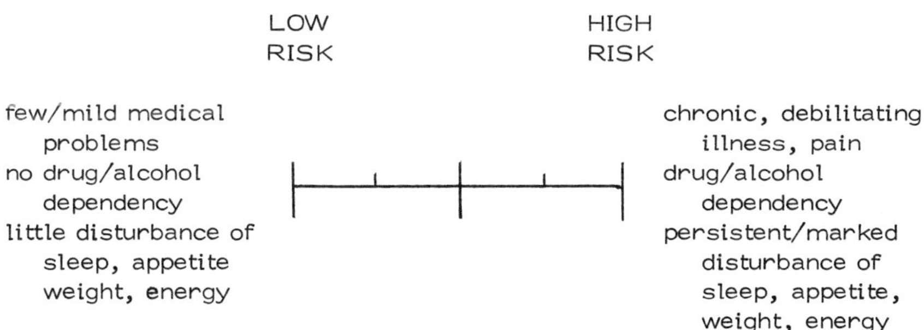

Past and Present Psychological Status

Gathering data about patients' past performance with respect to coping with life problems is valuable for predicting their future reactions to stress. Patients whose life patterns have been characterized by impulsivity, low frustration tolerance, poor vocational and/or social adjustment are more likely to resort to suicide when faced with stressful life problems. Similarly, patients who have required prior psychiatric treatment or previously attempted suicide by using a highly lethal means (e.g., a gun, jumping from a high building, etc.) are at special risk. The history of family suicide also increases the potential for self-harm.

Persons who demonstrate impaired reality testing, an organic brain disorder, psychosis, agitation, intense feelings of hopelessness or persistent self-recriminations are much more likely to act upon their suicidal ideas. The same is true of individuals who are poorly motivated for treatment.

LOW RISK	HIGH RISK
stable life pattern	unstable life pattern
no prior psychiatric treatment	prior psychiatric treatment
no prior suicide attempts	prior suicide attempt (high lethality)
mild depressive symptoms	prominent depressive symptoms
motivated for help	poorly motivated
few present psychiatric problems	impaired reality testing (OBD, psychosis, hopelessness, agitation, self-recrimination)

Suicidal Ideation

The probability of self-destructive behavior is greatly increased if patients have made specific plans for their death. If patients have made a detailed suicidal plan, selected a highly lethal method of suicide, and have the means readily available, immediate and decisive intervention is warranted. As a rule, the more bizarre, violent or potentially lethal the method of suicide, the greater the risk. Contemplated suicide by immolation, jumping from a high place, strangulation, throat slashing or using a gun, carries a worse prognosis than if a less deadly method such as taking an overdose of aspirin or wrist cutting is selected.

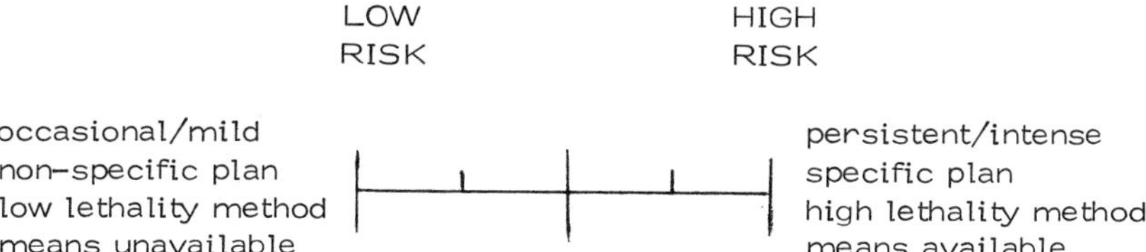

Suicide Assessment Form

We have assembled the above information to create the Suicide Assessment Form and have included it as part of Self-Assessment Exercise #3. Practice using it on the case history that follows. Circle the descriptors which apply to your patient and on the scale presented, mark your estimate of the suicidal risk for each category. You may find that in a particular category your patient simultaneously presents factors indicating both a high and low risk. Practice making these judgments, nevertheless. It is a skill that later will serve you well. Finally, indicate your overall judgment of risk at the bottom of the form. When working with actual patients, you should collect the same information and follow a similar evaluation procedure.

Now complete Self-Assessment Exercise #3 beginning on the following page.

Self-Assessment Exercise #3

1. Read the following case and complete the suicide assessment form which follows it to evaluate the patient for suicidal risk.

Case History

Mrs. Roberta Jorden is a 55-year-old Caucasian female, unemployed bank teller who sought consultation because of feeling increasingly depressed, tense and tired for several weeks. Many of her symptoms related to feelings about her children, marriage and an inability to maintain a job. During recent weeks, Mrs. Jorden suffered from persistent insomnia and appetite loss. She experienced occasional, nonspecific suicidal thoughts and had withdrawn from social activities that she formerly enjoyed. She described a tendency to neglect housework and spends much of her time in bed.

Mrs. Jorden related that she was hospitalized previously for depressive symptoms in 1969 and 1972 and had received electroconvulsive therapy (ECT). She had made three serious suicidal attempts by taking an overdose of medication. Mrs. Jorden presently is in good health, does not use alcohol, but takes diazepam, 5 mg. 4–5 x a day "in order to feel calm."

During the consultation, Mrs. Jorden appeared well groomed, She maintained a serious and somewhat depressive facial expression. Her speech and movements were slowed. Mrs. Jorden complained mainly of apathy towards life. Suicidal ideation was of mild intensity. There was no indication of a psychosis or organic brain disorder. Mrs. Jorden was willing to cooperate in receiving psychological help.

(This case will be continued.)

Now fill out the Suicide Assessment Form on the next page.

Self-Assessment Exercise #3 (Continued)

SUICIDE ASSESSMENT FORM

Circle all descriptors which characterize the patient. For each category, place a "✓" on the scale indicating your estimate of the suicidal risk.

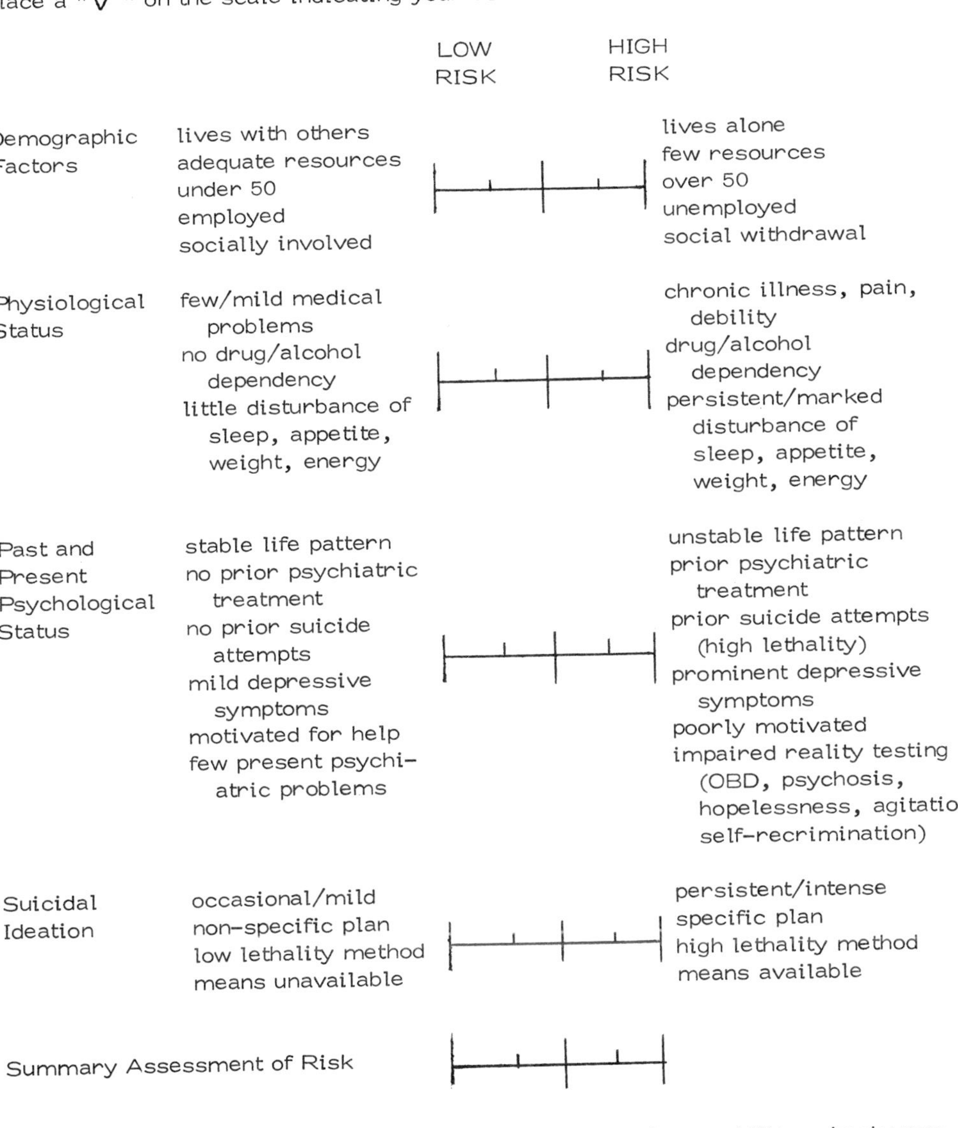

		LOW RISK — HIGH RISK	
Demographic Factors	lives with others adequate resources under 50 employed socially involved	|—'—|—'—|	lives alone few resources over 50 unemployed social withdrawal
Physiological Status	few/mild medical problems no drug/alcohol dependency little disturbance of sleep, appetite, weight, energy	|—'—|—'—|	chronic illness, pain, debility drug/alcohol dependency persistent/marked disturbance of sleep, appetite, weight, energy
Past and Present Psychological Status	stable life pattern no prior psychiatric treatment no prior suicide attempts mild depressive symptoms motivated for help few present psychiatric problems	|—'—|—'—|	unstable life pattern prior psychiatric treatment prior suicide attempts (high lethality) prominent depressive symptoms poorly motivated impaired reality testing (OBD, psychosis, hopelessness, agitation self-recrimination)
Suicidal Ideation	occasional/mild non-specific plan low lethality method means unavailable	|—'—|—'—|	persistent/intense specific plan high lethality method means available
Summary Assessment of Risk		|—'—|—'—|	

When you have completed this exercise to the best of your ability, check your answers with those on the following page.

Self-Assessment Exercise #3 - Feedback

SUICIDE ASSESSMENT FORM

Circle all descriptors which characterize the patient. For each category, place a "✓" on the scale indicating your estimate of the suicidal risk.

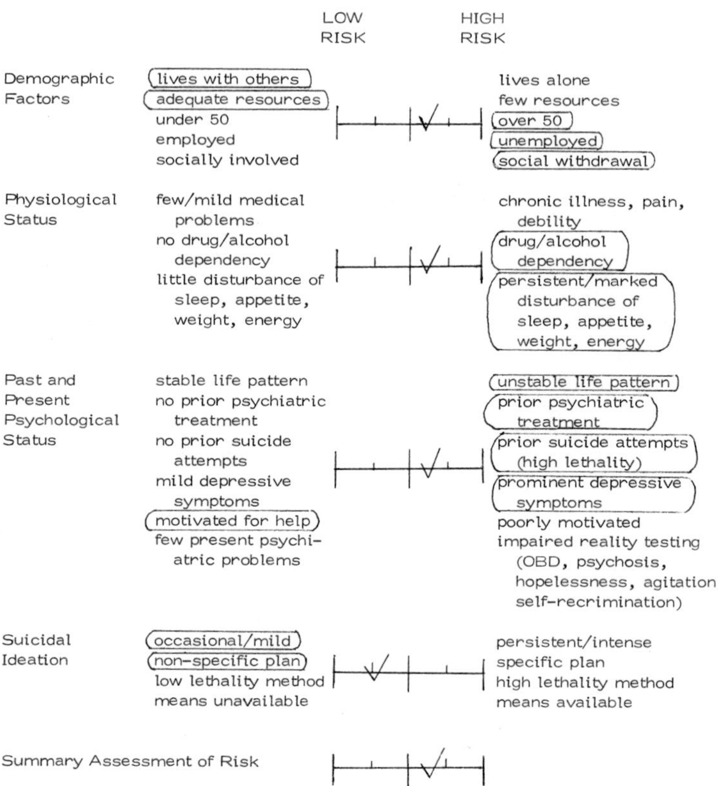

	LOW RISK	HIGH RISK
Demographic Factors	lives with others adequate resources under 50 employed socially involved	lives alone few resources over 50 unemployed social withdrawal
Physiological Status	few/mild medical problems no drug/alcohol dependency little disturbance of sleep, appetite, weight, energy	chronic illness, pain, debility drug/alcohol dependency persistent/marked disturbance of sleep, appetite, weight, energy
Past and Present Psychological Status	stable life pattern no prior psychiatric treatment no prior suicide attempts mild depressive symptoms motivated for help few present psychiatric problems	unstable life pattern prior psychiatric treatment prior suicide attempts (high lethality) prominent depressive symptoms poorly motivated impaired reality testing (OBD, psychosis, hopelessness, agitation, self-recrimination)
Suicidal Ideation	occasional/mild non-specific plan low lethality method means unavailable	persistent/intense specific plan high lethality method means available

Summary Assessment of Risk

If your answers correspond closely with those above, continue reading. If not, please reread the preceding section.

THERAPEUTIC INTERVENTION

The principles of therapeutic intervention can be applied both to individuals who have recently attempted suicide and those who are contemplating it.

Supportive Psychotherapy

The therapeutic approach to potentially suicidal persons deserves careful thought. A first task is to determine whether or not hospitalization is needed. Outpatient management for depressed patients is possible if your evaluation reveals three findings: that imminent suicidal action is unlikely; reliable family or friends are available to provide monitoring and support on an around-the-clock basis; and that you can count on being contacted immediately if the symptoms worsen. If all of these conditions cannot be met, then it is best to recommend hospitalization. Learn the procedures for initiating both voluntary admission and involuntary commitment to a hospital in your community.

Having determined the patient's status with respect to hospitalization, you can implement the following principles of supportive psychotherapy.

Directive guidance. Suicidal behavior usually is an effort to resolve a crisis during which the individual feels he can no longer endure present circumstances and is helpless to effect a positive change in the future. He feels without help or hope and asks, "If present suffering cannot be relieved in the future -- why go on?". The very intensity of feelings may impair the capacity to clearly define problems, much less take corrective action for solving them. It is the therapist-patient relationship that provides the basis for counteracting feelings of despair and hopelessness. In this regard, it is vital to skillfully use the following therapeutic principles.

First, you must assume overall responsibility for the patient's care -- his total care, if necessary. The therapeutic task is to supply the emotional support, guidance and sense of direction which the patient cannot provide for himself. By word and action you should convey a sense of authority -- kindly, but decisive. Having someone else "take over" provides a welcomed respite for most depressed patients. During this period, you become the coordinator of the patient's life, who with others is available around the clock until the crisis has passed. But this highly directive role is a temporary one. As the patient improves and is able to resume directing his own life, you should help him do so.

Environmental intervention. If the possibility of suicide is imminent, prompt and decisive intervention is needed. Patients must be separated from the means for self-harm and simultaneously provided with emotional support from "helping others". For many patients, this will call for hospitalization. Hospitalization can be used to give both patients and family members a time to recuperate from stress. For those who can be managed as outpatients, similar provisions are needed. Give direct advice about environmental problems, and arrange for therapeutic activities and medical care. According to the circumstances, you may prescribe an absence from the demands of work or school, obtain financial aid, or help initiate appropriate therapeutic activities. If it is feasible to do so, keep your patients involved and "on the job." Often, the structure and social interactions associated with a regular routine or job can be therapeutic. When the possibility of suicidal behavior is present, you are obligated to intervene to whatever degree necessary in order to mobilize resources, reduce stress and provide psychological support.

Ventilation. Most depressed persons experience a sense of relief when they can freely discuss their feelings and problems with another individual. Encourage patient communication by listening attentively, empathicly and nonjudgmentally. Help patients feel that they can literally talk about anything. You can learn a great deal about how and when to intervene by letting them talk first -- especially when they are new and a therapeutic relationship is not firmly established. Later, after learning about the details of his problems you will be in a better position to make meaningful comments.

Sometimes you may find it uncomfortable to listen to themes of despair, hopelessness and thoughts of self-destruction and feel inclined to switch the discussion to more neutral topics. However, for your patient's benefit, allow him first to express his feelings fully. Usually after the feelings have been vented, he will be more receptive to what you say. At that time, you can acknowledge his predicament but offer a more objective appraisal of the difficulties and suggest alternative solutions. Only when unguided history taking results in escalating disorganization or anxiety should you shift the patient's attention to a less disturbing topic.

Reassurance. The more disturbed the patient, the more important it is for you to provide reassurance. And both the type and timing of reassurance that you offer deserves consideration. The most important source of reassurance comes from an ongoing relationship with you since you represent the "lifeline" to survival. Most depressed patients feel less perplexed and hopeless when a calm, authoritative approach is taken toward their treatment -- that their therapist is "in command" of the situation and that all possible efforts are being made to provide protection and care. Keep communication channels open and make sure that patient access to helping others and yourself is possible twenty-four hours a day. Initial therapeutic meetings should be scheduled for specific times at a frequency proportionate to the patient's needs -- the greater the depression the more frequent the visits. Consultations need not last more than 15 to 20 minutes, and for outpatients, can be conducted by telephone between scheduled appointments. Accessibility to you is particularly important for socially isolated or high risk patients.

Attentive listening and empathic comments will assure the patient of your interest and understanding. Similarly, reassurance can be conveyed by maintaining optimism about therapeutic outcome even in the face of periodic setbacks. Comment positively about signs of progress, but avoid premature or superficial remarks such as, "Don't worry." or "Everything will be alright.", which do not reassure and can cause the patient to question whether you really understand his feelings. Identify which problems are most amenable to improvement, then direct words of hope in that area.

Finally, provide reassurance by carefully attending to your patient's physical and environmental needs. Prescribe medication to assure sleep, nutritious diets, arrange for adequate housing, and therapeutic relationships and activities.

Education. Even when patients are in the depth of depression, they should be told their symptoms are related to identifiable causes which can be alleviated and are time limited. They should be informed that others with comparable symptoms have benefited by treatment and have subsequently lived productive lives. Patients should be told about the details of therapy and what can be expected about the effectiveness of medications, potential side effects, etc. Giving information about depression and treatment will remove much of the uncertainty and fear that frequently accompanies emotional disorders. Family members, too, should be kept informed about the patient's condition and treatment.

It is important that patients learn that feelings however intense, are not reliable guides for action -- and that they can be resisted and overcome. Patients should be encouraged to participate in activities which are constructive and adaptive despite their present feeling of depression and lethargy, to minimize disappointments if a relapse occurs.

Explain that in the course of treatment there will be fluctuations of mood and progress will occur. Patients should be told that former energy levels, appetite and interest in life will return, but that progress can be gradual.

Now complete Self-Assessment Exercise #4 beginning on the following page.

Self-Assessment Exercise #4

1. It is likely that Mrs. Jorden's symptoms (reread the case presented in Self-Assessment Exercise #3) are early manifestations of a recurrent depressive illness and that without proper care she may resort to suicidal behavior. Her symptoms may fluctuate in intensity but probably will improve considerably with a proper course of therapy. Assume that after weighing the data, you elect to treat Mrs. Jorden as an outpatient on a trial basis. If her symptoms dramatically worsen, you can always hospitalize her. Using the principles of supportive psychotherapy outlined earlier, briefly describe how you would proceed with respect to the following therapeutic measures:

directive guidance

environmental intervention

ventilation

reassurance

education

When you have completed this exercise to the best of your ability, check your answers with those on the following page.

Self-Assessment Exercise #4 - Feedback

1. directive guidance

assume a kindly but authoritative role
help her to arrange daily activities and make decisions
strongly recommend psychological treatment

environmental intervention

make sure she has a responsible person with her at all times
have a responsible person keep and administer all medication
involve family members in her treatment
if her condition worsens or does not improve, arrange for hospitalization

ventilation

there is no apparent contraindication for allowing Mrs. Jorden to talk openly about her depression and worries; at this point she should be encouraged to communicate about anything that is on her mind -- her worries, her marriage, thoughts of suicide, etc.

reassurance

maintain an optimistic approach about the therapeutic outcome of her case
be readily available, scheduling frequent visits and communications by phone
make it clear that you are "in charge" and will help arrange her daily schedule, supply medication and medical care as needed
include the family and/or interested friends in providing continuous reassurance by their presence and scheduling other types of activities

education

remind her that she has had similar depressions and recovered from them
remind her that there will be "ups and downs" in treatment and that her chance for improvement is good
keep her informed about all treatment procedures, medications and therapy that you might recommend
help to encourage her to particpate in activities that will be therapeutic

Self-Assessment Exercise #4 - Feedback (Continued)

education

help her to realize that her feelings do not have to control her actions

help to educate the family about Mrs. Jorden's conditions, symptoms and treatment

If your answers correspond closely with those above, continue reading. If not, please reread the preceding section.

THERAPEUTIC INTERVENTION (CONTINUED)

Behavioral Therapy

Most of the commonly used methods of behavioral therapy are not appropriate for use with individuals who are actively suicidal. However the principles of rewarding and reinforcing adaptive behavior (participating in therapeutic activities, socializing, etc.) may be beneficial.

Pharmacologic Therapy

Prescribing medication for a depressed, potentially suicidal patient presents a therapeutic dilemma. On one hand, it is advantageous to relieve symptoms such as tension, depression and insomnia which further aggrevate your patient's distress. On the otherhand, any drug which you prescribe may be taken as an overdose. The situation is less problematic if your patient is hospitalized and medication can be closely monitored. For outpatients, prescribe medications in small dosages and assign a responsible relative or friend to keep and administer them. Your patient must be instructed to avoid alcohol and not take any other prescribed drugs without medical clearance.

Unfortunately there are no rapid-acting psychotropic drugs for the treatment of depressive symptoms as there are for anxiety, or the acute disorganization of psychosis. Most of the antidepressant medications have an onset of action ranging from 7 to 21 days. Nevertheless, consider a trial of medication for patients with a history of an extended depression (several weeks or more) which has not responded to supportive measures and, in which findings of decreased appetite and weight, fatigability, insomnia and constipation are prominent. See the chapter on "Pharmacologic Therapy" for a comprehensive discussion of the dosage, contraindications, etc. for the medications now to be described.

If the patient's findings indicate a tricyclic antidepressant (amitriptyline, doxepin or imipramine), administer an initial dose range of 75 to 150 mg. per day and increase it according to the recommended dosage schedule. It is rarely advisable to prescribe more than a week's supply of any of these medications because a relatively small overdose of tricyclic antidepressants (a 10 day's supply) can produce serious medical complications and even death. Lethality is increased if alcohol or other drugs have been take simultaneously.

If marked tension is associated with your patient's depression, prescribing tricyclic antidepressants with properites of increased sedation (doxepin and amitriptyline) may be effective. Occasionally, diazepam (Valium) 5 to 10 mg. BID to TID or chlordiazepoxide (Librium) 25 mg. BID to TID may provide relief. Insomnia, which is so troubling to many depressed persons, can be relieved by flurazepam (Dalmane) 15 to 30 mg. HS or diazepam, 10 mg. HS. Barbiturates and other hypnotics and sedatives are contraindicated for the treatment of insomnia because these drugs actually interfere with sound sleep, and if taken as an overdose, can be lethal. Central nervous system stimulants (amphetamines, methyphenidate, etc.) have no place in the treatment of depressed or potentially suicidal patients. If suicidal behavior is secondary to schizophrenia or manic-depressive illness, then hospitalization and/or treatment with anti-psychotic medications is indicated.

Electroconvulsive therapy (ECT) is a treatment form which is very effective in many patients for bringing about a rapid remission of intense depressive feelings and suicidal behavior. ECT is a safe treatment with few contraindications or sequelae, and for patients who are profoundly depressed and persistently suicidal, may be the treatment of choice.

Consultation and Referral

Treating suicidal patients requires a good deal of experience, skill and a capacity for tolerating emotional stress. Good clinical judgment dictates that if you prefer not to work with highly stressful patients, have commitments which prevent your being continuously available to them or feel that you lack sufficient expertise to deal with this specialized type of problem, then consultation and/or referral should be considered. Patients requiring medications, ECT or who have medical problems are best referred to a psychiatrist.

If, for the most part, you feel comfortable in helping patients work through their crises, but want the benefit of another opinion, then periodic consultation may be useful.

There are few psychological conditions for which it is more important to confer with interested family members and friends than in the case of possible suicide. With the patient's permission, it is important for you to meet with the family to obtain information and inform them about the patient's problems and treatment. Simultaneously, you can assess the family's characteristics and interactions to determine whether the members are a resource or liability with respect to treatment. Since referral and consultation requires sensitive handling, please read through the chapter on "Psychological Consultation and Referral."

Now complete Self-Assessment Exercise #5 beginning on the following page.

Self-Assessment Exercise #5

1. Briefly comment on the appropriateness of prescribing each of the following medications for Mrs. Jorden (presented in Self-Assessment Exercise #3).

   a. a tricyclic antidepressant

   b. a central nervous system stimulant (amphetamine)

   c. anti-insomnia medication

      (1) barbiturates

      (2) flurazepam (Dalmane)

2. In view of the fact that Mrs. Jorden has overdosed on pills before, how would you handle the administration of her medication, assuming that she will be treated on an outpatient basis?

3. Circle all of the medications listed below which are most likely to be lethal if taken as an overdose.

   a. barbiturates

   b. tricyclic antidepressants

   c. flurazepam (Dalmane)

   d. diazepam (Valium)

Self-Assessment Exercise #5 (Continued)

4. What behavioral changes should the family be advised to look for which may indicate that Mrs. Jorden's condition is worsening and should be hospitalized?

5. Under what circumstances would you seek consultation or referral for Mrs. Jorden?

6. When might ECT (electroconvulsive therapy) be suitable for someone who is depressed and/or potentially suicidal?

When you have completed this exercise to the best of your ability, check your answers with those on the following page.

Self-Assessment Exercise #5 - Feedback

1. a. A tricyclic antidepressant may be indicated for treatment of recurrent depressive reactions, particularly in cases of prolonged depression. Further evaluation is needed, but this treatment approach may have merit.

   b. amphetamines -- central nervous system stimulants (amphetamines) have no place in the treatment of depression and/or suicidal patients.

   c. anti-insomnia medication

      (1) barbiturates -- barbiturates are inappropriate from the standpoint that they may actually interfere with sound sleep and they also offer a potential hazard with respect to overdose; an overdose may be fatal

      (2) flurazepam (Dalmane) -- this would be a suitable medication given in 15 to 30 mg. HS for sleep difficulties. It is a safe medication even when taken in a large overdose.

2. Since Mrs. Jorden has overdosed with medication before, all medications should be given to responsible family members to keep and administer.

3. Medications which are potentially quite lethal if taken as an overdose are:

   a. barbiturates
   b. tricyclic antidepressants

4. Hospitalization is indicated if Mrs. Jorden shows signs of:

   worsening depressive and physical symptoms (insomnia, weight loss, etc.); agitation; suicidal thoughts increase in frequency, and/or become more specific; suicidal attempt made or threatened

5. Some reasons to seek consultation and/or referral are:

   personal feelings of discomfort in working with her; prefer not to work with high risk patients; lack of training or expertise; if special medical problems (hospitalization, use of medication, concomitant illnesses, etc.) arise

Self-Assessment Exercise #5 - Feedback (Continued)

6. ECT is indicated for persistently or severely depressed persons with a high risk for suicide for whom other therapeutic measures have been unsuccessful.

If your answers correspond closely with those above, continue reading. If not, please reread the preceding section.

SUMMARY

The potentially suicidal patient is experiencing a major life crisis in which your intervention can be decisive. The following therapeutic principles will help in your work with these patients:

Be alert to signs, behavior and statements suggestive of depression in your patients.

If you suspect the presence of suicidal ideas, explore them in detail.

If a suicidal risk is present, intervene decisively in your patient's life by mobilizing resources, and protecting him from impulses of self-harm.

Actively provide support and reassurance in the form of accessibility of yourself, therapeutic activities, medication and/or hospitalization.

Consider consultation and/or referral to another therapist if problems arise or if you have reservations about treating your patient.

In most cases, depression is time-limited and suicidal behavior can be prevented.

REFERENCES

Alvarez, A., The Savage God: A Study of Suicide, New York: Random House, 1972.

Flack, F. F., Draghi, S. C., Nature and Treatment of Depression, New York: Wiley, 1976.

Hatton, C. L., Valente, S. M., Rink, A., Suicide: Assessment and Intervention, New York: Appleton-Century-Crofts, 1977.

Rosenbaum, C. P., Beebe, J. E., Psychiatric Treatment - Crisis/Clinic/Consultation, New York: McGraw-Hill Co., 1975.

Schneidman, E. S., Fairberow, N. L., Litman, R. E., The Psychology of Suicide, New York: Science House, 1970.

CHAPTER 17. CHILDHOOD

Behavioral and emotional disorders of children are common and the advice of health care professionals is frequently sought to deal with them. These disorders range from severe psychotic states to mild school phobias, and generally evoke great concern in family members, teachers and community agencies involved in youth work. You should possess basic information about the diagnosis and treatment of these disorders.

LEARNING OBJECTIVES

By the time you complete this chapter, you should be able to do the following and apply the information to written case histories.

1. Define stress as it relates to childhood and describe how the individual is affected by the three factors listed below:

   a. sources of stress
   b. duration and frequency of stress
   c. the particular child's response to stress

2. Define and briefly describe the following problems of childhood:

   a. bowel and bladder incontinences
   b. eating problems
   c. sleep disorders
   d. tics and movement disorders
   e. speech disorders

f. hyperkinesis
g. learning disorders
h. fears and phobias
i. autism
j. reactions to illness and hospitalization
k. depressive disorders

3. For each of the given methods of therapeutic intervention listed below, describe the recommended approach and provide a rationale for its use in the management of problems of childhood:

a. supportive psychotherapy
b. behavioral therapy
c. pharmacologic therapy
d. consultation and referral

THE MAJOR CAUSE OF CHILDHOOD PROBLEMS

Behavior and emotional problems of children typically are the result of stress, the bodily and psychological tension resulting from factors which alter their existing emotional equilibrium.

Children are particularly sensitive to stress and it often plays a critical role in the development of behavior problems. Children may experience stress with a variety of symptoms including physical complaints, hyperactivity, muscular tension and feelings of anxiety. An examination of the source, frequency, duration and the individual child's reaction to stress is essential to effectively dealing with childhood problems.

Each child with behavior or psychological symptoms should be evaluated with reference to three sources of stress. These are <u>biological</u>, e.g., illness, dietary or physical deficit; <u>environmental</u>, e.g., moving to a new neighborhood, family problems, school problems, sibling rivalry, and; <u>psychological</u>, e.g., depression, psychosis and anxiety.

Stress is ever-present in some form, and a certain amount of it seems necessary to the development of a healthy personality. Stress is likely to produce a pathological outcome if it is severe and/or prolonged. Therefore, assessing the frequency and duration of stress is of utmost importance when evaluating childhood problems. Frequent stressful events, e.g., family fights, moves or rejection increase the likelihood of difficulties developing. If such stressful events extend over a long period of time the child may develop problematic psychological or behavioral mechanisms in order to cope with his/her situation.

A child's idiosyncratic response to stress is also important to consider. Some children become belligerent, confused, anxious or tearful under stress. Others become shy, withdrawn and uncommunicative. The characteristics of the child's reaction to stress may suggest the appropriate therapeutic intervention.

Now complete Self-Assessment Exercise #1 beginning on the following page.

Self-Assessment Exercise #1

1. Define stress as it relates to children.

2. List the three sources of stress which should be considered when evaluating problems in a child.

3. For the following case identify the source of stress, the child's response to it, and how the duration of stress may affect the future outcome.

   Sean is a six-year-old boy whose parents have separated because of marital problems. During this separation they continued to argue bitterly over various family matters. Sean has repeatedly wet his bed and had nightmares since his father moved out. His performance in school has steadily worsened as the family problems continued. Sean's school problems continued for several months as his parents attempted to resolve their problems.

   (a) Source of stress:

   (b) Sean's response to stress:

   (c) Affect of duration of stress:

When you have completed this exercise to the best of your ability, check your answers with those on the following page.

Self-Assessment Exercise #1 - Feedback

1. Stress is a bodily or mental tension resulting from factors that tend to alter an existent equilibrium. Children are particularly sensitive to stress.

2. The three factors important when evaluating stress are:

   a. sources of stress

   b. duration and frequency of stressful events

   c. the child's particular response to stress

3. a. The source of stress for Sean is his parents' separation and continued arguments.

   b. His response to this stress has been bedwetting, poor school performance and nightmares.

   c. The longer his parents are angry with each other the more serious his problems have become. The symptoms will likely remain or worsen until Sean's stress is reduced. His protracted trouble in school may affect his school performance for years to come.

If your answers correspond closely with those above, please continu reading on the next page. If not, please reread the preceding material.

COMMON CHILDHOOD PROBLEMS

During their developing years most children experience transient disturbances of sleep, learning, eating and other abnormalities. It is only when these difficulties persist, are severe or interfere with normal growth and social development that they warrant further evaluation and therapy. We shall now briefly outline some of the types of disorders which may occur. While the majority of these are stress related, a thorough medical examination should be completed on each child in order to rule out physiological causes. Except when they are marked, findings of the mental status examination are not so helpful in diagnosing psychopathology in children as in adults. More important to diagnose are persistent patterns of abnormal behavior, impaired social relationships and functioning in school.

Bowel and Bladder Incontinence

Bowel and bladder incontinence which result from stress, occur more often in male than female children but are not necessarily pathological unless they persistently occur after the age of 6 or 7. While loss of bowel or bladder control may be a solitary symptom, more often it occurs with other behavioral upsets such as tantrums, nightmares or other sleep disturbances. Loss of bladder control is more frequent while asleep and is called enuresis. It disappears in most children by adolescence. Loss of large bowel control typically occurs during waking hours and is termed encopresis and generally suggests more severe problems. Bladder and bowel control provide an arena in which the child may communicate strivings for independence or feelings of frustration with the parents. Problems of this nature generally reflect conflicts which parents have with respect to toilet training and their basic relationship with the child.

Eating Disorders

Eating disorders are common responses to both stress and physical illness and special care should be taken to rule out physical disease. There are three types of feeding problems: bulimia which is overeating, anorexia which is loss of appetite, and pica which is ingesting non-food items such as crayons, dirt, etc. Eating disturbances generally increase parental attention to the child and are unconsciously chosen by the child to express covert feelings which he is unable to verbalize.

Sleep Disturbances

Sleep disturbances are common in children and take the form of nightmares, night terrors, wakefulness and restlessness. Bedwetting and accumulated emotional tensions can also produce sleep disturbances. Lack of sound sleep itself accentuates feelings of irritability for parent and child alike.

Tics and Movement Disorders

Tics and motor disorders are sometimes displayed by an emotionally disturbed child. A tic is an involuntary movement of small groups of muscles, e.g., a blink, grimace or twitch of an extremity. It is a distracting and prominent symptom. Other abnormal movements include rhythmic rocking, head banging and hair pulling. These movements tend to be repetitive, rhythmic and represent a distrubance which merits further evaluation.

Speech Disorders

Transient speech disorders are common in developing children. However, if speech is significantly delayed or stuttering becomes marked or persistent special intervention may be indicated. Speech problems attract undesirable attention and subject a child to possible ridicule by peers and thus accentuating his discomfort.

Hyperkinesis

Hyperkinesis has gone by different diagnoses including minimal brain dysfunction (MBD), hyperactive child syndrome and others. The condition has been much studied in recent years and is believed to reflect a form of neurological disorder. It is characterized by a limited attention span, persistent hyperactivity, impulsivity and various learning disabilities. Children with this disorder often display emotional lability and behave in ways which provoke their peers and adults. The diagnosis of hyperkinesis is frequently misapplied to a variety of childhood disorders which may possess elements of learning disabilities and/or hyperactive behavior Careful psychological, medical and neurological evaluation should be conducted before this diagnosis is assigned to a child.

Learning Disorders

The diagnosis "learning disorder" is a non-specific term used to describe a variety of scholastic problems such as reading, recall, arithmetic, etc. Usually problems with learning are not isolated findings and regularly are accompanied by irritability, depression, poor peer relationships, signs of tension and others. Learning disorders can arise from a variety of emotional, environmental and medical factors. If the findings of scholastic difficulty are severe or worsen, especially if the child's I.Q. is normal, careful evaluation is indicated.

Fear and Phobias

Irrational fears (phobias) are so common in younger children that they are believed to be a part of normal development. Most tend to disappear as the child gets older. However, if they persist, worsen or interfere with socialization or school performance, definitive treatment is indicated. Fears are somewhat age dependent and fears of strangers and separation from parents is typical of younger children, while concerns of bodily harm are concerns expressed by older children. School phobias reflect a basic insecurity about leaving home and parents and should promptly be treated.

Autism

Autism is a relatively uncommon syndrome which becomes evident during the first two years of life. Autism is characterized by severe and varied types of emotional and perceptual disturbances. Autistic children act in a bizarre and puzzling fashion. They scream, bang their heads, rock incessantly, may be distant or overly responsive to stimuli and persons about them. These children often show severe disturbances of speech and unusual movements. It seems likely that autism is associated with some type of neurological deficit.

Reactions to Illness

Medical illness and hospitalization are often overlooked as sources of stress for children. The experience of illness and hospitalization is more traumatic for children than adults. Children may not show their distress so much in words as by social withdrawal, or the development of anxious behavior, bedwetting, etc. Children usually have many misconceptions, fantasies and fears about surgery and other medical treatment. Young children especially do not easily tolerate separation from their parents.

Depressive Disorders

Depression has recently been identified as a significant childhood problem. Children suffer from depression, i.e., feelings of low self-esteem, hopelessness, and lack of energy as do adults. Social withdrawal, expressed feelings of loneliness and sleep and appetite disturbances may signify the presence of depression.

Now complete Self-Assessment Exercise #2 beginning on the following page.

Self-Assessment Exercise #2

Match the correct diagnostic term from the list for the children's findings described below:

(a) enuresis
(b) encopresis
(c) autism
(d) hyperkinesis
(e) anorexia
(f) tic
(g) phobia

_____ 1. during intense arguments between his parents, six-year-old Bruce showed recurrent rapid blinking and twitching movements about his face

_____ 2. eight-year-old Susan refused to go near any furry animals and became tearful and frightened if forced to do so

_____ 3. 2½-year-old Robert demonstrated unusual behavior since birth; he stiffened and resisted being held or cuddled, he avoided physical contact and preferred solitary activities; he rarely spoke words

_____ 4. 11-year-old Tom wet his bed nightly despite a reduction of night time fluids, rewards or punishments by his parents

_____ 5. Billy, a 3rd grader, was described as being unusually talkative and restless in school; he was easily distracted by other children and had considerable problems in learning to read

_____ 6. 9-year-old George frequently lost control of his bowels during times of intense excitement or emotional stress

Indicate whether the following statements are true (T) or false (F).

_____ 7. Most children experience transient episodes of bedwetting, nightmares, and stuttering during their developmental years.

_____ 8. Phobias are rare phenomenon in normal children.

_____ 9. It is likely that the diagnosis of hyperkinesis (minimal brain damage) has been overused in recent years.

_____ 10. Physical illness can often give rise to the behavioral and emotional disorders of children.

When you have completed this exercise to the best of your ability, check your answers with those on the following page.

Self-Assessment Exercise #2 - Feedback

tic (F) 1. during intense arguments between his parents, six-year-old Bruce showed recurrent rapid blinking and twitching movements about his face

phobia (G) 2. eight-year-old Susan refused to go near any furry animals and became tearful and frightened if forced to do so

autism (C) 3. 2½-year-old Robert demonstrated unusual behavior since birth; he stiffened and resisted being held or cuddled; he avoided physical contact and preferred solitary activities; he rarely spo

enuresis (A) 4. 11-year-old Tom wet his bed nightly despite a reduction of night time fluids, rewards or punishmen by his parents

hyperkinesis (D) 5. Billy, a 3rd grader, was described as being unusually talkative and restless in school; he was easily distracted by other children and had considerable problems in learning to read

encopresis (B) 6. 9-year-old George frequently lost control of his bowels during times of intense excitement or emotional stress

The following statements are true (T) or false (F).

True 7. Most children experience transient episodes of bedwetting, nightmares, and stuttering during their developmental years.

False 8. Phobias are rare phenomenon in normal children.

True 9. It is likely that the diagnosis of hyperkinesis (minimal brain damage) has been overused in recent years.

True 10. Physical illness can often give rise to the behavioral and emotional disorders of children.

If your answers correspond closely with those above, please continue reading on the next page. If not, please reread the preceding material.

THERAPEUTIC INTERVENTIONS

Because of the wide variety of problems and the complexity of treating children, only general principles of treatment will be included in this section. Specific treatments for severe or chronic disorders, e.g., autism, persistent stuttering, encopresis are best referred for treatment to a specialist, i.e., a child psychiatrist, speech therapist, psychologist, social worker, etc.

Supportive Psychotherapy

As a general rule, young children do not verbalize their problems or conflicts. Rather, they simply enact them behaviorally in their play and games. It may be difficult to identify the source of their difficulties. For example, school pressures may be particularly stressful for an eight year old and in an attempt to cope with his feelings, he may displace his frustrations and at home become destructive, uncooperative and obstinant. The child may never say, "I'm upset about school," but rather express his feelings of frustration through his behavior at home.

Because most young children typically express their conflicts through their actions, most therapists who treat them use a therapeutic approach called "play therapy." Here, the natural inclination of the child to "play" and develop games about his inner feelings will provide clues to their problems as well as their methods of coping with them. Principles of directive guidance, education, ventilation, reassurance, and environmental intervention, as outlined in the chapter on "Supportive Psychotherapy," can be applied within the context of "play therapy." Although play therapy usually requires considerable training and experience, you can use a modified form of it to help diagnose and treat your patients.

Several steps should be followed when implementing play therapy. First, obtain an accurate history by talking to the child's parents, siblings and significant others (teachers, etc.). Data from these multiple sources will provide a more complete picture of the child and possibly suggest areas of conflict. Once this is accomplished you should begin relationship building with the child. Children will not usually communicate freely with an adult with whom they have not established rapport. Thus, you should spend time getting to know the child. Talk first about things that interest the child, e.g., TV programs, hobbies, etc. The child must sense that you care and are warm and accepting. Have available a selection of toys suitable for play therapy, e.g., a toy house, various dolls, water toys, stuffed animals, puppets, materials for drawing and simple games such as checkers. Let the child select and play unrestrictedly with the toys. Encourage free play with the toys and perhaps ask the child to make up a story about them. Then watch how they are used in play. Be alert for conflicts that might be expressed in the play. For instance, "mommy and daddy" dolls fighting, or "brother" dolls hurting younger children, school rooms that are angrily tossed about or other signs of intense feelings.

During play therapy, it is important that you facilitate expression of feeling rather than act as a teacher or parent. Avoid the temptation to tell the child what to do or prompt enactment of a suspected conflict. Maintaining a non-judgmental attitude about what you observe and letting the child proceed at his own emotional pace is most important. Occasionally, you can point out problem behaviors and encourage the child to consider the possible consequences of his play. As a facilitator, you can describe the prominent feeling which is being experienced either in terms of how the play figures feel or the child himself. For example, when a fight between a male and female doll is enacted, you might say, "It seems the man and woman are angry with each other. That can make children frightened. How about at your house?" By these comments about the play drama from a supportive adult, children can play through their feelings and experience a reduction of their anxiety. Play therapy can produce improvement in a child without the therapist being fully aware of the underlying dynamic factors.

Parents of troubled children generally have problems of their own which affect treatment, and counseling should be offered which will assist your care of the child. Many child therapists feel that consultations with the entire family are necessary to resolve and understand the complex factors affecting seriously disturbed children.

Now complete Self-Assessment Exercise #3 beginning on the following page.

Self-Assessment Exercise #3

Indicate whether the following statements are true (T) or false (F).

_____ 1. Persistent and/or severe stuttering or enuresis is best treated by a specialist, i.e., speech therapist, child psychiatrist, etc.

_____ 2. Given an opportunity to do so, most children under age 10 will verbalize the feelings and fears which trouble them.

_____ 3. "Play therapy" is often an effective technique for helping children work through their emotional problems.

_____ 4. Play therapy will likely have a more successful outcome if the therapist carefully structures the use of toys.

_____ 5. Play therapy will bring about improvement in a child's behavior only when the therapist fully understands the underlying psychodynamics of the child.

_____ 6. It is often useful to provide counseling for parents and family members of children who have serious behavioral problems.

Answer the questions following the case history of Ann, age 6.

Ann recently entered the first grade. Her family had moved frequently from city to city and her mother gave birth to an infant son shortly before school started. Ann began to experience "stomach aches and pains" and became tearful when asked to go to school. She frequently left school in mid-day to return home to be with her mother. Ann seemed tense, irritable and became easily tearful when frustrated.

7. What is the most likely diagnosis for Ann's behavior?

8. Would you recommend that she have a physical examination? Why?

Self-Assessment Exercise #3 (Continued)

9. What are some likely causes of her symptoms?

10. During a play therapy session, Ann uses a girl doll to hit an infant doll. Comment on the appropriateness of the following responses which the therapist could make.

"Children shouldn't hit one another -- especially when one is so much smaller."

"It looks like the girl is angry with the baby."

When you have completed this exercise to the best of your ability, check your answers with those on the following page.

Self-Assessment Exercise #3 - Feedback

True 1. Persistent and/or severe stuttering or enuresis is best treated by a specialist, i.e., speech therapist, child psychiatrist, etc.

False 2. Given an opportunity to do so, most children under the age of 10 will verbalize the feelings and fears which trouble them.

True 3. "Play therapy" is often an effective technique for helping children work through their emotional problems.

False 4. Play therapy will likely have a more successful outcome if the therapist carefully structures the use of toys.

False 5. Play therapy will bring about improvement in a child's behavior only when the therapist fully understands the underlying psychodynamics of the child.

True 6. It is often useful to provide counseling for parents and family members of children who have serious behavioral problems.

7. What is the most likely diagnosis for Ann's behavior?

   (School phobia)

8. Would you recommend that she have a physical examination? Why?

   (Yes. She may have medical problems which are contributing to her symptoms.)

9. What are some likely causes of her symptoms?

   (Frequent moves; new sibling; no friends; new environment.)

10. "Children shouldn't hit one another -- especially when one is so much smaller."

   (This is a judgmental comment and would produce guilt and shame. It might block future expression of her feelings.)

   "It looks like the girl is angry with the baby."

   (This is a descriptive statement which conveys understanding of Ann's feelings but doesn't provide criticism of her actions in play. The non-judgmental attitude would permit further "play

If your answers correspond closely with those above, please continue reading on the next page. If not, please reread the preceding material.

THERAPEUTIC INTERVENTIONS (CONTINUED)

Behavioral Therapy

Principles of behavioral therapy are widely used with children. In fact, behavior modification is the treatment of choice in many cases. One reason for this is that a behavior modification program easily can be learned by family members, teachers and others interested in the child's improvement. Complex skills or training are not needed. Because children are most likely to respond to nonverbal interactions, behavior modification has become very popular with child therapists.

You should ensure that the identified patient is not singled out as the sole cause of all family difficulties and that the parents do not misuse the method or become overly punitive. Insist that careful records be kept and reports of progress made regularly.

Specific behaviors such as temper tantrums, school phobias, refusal to do assigned chores, and poor grooming habits are potential symptoms for modification. Whether or not these behaviors are associated with severe psychopathology, a behavior modification program can be developed to improve them. Behavior modification can be used to complement play and other therapy forms.

A brief review of behavior modification techniques will help to illustrate the principles involved. You should first instruct the family about the principles of reinforcement and punishment, i.e., acceptable behaviors should be rewarded and unacceptable ones punished or ignored. A single target behavior should then be singled out. For the sake of illustration, let's focus on temper tantrums. For one week records should be kept by the parents of the timing, frequency and precipitating factors of the tantrums. The child then should be told that calm, socially accepted behaviors in response to frustration will be rewarded by candy or special privileges, while tantrums will be punished, e.g., by immediate loss of play privileges or temporary social isolation for a few minutes. It is very important to consistently reward desired behaviors, not simply punish the ones that are troublesome. Daily records are kept on the incidence of punishments and rewards. The rate of tantrum behavior should soon decrease. It is critical for treatment success that reward or punishment immediately follow the specified act. Delaying the reward or punishment will delay the development of adaptive behavior. The basic principles of rewarding desirable behavior and punishing unwanted ones may be used to treat phobias, reduce aggressive tendencies, promote adaptive responses, e.g., good grooming, etc.

It is important to remember that many parents and children "ignore" each other when all is going well. Rather, they should be encouraged to give positive "strokes" to one another when someone has done something pleasing, and not just reacting with criticism when unwanted responses occur. Initiating a behavior modification program for children requires special skills. If you are thinking of using behavior therapy on a regular basis, consider obtaining the training needed.

Pharmacologic Therapy

For several reasons, cautiously approach prescribing psychotropic medications for your young patients. When it comes to prescribing psychotropic medications for children, they cannot be considered small sized versions of adults and simply given lesser amounts. The criteria for prescribing drugs for children are not so well defined as is the case for adults. Drug dosage schedules are not well worked out, and the long-term affects of these potent medications on physical and psychological growth are largely unknown. Responses to these medications are unpredictable and must be carefully determined for each child. The incidence of side effects and complications is high. In the recent past, all too many children were treated with medications for reasons based mainly on the reports of teachers or parents and sometimes the medication was used to "solve" a variety of problems that could have been better handled by other forms of treatment. Before any medications are prescribed, a complete medical, psychological, educational, behavioral, and historical profile of the child should be developed. Only when all of these reports are analyzed and specific treatment goals are identified should drugs be used. Furthermore, if drugs are prescribed, care should be taken to follow the child's progress on a regular systematic basis. Records of behavior should be kept in school and at home, and the family should be regularly interviewed about the child's progress.

We shall comment only briefly on the use of specific psychotropics for children. We believe that in most cases these potent medications should be administered only by highly experienced pediatricians, child psychiatrists and others with comparable experience.

In the chapter on "Pharmacologic Therapy" we stated that central nervous system stimulants such as methylphenidate and amphetamines were not appropriate for the treatment of depressive syndromes and that they often caused many undesirable side effects. Interestingly, these psychostimulants act paradoxically and produce a calming, sedating effect on many children with symptoms of hyperkinesis. Many children become less tense and restless, are better able to concentrate and attend to school work. Methylphenidate seems to be more effective and causes fewer complications than amphetamines. Neither drug should be given to children under six, or those with symptoms of psychosis. Side effects of anorexia, impaired sleep and other physical disturbances are common. The long-term effect of central nervous system stimulants on developing children is still not well studied. Some evidence suggests that medical problems may later develop. If these drugs are prescribed, it should be for the least amount needed for symptom control and continued only for as long as is absolutely necessary. Specific dosage must be individualized for each child, but the usual range of methylphenidate is 5 to 30 mg. per day in divided doses.

Only in exceptional cases are anti-psychotic drugs (chlorpromazine, haloperidol, etc.) recommended for children. These medications are reserved for children with symptoms of psychosis, delusions, hallucinations, marked agitation or assaultive behavior. The incidence of extrapyramidal symptoms, oversedation, paradoxical responses and other complications is relatively high.

Childhood depressive disorders are not so well defined as is the case with adults, and it is much more difficult to identify which, if any, children would benefit from tricyclic anti-depressants such as imipramine, doxepin, etc. These drugs are not recommended for children under 12. Imipramine in doses of 25 or 50 mg. HS reduces enuresis in carefully selected children -- it is otherwise contraindicated. If depressive symptoms are problematic, then psychotherapy is indicated.

As in the case of other psychotropic drugs, there are few well substantiated indications for prescribing anti-anxiety drugs for children. Chronically tense or anxious children should receive a thorough medical, psychological and intellectual examination. Anti-anxiety drugs too often obscure underlying pathology which should receive definite treatment.

The diagnosis and treatment of the behavioral and emotional disorders of children is frequently a difficult and complex undertaking. It can involve the family, teachers, physicians and other experts for an indefinite period.

Consultation and Referral

For example, consultation with a child psychiatrist is indicated for accurate diagnosis, play therapy and prescribing any psychotropic drugs needed. Clinical psychologists provide the expertise for testing and conducting play therapy or designing behavior modification programs. Family physicians and pediatricians are needed to evaluate the presence of physical problems. Psychiatric social workers are often excellent therapists for treating family problems and childhood difficulties. Speech and learning specialists, teachers and recreational therapists are others whose expertise may be invaluable. Occasionally, long-term residential treatment or placement may be required and a social service consultation should be obtained. Most communities have mental health centers which provide facilities and trained personnel to diagnose and treat the disorders of children.

Now complete Self-Assessment Exercise #4 beginning on the following page.

Self-Assessment Exercise #4

1. For the case history below, briefly indicate the steps to follow for setting up a simple behavior modification program using the principles presented.

   Kevin, age eight, has to be repeatedly reminded to set the dinner table each evening. Various threats of punishment, scoldings, etc. have not changed his behavior. What would you instruct his parents to do?

Indicate whether the following statements are true (T) or false (F).

_____ 2. The criteria for prescribing psychotropic drugs for children are much less clear than those for adults.

_____ 3. Psychotropic medications are effective in dealing with most of the emotional disorders occurring in childhood.

_____ 4. A thorough medical, psychological and educational evaluation should be performed before prescribing any psychotropic medications for children.

_____ 5. Some psychotropic drugs, i.e., central nervous system stimulants and anti-psychotic medications may cause effects paradoxical to those experienced by adults.

Self-Assessment Exercise #4 (Continued)

Indicate the prescribing action you should take for each of the vignettes below. Assume that each child is in good physical health.

(a) prescribe no medication
(b) " an anti-anxiety medication
(c) " a central nervous system stimulant
(d) " a tricyclic anti-depressant
(e) " an anti-psychotic drug

_____ 6. The parents of 10-year-old Susan decided to separate and divorce. Two weeks after being informed of their intent, she shows evidence of depression, a mild sleep disturbance and trouble concentrating on her school work.

_____ 7. Since moving to his new neighborhood and school one month ago Tom, age 9, has been irritable, tense and restless. He complains of feeling "nervous" in school and states he would prefer to stay at home.

_____ 8. 12-year-old Keith has been noted by his teachers to be increasingly aggressive at school and has picked fights with several of his peers. He is often defiant and rude toward persons in authority. He can give no explanation for his behavior.

9. Roberta, a 2nd grader, showed persistent restless behavior, irritability and was unable to concentrate on her school work. Briefly list persons who likely should be consulted while attempting to diagnose and treat her symptoms.

When you have completed this exercise to the best of your ability, check your answers with those on the following page.

Self-Assessment Exercise #4 - Feedback

1. You should instruct his parents to:

   (a) keep a daily record of his table setting behavior for one week without commenting on his compliance

   (b) specify a specific reward to be given immediately for his compliance (a treat, points to be accumulated for going on an outing of his choice, etc.)

   (c) specify a specific punishment to be immediately administered for his non-compliance (interruption of play, loss of TV privileges, brief social isolation, etc.)

   (d) keeping a record of rewards and punishments which is regularly reviewed by Kevin and his parents to note his progress

   (e) consistent dealing with his behavior at each mealtime

   (f) periodic review of his progress with you

True 2. The criteria for prescribing psychotropic drugs for children are much less clear than those for adults.

False 3. Psychotropic medications are effective in dealing with most of the emotional disorders occurring in childhood.

True 4. A thorough medical, psychological and educational evaluation should be performed before prescribing any psychotropic medications for children.

True 5. Some psychotropic drugs, i.e., central nervous system stimulants and anti-psychotic medications may cause effects paradoxical to those experienced by adults.

(a) 6. The parents of 10-year-old Susan decided to separate and divorce. Two weeks after being informed of their intent, she shows evidence of depression, a mild sleep disturbance and trouble concentrating on her school work.

Self-Assessment Exercise #4 - Feedback (Continued)

(a) 7. Since moving to his new neighborhood and school one month ago Tom, age 9, has been irritable, tense and restless. He complains of feeling "nervous" in school and states he would prefer to stay at home.

(a) 8. 12-year-old Keith has been noted by his teachers to be increasingly aggressive at school and has picked fights with several of his peers. He is often defiant and rude toward persons in authority. He can give no explanation for his behavior.

9. Persons who should likely be involved in consultation about her symptoms are her parents, teachers, pediatricians to evaluate her physical health, a clinical psychologist for testing; and possibly a child psychiatrist for psychotherapy and/or drug treatment.

If your answers correspond closely with those above, please continue reading on the next page. If not, please reread the preceding material.

SUMMARY

Childhood emotional and behavioral problems often are linked to biological, environmental and psychological stresses. Childrens' reactions to stress usually are revealed in their play and activities. For this reason, play-oriented treatment and behavior modification programs are often successful forms of therapy. Psychotropic medications are rarely indicated for most cases of childhood disorders. Usually the expertise of several specialists are needed to help resolve the more persistent or serious problems.

REFERENCES

Anders, T. F. and Ciaranello, R. D., "Psychopharmacology of Childhood Disorders," Psychopharmacology: From Theory to Practice, New York: Oxford University Press, 1977.

Anders, T. F. and Ciaranello, R. D., "Pharmacological Treatment of the Minimal Brain Dysfunction Syndrome," Psychopharmacology: From Theory to Practice, New York: Oxford University Press, 1977.

Freud, A., Normality and Pathology in Childhood: Assessments of Development, New York: International Universities Press, 1966.

Harrison, S. and McDermott, J., Childhood Psychopathology, New York: International Universities Press, 1972.

Johnson, D. J. and Myklebut, H. R., Learning Disabilities, New York: Grune and Stratton, 1967.

Looff, David H., Getting to Know the Troubled Child, Knoxville: University of Tennessee Press, 1976.

Rexford, Eveoleen N., et al, Infant Psychiatry: New Synthesis, New Hav and London: Yale University Press, 1976.

Rutter, M. and Hersov, L., Child Psychiatry: Modern Approaches, Philadelphia: J. B. Lippincott, 1976.

Steinhauer, P. D. and Rae-Grant, Q., Psychological Problems of the Child and His Family, Toronto: Macmillan, 1977.

Strauss, Susan, Is It Well With the Child?, Garden City, New York: Doubleday, 1975.

Wender, Paul H., The Hyperactive Child, New York: Crown Publishers, 1973.

Wing, Lorena, Autistic Children, New York: Brunner/Mazel, 1972.

CHAPTER 18. ADOLESCENCE

Adolescence is a time of rapid and profound psychological and biological development during which sexual maturation and major changes in body size and configuration occur. These physical changes, plus a growing sense of urgency to establish a personal identity and become autonomous produces considerable stress for the typical adolescent. One measure of the stress and turmoil of adolescence is the dramatic increase of psychopathology of all types, ranging from transient adjustment reactions to full-blown affective and schizophrenic disorders. Parents and teenagers alike often feel confused, and at times overwhelmed by this stage of life. As a health care professional it is likely that you will be called upon to evaluate and assist with problems which involve adolescents and their families. In this chapter we will review psychologically important aspects of adolescence, indications of psychopathology and various treatment strategies.

LEARNING OBJECTIVES

By the time you complete this chapter, you should be able to do the following and apply the information to written case histories.

1. Briefly describe the three developmental tasks of adolescents.

2. Briefly describe the findings suggestive of behavioral or emotional disorders typical of adolescence.

3. For each of the methods of therapeutic intervention listed below, describe the recommended treatment approach and provide a rationale for its use in the management of the problems of adolescents.

   a. supportive psychotherapy
   b. behavioral therapy
   c. pharmacologic therapy
   d. consultation and referral

DEVELOPMENTAL TASKS OF ADOLESCENTS

Many clinicians view adolescence as a unique period of life that serves as a transition between childhood and the adult years -- a time during which social, emotional and intellectual skills are developed in preparation for adult responsibilities. In order to mature normally, teenagers must master three developmental tasks -- establishing a personal identity, adapting to changes associated with physical growth and sexual maturation, and becoming more self-reliant and autonomous with respect to their family. Failure to achieve at least minimal success in these tasks can lead to emotional and behavioral disorders.

It is during this time that teenagers should increasingly develop a sense of personal identity and unique individuality. They must critically reexamine the life view and values of their parents, and accept or modify them for themselves. They should be forming ideas of a life work and vocation which most suits them. In order that they achieve greater self-sufficiency apart from their families, adolescents turn more and more to their peers for emotional support and companionship. They are particularly influenced by peer ideas, and teenagers often feel conflicted about whether to follow established family standards or adopt the new and untried ones of their friends. Establishing personal guidelines about work, study, sexual behavior, drug use and management of finances are a few of the issues which must be resolved. The family is less important for personal survival than during earlier years but still serves as a needed source of support and nurturing. Many parents find that dealing with their teenagers is a puzzling and frustrating experience and may respond by becoming overly authoritarian or "throw up their hands" in desperation and discontinue providing any behavioral guidelines. Either extreme can cause conflicts which lead to impaired school performance, truancy, abuse of intoxicating substances or psychological symptoms.

Physical changes and sexual maturation often become a major source of concern for adolescents. Rapid increases in body size, weight and strength result in a new and unfamiliar body image which requires months or years to fully assimilate. Medical illness and treatment are particularly threatening at this time of dramatic physical change. It is important to supportively deal with the fears that adolescents have about their bodies and disease. The onset of puberty and heightened sexual feelings may give rise to numerous conflicts, guilt and self-doubt. Despite a more "enlightened and permissive" approach to sexuality in our society, the introduction of sex education courses in our schools, and the advent of various birth control devices, unplanned pregnancy and venereal disease among teenagers has reached epidemic proportions. Obviously, much remains to be done to help these young persons adapt to the biological aspects of adolescence.

INDICATIONS OF PSYCHOPATHOLOGY

Because of the stresses and developmental changes inherent during adolescence, these years are often characterized by transient episodes of depression, anxiety, unpredictable behavior, moodiness and other psychological symptoms. Preoccupation with bodily symptoms and changes, transient phobias, insomnia or eating disturbances are typical. More serious emotional conditions including affective and schizophrenic disorders also may begin during the mid to late teen years and it is sometimes difficult to distinguish between the psychological findings which are associated with normal development and those indicative of psychopatholog Behavioral disturbances in the form of learning difficulties, defiance toward authority figures and drug or alcohol abuse often occur. It is useful diagnostically to perform a mental status examination and gather information about particular areas of personal functioning to determine whether or not serious psychopathology is present.

Mental status examination findings take on increasing diagnostic significance as each individual matures and moves through childhood and adolescence. Reality testing progressively improves and personal wishes and feelings are more readily distinguished from reality. Thought pattern are more goal directed and coherent, and adult-type logic is used. Teenagers are also better able to verbalize their feelings and thoughts than whe they were younger. By mid to late adolescence, mental status examinatio findings provide a relatively reliable source of data for formulating diagnoses. Especially significant are M.S.E. findings which disclose intense depression or anxiety, eccentric or delusional thinking, suicidal ideation, disorientation and memory impairment, inappropriate or excessive affect and hallucinations. These findings carry the same pathological significanc in adolescents as in adults.

Other indications suggestive of psychopathology are any intense psychological symptoms which persist longer than a week or two or that progressively worsen. Also significant is an inability to form meaningful persona relationships or the progressive deterioration of performance at work or school. Persistent social withdrawal, apathy toward activities which formerly were enjoyed and chronic insomnia and/or weight loss warrant careful evaluation.

Because many schizophrenic, affective and anxiety disorders begin during adolescence, we suggest that you read the chapters in this book on those topics in order to be thoroughly familiar with the typical findings of those diagnostic categories.

Now complete Self-Assessment Exercise #1 beginning on the following page.

Self-Assessment Exercise #1

1. List at least three developmental tasks of adolescents.

2. Circle findings from the following which suggest the presence of psychopathology in adolescents:

   (a) delusions

   (b) transient episodes of irritability

   (c) hallucinations

   (d) episodic appetite disturbances

   (e) impaired reality testing

   (f) suicidal ideation

   (g) persistent social withdrawal

   (h) steady decline in school performance

Indicate whether the following statements are true (T) or false (F).

_____ 3. M.S.E. findings are more reliable indicators of psychopathology in adolescents than in younger children.

_____ 4. The onset of schizophrenic and serious affective disorders is more common in adolescence than in childhood.

_____ 5. Most teenagers look increasingly to their peers for emotional support than to their family.

When you have completed this exercise to the best of your ability, check your answers with those on the following page.

Self-Assessment Exercise #1 - Feedback

1. Three major developmental tasks of adolescents are:

   establishing a personal and sexual identity
   becoming increasingly autonomous from the family
   dealing with the biological and psychological changes of puberty

2. The following findings suggest the presence of psychopathology in adolescents:

   (a) delusions

   (c) hallucinations

   (e) impaired reality testing

   (f) suicidal ideation

   (g) persistent social withdrawal

   (h) steady decline in school performance

True 3. M.S.E. findings are more reliable indicators of psychopatholo in adolescents than in younger children.

True 4. The onset of schizophrenic and serious affective disorders is more common in adolescence than in childhood.

True 5. Most teenagers look increasingly to their peers for emotional support than to their family.

If your answers correspond closely with those above, please continue reading on the next page. If not, please reread the preceding material.

THERAPEUTIC INTERVENTIONS

Supportive Psychotherapy

Emotional problems of adolescents generally can be treated with the same therapy techniques that are used with adults. However, it is necessary to allow for some age-related characteristics of teenagers, in particular, their strivings to be self-sufficient and wariness about authority figures. Keeping in mind the following general principles will facilitate your work with teenagers -- whatever their psychopathology may be.

It is valuable that you have a comprehensive picture of your patients' problems. Therefore, complete an indepth assessment of their life circumstances including their current activities, family and social relationships, school performance, sexual habits, medical history and current interests. Adolescents often will attempt to exert pressure for you to "take sides" in their conflicts with others, such as their teachers and parents. Although you should remain sympathetic to their cause, maintain an objective perspective rather than allying too closely with your patients' point of view. Many adolescents will need time to develop trust in you before they can freely express themselves. Since a therapeutic relationship is the foundation upon which all treatment rests, help them build trust in you by showing your concern and a nonjudgmental attitude.

Directive guidance. Most adolescents resent being "lectured" or in other ways belittled. They may need counsel about many areas of their life, but they resist being "told what to do." In this regard, you should speak authoritatively without being authoritarian. Your advice more likely will be received if it is presented in the form of a "suggestion" or "possibility" rather than as a directive. Introducing your comments in a somewhat tentative fashion like, "Have you thought of doing...?" or "I wonder what would happen if...?" or "Perhaps if you approach the problem in another way it might work out better," is preferable to more emphatic statements.

Teenagers respond better to a less structured "rap session" type of interview rather than one which is formal or overly structured. They appreciate being considered as active participants in the therapeutic process and in any decisions which affect them. Only at times when they seem immobilized by strong feelings or are about to take actions which would adversely effect them, should you take a very firm stand.

Ventilation. Most adolescents desire an opportunity to talk with others about their feelings, ideas and worries -- they need to feel understood. But it is rare for them to discuss personal matters with family members. Rather, they usually turn to their peers who can supply emotional support but little authoritative advice. As an interested and objective professional, you may be able to meet their needs for someone in whom they can confide.

Teenagers are more likely to "open up" to you if they sense your concern and what they reveal is kept private. It is important that all that is said be held confidential unless they have given you permission to talk with others about them. If they are brought for consultation by parents or others, it is generally best to interview the teenager first. Later, if you plan to confer with the parents, ask if your patient would like to remain during the discussion.

Reassurance. Careful attention should be paid to providing reassurance and building self-esteem during the therapy of young persons. Every effort should be made to reinforce successful coping mechanisms and emphasize any special capabilities and assets which they may have. Review with them their previous accomplishments. Without minimizing their current difficulty, it is supportive to place your patients' problems in perspective -- to point out that many of their difficulties are time limited and that many others have lived through and mastered similar upsets. It is reassuring for them to learn that their problems are neithe unique nor hopeless. Defining their problems and proposing possible solutions is also very reassuring. Finally, your dependable presence, therapeutic optimism and ongoing concern provides invaluable hope and reassurance.

Environmental intervention. Be sure that you are familiar with your patients' daily routine and life setting. As with younger children, the treatment of teenagers often requires you to directly intervene on their behalf to make their environment more favorable. For example, you may be called upon to arrange a change of school schedule, consult family members about problems within the home or contact agencies about arranging vocational training. You should take care not to be "manipulated" by your patients and take on responsibilities that could be handled by them. Neither should they be allowed to avoid important responsibilities or growth opportunities (school, work, etc.) simply because they are difficult to face. With your support, adolescents should be encouraged to deal with their life problems as fully as possible. Occasionally, a structured therapeutic environment is needed and placement in a residential treatment setting such as a "foster home" or a hospital may be indicated. As much as possible, try to achieve for your patients an environment which assures privacy, emotional support and provides worthwhile relationships and activities.

Behavioral Therapy

Behavioral modification can be adapted to the therapy of adolescents with specific behavioral problems. As described in the chapter on "Behavioral Therapy," rewarding adaptive behaviors and neither selectively overlooking or punishing undesirable ones is the regimen to follow.

After setting behavioral standards and outlining rewards and punishments, parents should award or withdraw privileges such as the use of the car, dating permission, etc. in accordance with the adolescent's behavior. Generally, it is best to consult an expert for designing a special therapy program if severe behavioral problems exist.

Pharmacologic Therapy

The indications for pharmacologic treatment of older adolescents closely resemble those outlined for adults in the chapter on "Pharmacologic Therapy." Psychotropic drugs should be recommended only for the treatment of well defined target symptoms. Anti-anxiety drugs can be prescribed for the symptoms of psychological and physical distress associated with intense anxiety. Neuroleptics are reserved for symptoms of marked agitation, assaultiveness or symptoms of psychosis, including delusions or hallucinations. Tricyclic anti-depressants are usually warranted only for teenagers who show signs of a major depressive disorder.

Younger and smaller adolescents should be given doses of psychotropic medications in proportion to their body weight. Special caution should be exercised when prescribing medications for younger teenagers, those from 11 to 13. They may experience a paradoxical reaction in which their behavior is opposite to that which is usually expected from a drug, i.e., they may become hyperactive after receiving a sedative. Most teenagers resist taking medications on a regular basis if the drugs cause unpleasant side effects or in other ways make them feel different from their peers.

Consultation and Referral

As with younger children, consultation with numerous specialists is often required when helping adolescents deal with their problems. For teenagers with severe emotional disorders such as psychosis or recurrent anti-social behavior, referral to an experienced psychiatrist or psychologist for diagnosis and treatment is indicated. Consultation should also be requested if hospitalization or placement in a residential treatment center becomes necessary. Such placement usually can be expedited by a psychiatrist or an experienced psychiatric social worker. Most adolescents should be referred to a physician for a thorough medical evaluation to rule out physical causes of their behavioral or emotional disorders. Regional mental health centers can be consulted for adolescent outpatients who need psychotherapy. Consider consulting educational specialists if your patients have academic problems or need special vocational training.

Now complete Self-Assessment Exercise #2 beginning on the following page.

Self-Assessment Exercise #2

Read the case vignettes and answer the questions which follow.

1. Tom, aged 14, formerly a good student, recently has been performing poorly in school. He seems to lack motivation for his studies and prefers watching TV or talking with his friends. His concerned parents ask that you meet with him. Tom does not show signs of serious psychopathology and he is puzzled about his academic apathy.

   Comment on the therapeutic appropriateness of each of the following statements that you might make.

   (a) "Tom, you've got a good mind. Now I want you to get a hold of yourself and start cracking these books -- at least three hours a day."

   (b) "You seem temporarily disinterested in school right now. What do you think is causing your problem -- what might help?"

   (c) "Your success in school is your responsibility. It's up to you to decide what to do about studying."

Self-Assessment Exercise #2 (Continued)

2. Sixteen-year-old Susan broke up with her boyfriend. Over the past two weeks she has been intermittently tearful, anorexic and complained of not being able to concentrate on her studies. Her parents, being somewhat overly concerned, request a consultation with you. At the time of the consultation, Susan's mother accompanies her and asks to speak with you privately before your interview with Susan.

   (a) Should you first see Susan or her mother? Why?

   In the interview, Susan recites a long list of complaints against her parents. She feels that they are "overprotective" and expresses resentment that they won't allow her to stay out as late as her friends and make her do "too much" housework. Susan asks that you tell her parents to "ease up" on her.

   (b) Should you comply with Susan's request? Why?

Self-Assessment Exercise #2 (Continued)

Indicate whether the following statements are true (T) or false (F).

_____ 3. Most teenagers prefer counselors who are direct and "lay it on the line" by telling them clearly what should be done to solve their problems.

_____ 4. In most instances, a physical examination is not indicated for adolescents who become significantly depressed and show evidence of weight loss and insomnia.

_____ 5. The dosage schedules and indications for prescribing psychotropic drugs to adolescents is similar to those of adults.

_____ 6. During treatment with adolescents, therapists are less likely called upon for environmental intervention than is the case with adult patients.

_____ 7. Relatively few teenagers object to taking psychotropic drugs on a regular basis.

_____ 8. Psychotropic drugs should be prescribed for adolescents only to treat specific target symptoms.

_____ 9. The supportive therapy of teenagers regularly involves consultation/referral with a variety of professionals and agencies.

_____ 10. Principles of behavioral modification are difficult to apply successfully to the behavior problems of adolescents.

When you have completed this exercise to the best of your ability, check your answers with those on the following page.

Self-Assessment Exercise #2 - Feedback

1. (a) "Tom, you've got a good mind. Now I want you to get a hold of yourself and start cracking these books -- at least three hours a day."

   This statement is much too directive. Even though the advice is well intended, it is likely to be resisted. A better approach would be to explore Tom's perception of his study problems and see if he can arrive at a suitable approach for doing his homework. Offer "suggestions" if he can't come up with some ideas for help.

   (b) "You seem temporarily disinterested in school right now. What do you think is causing your problem -- what might help?

   This comment focuses on the trouble at hand and encourages Tom to participate in defining the problem causes and solutions. If Tom falters in identifying his problem, then you might offer some observations.

   (c) "Your success in school is your responsibility. It's up to you to decide what to do about studying."

   This comment leaves Tom pretty much to his own devises. It would be unusual for him to be able to solve his difficulty without some outside guidance. He likely will need some definitive help from you.

2. (a) No. Susan should be interviewed first. As a general rule, seeing the adolescent first will help to build a feeling of trust and support However, if Susan specifically requests that her mother be preser her wishes should be granted.

   (b) No. You should not propose to intervene or side with Susan until you have more information. Susan's explanations reflect her perception of things and may be considerably biased. Even if she is not being treated fairly at home; this issue should be cautiously approached with her parents. If they feel alienated or unduly coerced by treatment they may discontinue therapy.

Self-Assessment Exercise #2 - Feedback (Continued)

The following statements are true (T) or false (F).

False 3. Most teenagers prefer counselors who are direct and "lay it on the line" by telling them clearly what should be done to solve their problems.

False 4. In most instances, a physical examination is not indicated for adolescents who become significantly depressed and show evidence of weight loss and insomnia.

True 5. The dosage schedules and indications for prescribing psychotropic drugs to adolescents is similar to those of adults.

False 6. During treatment with adolescents, therapists are less likely called upon for environmental intervention than is the case with adult patients.

False 7. Relatively few teenagers object to taking psychotropic drugs on a regular basis.

True 8. Psychotropic drugs should be prescribed for adolescents only to treat specific target symptoms.

True 9. The supportive therapy of teenagers regularly involves consultation/referral with a variety of professionals and agencies.

False 10. Principles of behavioral modification are difficult to apply successfully to the behavior problems of adolescents.

If your answers correspond closely with those above, please continue reading on the next page. If not, please reread the preceding material.

SUMMARY

Adolescence is a time of great developmental change and physical and emotional growth. It is also a stage of life characterized by considerable turmoil and unrest for the teenager and his family. It is important to distinguish between the transient emotional disorders of normal adolescence and findings which indicate serious psychopathology. The approach to the diagnosis and treatment of adolescent problems closely resembles those used with adults, but some age-related modifications are indicated.

REFERENCES

Cantwell, D. , "Psychopharmacologic Treatment of the Minimal Brain Dysfunction Syndrome," Psychopharmacology in Childhood and Adolescence, New York: Basic Books, Inc., 1977.

Freeman, R. D., "Minimal Brain Dysfunction, Hyperactivity and Learning Disorders: Epidemic or Episode?" The Hyperactive Child and Stimulant Drugs, Chicago: University of Chicago Press, 1976.

Hamburg, B. A., "Coping in Early Adolescence," American Handbook of Psychiatry, New York: Basic Books, 1974.

King, S. H., "Coping and Growth in Adolescence," Annual Progress in Child Psychiatry and Child Development, New York: Brunner/Mazel, 1974.

Nicholi, A. M., Jr., "The Adolescent," Harvard Guide to Modern Psychiatry, Cambridge: Belknap Press of Harvard University Press, 1978.

Offer, D. and Offer, J., "Normal Adolescence in Perspective," Current Issues in Adolescent Psychiatry, New York: Brunner/Mazel, 1973.

Werry, J. S., "The Use of Psychotropic Drugs in Children," J. Am. Acad. Child Psychiatry, 16:446, 1977.

CHAPTER 19. GRIEF AND TERMINAL ILLNESS

In years past man has devoted considerable time to studying birth and the life cycle, but until very recently relatively little has been done to investigate the process of dying and the ways in which individuals cope with loss and grief. Within the past decade, however, considerable time and research has been devoted to the study of loss, dying and death. From this newly derived knowledge have come insights which can significantly improve the care of terminally ill patients and their families. In this chapter we will review typical patient and family responses to terminal illness, fears commonly associated with death, characteristic findings of normal and pathological grief reactions, and therapeutic interventions which can be used to help dying and grieving persons.

LEARNING OBJECTIVES

By the time you complete this chapter, you should be able to do the following and apply the information to written case histories.

1. Describe and distinguish between grief, bereavement and anticipatory grief.
2. Describe five or more patient responses which may indicate pathological bereavement.
3. Briefly characterize the responses of dying persons to their impending death as described by Kubler-Ross.
4. Describe four or more fears commonly experienced by dying persons.

5. For each of the methods of therapeutic intervention listed below, describe the recommended approach and provide a rationale for its use in the management of dying patients and their families.

   a. supportive psychotherapy
   b. behavioral therapy
   c. pharmacologic therapy
   d. consultation and referral

GRIEF AND BEREAVEMENT

Grief and bereavement represent the behavioral responses to a significant loss of any kind, be it a relationship, physical health or life itself. In this chapter we shall distinguish between acute grief which is the emotional response to a major loss and bereavement, the ongoing process during which one gradually adapts to loss.

The symptoms of acute grief such as might occur after the death of a loved one resemble those of a depressive syndrome and include feelings of sadness, emptiness and a general disinterest in activities which formerly were enjoyed. Intermittent tearfulness, restlessness, impairment of appetite and sleep, decreased concentration, easy fatigability and various bodily complaints are regularly experienced by grieving persons. Also present are self-directed recriminations and regrets, usually relating to missed opportunities to show appreciation and love toward the deceased. During the acute phase of grief, it is common for close family members to experience feelings of unreality (depersonalization), illusions or limited hallucinatory episodes. Surviving spouses or parents often report that they hear footsteps or a voice calling their name which is attributed to the dead person. This phenomenon is so widely experienced that is is considered by many clinicians as a part of normal grieving. Other frequent, but rarely stated feelings, are those of resentment at being left and abandoned by the person who has died. Such feelings of anger toward the dead or dying usually evoke considerable guilt and seldom are openly expressed. The intensity of acute grief usually lessens within several weeks and former activities and relationships are gradually resumed.

Bereavement, or mourning as it is sometimes called, is the extended process lasting months or longer during which individuals gradually assimilate and adjust to their loss. During bereavement, episodes of acute grief are experienced each time a reminder of the lost relationship is encountered. A familiar song, or place or activity which is associated with the dead person may evoke another wave of tearfulness, sadness and sense of loss. Initially, the reminders of the lost relationship are frequent and interfere with routine tasks and relationships. Many deeply bereaved persons feel that they never again will be able to resume a normal life; but in time the intensity of grief lessens. Gradually, the ties to the lost loved one are severed and new activities and relationships begin to replace the old. Interest and involvement in living is resumed. In most instances, the bereavement process noticeably subsides within a few months and sleep, appetite and physical stamina return to previous levels. In most cases, by the end of several months, acute recurrences of grief occur only at times of particular emotional significance such as holidays, birthdays, etc.

We usually think of grief and bereavement as responses which follow a loss or death. But the grieving process also can occur in anticipation of death, as in the instance of a patient and his family who are informed that he has an incurable illness. The grieving process is activated by the realization of death in the immediate future. Anticipatory grief is an emotionally painful process for the patient and loved ones alike. Nevertheless, research has shown that family members make a better long-term adjustment to the death of a loved one if they have time to gradually accustom themselves to the loss and say their "goodbyes" than in instances when death was sudden and unexpected.

In some cases, grief responses may take on pathological overtones and warrant special therapeutic intervention. Findings of a pathological grief reaction include steadfast denial of the death or a persistent wish to die and "join" the lost one. Development of an elated mood, an inability to feel or openly express sadness and intense grief responses which do not significantly lessen within a few months also are abnormal findings. Excessive use of alcohol or drugs, persistent severe insomnia and weight loss are physical findings which indicate an abnormal grieving process. Finally, symptoms of unrelenting depression or the development of delusions or hallucinations all point toward a psychopathological response.

Now complete Self-Assessment Exercise #1 beginning on the next page.

Self-Assessment Exercise #1

1. Define and briefly characterize:

   grief

   bereavement

   anticipatory grief

2. Assume that each of the patient findings below have occurred within two weeks of the death of a loved one. In the space provided, indicate whether the findings associated with grief are likely to be:

   P - "pathological" or N - "normal"

_____ sleep disturbance

_____ feelings of unreality

_____ intermittent denial of the death

_____ feelings of tension and restlessness

_____ marked agitation

_____ steadfast belief that the deceased was not dead but kidnapped

_____ decreased concentration

_____ feelings of elation

_____ thoughts of suicide

_____ regrets about not showing love toward the deceased

_____ hesitant expressions of anger about being abandoned by the deceased

_____ persistent, elaborate hallucinatory experiences

When you have completed this exercise to the best of your ability, check your answers with those on the following page.

Self-Assessment Exercise #1 - Feedback

1. Grief is the emotional response to a significant loss. Grief includes the many findings typical to a depressive reaction, e.g., sadness, tearfulness, insomnia, etc.

   Bereavement is the ongoing process by which an individual gradually accomodates to an important loss; it involves reexperiencing acute grief each time the individual is reminded of his loss; gradually the intensity of grief subsides and new interests develop.

   Anticipatory grief is a grief reaction which occurs in advance of an expected loss; it consists of typical findings of depression.

2.

N sleep disturbance

N feelings of unreality

N intermittent denial of the death

N feelings of tension and restlessness

P marked agitation

P steadfast belief that the deceased was not dead but kidnapped

N decreased concentration

P feelings of elation

P thoughts of suicide

N regrets about not showing love toward the deceased

N hesitant expressions of anger about being abandoned by the deceased

P persistent, elaborate hallucinatory experiences

If your answers correspond closely with those above, please continue reading on the next page. If not, please reread the preceding material.

COMMON RESPONSES OF DYING PATIENTS

Among the more informative studies of dying patients are those of Kubler-Ross. She has described five general reactions which many patients experience during the course of their terminal illness. All of these reactions are not necessarily found in every patient nor do they always follow an unvarying sequence. Nevertheless, these patterns of behavior are sufficiently common and important to deserve discussion. Incidentally, comparable responses can sometimes be observed in family and friends of dying persons as they anticipate their impending loss.

Most persons initially respond to learning that they have a terminal illness with denial, i.e., the emotional and intellectual disclaiming that a fact is true. Although most individuals, when asked, will intellectually acknowledge their mortality, the idea of personal death usually is treated as an event which will occur at some "distant future time" and is quickly dismissed from their minds. A full appreciation of the implications of one's own death is likely impossible. To contemplate loss of all relationships and all else that is loved and valued and meaningful, is indeed, threatening. No wonder then that the coping mechanism of denial is prominently called into play. It takes time for the impact of approaching death to be assimilated by the patient and loved ones alike. When presented with their prognosis, it is common for patients to initially respond with shock, emotional numbness and disbelief. Later, they may gradually experience waves of acceptance alternating with denial. Some patients seek alternative explanations for their symptoms, perhaps consulting other physicians and hoping for a more favorable opinion, while others continue denying the facts and live as if nothing were wrong with them. Eventually, for most persons, denial gradually gives way to at least a partial acceptance of their circumstances.

When the intensity of denial lessens somewhat, many patients then may respond with anger toward fate, God or any others who can be blamed for their predicament. Many patients feel that their illness is unjustified or a form of punishment and ask, "Why me?", questioning terrible things they have done to deserve such a fate. For awhile they may vent their frustrations on family, friends and other caregivers.

Many individuals may next deal with their impending death by engaging in a type of bargaining. They begin to act in ways which they believe are especially pleasing to God or the physician, and thereby, their disease and its consequences may yet be undone. They hope that by personal sacrifice or performing good deeds, they will be spared and given a reprieve from suffering and death.

But sooner or later, despite denial, threats and bargaining, the implications of their deteriorating condition become increasingly evident. Faced with the daily reality of progressive debility and helplessness and the imminent loss of valued relationships, a reaction of grief sets in. This grief response possesses all the characteristics of that described earlier -- feelings of despair and hopelessness, accompanied by all of the other physical and psychological findings commonly associated with depression.

Eventually, many dying persons come to terms with their fate and give up their struggle to survive. Much of their anger and depression subside and they gradually become more quiet and withdraw their emotional investment in the activities and relationships which were once so important. They seem at peace and reconciled to death. They are prepared to relinquish their hold on life.

The responses of dying patients described by Kubler-Ross vary considerably in intensity and in sequence from individual to individual. Occasionally, some patients become fixated at one response or another, or develop significant psychopathology. Your task in those cases is to provide for them understanding, comfort and patience using the principles to be described later in this chapter.

FEARS OF DYING PATIENTS

A number of fears are evoked in dying persons. All too often these patients must suffer their anxieties in silence because of the taboos which surround the topic of death. As a caregiver, you may be in a position to encourage your patients to express and deal with their fears as they surface. Some patients will openly verbalize their fears while others may attempt to hide or suppress them. Because their particular worries about death are determined by diverse factors such as cultural ethical beliefs, background, age and others, it is necessary that you identify and address the fears particular to each person. We will now discuss briefly the most common fears of dying patients.

Non-Being

Many patients fear that their unique, personal identity will cease. For persons without a religious orientation and belief in an after-life, this fear can be difficult to counteract. Little can be said to console or prepare one for the prospect of non-existence. Nevertheless, it may comfort them to talk about their feelings.

Loss of Autonomy and Self-Determination

Many persons worry that because of their progressive weakness and debility, they will be reduced to a helpless, dependent state. They usually are concerned that because our society so highly esteems traits of independence and autonomy, they will be shamed or less valued as individuals.

Experiencing Intolerable Pain

Many persons fear that their disease or the act of dying will cause intense pain from which they cannot escape. Many are concerned that analgesic medications will be insufficient to control their pain and that they will "breakdown" emotionally.

Changes in Body Image and Disfigurement

Persons with wasting illnesses such as cancer or who have had surgical procedures such as breast removal or a colostomy, often express concerns that their loved ones will find them physically repulsive and will reject or abandon them.

Abandonment

Many individuals express fears that their disease or dying state will cause others to avoid or abandon them altogether. Rejection and loneliness further adds to their distress.

Punishment After Death

Some religiously-oriented patients fear that after death they will face judgment and damnation because of wrongdoings which were committed in this life. A clergyman of the patient's particular faith can be of considerable value to deal with this fear.

Becoming a Burden to Others

Worries about the financial and emotional burden which their illness and death brings to family members is a preoccupation of many dying patients. They fear that family members will be deprived or eventually become resentful because of the considerable expense, time and obligations involved in caring for one who has so little to give in return.

Now complete Self-Assessment Exercise #2 beginning on the next page.

Self-Assessment Exercise #2

1. Kubler-Ross described five behavioral responses which many persons demonstrate during a terminal illness. Briefly describe the five and list them in the typical sequence in which they occur.

   (a)

   (b)

   (c)

   (d)

   (e)

2. Indicate whether the following statements are true (T) or false (F).

______ a. most persons initially respond with intense depression when informed that they have a life threatening illness

______ b. the responses of patients to terminal illness as described by Kubler-Ross invariably follow the same sequence in all individuals

______ c. the presence of denial during a terminal illness often aids adaptation to a painful reality

______ d. most dying patients spontaneously talk about their fears

______ e. most persons have in common the same three fears of dying

Self-Assessment Exercise #2 (Continued)

3. Using the information in the preceding section, indicate fears connected with dying likely to be present in the terminally ill patients described below.

   (a) a self-made businessman who has taken great satisfaction during his life by being independent and productive

   (b) a middle-aged woman from a low-income family who has had a breast removed because of cancer

If your answers correspond closely with those above, please continue reading on the next page. If not, please reread the preceding material.

Self-Assessment Exercise #2 - Feedback

1. Kubler-Ross described these five responses to the presence of a terminal illness.

   (a) denial - a "refusal" (inability) to accept their illness and its implication.

   (b) anger - anger felt towards fate, God or others who may be "responsible" for the illness.

   (c) bargaining - an attempt to exchange a change in prognosis for good behavior and personal concession.

   (d) grief - a depressive response to the anticipated loss of life.

   (e) acceptance - reconciled to impending death.

2.

False a. Most persons initially respond with intense depression when informed that they have a life threatening illness.

False b. The responses of patients to terminal illness as described by Kubler-Ross invariably follow the same sequence in all individuals.

True c. The presence of denial during a terminal illness often aids adaptation to a painful reality.

False d. Most dying patients spontaneously talk about their fears.

False e. Most persons have in common the same three fears of dying.

3. The individuals described below are likely to have these specific fears associated with dying.

   (a) Dying persons who have placed particular importance on being independent and productive during their lifetime often fear becoming helpless and a burden to others.

   (b) This woman will likely have fears associated with changes in body image (breast removal), that family members will find her physically repulsive and because of limited finances she may be a burden to others.

THERAPEUTIC INTERVENTIONS

Supportive Psychotherapy

Working with terminally ill persons tends to evoke in caregivers the same fears about death as those experienced by the patients themselves. As a consequence, caregivers who are not in control of their own feelings may defensively begin to emotionally withdraw from their patients. At the time when dying persons most need closeness and support, "helping others" may spend less and less time with them, and in other ways, disengage themselves from the relationship. It is natural to want to avoid situations or persons that threaten and disturb us. However, as health care professionals, it is our responsibility in this unique situation to meet patient needs regardless of our personal discomfort.

Your supportive role in the management of dying patients and their families is a very important one. We will now discuss treatment techniques which are useful with terminally ill patients and their families.

Directive guidance. Terminal illness follows a changing course and you should match your interventions to the needs of your patients and their families. Although you are the authoritative professional who is "in charge" of treatment, as much as possible encourage patient self-determination and participation in making decisions. As a general rule, you should discourage emotionally made decisions which, if enacted, may have far-reaching consequences; for example, abruptly selling the family home, moving to a distant city, and so forth. Help patients set and accomplish goals which are in keeping with their remaining capabilities. Anticipate that as patient debility increases, they will become physically and psychologically regressed and more dependent. When that occurs, allow them to emotionally "lean" on you. Encourage patient involvement in satisfying activities intervening only if they over-extend themselves.

Education. Severely ill patients and their families often have many misconceptions about disease and death, and you will be able to counteract their uncertainties by providing authoritative information. Some patients want to be told the specific details of their condition while others prefer to remain relatively uninformed. Your patients will provide clues about what and how much information they want to receive by the themes of their questions, their emotional response to information given, and their nonverbal behavior. Do not attempt to hid unfavorable findings from your patients who ask for information. Even if they are not told explicitly about their condition, patients intuitively "know" when their condition is deteriorating. They can "read between the lines" of a knowing glance, a significant pause and emotional nuances of their care givers.

Any attempt to deliberately mislead or minimize the gravity of their prognosis will serve only to make them distrust you. They need honest answers to their questions which are tactfully and sensitively worded.

Encourage patients to ask any questions which they may have. Keep patients informed about medical interventions which are needed, including any potential complications or side effects that may arise. It is often helpful to prepare them for psychological ups and downs of their conditions by making such statements as, "Don't be surprized if you feel frustrated...worried...etc. from time to time." Keep family members and friends fully informed about the course of the illness and treatment. It is especially important that grieving persons be told about the variety of psychological and physical manifestations of normal bereavement. Many worry needlessly that their intense feelings may be indicative of incipient mental illness.

Ventilation. One of the most therapeutic experiences for dying patients is an opportunity to verbalize their thoughts, fears and feelings. It is distressing to listen to persons whose thoughts are preoccupied with themes of loss, fear and death, but their opportunity to "unload" to a sympathetic listener provides them with considerable emotional relief. Encourage silent patients to express their feelings -- whatever they may be. Their reluctance for open communication usually reflects a fear of their losing emotional control. One way of approaching their silence is to say, "You probably have some feelings or questions about your condition -- most persons do. I'd like to hear about them if you are willing to share them with me." If they still remain reluctant to talk about themselves, then let the matter rest until a later time.

During the course of their illness, many persons respond with an outpouring of intense feelings such as anxiety, anger or despair. At these times listen attentively and empathically -- providing support, but not interrupting the flow of feeling. Only if talking about their condition clearly leads to escalating depression or thought disorganization should you divert them to more neutral topics. For the patients' well-being, it is generally more therapeutic to allow them to fully ventilate their feelings.

Note carefully any special words which patients select when referring to their condition and use the same words when communicating with them. For example, it is emotionally significant whether a patient with a malignancy describes his illness vaguely as "a tumor of some sort" or states, "I have cancer." By their words, patients will reveal the level of emotional communication which they can handle. Follow their lead. Be sure to allow opportunity for family members to express their feelings and ask questions. In answering their questions about prognosis and treatment, assume that what you say likely will be conveyed back to your patient.

Reassurance. Your sense of hope tempered optimism and concern is vital for the day-to-day morale of terminally ill patients and their families. Your presence, willingness to listen and answer questions is greatly valued. Do not give superficial or unrealistic reassurances, but daily try to convey some degree of optimism.

The meaning of time changes for dying patients. Their "future" comes to mean days and weeks instead of months and years. By using statements such as, "See you tomorrow." or "We'll meet again next week at the regular time." subtle reassurance can be given that they have a future, albeit a limited one. Finally, it is important to identify and alleviate the many fears which seriously ill persons have. Make it unequivocally clear that they will receive sufficient medications to control pain and that they will be well cared for.

Environmental intervention. An important aspect of treatment for patients is their environment and physical care. Make sure that whether patients are hospitalized or reside at home their environment is pleasant, clean and offers opportunity for gratifying activities and relationships. Many persons take comfort in having around them personal objects such as pictures, a favorite chair, etc. which have particular sentimental value. They usually prefer a daily routine which is predictable with regards to activities, meals, and social interactions. Keep patients appropriately involved with worthwhile activities -- but not just busy work. Most appreciate visits with friends and relatives. Many individuals request to die at home in the presence of family members and surrounded by familiar objects that carry special value and meaning. If possible, their wishes should be granted. Others may require the specialized care which can be given only in a hospital or hospice, a residential treatment center for terminally ill patients.

Behavioral Therapy

Other than following principles of behavioral modification which reward adaptive behavior, i.e., treatment compliance, and selectively ignores maladaptive behavior (excessive demandingness, whining) this form of treatment has limited applicability to dying patients.

Now complete Self-Assessment Exercise #3 beginning on the next page.

Self-Assessment Exercise #3

Using the principles of supportive psychotherapy just presented, describe the correct therapeutic approach for the responses of the following patient.

George Stanton, a middle-aged executive, was recently informed that he had a chronic form of leukemia. He has a wife and two high school aged children and works for a company which provides liberal health insurance benefits.

(1) A few days after receiving the news of his condition, Mr. Stanton in a somewhat agitated condition states that his "time is running out," and that he would like to sell his home and take his family to the South Pacific to live out his remaining days. His family is uneasy about the idea and he asks your advise. Would you encourage or discourage his move? Why?

(2) During the course of Mr. Stanton's treatment it will be necessary to give him medication which will produce unpleasant side effects. He is a worrier and asks if the treatment will make him sick. Should you tell him the truth and accentuate his worry or let him find out for himself? Why?

Self-Assessment Exercise #3 (Continued)

(3) During the early weeks of his treatment, Mr. Stanton talks endlessly about his health, financial worries, and regrets of his earlier life. During his narration, he frequently becomes temporarily distraught and fearful. His wife asks if he should not be diverted to less troubling topics. What would you tell her to do?

(4) In addition to a comprehensive medical regimen, what ways can you provide ongoing reassurance to Mr. Stanton and his family?

When you have completed this exercise to the best of your ability, check your answers with those on the following page.

Self-Assessment Exercise #3 - Feedback

1. You should discourage his impulsive decision to make such an abrupt change in his life curcumstances. He needs time to talk over with his family the implications of such a move for all. Understandably, he is very upset and needs time to talk over his distress and feelings. Decisions involving major changes should be delayed until they have been carefully explored.

2. By all means advise him in advance that he may experience some unpleasant side effects, even if it causes him some worry. It is important to deal directly and honestly with patients. He needs a therapeutic relationship which he can count on -- one without deception or surprises.

3. He needs an ample opportunity to express his feelings and talking about them will relieve his emotional tensions. On the other hand, if he becomes increasingly distraught or anxious when he discusses unpleasant topics, then he should be diverted to less unsettling subjects.

4. Reassurance can be provided by your ready availability, therapeutic optimism, willingness to listen and answer questions, and ongoing commitment to his well being.

If your answers correspond closely with those above, please continue reading on the next page. If not, please reread the preceding material.

THERAPEUTIC INTERVENTIONS (CONTINUED)

Pharmacologic Therapy

The selective use of prescribed medications can add comfort to dying patients.

Certainly, pain control is a primary concern of medical treatment. Although we will not discuss them in a specific way, many types and combinations of analgesic drugs are now available which can effectively lessen pain. Patients should be informed early in treatment that they will be given whatever medications are needed to maintain their comfort. Many therapists mistakenly undertreat terminal patients experiencing pain, fearing that drug dependency may become problematic. Drug tolerance and side effects such as discoordination and constipation often develop in patients regularly taking analgesic medications, but in most cases, maintaining pain control far outweighs the risks of these complications. These side effects can be minimized somewhat by carefully selecting drugs, using low starting doses and then increasing the amount as patient needs dictate. Also, combining certain analgesics with other drugs may enhance their effectiveness, reduce the dose required for pain control, and thereby minimize undesirable side effects.

Many chronically ill persons are troubled with insomnia and this symptom, too, can be successfully treated. Flurazepam given 15 to 30 mgs. about 30 minutes before bedtime will produce restful sleep for most persons. This medication is usually well tolerated but may interact with any analgesics which are simultaneously taken. Excessive sedation may result.

Patients (and family members) often request medication to relieve symptoms of "nervousness." Anti-anxiety medications (diazepam, chlordiazepoxide) are suitable for treating specific target symptoms of restlessness, apprehension and the physical accompaniments of anxiety. However, these drugs lose their effectiveness if taken continuously for longer than a few days. They should be taken only intermittently to moderate intense discomfort. Diazepam, 2 to 5 mgs. taken two to three times a day during periods of peak anxiety generally will provide some tension relief. Diazepam may interact with analgesics taken and cause excessive sedation. Patients and their families should be told that some anxiety and tension are to be expected, and that not all symptoms of nervousness warrant pharmacologic therapy. Routinely prescribing sedative drugs for grieving persons is ill advised and may interfere with the normal process of bereavement. If patients become uncomfortably tense then, of course, anti-anxiety medications can be prescribed.

Antidepressant medications such as tricyclic antidepressants (imipramine, doxepin, amytriptyline) generally are not indicated for treating either the depressive symptoms associated with terminal illness or the grief reaction following the death of a loved one. In most cases, the grief experienced is an expected consequence of loss and, therefore, is not likely to respond to medications which are primarily designed to counteract a biochemical deficiency of the central nervous system. However, a trial regimen of tricyclic anti-depressants may be considered for persons who develop unusually severe depressive symptoms which persist longer than several weeks and do not respond to psychological support.

Occasionally, some persons will develop intense anxiety, agitation or symptoms of psychosis during the course of their grief. For these individuals anti-psychotic medications can be prescribed to lessen the intensity of agitation, delusions and hallucinations. In such cases, haloperidol, thiothixene or other neuroleptics may be appropriate medications. Dosages, side effects and possible contraindications for these psychotropic drugs are found in the chapter on "Pharmacologic Therapy."

Consultation and Referral

The effectiveness of your therapeutic interventions with dying patients and their families can be increased by making use of the expertise of other specialists. Of course, the medical status of physically ill persons should be continuously monitored by physicians. For patients who prefer receiving treatment at home, arranging for the services of a visiting nurse may be indicated. Many persons with terminal illness may have business or legal problems which warrant the counsel of a lawyer, accountant or insurance representative. For religiously-oriented patients and their families, clergymen can provide invaluable comfort and assistance, and their services should become an integral part of the treatment regimen. Occasionally, consultations with a psychiatrist is indicated if severe depression or psychosis occurs which does not respond to supportive measures and medications. Finally, various self-help groups comprised of persons with similar fatal diseases may be available in your community to help provide comfort and emotional support.

Now complete Self-Assessment Exercise #4 beginning on the following page.

Self-Assessment Exercise #4

1. From the treatment options below, indicate the most appropriate action to take regarding prescribing drugs. Briefly state the rationale for your action.

   (a) prescribe no medication
   (b) " an anti-depressant medication (imipramine)
   (c) " an anti-psychotic medication (haloperidol)
   (d) " an anti-anxiety medication (diazepam)
   (e) " a hypnotic (flurazepam)
   (f) " a sedative (phenobarbital)

_____ (1) during an intense grief reaction an older woman becomes increasingly agitated and insists that a neighbor has cast a spell upon her

_____ (2) two days after the death of her sister, a young woman complains that she can't stop crying and requests an anti-depressant medication to lift her spirits

_____ (3) an older man is troubled by recurrent insomnia three weeks after the death of his wife

_____ (4) during the course of her husband's terminal illness the wife becomes increasingly tense and restless; she complains of episodes of rapid pulse and "nervousness"

Self-Assessment Exercise #4 (Continued)

2. Indicate whether the following statements are true (T) or false (F).

_____ (a) using present day medications, pain control can be assured for most terminally ill patients

_____ (b) psychotropic drugs may increase the depressant effect of simultaneously given analgesics

_____ (c) anti-anxiety medications should be routinely prescribed for most dying patients

_____ (d) anti-depressant medications are usually effective in reducing the symptom of acute grief reactions

_____ (e) most dying patients should be seen by a psychiatrist

_____ (f) the potential for developing drug dependency in dying patients warrants a policy of very conservative use of analgesics

When you have completed this exercise to the best of your ability, check your answers with those on the following page.

Self-Assessment Exercise #4 - Feedback

1.

__C__ (1) The woman demonstrates symptoms of psychosis and agitation. A neuroleptic such as haloperidol is indicated.

__A__ (2) Tearfulness and depressive feelings are a natural response to the death of a loved one. No anti-depressant medications are indicated.

__E__ (3) With persistent insomnia of this duration, a short-term use of flurazepam is indicated.

__D__ (4) The periodic use of diazepam may relieve the psychological and physical symptoms associated with tension.

2.

__True__ (a) Using present day medications, pain control can be assured for most terminally ill patients.

__True__ (b) Psychotropic drugs may increase the depressant effect of simultaneously given analgesics.

__False__ (c) Anti-anxiety medications should be routinely prescribed for most dying patients.

__False__ (d) Anti-depressant medications are usually effective in reducing the symptom of acute grief reactions.

__False__ (e) Most dying patients should be seen by a psychiatrist.

__False__ (f) The potential for developing drug dependency in dying patients warrants a policy of very conservative use of analgesics.

If your answers correspond closely with those above, please continue reading on the next page. If not, please reread the preceding material.

SUMMARY

Recent research has provided new information and understanding about grief and the behavior of terminally ill patients. Aided by this knowledge, your therapeutic intervention can provide considerable comfort to dying patients and their families.

REFERENCES

Barton, D., _Dying and Death: A Clinical Guide to Care Givers_, Baltimore: Williams and Wilkins Co., 1977.

Kubler-Ross, E., _On Death and Dying_, London: Macmillan, 1969.

Lindemann, E., "Symptomatology and Management of Acute Grief," _Amer. J. Psych._, 101:141 - 148, 1944.

Schneidman, E. S., _Deaths of Man_, Baltimore: Penguin Books, Inc., 1974.

Weisman, A. D., _On Dying and Denying: A Psychiatric Study of Terminality_, New York: Behavioral Publications, 1972.